...TY LAW IN BRITAIN

The concept of reasonable adjustment (alternatively known as reasonable accommodation) is rapidly gaining significance for countries throughout Europe and beyond. Directive 2000/78/EC required all EU Member States to ensure that, by the end of 2006 at the latest, reasonable accommodation obligations would operate to protect disabled people from unequal treatment in the context of employment. The new United Nations Convention on the Rights of Persons with Disabilities will require ratifying States to impose such obligations in a broad range of situations.

This book provides a detailed and critical analysis of the current and potential role of reasonable adjustment duties in British law. It explores the notion of the anticipatory reasonable adjustment duty—a notion which is, in many respects, distinctively British. It probes the relationship between reasonable adjustment and other concepts, including indirect discrimination and positive discrimination. Drawing particularly on US debates, potential sources of resistance to the duties are exposed and an attempt is made to suggest pre-emptive counter strategies. Attention is also given to issues of legal reform and rationalisation—issues of immense topicality and importance in view of the recent British move towards a single Equality Act.

In short, this book examines the current and potential role of reasonable adjustment duties in Britain. It will be of interest to lawyers, policy-makers and students working in the field of disability rights. It will also be of interest to all those concerned with the operation and development of equality law and policy more generally, both in Britain and beyond.

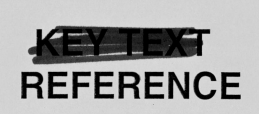

D1355091

Disability and Equality Law in Britain

The Role of Reasonable Adjustment

Anna Lawson

·HART·
PUBLISHING

OXFORD AND PORTLAND, OREGON
2008

Published in North America (US and Canada) by
Hart Publishing
c/o International Specialized Book Services
920 NE 58th Avenue, Suite 300
Portland, OR 97213–3786
USA
Tel: +1 503 287 3093 or toll-free: (1) 800 944 6190
Fax: +1 503 280 8832
E-mail: orders@isbs.com
Website: http://www.isbs.com

Hart Publishing Ltd, 16C Worcester Place, Oxford, OX1 2JW
Telephone: +44 (0)1865 517530 Fax: +44 (0)1865 510710
E-mail: mail@hartpub.co.uk
Website: http://www.hartpub.co.uk

British Library Cataloguing in Publication Data
Data Available

ISBN: 978-1-84113-828-2

Typeset by Columns Design Ltd, Reading
Printed and bound in Great Britain by
TJ International Ltd, Padstow, Cornwall

This book is dedicated to my parents, Bruce and Catherine Lawson. I owe everything to their unfailing love, support and guidance. Without the endless hours they spent reading academic material onto tape for me over many years, I would not have been able to attend university—let alone to have had a university career. Their selfless readiness to help anybody in trouble, their willingness to stand up for fairness and compassion, and their tremendous warmth and generosity of spirit are inspirational. So too is their immense capacity for hard work and many other things besides. I have greatly valued the interest they have taken in the progress of this book.

The book is in memory of Hamlet—my first guide dog with whom I had the honour to spend nine and a half years. After a well-earned retirement, in which he reigned over my parent's house, he died on 23 July 2008 while I was keeping him company and in the final stages of updating this book.

'Goodnight, sweet prince, and flights of angels sing thee to thy rest!'

Acknowledgements

This book was made possible by a period of research leave funded by the Arts and Humanities Research Council. The assistance of my team of support workers, funded through the Access to Work scheme, was also absolutely vital. So too were the services provided by the RNIB and University of Leeds Transcription Centre.

As always, I am very grateful indeed to the people who acted as my support workers—all of whom are friends who put in a degree of effort and skill which far exceeded the pay. Accordingly, I would like to thank Helena and Melanie for spending months over a steaming scanner and for being willing to work long and unsociable hours when I needed material urgently. I would like to thank Sarah for her meticulous proofreading and her willingness to trek to my office at short notice in emergencies. I would also like to thank Clare for her reference-checking and for staying up all night to help finalise the book and print it out and, especially, for keeping her sense of humour throughout!

Special thanks are due to David. Not only has he allowed me to use his house as a peaceful haven in which to work (even when I was at my most stressed and anti-social) but he has also provided expert help, at all stages of the book, with a huge range of different tasks. He has made awkward pdf documents accessible, navigated inaccessible websites, battled with the eccentricities of formatting which dogged the earlier drafts, proofread and found and checked countless references. He has worked on this book almost as hard as I have and I certainly could not have written it without him.

The book has benefited greatly from the extremely helpful comments and insights of Lisa Waddington and Caroline Gooding. I am deeply grateful to them for taking the trouble to wade through an earlier draft at times in which they were both already under considerable pressure. I am also very grateful to Dagmar Schiek and Colin Low for their comments on parts of an earlier draft and for all their help. Sincere thanks are also due to Jenny White, David Sparrow and Martin Crick—for providing me with various documents and pieces of information— and to Sandra Fredman for supporting my AHRC application.

I would like to thank my family, friends and colleagues for their patience, their understanding and their support. In particular, I would like to thank Amrita (who has also been writing a book) and Sarah (who has been writing a dissertation) for their solidarity; Michael, for the wisdom of an old hand; Jane, for all the lost texts; and Juliet for her remarkable strength and sparkle.

Finally, I would like to acknowledge the invaluable input of Richard Hart and his colleagues (especially Rachel Turner, Mel Hamill, Tom Adams, Jo Choulerton and Rachel O'Dowd). Their combination of the personal touch and scrupulous professionalism is unique in my experience. I have been constantly surprised by the degree of care which they have taken and the level of support which they have provided.

Contents

Contents

Table of Cases

Table of Cases

Table of Legislation

National Legislation

Netherlands

Sweden

United Kingdom

United States

EC Legislation

International Treaties and Conventions

1

Introduction

1. Purpose and Scope

T
HE FOCUS OF this book is the concept of reasonable adjustment—a concept which, outside Britain, is more commonly termed 'reasonable accommodation'. It is a concept which has attracted surprisingly little academic scrutiny in Britain despite the fact that it has generated a wealth of literature in the United States. It is nevertheless a concept which British law explicitly adopted well over a decade ago and one which has been crafted by that law into a form it has taken in no other country. Further, it is a concept which raises interesting theoretical questions for equality and non-discrimination law and one which has the potential to touch the lives of almost every person in Britain.

Reasonable adjustment (or accommodation) duties require duty-bearers to recognise that individuals with certain characteristics (such as a physical, sensory, intellectual or psychosocial impairment or a particular religious belief) might be placed at a disadvantage by the application to them of conventional requirements or systems. In the words of Lisa Waddington,

> [t]he obligation to make a reasonable accommodation is based on the recognition that, on occasions, the interaction between an individual's inherent characteristics, such as impairment, sex, religion or belief, and the physical or social environment can result in the inability to perform a particular function or job in the conventional manner. The characteristic is therefore relevant in that it can lead to an individual being faced with a barrier that prevents him or her from benefiting from an … opportunity that is open to others who do not share that characteristic. The resulting disadvantage is exclusion from the job market, or a restricted set of … opportunities.[1]

Such duties thus require duty-bearers to recognise the disadvantage which would result from treating relevant individuals in the same way as they treat others. In

---

[1] L Waddington, 'Reasonable Accommodation' in D Schiek, L Waddington and M Bell (eds), *Cases, Materials and Text on National, Supranational and International Non-Discrimination Law* (Oxford, Hart Publishing, 2007) 631 (footnotes omitted).

addition, they require duty-bearers to take reasonable steps to remove that disadvantage by treating relevant individuals differently from the way in which they treat others.

This book aims to provide a detailed account of the reasonable adjustment duties currently imposed by British human rights and non-discrimination law; to consider their positioning amongst other concepts at work in British equality law; and to identify strengths and potential sources of weakness in their design and implementation. More broadly, its purpose is to provide a critical analysis of reasonable adjustments that will assist in the development of successful and effective obligations—obligations which will play an important role in facilitating the full inclusion and participation in society of those in whose favour they operate.

At present, British statutory reasonable adjustment duties operate in favour only of disabled people.[2] The question of whether their reach should be extended to other groups is an important one, which will be considered further in chapter four. For present purposes, however, it is useful to stress the strength of the link between disability and the British concept of reasonable adjustment. Any book about the latter is necessarily also a book about the former.

It should also be stressed that this is a book about Britain. Its aim is to explain and to evaluate the development and operation of the law applying in England, Wales and Scotland.[3] In order to assist this analysis, however, references will frequently be made to comparable law operating in other jurisdictions. US law is of particular interest in this regard because it provided the inspiration and the role model for much of the relevant British law. In addition, the literature on US reasonable accommodation duties contains much of relevance to Britain. Accordingly, US law and literature will be heavily drawn upon. This is not a comparative study, however, and no attempt will be made to provide a comprehensive account of relevant law in any country other than Britain.

An analysis of British reasonable adjustment law has been made particularly timely by a number of developments at the national, European and international levels. At the national level, the Government has promised to rationalise and harmonise current non-discrimination law concepts and provisions (including those relating to reasonable adjustment) by bringing them within the ambit of a single Equality Act. Its Green Paper on this subject—the Discrimination Law Review[4]—was published in June 2007 and generated lively debate. After a period of consultation and discussion, the Government published its detailed response

---

[2] Although case law indicates that analogous duties to make reasonable adjustments on grounds of religion may well be imposed by human rights law. See ch 2, fnn 127–8 below and accompanying text and ch 4, section 5 below.

[3] Some but not all of this law also applies to Northern Ireland.

[4] Department for Communities and Local Government, *Discrimination Law Review—A Framework for Fairness: Proposals for a Single Equality Bill for Great Britain* (London, Stationery Office, 2007).

on 21 July 2008.[5] It plans to introduce a Bill, based on the proposals set out in that document, in the next parliamentary session.[6]

Any attempt to harmonise British non-discrimination legislation will necessarily raise some of the questions addressed in this book: What are reasonable adjustment duties and how do they differ from other equality and non-discrimination concepts? Is there a need for them in the disability context or could the same results be achieved by concepts such as indirect discrimination, which already apply to the other grounds? If they are required for disability, should they be extended to cover other grounds too?

At the European level, the Employment Equality Directive 2000[7] required all Member States to make provision for reasonable accommodation to be afforded to disabled people in the contexts of employment and occupation by the end of 2006 at the latest. All European Union countries are therefore now required to have some form of reasonable adjustment or accommodation law. Such laws are new to many of these countries, however, and there is therefore considerable interest in the experiences of countries in which they have enjoyed a longer history. As the first European country to introduce such laws, the United Kingdom provides an obvious point of reference. This interest is likely to intensify now that the European Commission has published a Draft Directive, which would extend the obligation to provide reasonable accommodation into the arena of goods and services. This Draft Directive includes a duty to remove barriers on an anticipatory basis, which may well have been inspired by British reasonable adjustment law.[8]

At the international level, the United Nations Convention on the Rights of Persons with Disabilities opened for signature in March 2007 and entered into force on 3 May 2008.[9] It requires signatory States, among other things, to protect their disabled citizens from discrimination in all areas of life. For these purposes, discrimination is defined so as to include the notion of reasonable accommodation or adjustment. A great many countries outside the European Union are thus also likely to be required to introduce reasonable accommodation obligations and therefore to search for inspiration as to how this might best be achieved.

British reasonable adjustment law will be of interest to many of these countries. Its law is not as old as that of countries such as the United States or Australia but, in some respects, it may provide a more positive role model. British reasonable adjustment law may be more accessible than Australian reasonable adjustment law—which is embedded within the indirect discrimination provisions of the Commonwealth Disability Discrimination Act 1992 and does not

---

[5] Government Equalities Office, *The Equality Bill: Government Response to the Consultation* (London, Stationery Office, 21 July 2008).

[6] *Ibid*, Executive Summary para 28.

[7] Directive 2000/78/EC establishing a general framework for equal treatment in employment and occupation, [2000] OJ L 303/16.

[8] See ch 2, fnn 212–18 below and accompanying text.

[9] See ch 2, section 3 below.

itself make an explicit appearance[10]—and it has not yet been hampered by a backlash such as that which has affected the US law.[11] The fact that it is heavily based on statute and code of practice may also make it more useful to countries needing to introduce reasonable accommodation duties for the first time than the more judicially driven type of approach evident in countries such as Canada.[12]

In short, Britain possesses one of the strongest and most successful reasonable adjustment regimes in the world. It is therefore a subject of importance to people outside as well as inside the country. It is also one which features large on the Government's reform agenda. Notwithstanding all of this, it is an issue which has lurked in the shadows and been the object of academic neglect. This book aims to bring British reasonable adjustment law out of its hiding place and nudge it towards the exposure of academic debate and analysis.

The topic is a complex one and, in order to assist the discussion in subsequent chapters, some background and context will be provided here. The next Section will refer to the early development of reasonable accommodation or adjustment duties in the United States to which the origins of the British duties can be traced. This will be followed by a very brief overview of the emergence and location of reasonable adjustment obligations in British law. After that, a few words will be devoted to the establishment of a single Equality Commission and the current progress towards the formulation of a single Equality Bill. Some consideration will then be given to the social model of disability and to the terminology that is frequently connected with it. Finally, some indication of the structure of the rest of the book will be provided.

---

[10]   See, for useful accounts of current Australian law on reasonable adjustment, *Employment and the Disability Discrimination Act: Guidance and Information from the Human Rights and Equal Opportunities Commission* available at http://www.humanrights.gov.au/disability_rights/faq/Employment/employment_faq_1.html#adjustment (last accessed 29 April 2008); and Productivity Commission, *Inquiry Report: Review of the Disability Discrimination Act 1992* (AGCNCO, 2004) available at http://www.pc.gov.au/inquiry/dda/docs/finalreport (last accessed 29 April 2008). I am very grateful to Graeme Innes for assistance with these references. See also, more generally, ME Tyler, 'The Disability Discrimination Act 1992: Genesis, Drafting and Prospects' (1993) 19 *Melbourne University Law Review* 211; and M Jones and LA Basser Marks, 'The Limitations on the Use of Law to Promote Rights: An Assessment of the Disability Discrimination Act 1992' in M Hauritz, C Sampford and S Blencowe (eds), *Justice for People with Disabilities: Legal and Institutional Issues* (Sydney, The Federation Press, 1998).

[11]   See generally the essays in L Hamilton Krieger (ed), 'Backlash Against the ADA: Interdisciplinary Perspectives and Implications for Social Justice Strategies' (2000) 21 *Berkeley Journal of Employment and Labor Law.*

[12]   See generally D Lepofsky, 'The Canadian Judicial Approach to Equality Rights: Freedom Ride or Roller Coaster?' (1992) 55 *Law and Contemporary Problems* 167; and JE Bickenbach, 'The ADA v the Canadian Charter of Rights: Disability Rights and the Social Model of Disability' in L Pickering Francis and A Silvers (eds), *Americans with Disabilities: Exploring Implications of the Law for Individuals and Institutions* (New York, Routledge, 2000).

2. The Emergence of Reasonable Accommodation Duties in the United States

The term 'reasonable accommodation' was born in the United States and was first used in connection with a duty to accommodate the religious beliefs of employees. Such a duty was created in 1972 by way of an amendment to the Civil Rights Act 1964.[13] It required an employer to 'reasonably accommodate to an employee's or prospective employee's religious observance or practice' unless this would impose 'undue hardship on the conduct of the employer's business'.[14] This provision, however, has been restrictively interpreted and consequently imposes only minimal obligations.[15]

Duties to make reasonable adjustments or accommodations in favour of disabled people also originate in the United States. These duties, although not expressly stated in the Rehabilitation Act 1973,[16] were introduced by its accompanying interpretive regulations[17] in what has been described as 'a remarkable example of legislating via administrative rule-making'.[18] The Rehabilitation Act is thus an important statute. It prohibits discrimination against disabled people and, by virtue of its accompanying regulations, imposes a duty to make reasonable accommodations in their favour. Its reach is limited, however, in that it extends only to federal government and to organisations which receive funding from it or which supply it with goods or services.

It was only on the enactment of the Americans with Disabilities Act 1990 (ADA)[19] that protection from disability discrimination was extended to the private sector. This Act is closely modelled on the Rehabilitation Act 1973, which continues in force.

Title I of the ADA deals with employment and applies to all employers with 15 or more employees. It imposes a duty to make reasonable accommodation subject to the limit of undue hardship.[20] Although duties to make adjustments appear throughout the ADA, the language of 'reasonable accommodation' and 'undue hardship' does not. In Title III (which deals with 'public accommodations' consisting of the provision of goods, services and amenities to the public by private entities), for instance, different terminology appears. Like Title I, it imposes duties to make adjustments but refers to them as duties to make

---

[13] Equal Employment Opportunity Act 1972 (amending the Civil Rights Act 1964, 42 USC s 2000-e).

[14] *Ibid*, s 701(j).

[15] See eg *Ansonia Board of Education v Philbrook*, 479 US 60 (1986); and *Trans World Airlines v Hardison*, 432 US 63 (1977).

[16] 29 USC s 701 et seq.

[17] 28 CFR Part 41 (Department of Justice); 29 CFR Part 32 (Department of Labor); 45 CFR Part 84 (Department of Health and Human Services).

[18] B Doyle, *Disability Discrimination and Equal Opportunities: A Comparative Study of the Employment Rights of Disabled Persons* (London, Mansell, 1995) 221.

[19] 42 USC s 12101 ff.

[20] 42 USC s 12111(8).

'reasonable modifications' subject to the limit of what is 'readily achievable'[21]—a less demanding limit than that of 'undue hardship'.

The advent of the ADA undoubtedly acted as a powerful catalyst for the enactment of the Disability Discrimination Act 1995 (DDA) in Britain. Indeed, its influence has been impressively far-reaching, and numerous countries across the globe have now followed the lead it provides and introduced laws prohibiting disability discrimination. It should nevertheless be pointed out that, while the British DDA owes its existence in large part to the ADA, it by no means mirrors all of the ADA's provisions.

3. The Emergence and Location of British Reasonable Adjustment Duties

Duties to make reasonable adjustments were introduced into British non-discrimination law by the DDA in 1995.[22] In essence, they require duty-bearers to take reasonable steps to remove a disadvantage to which a disabled person (or a group of disabled people) would otherwise be subjected by some aspect of the duty-bearer's operations. These duties apply to all areas covered by the DDA and are therefore imposed on a wide range of social actors (including employers, education providers, examination and qualification bodies, providers of goods and services, public authorities and private clubs).

The significance of the role played by reasonable adjustment obligations in disability non-discrimination law is widely recognised. It is often described as 'central'[23] to such law, as its 'cornerstone'[24] or 'core'[25] and as its 'most important aspect'.[26] So significant is the role of these duties that it is no exaggeration to suggest that such legislation would be ineffective without them.[27] Unsurprisingly therefore they have been described as 'what should be the most incisive weapon

---

[21] 42 USC s 12181(9).

[22] For critical analysis of this statute, as it was originally enacted, see eg B Doyle, 'Enabling Legislation or Dissembling Law? The Disability Discrimination Act 1995' (1997) 60 *Modern Law Review* 64; and C Gooding, *Blackstone's Guide to the Disability Discrimination Act 1995* (London, Blackstone Press, 1996).

[23] See eg R Lissack and A Short, 'Disability Discrimination Act: A Reasonable Approach to Reasonable Adjustment' (2005) 66 *Employment Law Journal* 10 at 10.

[24] See eg Department for Communities and Local Government, *Discrimination Law Review—A Framework for Fairness* (n 4 above) para 1.54; and M Diller, 'Judicial Backlash, the ADA and the Civil Rights Model' (2000) 21 *Berkeley Journal of Employment and Labor Law* 19 at 31.

[25] See eg SJ Schwab and SL Willborn, 'Reasonable Accommodation of Workplace Disabilities' (2003) 44 *William and Mary Law Review* 1197 at 1201.

[26] C Gooding and C Casserley, 'Open for All? Disability Discrimination Laws in Europe Relating to Goods and Services' in A Lawson and C Gooding (eds), *Disability Rights in Europe: From Theory to Practice* (Oxford, Hart Publishing, 2005) 149.

[27] See eg Doyle, *Disability Discrimination and Equal Opportunities* (n 18 above) 245; G Quinn, 'Disability Discrimination Law in the European Union' in H Meenan (ed), *Equality Law in an Enlarged European Union: Understanding the Article 13 Directives* (Cambridge, Cambridge University

in the fight against disability discrimination'[28] and as 'the key to breaking down the walls of myth and ignorance that have limited opportunities for individuals with disabilities'.[29]

Fundamental though these duties are acknowledged to be in the disability context, the DDA is the only British non-discrimination statute to impose them. This represents a significant departure from the template laid down in the Sex Discrimination Act 1975 (SDA) and the Race Relations Act 1976 (RRA). It is not, however, the only departure. Another important difference between the DDA and these other statutes is its asymmetrical structure. This means that, while treating a woman more favourably than a man is generally prohibited by the SDA, treating a disabled person more favourably than a non-disabled person is not prohibited by the DDA. The DDA's protection extends only to disabled people, whereas the SDA and the RRA afford protection to members of both sexes and to members of all racial or ethnic groups.

Accordingly, the DDA departs from the symmetrical structure of the SDA and the RRA. Unlike them, it does not require strict neutrality on the specified ground. It does not require identical treatment. It permits disabled people to be treated more favourably than non-disabled people and, where its reasonable adjustment duties operate, it requires them to be treated differently from non-disabled people. As Baroness Hale has observed,

> [i]n the Sex Discrimination Act and Race Relations Act, men and women or black and white, as the case may be, are opposite sides of the same coin. Each is to be treated in the same way. Treating men more favourably than women discriminates against women. Treating women more favourably than men discriminates against men. Pregnancy apart, the differences between the genders are generally regarded as irrelevant. The 1995 Act, however, does not regard the differences between disabled people and others as irrelevant. It does not expect each to be treated in the same way. It expects reasonable adjustments to be made to cater for … disabled people.[30]

Other judges have accordingly acknowledged that the DDA is an 'innovative'[31] piece of legislation which presents 'novel questions of interpretation'.[32] Observations such as these clearly indicate that the reasonable adjustment duties, which lie at the heart of this statute, merit careful study and analysis.

Express and clearly defined reasonable adjustment duties have thus taken shape in British non-discrimination law. Analogous duties, though less sharply defined, have also been developed in the context of human rights law. European

---

Press, 2007) 268–9; and P Hughes, 'Disability Discrimination and the Duty to Make Reasonable Adjustments' (2004) 33 *Industrial Law Journal* 358 at 365.

[28] Doyle, *Disability Discrimination and Equal Opportunities* (n 18 above) 233.

[29] J Cooper, 'Overcoming Barriers to Employment: The Meaning of Reasonable Accommodation and Undue Hardship in the Americans with Disabilities Act' (1991) 139 *University of Pennsylvania Law Review* 1423 at 1456.

[30] *Archibald v Fife Council* [2004] UKHL 32, [2004] IRLR 197 [47].

[31] *Smith v Churchill Stairlifts plc* [2005] EWCA Civ 1220 [1] (Maurice Kay LJ).

[32] *Clark v Novacold* [1999] IRLR 318 (CA) [2] (Mummery LJ).

human rights instruments (such as the European Convention on Human Rights and the European Social Charter) do not explicitly refer to a duty to make adjustments. Nevertheless, it is possible to identify traces of such duties in the reasoning of the European Court of Human Rights and the European Committee of Social Rights. Indeed, some sort of human rights-based duty to make adjustments appears to operate on grounds of religious belief as well as on grounds of disability.

At the international level, the recent formulation and adoption of the United Nations Convention on the Rights of Persons with Disabilities has provided an opportunity to insert explicit reasonable accommodation duties into the very heart of a binding human rights instrument. It is likely that the United Kingdom will ratify this treaty by the end of 2008.[33]

4. Progress Towards a Single Equality Commission and a Single Equality Act

4.1 Equality Commissions

The SDA established the Equal Opportunities Commission and the RRA established the Commission for Racial Equality. These were independent, government-funded bodies set up to promote the implementation and enforcement of the RRA and the SDA respectively and to provide government with relevant advice and information. The DDA, however, made no provision for the establishment of such a commission. Instead, it provided for the establishment of the National Disability Council, which had much more limited powers than those of the Commissions dealing with race and gender. Unlike those Commissions, for instance, there was no provision for the Council to support litigants or to investigate apparent patterns of non-compliance.

The National Disability Council was created in January 1996. The following year a Labour Government was elected and it set about creating a more powerful enforcement body.[34] The Disability Rights Commission Act 1999 paved the way for the replacement of the National Disability Council by the Disability Rights Commission (DRC) in 2000.

The DRC was given powers analogous to those of the other Commissions. It undoubtedly played an active and highly significant role in the promotion of

---

[33] 'UN Convention on Disability Rights' Statement released by Ann McGuire, Minister for Disabled People (London, Department for Communities and Local Government, 6 May 2008).
[34] See eg the terms of reference of the Disability Rights Task Force, *From Exclusion to Inclusion* (London, Department for Education and Employment, 1999).

disability equality in Britain and in the development of the entitlements conferred on disabled people by the DDA.[35] Frequent references will be made to its work throughout this book.

Prompted by the demands of the Employment Equality Directive to extend non-discrimination protection to the grounds of age, sexual orientation and religion and belief, the Government decided to establish a single commission to cover all grounds of discrimination and also to have a remit to cover human rights. Accordingly, the Equality Act 2006 made provision for the setting up of what has become known as the Equality and Human Rights Commission.[36] This came into being in October 2007 and has replaced the DRC along with the Equal Opportunities Commission and the Commission for Racial Equality. It is therefore this body which is now charged with the responsibility of providing assistance with the enforcement of the DDA, including its reasonable adjustment obligations, and of providing relevant information and advice to the Government.

4.2 Equality Act

Although the terms 'non-discrimination law' and 'equality law' are often used interchangeably, they will generally be used in this book to carry slightly different meanings. 'Non-discrimination law' will be reserved for law which prohibits discrimination. 'Equality law', on the other hand, will be used in a broader sense to refer to all law which aims to promote equality. The latter term therefore extends beyond law prohibiting discrimination to cover positive duties to promote equality, law relating to positive action, and those elements of human rights law which seek to further equality.

In addition to the creation of a single Equality Commission, the Government is committed to the introduction of a single Equality Act. Such an Act would cover all the existing strands covered by British non-discrimination law and would provide an opportunity to harmonise and simplify the current mass of unnecessarily complex and inconsistent statutory provisions on the subject—a mass which has been described by Lord Lester as a 'tangled thicket of inconsistent and incomplete legislation in urgent need of coherent reform'.[37] In order to inform the development of such an Act, the Government commissioned two reviews, both of which reported in 2007—the Equalities Review and the Discrimination Law Review.

---

[35] See generally DRC, 'DRC Legal Achievements: 2000–2007' (2007) 12 *DRC Legal Bulletin (Legacy Edition)*.

[36] Equality Act 2006, Part 1. See generally C O'Cinneide, 'The Commission for Equality and Human Rights: A New Institution for New and Uncertain Times?' (2007) 36 *Industrial Law Journal* 141.

[37] Lord Lester, 'Some More Equal than Others', *The Times*, 14 January 2003.

The Equalities Review was charged with the task of providing an 'independent investigation of the causes of persistent discrimination and inequality in British society'.[38] It was chaired by Trevor Phillips and composed of equality experts drawn from a variety of backgrounds. Its report, published in February 2007, makes fascinating reading and will be drawn upon in subsequent chapters.

The Discrimination Law Review was set up in February 2005 and charged with the task of assessing current non-discrimination legislation and considering how it might be harmonised and simplified. Such a review is clearly a necessary pre-condition of any attempt to produce a single Equality Bill. It was initially co-ordinated by the Department for Trade and Industry. A number of other Government Departments were heavily involved in the Review, however, and responsibility for it was moved to the Department for Communities and Local Government before it was published in June 2007.[39]

As mentioned above, the consultation paper produced by the Discrimination Law Review has sparked intense debate. It is hoped that this book will contribute to this debate and that before too long some of the law described in it will have changed. Proposals made by the Government in the Discrimination Law Review and in its recent response to the consequent consultation will be considered at relevant points throughout the text which follows.

5. The Social Model of Disability

Disability activists have reacted against what they have termed 'medical' or 'individual' understandings of disability.[40] According to these understandings, disability is viewed as a problem located within the particular individual who has the physical, sensory, intellectual, psycho-social or other impairment or condition. The responses to disability-related disadvantage generated by such understandings are likely to focus on measures targeted exclusively at the disabled individual. They might include attempts to cure the impairment or condition

---

[38] Equalities Review, *Fairness and Freedom: The Final Report of the Equalities Review* (London, Stationery Office, 2007) 13.

[39] Department for Communities and Local Government, *Discrimination Law Review—A Framework for Fairness* (n 4 above). See generally C McCrudden, 'Equality Legislation and Reflexive Regulation: A Response to the Discrimination Law Review's Consultative Paper' (2007) 36 *Industrial Law Journal* 255.

[40] See eg M Oliver, *The Politics of Disablement* (Basingstoke, Macmillan, 1990); M Oliver, *Understanding Disability: From Theory to Practice* (Basingstoke, Macmillan, 1996); J Campbell and M Oliver, *Disability Politics: Understanding our Past, Changing our Future* (New York, Routledge, 1996); T Shakespeare, 'Disability, Identity and Difference' in C Barnes and G Mercer (eds), *Exploring the Divide: Illness and Disability* (Leeds, Disability Press, 1996); C Barnes, 'A Working Social Model? Disability, Work and Disability Politics in the 21st Century' (2000) 20 *Critical Social Policy* 441; C Barnes and G Mercer, *Disability* (Malden, Polity Press, 2003); M Priestley, 'Constructions and Creations: Idealism, Materialism and Disability Theory' (1998) 13 *Disability and Society* 75; V Finkelstein, 'Representing Disability' in J Swain, S French, C Barnes and C Thomas (eds), *Disabling Barriers—Enabling Environments* (London, Sage, 2004).

through medical intervention or to correct it through the provision of aids such as hearing aids or spectacles. Should cure or correction prove impossible, attempts might be made to rehabilitate an individual by training them in skills such as the use of a long cane or an electric wheelchair. The emphasis of this individual-orientated approach is on adapting the individual so as to enable them to function in the world around them.

Although measures such as these have an important role to play in maximising the independence of disabled people, an exclusive focus upon them ignores a crucial dimension of the experience of being disabled. It is for this reason that, in the 1970s, British disabled people's organisations began to develop an alternative 'social model' understanding of disability.[41] The power of this model has undoubtedly gained considerable strength and momentum from the work of a number of highly influential disabled British social scientists.[42]

The social model draws attention to the external societal forces which operate to exclude and to marginalise people with impairments. These societal barriers take many forms. They might include architectural barriers (such as high kerbs), legal barriers (such as laws denying people with certain impairments a right to vote or to have children), organisational barriers (such as inflexible time-tabling of classes or work) and simple prejudice and hostility. The disabling effect of these barriers on people with impairments is the subject to which proponents of the social model direct attention. The term 'disability', in this social model sense, is thus reserved for

> the loss or limitation of opportunities to take part in the normal life of the community on an equal level with others due to physical and social barriers.[43]

A social model approach is one which focuses on the process through which people with impairments are disadvantaged and oppressed by the operation of external societal barriers.

The social model has not been free from academic controversy.[44] This has largely concerned its inability to address the entirety of the experience of, and the limitations imposed on, disabled people.[45] The social model is designed to focus on the process of disablement through societal barriers and is not concerned with non-social issues, such as the symptoms of particular impairments in particular individuals and the restrictions that such impairments will inevitably impose on their ability to function.

---

[41] See eg Union of Physically Impaired Against Segregation, *Fundamental Principles of Disability* (London, UPIAS/Disability Alliance, 1976).

[42] See eg the works of Oliver, Barnes and Finkelstein cited in n 40 above. See also more generally C Barnes, 'Disability, Disability Studies and the Academy' in Swain, French, Barnes and Thomas (eds), *Disabling Barriers* (n 40 above).

[43] Disabled People's International, *Proceedings of the First World Congress* (Singapore, DPI, 1982).

[44] For a concise and lucid account of the causes and nature of some of these debates, see C Thomas, 'How is Disability Understood? An Examination of Sociological Approaches' (2004) 19 *Disability and Society* 569.

[45] See eg T Shakespeare, *Disability Rights and Wrongs* (London, Routledge, 2006).

Nevertheless, perhaps because of its limitations and its simplicity, the social model represents an extremely potent political instrument the influence of which has spread throughout the world. British disabled people and their organisations have relied on it to call upon policy-makers and legislators for laws and policies designed to break down disabling social barriers. Non-discrimination law, with well-crafted reasonable adjustment duties, is clearly one such law.[46] Importantly, however, it is not the only one and is not looked to as the sole solution to the problems of exclusion and marginalisation faced by British disabled people. Considerable campaigning effort has been devoted to the introduction of other forms of law or policy on issues such as independent living and welfare benefits.

Strict adherence to the social model understanding of disability has implications for terminology. The logical consequence of adherence to it is that the term 'disability' is reserved for the disadvantage caused to people with impairments by externally-imposed social barriers. Many of those who adopt a social model approach (particularly in Britain) therefore favour the language of 'people with impairments' and 'disabled people'. This is because in strict social model terms, while it makes sense to speak of people being 'disabled' by social barriers, it is illogical to refer to people as having 'disabilities'. The term 'people with disabilities', however, is favoured by many disability campaigners outside the United Kingdom (including those influential in the drafting of international human rights instruments) because it positions 'people' before disability or impairment.[47]

In this book, the social model language of 'disabled people' and 'people with impairments' will generally be used. It will sometimes be necessary to depart from this terminology, however, in order to take into account the fact that statutes have given the term 'disabled' different and quite particular meanings.

6. Structure of the Book

This book will be divided into five substantive chapters. The first of these, chapter two, will explore the extent to which duties akin to reasonable adjustment duties emerge from human rights law. The second, chapter three, will set out the law relating to reasonable adjustment duties laid down by the DDA.

Chapters four and five will be concerned with the relationship between reasonable adjustment and other equality and non-discrimination concepts.

---

[46] See generally C Barnes, *Disabled People in Britain and Discrimination: A Case for Anti-Discrimination Legislation* (London, Hurst/BCODP, 1991).

[47] See eg G Quinn, 'The Human Rights of People with Disabilities under EU Law' in P Alston, M Bustello and M Keenan (eds), *The EU and Human Rights* (Oxford, Oxford University Press, 1999) 285. For a thought-provoking discussion of the relationship between the social model and the UN Convention on the Rights of Persons with Disabilities, see R Kayess and P French, 'Out of Darkness into Light? Introducing the Convention on the Rights of Persons with Disabilities' (2008) 8 *Human Rights Law Review* 1.

Chapter four will focus on the way in which it interacts with and compares to other concepts which prohibit discrimination. It will cover the non-discrimination concepts included in the DDA itself and also the concept of indirect discrimination, which, though not included in the DDA, has an important role to play in British equality law.

Chapter five will address concepts associated with the taking of positive measures to counter disadvantage and promote equality. It will explore the relationship between the duty to make reasonable adjustments and the disability equality duty, which requires public sector bodies to have due regard to the promotion of disability equality in all aspects of their functioning. It will also consider the notions of positive action and positive discrimination and the question of whether the duty to make reasonable adjustments should be classified in either of these ways.

Chapter six, the last of the substantive chapters, will attempt to identify some of the potential barriers to successful implementation and development of reasonable adjustment duties. It will also explore ways in which these might be addressed. Although the focus of this chapter remains British reasonable adjustment duties and their development, it will draw heavily upon US literature and experience.

2

Duties to Make Adjustments and Human Rights

1. Introduction

THE EMERGENCE AND development of British non-discrimination law has not taken place within a broad framework of human rights. Indeed, non-discrimination statutes were enacted more than two decades before the Human Rights Act 1998 placed human rights clearly on the domestic agenda. Although these Acts were not confined to employment, it undoubtedly provided their prime focus at least in the early years.[1] The prime focus of human rights law, on the other hand, is the activity of public authorities. The original gap between non-discrimination and human rights in Britain is also demonstrated by the fact that the Commissions set up to support the non-discrimination legislation relating to race, gender and disability were given no clear human rights mandate.

In recent years, however, the originally sharp divide between non-discrimination and human rights has begun to blur. The discharge of public functions has been brought within the ambit of non-discrimination legislation and public authorities have been placed under statutory duties to promote race, gender and disability equality. Part 1 of the Equality Act 2006 provided for the establishment of a single Equality and Human Rights Commission to replace the three pre-existing Commissions. This represents an explicit recognition of the obvious overlap between the concerns of non-discrimination and human rights law.[2]

In the disability context, British reasonable adjustment duties tend to be associated with non-discrimination law rather than human rights law. This is unsurprising given that such duties were given statutory effect by the Disability

---

[1] See generally N Bamforth, 'Conceptions of Anti-Discrimination Law' (2004) 24 *Oxford Journal of Legal Studies* 693 at 693–4.

[2] S Spencer, 'Partner Rediscovered: Human Rights and Equality in the UK' in C Harvey (ed), *Human Rights in the Community* (Oxford, Hart Publishing, 2005); and C Gearty, 'Can Human Rights Provide Real Equality?', Legal Action Group annual lecture, 19 November 2007, available at http://www.conorgearty.co.uk/pdfs/Legal_Action_group_GEARTY2007.pdf (last accessed 29 April 2008).

Discrimination Act 1995 (DDA). Their exact nature and shape will be examined in the next chapter. Their statutory skeleton, as will be seen, is laid out in precise and technical detail and flesh has now been added to it by case law.

Reasonable adjustment obligations have, however, also emerged in the context of human rights law. Although their existence has now been acknowledged (both implicitly and explicitly) in various international and European instruments and case law, they are defined with much less precision and technicality in this context than they are in the DDA. It is the purpose of this chapter to identify and explore the nature and scope of these human rights based reasonable adjustment duties.

In Section 2 of this chapter, the argument that disabled people will only truly be able to enjoy the universal human rights conferred on them if some sort of reasonable adjustment duty is recognised will be outlined. In Section 3, attention will be turned to what is now the foremost international instrument on the human rights of disabled people—the United Nations Convention on the Rights of Persons With Disabilities (CRPD). Section 4 will examine relevant developments under the European Convention on Human Rights (ECHR) and the European Social Charter (ESC). Although the United Kingdom is a signatory to both instruments, the impact of the former on domestic law has been more significant than the latter, largely due to its more powerful enforcement machinery (in the form of the European Court of Human Rights) and to its incorporation into domestic law by the Human Rights Act 1998. This distinction will be reflected in the text which follows—the ECHR being given more emphasis than the ESC. In Section 5 some consideration will also be given to the European Union and the role of relevant human or fundamental rights within it. Relevant provisions of the Employment Equality Directive[3] will be outlined at this point because, although that instrument emerged from non-discrimination principles that were not exclusively driven by a human rights agenda, its requirements are inextricably bound up with the European Union's growing concern with human or fundamental rights.

---

[3] Directive 2000/78/EC establishing a general framework for equal treatment in employment and occupation, [2000] OJ L 303/16.

2. The Role of Reasonable Adjustment in Ensuring the Genuine Universality of Human Rights

2.1 The Traditional Invisibility of Disabled People

Modern human rights regimes date back to the years following the Second World War.[4] At the international level, the Universal Declaration of Human Rights was issued in 1948 and, at the European level, the European Convention on Human Rights was elaborated in 1950. At both the international and the European levels, a distinction has traditionally been made between civil and political rights on the one hand and social, cultural and economic rights on the other. The former are protected, within the United Nations framework, by the International Covenant on Civil and Political Rights 1966 (ICCPR) and, at the European level, by the ECHR. The latter are protected, within the UN framework, by the International Covenant on Economic, Social and Cultural Rights (ICESCR) and, at the European level, by the European Social Charter. These instruments require States to confer and protect the relevant rights on a universal basis. They are thus obliged to confer them on all citizens, including those who happen to be disabled.

Civil and political rights include the right to life,[5] to be free from torture and inhuman or degrading treatment,[6] to liberty and security of person,[7] to associate freely with others,[8] and to vote and take part in the political life of one's country.[9] They also include the right to be free from discrimination.[10] Economic, social and cultural rights include the right to education,[11] to work,[12] to health[13] and to an adequate standard of living.[14]

---

[4] See generally MA Glendon, *A World Made New: Eleanor Roosevelt and the Universal Declaration of Human Rights* (New York, Random House, 2001); and AWB Simpson, *Human Rights and the End of Empire: Britain and the Genesis of the European Convention* (New York, Oxford University Press, 2001).

[5] ICCPR Art 6.

[6] ICCPR Art 7.

[7] ICCPR Art 9. See also Art 8, concerning freedom from slavery, and Art 12, concerning liberty of movement.

[8] ICCPR Art 22. See also Art 23, concerning family rights; Art 24, concerning the protection of children; and Art 17, concerning privacy.

[9] ICCPR Art 25.

[10] ICCPR Art 26.

[11] ICESCR Art 13.

[12] ICESCR Art 6.

[13] ICESCR Art 12. See generally K Tomasevski, 'The Right to Health for Persons with Disabilities' in T Degener and Y Koster-Dreese (eds), *Human Rights and Disabled Persons: Essays and Relevant Human Rights Instruments* (Dordrecht Netherlands, Martinus Nijhoff Publishers, 1995).

[14] ICESCR Art 11.

These rights, if appropriately granted and protected, would undoubtedly go a considerable way towards solving the problems of exclusion, neglect and humiliation which disabled people all over the world continue to experience.[15] Traditionally, however, the potential of these universally conferred human rights to effect improvements in the lives of disabled people has been disturbingly underdeveloped. The invisibility of disabled people as subjects of human rights law has often been identified as the principal explanation.[16]

This invisibility has arisen from the separation of disabled people from society's mainstream—a separation caused by their inability to access mainstream facilities due to physical and social barriers. Even if their exclusion and humiliation are noticed, lawyers, policy-makers and others have frequently failed to recognise such marginalisation as involving any form of violation of human rights. Too often, it has been attributed to the disabled person's impairment rather than to an inadequate social response to that impairment.

For at least the past four decades, the Disability Movement has striven to challenge the assumption that unless a person with an impairment can be cured or corrected (eg through a hearing aid or drugs) they must remain outside the mainstream of their society and, unable to participate in education or employment, become dependent on welfare or charity for their survival. It has argued that disabled people should be valued as equals. They should be viewed, not merely as somewhat burdensome objects of pity or charity, but as human beings who, like their non-disabled counterparts, are entitled to enjoy the fundamental human rights granted to all. In the words of Gerard Quinn and Theresia Degener, in a highly influential report on the treatment of disability in the UN human rights system, 'the answer to invisibility is an insistence on the equal application of all human rights to persons with disabilities'.[17] The 'equal application' of human rights to disabled people, however, is not an entirely straightforward matter.

---

[15]   See generally L Despouy, *Human Rights and Disabled Persons,* Human Rights Studies Series No 6, sales no E.92.XIV.4 (Geneva, UN Publications, 1992).

[16]   See eg, in the context of the ECHR, L Clements and J Read, *Disabled People and European Human Rights: A Review of the Implications of the 1998 Human Rights Act for Disabled Children and Adults in the UK* (Bristol, Policy Press, 2003); and L Clements and J Read, 'The Dog that Didn't Bark: The Issue of Access to Rights under the ECHR by Disabled People' in A Lawson and C Gooding (eds), *Disability Rights in Europe: From Theory to Practice* (Oxford, Hart Publishing, 2005); and, in the context of the UN, G Quinn and T Degener, 'Expanding the System: The Debate about a Disability-Specific Convention' in G Quinn and T Degener (eds), *Human Rights and Disability: The Current Use and Future Potential of United Nations Human Rights Instruments in the Context of Disability* (Geneva, UN, 2002).

[17]   G Quinn and T Degener, 'The Moral Authority for Change: Human Rights Values and the Worldwide Process of Disability Reform' in Quinn and Degener (eds), *Human Rights and Disability* (n 16 above) para 1.4(c).

2.2 Equal Application of Human Rights

The concept of equality has attracted debate and analysis for many centuries.[18] A detailed account of that debate is beyond the scope of this work. Nevertheless, for present purposes, an understanding of the distinction that is frequently drawn between notions of formal and substantive equality is important.[19]

Formal equality is based on the Aristotelian notion that likes should be treated alike—that similarly situated people should be treated in the same way despite irrelevant differences in their circumstances. Its focus is therefore on requiring identical treatment. It would insist, for instance, that a university treat identically qualified applicants in the same way regardless of the fact that they might have different genders, racial backgrounds or physical impairments. It would insist that employers offer promotion to identically situated people on the same basis regardless of such differences; that hospitals offer them beds on the same basis; that electoral authorities allow them to vote on the same basis; and that public housing services offer them accommodation on the same basis. Clearly, the application of a system of formal equality begs the question of what should be regarded as a relevant difference and who should be treated as similarly situated.[20]

Substantive equality, however, looks beyond the limits of identical treatment to the measures which may be required in order to counter disadvantage and to facilitate equality of opportunity or even equality of outcome. It therefore requires difference, resulting from factors such as disability, to be acknowledged and to elicit different treatment where identical treatment would cause disadvantage. It would thus require education providers not simply to issue all students with identical printed examination questions but to ensure that those questions were issued to a blind student in an appropriate alternative format. It would require electoral authorities not simply to declare that all citizens were entitled to vote but to ensure that the places in which voting took place were accessible to wheelchair-users.

A distinction which reflects the division between notions of formal and of substantive equality has been developed by Ronald Dworkin.[21] He distinguishes

---

[18] See generally I Hampscher-Monk, *A History of Modern Political Thought: Major Political Thinkers from Hobbes to Marx* (Oxford, Blackwell, 1992); S Darwall (ed), *Equal Freedom* (Ann Arbor, Michigan University Press, 1995); L Pojman and R Westmoreland (eds), *Equality: Selected Readings* (Oxford, Oxford University Press, 1997); and M Clayton and A Williams (eds), *The Ideal of Equality* (Basingstoke, Palgrave Macmillan, 2002).

[19] See generally S Fredman, *Discrimination Law* (Oxford, Oxford University Press, 2002) ch 1; S Fredman, 'Equality: A New Generation?' (2001) 30 *Industrial Law Journal* 145; C Barnard and B Hepple, 'Substantive Equality' (2000) 59 *Cambridge Law Journal* 562; and A Hendriks, 'The significance of equality and non-discrimination for the protection of Disabled Persons' in Degener and Koster-Dreese (eds), *Human Rights and Disabled Persons* (n 13 above).

[20] R Westen, 'The Empty Idea of Equality' (1982) 95 *Harvard Law Review* 537. See also E Holmes, 'Anti-Discrimination Rights Without Equality' (2005) 68 *Modern Law Review* 175.

[21] R Dworkin, *A Matter of Principle* (Oxford, Oxford University Press, 1986) 190–98 and 205–13.

the equal treatment of people, in terms of the division of resources, from the treatment of people as equals. The latter type of treatment is a manifestation of commitment to the view that people are entitled to equal concern and respect from the State. Such a commitment will require treatment which is not identical in situations where treating everybody in the same way would demonstrate a lesser degree of concern and respect for certain individuals because of their particular circumstances. This distinction is succinctly expressed by Nicholas Bamforth in the following words:

> A crucial difference between equal treatment and treatment as equals lies in the comparison which each involves. Equal treatment requires only a crude evaluation of whether two people or actions are sufficiently 'the same' that they merit similar treatment. Treatment as equals, by contrast, involves a fuller and more flexible conception of equality. The question is not 'whether any deviation' from equal treatment is permitted, but instead 'what reasons for deviation are consistent with equal concern and respect'.[22]

The use of the term 'equality' to cover notions of treatment as equals has not been free from controversy. It has been argued that it constitutes little more than a rhetorical device by which to express the principle that the well-being of every human being matters.[23] Attention should consequently be directed to the values or the 'moral goods' on which legal regimes which purport to be justified by reference to such principles are in fact based.[24]

The facilitation of social inclusion and of participation in society may be regarded as important values, which underlie and shape non-discrimination and much of human rights law.[25] Concepts of autonomy and freedom also play an important role.[26] The value which is perhaps most frequently mentioned in connection with human rights, however, is that of human dignity.[27]

---

[22] Bamforth, 'Conceptions of Anti-Discrimination Law' (n 1 above) 712—drawing upon Dworkin, *ibid*, 209.

[23] See eg J Raz, *The Morality of Freedom* (Oxford, Oxford University Press, 1986) 217–28.

[24] *Ibid*.

[25] See generally H Collins, 'Discrimination, Equality and Social Inclusion' (2003) 66 *Modern Law Review* 16; C Barnard, 'The Future of Equality Law: Equality and Beyond' in C Barnard, S Deakin and GS Morris (eds), *The Future of Labour Law* (Oxford, Hart Publishing, 2004); and F Mégret, 'The Disabilities Convention: Human Rights of Persons with Disabilities or Disability Rights?' (2008) 30 Human Rights Quarterly 494.

[26] See eg Raz, *The Morality of Freedom* (n 23 above). See also the Opinion of the Advocate General in Case C-303/06 *Coleman v Attridge Law* OJ C 237, 30 September 2006, p 6, (31 January 2008) [7]–[14] where 'human dignity' and 'personal autonomy' are identified as the values underlying equality.

[27] See generally G Moon and R Allen, 'Dignity Discourse in Discrimination Law: A Better Route to Equality?' [2006] *European Human Rights Law Review* 610; C McCrudden, 'Human Dignity' Working Paper No 10/2006 (April 2006), University of Oxford Faculty of Law, Legal Studies Research Paper Series, available at http://papers.ssrn.com/Abstract=899687 (last accessed 2 March 2008); DG Reaume, 'Discrimination and Dignity' (2003) *Louisiana Law Review* 645; D Feldman, 'Human Dignity as a Legal Value Part I' [1999] *Public Law* 682 and 'Part II' [2000] *Public Law* 61; and DC Galloway, 'Three models of (in)equality' (1993) 68 *McGill Law Review* 64.

Dignity has particular resonance for disabled people. In the words of Gerard Quinn and Theresia Degener,

[r]ecognition of the value of human dignity serves as a powerful reminder that people with disabilities have a stake in and a claim on society that must be honoured quite apart from any considerations of social or economic utility. They are ends in themselves and not means to the ends of others. This view militates strongly against the contrary social impulse to rank people in terms of their usefulness and to screen out those with significant differences.[28]

A commitment to respect for human dignity requires a focus not on sameness or identical treatment but on individual flourishing. Connor Gearty adopts this view, arguing that the language of human rights

asserts that we are all equal in view of our humanity and ... our dignity ... demands that we each of us be given the chance to do the best we can, to thrive, to flourish, to do something with ourselves.[29]

For this reason respect for dignity will sometimes require treatment which is different rather than treatment which is identical.[30]

Notions of substantive equality or the treatment of people as equals are of fundamental importance in human rights law. They underlie the references which are frequently made to the idea that democratic society is 'founded on the principle that each individual has equal value' and that their rights should be protected accordingly.[31] The right to equality in this sense has been described as 'one of the oldest and most well-recognised of fundamental human rights'.[32] Indeed, it played an important part in shaping such venerable documents as the French Declaration of the Rights of Man and the Constitution of the United States of America.[33]

The principle that all human beings must be valued and protected as equals also shapes the rhetoric of the current international human rights framework.

---

[28] Quinn and Degener, 'The Moral Authority for Change' (n 17 above) para 1.1.

[29] *Can Human Rights Survive?* (Cambridge, Cambridge University Press, 2006) 50.

[30] See generally Moon and Allen, 'Dignity Discourse in Discrimination Law' (n 27 above) 635–9. For arguments that the notion of dignity is highly context and time dependent and that its substantive content is therefore not fixed or unvarying, see E Grabham, 'Law v Canada: New Directions for Equality Under the Canadian Charter' (2002) 22 *Oxford Journal of Legal Studies* 654; and McCrudden, 'Human Dignity' (n 27 above). For similar arguments in relation to human rights generally, see S Sedley, 'Human Rights: A Twenty-First Century Agenda' [1995] *Public Law* 386.

[31] *Ghaidan v Godin-Mendoza* [2004] UKHL 22 [132] (Baroness Hale). See further B Hale, 'The Quest for Equal Treatment' [2005] *Public Law* 571 and, for critical analysis of the concept of equal human worth and its constitutional role, L Pojman, 'On Equal Human Worth: A Critique of Contemporary Egalitarianism' in Pojman and Westmoreland (eds), *Equality: Selected Readings* (n 18 above); and J Jowell, 'Is Equality a Constitutional Principle?' (1994) 47 *Current Legal Problems* 1.

[32] C Barnard, 'The Principle of Equality in the Community Context: P, Grant, Kalanke and Marschall—Four Uneasy Bedfellows?' (1998) 57 *Cambridge Law Journal* 352 at 362.

[33] See generally T Paine, *Rights of Man* (Indianapolis, Hackett Publishing, 1992) and AH Kelly, W Harbison and H Belz, *The American Constitution: Its Origin and Development* (New York, W Norton and Company, 1991).

The Universal Declaration of Human Rights 1948, for instance, asserts that 'all human beings are born free and equal in dignity and rights'[34] and describes the recognition of the 'inherent dignity' and the 'equal and inalienable rights of all members of the human family' as the 'foundation of freedom, justice and peace in the world'.[35] These 'equal and inalienable' rights are thus inextricably linked to and 'derived from the inherent dignity of the human person'.[36]

The idea that different treatment may sometimes be required in order to ensure that the human rights of certain individuals enjoy the same degree of respect, concern and protection as that accorded to the rights of others is by no means a new one in the international arena. As early as 1935, the Permanent Court of International Justice observed that

> equality in fact may involve the necessity of different treatment in order to attain a result which establishes an equilibrium between different situations.[37]

It is an idea which has been expressly articulated by both the UN's Human Rights Committee and its Committee on Economic Social and Cultural Rights. In its General Comment No 18 the Human Rights Committee stressed that Article 26 of the ICCPR—which requires civil and political rights to be enjoyed on a non-discriminatory basis—may sometimes go beyond requiring mere formal equality and demand different treatment.[38] These views are reflected in the Committee on Economic Social and Cultural Rights' General Comment No 5.[39] It is therefore no surprise that the Conventions on race and gender expressly authorise affirmative action measures which aim to counter the particular forms of disadvantage and discrimination experienced by relevant groups.[40] Article 5(4) of the recently adopted CRPD makes similar provision, although, unlike the equivalent provisions relating to race and gender, it is not subject to the limitation that 'these measures shall be discontinued when the objectives of equality of opportunity and treatment have been achieved'.

In the context of human rights, then, recognition of the need to accord equal respect and concern to all human beings carries with it an obligation on States to ensure that, where appropriate, certain individuals are treated differently from others. Treating them in the same way as others would be to fail to recognise

---

[34] Universal Declaration of Human Rights 1948 Art 1.

[35] *Ibid*, Preamble.

[36] Preamble to both the ICCPR and the ICESCR.

[37] PCIJ, Advisory Opinion of 6 April 1935 on the *Minority Schools in Albania* case (Series A/B no 64) 19.

[38] UN Official Records, Supp No 40, 1989 (A/45/40) pp 173–5, para 8.

[39] General Comment No 5 'Persons with Disabilities' adopted by the Committee on Economic, Social and Cultural Rights at its 11th session in 1994 (UN Doc E/1995/22). For discussion of the background to this General Comment, see P Alston, 'Disability and the International Covenant on Economic, Social and Cultural Rights' in Degener and Koster-Dreese (eds), *Human Rights and Disabled Persons* (n 13 above).

[40] International Convention on the Elimination of Discrimination Against Women 1979, Art 4(1); and International Convention on the Elimination of Racial Discrimination 1965, Art 1(4).

significant differences in their circumstances and would result in a lesser degree of respect for, or protection of, their basic human rights. Adherence to the concept of formal equality alone would thus represent an inadequate response. Some notion of substantive equality is therefore inherent in the effective recognition of universal human rights. The nature of the different treatment required in any particular case will depend on the needs and circumstances of the individuals concerned.

2.3   Reasonable Adjustment and the Human Rights of Disabled People

In the context of disability, the importance of responding to the differing needs and circumstances of each individual, as a pre-condition of effective human rights protection, was recognised in the World Programme of Action concerning Disabled Persons. This was adopted by the UN General Assembly in 1982. According to it,

> [t]he principle of equal rights for the disabled and non-disabled implies that the needs of each and every individual are of equal importance, that these needs must be made the basis for the planning of societies, and that resources must be employed in such a way as to ensure, for every individual, equal opportunity for participation.[41]

These words were echoed a decade later in both the non-binding Standard Rules on the Equalization of Opportunities for Persons with Disabilities,[42] and the Committee on Economic Social and Cultural Rights' General Comment No 5.[43] Given the stress they placed on responding appropriately to the needs and circumstances of a particular disabled individual, the emergence of some form of reasonable adjustment or accommodation duty was perhaps inevitable.

The concept of reasonable adjustment, or reasonable accommodation, was explicitly acknowledged to be an integral element of equality in General Comment No 5. The Committee on Economic, Social and Cultural Rights there stressed that Article 2(2) of the ICESCR required States to ensure that the rights conferred by that Convention should be enjoyed by all citizens without any discrimination on the ground of disability.[44] For this purpose, it specified that disability-based discrimination included

---

[41]   General Assembly Resolution 37/52 (3 December 1982) para 25.

[42]   Standard Rules on the Equalization of Opportunities for Persons with Disabilities adopted by General Assembly Resolution 48/96 of 20 December 1993, paras 25 and 26.

[43]   General Comment No 5 'Persons with Disabilities' (n 39 above) para 17.

[44]   According to the Committee, disability is included in Art 2(2)'s reference to 'other status': General Comment No 5 'Persons with Disabilities' (n 39 above) para 5.

any distinction, exclusion, restriction or preference, or denial of reasonable accommodation based on disability which has the effect of nullifying or impairing the recognition, enjoyment or exercise of economic, social or cultural rights.[45]

It is not difficult to imagine scenarios in which the denial of a reasonable adjustment would nullify the recognition or enjoyment of such rights. The right to education, for instance, would be meaningless for children with sensory impairments, such as blindness or deafness, without some provision for information and communication to be made accessible to them. The right to health would be illusory for people with mobility impairments if medical advice and treatment were made available only in physically inaccessible buildings. The right to work would be effectively nullified for many disabled people if employers were entitled to treat them in exactly the same way as their non-disabled colleagues without any obligation to consider adapting timetables, physical features or equipment to accommodate their needs.

Some notion of reasonable accommodation or adjustment also seems to have been recognised in the context of civil and political rights prior to the CRPD. This is well illustrated by the decision of the Human Rights Committee in *Hamilton v Jamaica*.[46] *Hamilton* concerned a prisoner whose legs were paralysed and who was detained in the standard accommodation of death row. Because of his physical impairment, he was unable to slop out his cell and to climb onto the bed. The failure of the State to ensure that he was held in conditions that were adapted to meet his needs was found to constitute a failure to treat a detained person with humanity and respect, contrary to Article 10 of the ICCPR.

In summary, even before the CRPD, there was an understanding that the human rights of disabled people would be effectively enjoyed and protected only if their different circumstances and needs were recognised and, where reasonable, accommodated. The CRPD, as will be seen in the next Section, builds on this understanding. Indeed, one of its central aims is to clarify this understanding and to give it context. It is also neatly encapsulated in the following words of the British Disability Rights Commission:

> Starting from a human rights perspective means recognising that human beings do not all start from the same place. The approach recognises that as we tackle the differing dimensions to exclusion, address multiple exclusion and the cumulative effect of different forces on the individual ... we do not lose sight of that individual. This focus on the individual means that barriers need to be actively dismantled and reasonable adjustments made to ensure equitable outcomes for all people ... The DRC hopes that

---

[45] General Comment No 5 'Persons with Disabilities' (n 39 above) para 15.

[46] Communication No 616/1995, Views adopted by the Committee on 28 July 1999 (CCPR/C/66/D/616/1995). For a similar case decided by the European Court of Human Rights, see *Price v UK* App No 33394/96 (2001) 34 EHRR 1285; and, for a similar decision of the Inter-American Commission on Human Rights, see The Case of Victor Rosario Congo, Annual Report of the Inter-American Commission on Human Rights, Report 63/99, Case 11.427, Ecuador, OEA/Ser.L/V/II.102, Doc 6 Rev (1999) (discussed in A Kanter, 'The Globalization of Disability Rights Law' in P Blanck (ed), *Disability Rights* (Hants, Ashgate Publishing, 2005) 508–11).

one day we will get to the situation where human rights and disability rights are regarded as one in the same and where there is a thriving human rights culture in this country.[47]

3. Reasonable Adjustments Under the United Nations Convention on the Rights of Persons with Disabilities

3.1 Purposes and Obligations

3.1.1 The Clarification of Existing Rights

The CRPD, together with its accompanying optional protocol, was adopted by the General Assembly on 13 December 2006 and opened for signature on 30 March 2007.[48] It received more signatures from States Parties on its opening day than have been received by any other UN human rights Convention. The CRPD entered into force on 3 May 2008 and its Optional Protocol entered into force thirty days after that. It is the first binding UN disability-specific instrument and its implementation is to be monitored and supported by a new Committee on the Rights of Persons with Disabilities.[49]

The CRPD was described by Kofi Annan, the outgoing Secretary-General, as a 'remarkable and forward-looking document' which marks

the dawn of a new era—an era in which disabled people will no longer have to endure the discriminatory practices and attitudes that have been permitted to prevail for all too long.[50]

Similar enthusiasm was displayed by leading figures in the disability movement. According to Venus Ilagan, the chair of Disabled Peoples International, speaking on the day the substantive terms of the Convention were finalised,

[t]oday, August 25, 2006, is a day to celebrate! We have achieved something that has long been the dream of our membership: A UN Convention on our human rights....

---

[47] Parliamentary Briefing released prior to a House of Lords balloted debate on human rights on 22 March 2007.

[48] See generally A Kanter (ed), *Special Issue of Syracuse Journal of International Law and Commerce*, vol 34, Spring 2007; O Arnardottir and G Quinn (eds), *The UN Convention on the Rights of Persons with Disabilities: European and Scandinavian Perspectives* (Leiden, Martinus Nijhoff, 2008); R Kayess and P French, 'Out of Darkness into Light? Introducing the Convention on the Rights of Persons with Disabilities' (2008) 8 *Human Rights Law Review* 1; Mégret, 'The Disabilities Convention' (n 25 above); and C Parker and L Clements, 'The UN Convention on the Rights of Persons with Disabilities: A New Right to Independent Living?' [2008] *European Human Rights Law Review* 508.

[49] CRPD Art 34.

[50] Secretary-General's Message on the Adoption of the CRPD, available at http://www.un.org/apps/sg/sgstats.asp?nid=2362 (last accessed 29 April 2008).

> The draft instrument accepted here today recognizes and entrenches our rights in the UN Human Rights framework, and in this way is a huge victory for us all.[51]

These words allude to the important role played by disabled people and their organisations in the elaboration and adoption of the CRPD. Insisting on the motto 'nothing about us without us', they played an unprecedented role in the history of UN treaty-making. According to Ambassador Don MacKay, who chaired the meetings in which the terms of the CRPD were finalised,

> [t]his is an extraordinarily far-reaching convention … When I first became involved in the process I would not have seen States being able to reach out as far as they have on the issues in the Convention. The credit for that undoubtedly goes to colleagues from civil society who have been so actively engaged in the process in such large numbers. They have constantly cajoled, urged, entreated, pressured, argued and very very effectively persuaded governments to keep shifting the boundaries of the envelope in so far as the Convention is concerned. I am very pleased that that has happened.[52]

In view of such enthusiasm, it may be tempting to believe that the CRPD confers new rights on disabled people.[53] This, however, was not its purpose. It was elaborated in order to ensure that the rights already conferred on all human beings in signatory states by instruments such as the ICESCR and the ICCPR might genuinely be enjoyed by disabled people on an equal basis with others. The realisation of this aim would nevertheless represent a giant leap forward towards a world in which disabled people were meaningfully included and valued. It is this possibility which has justifiably generated so much enthusiasm.

The task confronting the drafters of the CRPD was thus the challenging one of articulating pre-existing rights so as to give them particular relevance to the lives of disabled people. Disability activists insisted that, regardless of political pressure to reach agreement, no compromise could be made on the standard of the rights to be set out in the new instrument. A new disability-specific convention would be worth having only if its elaboration of the human rights to be enjoyed by disabled people was set at a standard no lower than that set for non-disabled people.[54] With this in mind, the International Disability Caucus (set up to co-ordinate the work of disabled people's organisations during the drafting process) issued a statement in which it set out a number of examples of issues and principles that it considered essential to include in the Convention and

---

[51] Disabled Peoples International, 'Message from the Chairperson', available at http://v1.dpi.org/lang-en/resources/details.php?page=685 (last accessed 29 April 2008).

[52] Press conference on the adoption of the Convention on the Rights of Persons with Disabilities, UN Headquarters, New York, 6 December 2006.

[53] For thought-provoking discussion of the extent to which this Convention does in fact create new rights, see Mégret, 'The Disabilities Convention (n 25 above).

[54] See eg E Rosenthal and CJ Sundram, 'Recognizing Existing Rights and Crafting New Ones: Tools for Drafting Human Rights Instruments for People with Mental Disabilities' in S Herr, L Gostin and H Koh (eds), *The Human Rights of Persons with Intellectual Disabilities* (Oxford, Oxford University Press, 2003) 470–71 and 474–7.

without which it would 'fall short'.[55] Among these were the prohibition of 'any deprivation of liberty on the basis of disability' and 'any medical and other intervention which is made against the informed consent of persons with disabilities'; equal access to health care and rehabilitation; the right to live in the community and to fully inclusive mainstream education; the provision of accessible information and infrastructure; and the establishment of a rigorous monitoring system operating with the involvement of disabled people's organisations.

The concern that the standard of rights articulated for disabled people must be equivalent to that applying to non-disabled people animated the debates over every substantive Article in the Convention. It is thus to be hoped that it will not be possible to interpret any of the provisions to emerge from such debates so as to legitimise a lower standard of protection for the rights of disabled people. Article 4(4) offers an additional safety net by providing that the Convention should not in any way derogate from stronger obligations imposed on a particular State either by national or by international laws. It would thus make it impossible for a State to argue that the CRPD sets a lower standard than that set by the ICCPR or the ICESCR and thereby exempts it from satisfying the higher standard.

3.1.2 General Principles and Obligations

The CRPD itself contains a number of Articles, in addition to the 26 paragraphs of its preamble, the function of which is to make clear its purpose and its underlying principles. According to Article 1, its purpose is

> to promote, protect and ensure the full and equal enjoyment of all human rights and fundamental freedoms by all persons with disabilities, and to promote respect for their inherent dignity.

The principle of equality is thus given a central place. The preamble refers to 'the profound social disadvantage' currently experienced by disabled people, to the fact that most of them live in conditions of poverty and to the fact that they continue to encounter 'barriers in their participation as equal members of society'.[56] It is acknowledged that, although the UN Charter recognises that 'all members of the human family' have 'equal and inalienable rights', there is a need for disabled people to be guaranteed the full enjoyment of these rights 'without discrimination'.[57] Further, paragraph (h) declares that discrimination against any person on the basis of disability is a violation of the inherent dignity and worth of the human person.

---

[55] 'IDC Final Statement to States Delegates at Ad Hoc Committee 6th Session'. See further P Wright, 'When to Hold 'Em and When to Fold 'Em: Lessons Learned from Enacting the Americans with Disabilities Act' in M Breslin and S Yee (eds), *Disability Rights Law and Policy: International and National Perspectives* (Ardsley NY, Transnational Publishers inc, 2002).

[56] CRPD preamble, paras (y), (t) and (k) respectively. See also para (e).

[57] *Ibid*, paras (a) and (c).

Article 3 contains eight paragraphs, which set out the underlying principles of the CRPD and are intended to inform its interpretation. Paragraph (a) refers to respect for the 'inherent dignity', 'autonomy' and 'independence' of the individual, and paragraph (d) to respect for 'difference' and 'human diversity'. Other paragraphs refer to 'non-discrimination', 'equality of opportunity', 'accessibility' and 'full and effective participation and inclusion in society'.[58] Reference is also made to the principle of gender equality[59] and to that of respect for the identity and the evolving capacities of disabled children.[60] Given the explicit reference to gender and to childhood, it is perhaps surprising that there is no mention of race or of older people in Article 3.[61]

Article 4 sets out the 'general obligations' of States under the Convention. Article 4(1) lists a range of strategies which must be adopted in pursuance of the general obligation to ensure the full realisation of all human rights by disabled people. These include refraining from practices inconsistent with the Convention[62]; mainstreaming disability perspectives into all policies and programmes[63]; introducing legislative, administrative and other measures to secure relevant rights for disabled people[64]; and taking positive steps to promote the development and availability of universal design, of assistive technology and of professionals appropriately trained in the provision of relevant skills, essential to the realisation of human rights (for example, the use of assistive technology or mobility aids such as long canes, assistance dogs and wheelchairs).[65] These obligations are supplemented by the duty, imposed on States by Article 8, both to raise awareness of the contribution and potential of disabled people and also to counter stereotypes and to promote positive images of disability. Article 4(3) requires States to 'closely consult with and actively involve' disabled people's organisations in their implementation of the CRPD and other policies affecting disabled people.

Finally, it should be noted that the CRPD covers both civil and political rights and economic, social and cultural rights. The traditional tendency to draw fairly sharp distinctions between these two types of right (as illustrated by the different regimes set up by the ICCPR and the ECHR on the one hand and the ICESCR and the ESC on the other) has long been challenged. It has frequently been argued that it will be possible to confer meaningful human rights on disabled

---

[58] CRPD Art 3(b), (e), (f) and (c) respectively.

[59] *Ibid*, Art 3(g). See further Art 6.

[60] *Ibid*, Art 3(h). See further Art 7.

[61] Although some reference is made to such issues in para (p) of the preamble. See, on the issue of older people, H Meenan, 'Disability and Age: Achieving Freedom for All' (paper delivered at The Human Rights of People With Disabilities: Extending Freedom to All seminar, London School of Economics Centre for the Study of Human Rights, London, March 2006).

[62] CRPD Art 4(1)(d).

[63] *Ibid*, Art 4(1)(c).

[64] *Ibid*, Art 4(1)(a) and (b).

[65] *Ibid*, Art 4(1)(f) and (g) respectively.

people, and indeed on everybody else, only if the interdependence and indivisibility of both types of right is acknowledged.[66] This point is undoubtedly recognised in the CRPD, the structure of which reflects issues of relevance to the lives of disabled people rather than technical distinctions between different categories of right.[67] There is nevertheless one respect in which the two types of right are treated differently.

In conformity with long-standing tradition, the CRPD makes provision for economic, social and cultural rights but not civil and political rights to be implemented on a progressive basis.[68] This reflects the conventional view that the effective implementation of the former type of right is likely to require the investment of resources to a much greater extent than is implementation of the latter. This view, however, is itself challenged by the interpretation given to various civil and political rights in the CRPD.[69] The right to liberty, for instance, is interpreted in such a way as to ground a right to reject institutional living arrangements and to choose to live in the community (with appropriate support from the State)[70]; and also to maximise one's personal mobility (through, for example, training in mobility skills and the use of assistive aids).[71] Similarly, the right to freedom of expression and opinion is interpreted in such a way as to impose an obligation on States to accept and facilitate, in connection with official communications, the use of 'sign languages, Braille, augmentative and alternative communication, and all other accessible means, modes and formats of communication' by disabled people.[72]

It is fitting to close this Section with the following words of Sheikha Hissa Al-Thani, the UN Special Rapporteur on Disability:

---

[66] See eg Alston, 'Disability and the International Covenant on Economic, Social and Cultural Rights' (n 39 above); G Quinn, 'The International Covenant on Civil and Political Rights and Disability: A Conceptual Framework' in Degener and Koster-Dreese (eds), *Human Rights and Disabled Persons* (n 13 above); Quinn and Degener, 'The Moral Authority for Change' (n 17 above) para 1.2; T Degener, 'Disability as a Subject of International Human Rights Law and Comparative Discrimination Law' in Herr, Gostin and Koh (eds), *The Human Rights of Persons with Intellectual Disabilities* (n 54 above) 151 at 155; A Dander, 'The Right to Treatment of Persons with Psychosocial Disabilities and the Role of the Courts' (2005) 28 *International Journal of Law and Psychiatry* 155; R Gavison, 'On the Relationship Between Civil and Political Rights and Economic and Social Rights' in JM Coicaud, MW Doyle and AM Gardner (eds), *The Globalization of Human Rights* (Tokyo, UN University Press, 2003); H Shue, *Basic Rights: Subsistence, Affluence and US Foreign Policy* (Princeton, Princeton University Press, 1996); and S Fredman, *Human Rights Transformed* (Oxford, Oxford University Press, 2008).

[67] See generally Kayess and French, 'Out of Darkness into Light?' (n 48 above).

[68] CRPD Art 4(2). See also Art 2(1) of the ICESCR and General Comment No 3 'The nature of States parties' obligations', adopted by the Committee on Economic, Social and Cultural Rights at its fifth session in 1990 (UN Doc E/1991/23). See also Art 4 of the Convention on the Rights of the Child 1989.

[69] See generally Kayess and French, 'Out of Darkness into Light?' (n 48 above).

[70] CRPD Art 19.

[71] *Ibid*, Art 20.

[72] *Ibid*, Art 21.

This Convention has risen from the very core of the human rights principles of the United Nations. It is founded on the principles of dignity and justice; and rooted in the concepts of inalienability, universality and indivisibility of human rights. It highlights the right to full participation, and rests upon the notion of equality without distinctions; underlines the right to enjoyment without discrimination; stresses the belief in the dignity and worth of all human beings, and their right to equality and protection by the law.[73]

3.2   Reasonable Adjustment Under the CRPD

The concept of reasonable adjustment, though referred to in terms of reasonable accommodation, is firmly embedded in the Convention. It is explicitly mentioned in the substantive Articles dealing with education,[74] employment,[75] liberty and security of person[76] and, though in slightly different terms, in the Article dealing with access to justice.[77] Further, largely as a result of Articles 2 and 5, it is an implicit element of almost every one of the substantive Articles. As Kayess and French observe,

> [t]he incorporation of a State obligation to ensure that reasonable accommodations are made to facilitate the exercise by persons with disability of CPRD [*sic*] rights is perhaps the most fundamental instrumental element of the Convention.[78]

Article 5(2) requires signatory States to 'prohibit all discrimination on the basis of disability'. Such discrimination is defined in Article 2 as follows:

> any distinction, exclusion or restriction on the basis of disability which has the purpose or effect of impairing or nullifying the recognition, enjoyment or exercise, on an equal basis with others, of all human rights and fundamental freedoms in the political, economic, social, cultural, civil or any other field. It includes all forms of discrimination, including denial of reasonable accommodation.

As will be apparent, this is an extremely broad definition. It is broader and more far-reaching in its application than any of the definitions of discrimination to be found in current British law.

Reasonable accommodation is itself defined in Article 2 as:

---

[73] 'Convention on the Rights of Persons with Disabilities: A Progressive Human Rights Instrument' statement by the Special Rapporteur on Disability to the UN Human Rights Council, Geneva, September 2006, available at www.un.org/esa/socdev/enable/rapporteur.htm (last accessed 29 April 2008).

[74] CRPD Art 24(2)(c) and Art 24(5).

[75] CRPD Art 27(1)(i).

[76] CRPD Art 14(2).

[77] CRPD Art 13(1). This refers to the 'provision of procedural and age appropriate accommodations'.

[78] Kayess and French, 'Out of Darkness into Light?' (n 48 above) section 5D.

necessary and appropriate modification and adjustments not imposing a disproportionate or undue burden, where needed in a particular case, to ensure to persons with
disabilities the enjoyment or exercise on an equal basis with others of all human rights
and fundamental freedoms.

This makes it clear that a duty to provide reasonable accommodation requires
States to impose positive obligations on employers, educators, public authorities
and others to identify barriers in the way of a disabled person's enjoyment of
their human rights and to take appropriate steps to remove them. The emphasis
is on the barriers which operate in a particular case and thus on the need to
respond to the specific circumstances of the individual disabled person in
question. The solutions required must be appropriate to that person. They may
simply require cost-free changes to be made to standard practices but they may
also require cost-intensive measures, such as the purchase of additional equipment or support, or the installation of improved physical access.

Article 2, like section 21 of the DDA, refers to 'disabled persons' in the plural. It
is therefore possible that an expansive interpretation of its definition of reasonable accommodation would give birth to anticipatory duties of the type which
now flourish under the DDA.[79] Such a possibility, however, was clearly not
contemplated in any of the pre-CRPD discussions. Further, the Convention
imposes specific obligations relating to accessibility and to universal design.[80]
These obligations would clearly cover much of the same ground as would
anticipatory reasonable adjustment duties. Both would require steps to be taken,
regardless of the appearance on the scene of a particular disabled person, to
remove disabling barriers and to ensure that access to products, information and
the built environment was maximised. Thus, although it will remain open to
States to choose to adopt anticipatory duties in their own domestic systems, it is
highly unlikely that this specific form of legal obligation will be required by the
Disability Committee. What is beyond doubt is that States will be required to
introduce individualised reasonable accommodation duties which are responsive
to the circumstances of the particular case.

As Article 2 makes clear, the reasonable accommodation duty contemplated in
the Convention is subject to a defence of 'disproportionate or undue burden'.[81]
The term 'disproportionate' here means that it is the impact of making the
relevant modification on the particular business or entity that will matter—
simple absolute figures are therefore not the central issue. Thus, a particular
adjustment is much less likely to amount to a disproportionate hardship for a
large, wealthy firm than it would be for a small business. A business in a wealthy

---

[79]   See further ch 3, section 3 below.

[80]   CRPD Arts 9 and 4(1)(f) respectively. 'Universal design' is defined in Art 2 as 'the design of
products, environments, programmes and services to be usable by all people, to the greatest extent
possible, without the need for adaptation or specialized design'.

[81]   For criticism of this wording, see Kayess and French, 'Out of Darkness into Light?' (n 48 above)
section 5D.

country, with access to State subsidies, is also less likely to be able to prove that a particular adjustment would be a disproportionate hardship than is an equivalent business in a poorer country with no State support. Thus, while the CRPD requires all signatory States to introduce reasonable accommodation duties, their practical manifestations are likely to differ markedly from country to country.

Article 5(3) provides:

> In order to promote equality and eliminate discrimination, States Parties shall take all appropriate steps to ensure that reasonable accommodation is provided.

This would appear to require States not only to impose reasonable accommodation obligations on employers, service providers and others but also to take steps to raise awareness of their existence and nature and to facilitate their enforcement.[82]

As already mentioned, a failure to make reasonable accommodation is included in the definition of discrimination in Article 2. States are therefore required to prohibit such failures by Article 5(2) and to do so immediately, as the right to be free from discrimination is a civil and political right to which the principle of progressive realisation does not apply.[83] Reasonable accommodation obligations, however, depart from the traditional conception of the obligations flowing from civil and political rights in that they are highly proactive in nature and likely to require the spending of money.

Because of the expenditure associated with reasonable accommodation, its positioning within the domain of civil and political rights was not free from controversy in the CRPD negotiations. It should be stressed, however, that the concepts of 'reasonableness' and 'undue burden' will themselves inject some degree of progressive realisation into the implementation of reasonable accommodation duties. These concepts are inherently sensitive to the particular circumstances not only of the disabled individual in need of an accommodation but also to the circumstances of those on whom the duties fall. These circumstances are likely to change over time with the result that an accommodation that may at one time be considered to impose an undue burden would, at a later point, not be so regarded.

Finally, it is worth noting the peculiar bridging role played by the concept of reasonable accommodation in the context of human rights law. As has been seen, it may legitimately be regarded as an integral element of non-discrimination. This situates it within the realms of civil and political rights. Its function, however, is to ensure that rights of all kinds—whether they are classified as economic, social and cultural rights or as civil and political ones—become available, in a meaningful sense, to disabled people. It thus directly challenges the traditional clear-cut division between civil and political rights, on the one hand, and economic, social and cultural ones, on the other.

---

[82] See also the awareness-raising obligations imposed on States by CRPD Art 8.
[83] See n 68 above and accompanying text.

The concept of reasonable accommodation (together with other related concepts such as accessibility and universal design) operate to move the CRPD away from many of the dichotomies for which human rights law has often been criticised. It is not structured according to whether rights are civil or political on the one hand or economic, social or cultural on the other. Neither does it allow some rights to be regarded as imposing negative cost-free obligations and others as imposing positive resource-demanding obligations. Instead, the CRPD acknowledges and demands that, in relation to every one of its substantive rights, inaction and non-interference by States will not suffice. Positive steps are also required. For these reasons, together with its history of involvement and participation from disabled people themselves,[84] the CRPD appears entirely consistent with the conception of human rights recently advanced by Sandra Fredman.[85]

Fredman draws upon the capability theory developed by Amartya Sen and applied in the human rights context by Martha Nussbaum.[86] Like them, she argues that freedom should not be understood as simply the absence of interference or repression. Freedom should instead be regarded as a more positive and dynamic concept, carrying obligations to remove sources of 'unfreedom' that may hinder particular citizens from achieving or becoming what they regard as of value or that prevent them being treated with dignity and respect.[87] This positive notion of freedom, Fredman argues, underlies human rights law and demands positive action from the State in order to ensure that rights are genuinely conferred on all. She concludes:

> Positive duties arising from human rights can no longer be ignored, or hidden behind artificial distinctions between different categories of rights. The fundamental values of freedom, equality, democracy, and solidarity which underpin all human rights entail the recognition of both positive duties and duties of restraint. The challenge is to fashion those duties in a way which is not only coherent and sustainable, but which advances those values.[88]

---

[84] See nn 51–2 above and accompanying text.

[85] Fredman, *Human Rights Transformed* (n 66 above).

[86] See generally A Sen, *Development as Freedom* (Oxford, Oxford University Press, 1999); and M Nussbaum, *Women and Human Development* (Cambridge, Cambridge University Press, 2000). For an application of this approach in the context of human rights and disability, see M Stein, 'Disability Human Rights' (2007) 95 *California Law Review* 75; and, for discussion of its relationship with the social model of disability, see T Burchardt, 'Capabilities and Disability: The Capabilities Framework and the Social Model of Disability' (2004) 19 *Disability and Society* 735.

[87] See in particular Fredman, *Human Rights Transformed* (n 66 above) ch 1.

[88] Fredman, *Human Rights Transformed* (n 66 above) 240. It should be added that the value of 'democracy' is supported by a number of provisions in the CRPD which stress the importance of involving disabled people and their organisations in its implementation.

4. Reasonable Adjustment and Human Rights Within the Council of Europe

4.1 The Council of Europe

The Council of Europe was established in 1949 and given the task of overseeing the 'maintenance and further realisation' of human rights in the European region.[89] It has adopted a multiplicity of conventions and treaties, many of which have relevance to disabled people. For present purposes, however, only the two most prominent of these instruments will be considered in any depth. These are the European Convention on Human Rights 1950 (ECHR) and the European Social Charter 1961 (ESC).

As has been indicated above, the ECHR and the ESC reflect the ICCPR and the ICESCR in the general distinction they make between civil and political rights on the one hand and economic social and cultural rights on the other. The ECHR, which deals largely with civil and political rights, is supported by the European Court of Human Rights (ECtHR) to which complaints may, in certain circumstances, be brought by individual citizens of signatory States. The Human Rights Act 1998, by providing that the rights conferred by the ECHR should be directly enforceable in British courts, has dramatically increased the domestic profile of this Convention.

The ESC, together with the economic, social and cultural rights it protects, has traditionally occupied a much less prominent place in public consciousness. Until the Additional Collective Complaints Protocol 1995[90] came into force, the enforcement mechanism consisted solely of periodic reporting to the Council of Europe and to what is now entitled the European Committee of Social Rights. The 1995 Protocol, however, introduced a mechanism for collective complaints to be lodged by authorised international and national NGOs. Regrettably, the United Kingdom has not ratified this Protocol with the result that collective complaints may not be brought against it. A revised version of the Social Charter was produced in 1996. Although the United Kingdom signed this in November 1997, it has not yet ratified it. Accordingly, the terms of the original Charter continue to apply in the UK.

In the following two Sections, the relevance of the concept of reasonable accommodation to the rights laid down in the ECHR and the ESC will be

---

[89]   Statute of the Council of Europe 1949, Art 1(b).

[90]   Additional Protocol to the European Social Charter providing for a system of collective complaints, Council of Europe Treaty Series No 158. See further R Brillat, 'A New Protocol to the European Social Charter Providing for Collective Complaints' (1996) 1 *European Human Rights Law Review* 52; D Harris, 'The Collective Complaints Procedure' in *Council of Europe: The Social Charter of the 21st Century* (Strasbourg, Council of Europe Publishing, 1997); and H Cullen, 'The Collective Complaints Mechanism of the European Social Charter' (2000) 25 *European Law Review Supplement* (Human Rights Survey) 18.

considered. It is useful, however, to set that discussion against the backdrop of other disability-related policy and strategy work being carried out by the Council of Europe. Although by no means its first initiative on disability equality,[91] the Council of Europe's current 10-year Action Plan to promote the rights and full participation of disabled people undoubtedly now represents the primary reference point in this area.

The Action Plan was adopted by the Committee of Ministers on 5 April 2006 and formed the subject-matter of a subsequent Recommendation to Member States.[92] Member States are thus urged to 'integrate as appropriate in their policy, legislation and practice the principles' and to 'implement the actions' set out in the Plan.[93] The Council of Europe undertakes to assist Member States in this regard by providing them with recommendations, advice and information.[94]

The Plan identifies, as its fundamental principles:

Non-discrimination; equality of opportunities; full participation in society of all persons with disabilities; respect for difference and acceptance of disability as part of human diversity; dignity and individual autonomy including the freedom to make one's own choices; ... [and] participation of disabled people in all decisions affecting their lives, both at individual level and at society level through their representative organisations.[95]

'Universal Design principles, ... training and mainstreaming' are described as 'vital elements' of its implementation strategy.[96] The need to ensure that laws and policies include the notion of 'reasonable adjustment' is expressly mentioned in the contexts of access to culture, the arts, sport, leisure and tourism[97]; of education[98]; and of employment.[99] It would also appear to play an essential, if implicit, role in the 'fundamental principles' of the Plan and therefore to underlie the entire document. Unlike the CRPD, however, the Plan does not expressly acknowledge the fundamental and far-reaching nature of the role of reasonable accommodation and defines neither the concept of 'reasonable adjustment' itself nor its relationship with other concepts such as that of 'non-discrimination'.

---

[91] See, eg, 'A Coherent Policy for the Rehabilitation of Persons with Disabilities', Recommendation of the Committee of Ministers, No R (92) 6, 1992; and 'Malaga Political Declaration: Improving the Quality of Life for People with Disabilities, Enhancing a Coherent Policy for and Through Participation', Second Council of Europe Ministerial Conference in Disability, Malaga, 2003.

[92] 'The Council of Europe Action Plan to Promote the Rights and Full Participation of People with Disabilities in Society: Improving the Quality of Life of People with Disabilities in Europe 2006–2015', Recommendation of the Committee of Ministers, No R (2006) 5, 2006.

[93] *Ibid*, para (a).

[94] *Ibid*, para 2.1.

[95] *Ibid*, para 2.7.

[96] *Ibid*, para 1.5.

[97] *Ibid*, para 3.2.1.

[98] *Ibid*, para 3.4.2.

[99] *Ibid*, para 3.5.3.

4.2 Reasonable Adjustment and the ECHR

4.2.1 The ECHR and the Human Rights Act 1998

The ECHR has been influential over UK law since its ratification in 1950. However, as has already been mentioned, its influence increased dramatically in 2000 when the Human Rights Act 1998 (HRA) incorporated it into domestic law. The HRA provides for direct reference to be made to its provisions and jurisprudence in domestic courts and requires those courts to reach decisions which, so far as possible, are compatible with Convention rights.[100] It allows individuals who consider that their Convention rights have been infringed by public authorities to issue proceedings in domestic courts.[101]

In this discussion of ECHR rights, reference will be made to a number of HRA cases as well as to decisions of the ECtHR. While these HRA cases have obvious relevance within the United Kingdom, their practical significance to other signatories of the ECHR is limited. Some reference will be made, at the end of the discussion, to the greater willingness to find violations of Convention rights which often appears to be evident in these domestic cases than in the decisions of the ECtHR.[102]

4.2.2 The Right to be Free from Discrimination

The starting point for any consideration of reasonable adjustment under the ECHR is its non-discrimination provision, Article 14. According to this,

> [t]he enjoyment of the rights and freedoms set forth in this Convention shall be secured without discrimination on any ground such as sex, race, colour, language, religion, political or other opinion, national or social origin, association with a national minority, property, birth or other status.

As will be immediately apparent, disability is not included in the list of prohibited grounds. Nevertheless, there can be little doubt that it falls within the catch-all phrase of 'other status'.[103]

Article 14 affirms the view that human rights must be enjoyed by all on an equal basis. It is limited, however, in that, although it does not require the discrimination concerned to amount to an actual violation of a right set out in the substantive provisions of the Convention, it does require it to amount to an interference with the enjoyment of such a right. The case must fall within the

---

[100] Human Rights Act 1998 ss 2 and 3.

[101] Human Rights Act 1998 ss 6 and 7.

[102] See generally on the ECHR and disabled people, P Bartlett, O Lewis and O Thorold, *Mental Disability and the European Convention on Human Rights* (Leiden, Martinus Nijhoff, 2007); Clements and Read, *Disabled People and European Human Rights* (n 16 above); and A Lawson, 'Disabled People and the Human Rights Act 1998: A Right to be Human?' in Harvey (ed), *Human Rights in the Community* (n 2 above).

[103] See eg *Botta v Italy* Series A no 66 (1998) 26 EHRR 241 although, as will be explained below, no violation of the Article was found to have occurred for other reasons.

ambit of one of the substantive provisions of the ECHR before any issue of discrimination under Article 14 may be considered.[104] Unsurprisingly, this limitation has attracted criticism.[105] The problem is addressed by Protocol 12, which came into force on 1 April 2005, and confers the much broader right to be free from discrimination in 'the enjoyment of any right set forth by law'.[106] Regrettably, however, the United Kingdom has not ratified this Protocol because of nervousness as to its potential scope.[107]

The distinction between direct and indirect discrimination—so fundamental to much of domestic non-discrimination law—has, until recently, not played an important part in Article 14 jurisprudence.[108] In contrast with the traditional British approach to direct discrimination, Article 14 is subject to a general justification defence. It will not be violated if it can be shown that there was an objective and reasonable justification for the alleged discriminatory treatment.

There was no clear recognition of the concept of indirect discrimination in Article 14 case law until the decision of the Grand Chamber of the ECtHR in *DH v Czech Republic* in November 2007.[109] This case concerned the placement of Roma children in segregated schools for children with 'mental handicaps'[110] where, it was accepted, they received a 'substantially inferior education' to that received by children in mainstream schools.[111] It was argued that the rate of such placement was disproportionately high compared to that of non-Roma children and that it amounted to a violation of the Article 14 right of Roma children to be free from discrimination in connection with their right to education under Article 2 of Protocol 1.

The Grand Chamber, reversing an earlier decision of a Chamber of the Court's Second Section,[112] held that Article 14 had indeed been violated. It explicitly

---

[104] See eg *Abdulaziz, Cabales and Balkandali v UK* App Nos 9214/80, 9473/81, 9474/81 (1985) 7 EHRR 471; and *Botta v Italy* (n 103 above).

[105] See eg K Monaghan, 'Limitations and Opportunities: A Review of the Likely Domestic Impact of Article 14 ECHR' (2001) *European Human Rights Law Review* 167; R Wintermute, 'Within the Ambit: How Big is the "Gap" in Article 14 ECHR?' (2004) *European Human Rights Law Review* 366.

[106] See generally J Schokkenbroek, 'A New European Standard Against Discrimination: Negotiating Protocol No 12 to the European Convention on Human Rights' in J Niessen and I Chopin (eds), *The Development of Legal Instruments to Combat Racism in a Diverse Europe* (Leiden, Martinus Nijhoff, 2004); and *Non-Discrimination: A Human Right—Proceedings of a Seminar Marking the Entry into Force of Protocol 12 of the European Convention on Human Rights* (Strasbourg, Council of Europe Publishing, 2006).

[107] See Hansard HL, 617, 37 (11 October 2000), 13–14 (23 October 2000), and 45 (25 October 2000). For criticism of the UK position, see R Wintemute, 'Filling the Article 14 "Gap": Government Ratification and Judicial Control of Protocol No 12 ECHR, Part 2' (2004) *European Human Rights Law Review* 484; and S Fredman, 'Why the UK Government should sign and ratify Protocol 12' (2002) 105 *Equal Opportunities Review* 21.

[108] For discussion of domestic jurisprudence relating to Art 14 and the concept of indirect discrimination, see C McCrudden, 'Equality and Non-Discrimination' in D Feldman (ed), *English Public Law* (Oxford, Oxford University Press, 2004) ch 11.

[109] *DH v Czech Republic* App No 57325/00 (13 November 2007).

[110] This is the language used in the judgment. See eg, *ibid*, [41].

[111] *Ibid*, [135].

[112] *DH v Czech Republic* App No 57325/00 (7 February 2006).

acknowledged, for the first time, that Article 14 embraced the notion of 'indirect discrimination'.[113] It ruled that the Article did not require a discriminatory intent to be established.[114] It also removed the uncertainty which had previously existed as to whether statistical evidence might be adduced in order to prove the disproportionate impact of an apparently neutral measure. The court, which had regard to the practice of the European Court of Justice and various UN bodies, accepted that statistical evidence should be admissible for these purposes.[115] Once a prima facie case of discrimination had been made out, the burden of proof would shift to the respondent State to show the existence of an 'objective and reasonable justification'.[116] This justification defence would not be established unless the State could demonstrate that the challenged measure pursued a legitimate aim and that the means employed to achieve it were proportionate.[117]

On the facts of *DH*, statistical evidence was held to raise the presumption of indirect discrimination.[118] This indicated that Roma children were disproportionately affected by the procedures established by the State for placing children in special schools. The State attempted to rebut the indirect discrimination presumption by arguing that the placement of children in such schools furthered the legitimate aim of adapting educational provision for the needs of children with low intellectual ability. The tests on which recommendations for placements in special schools were based were entirely objective and had no reference to ethnicity. The court rejected this argument, however, holding that the tests had been developed without regard to Roma-specific cultural and linguistic factors.[119]

It was not necessary, on the facts of *DH*, for the Court to confront the question of the legitimacy of the Czech system of segregated education for disabled children. It accepted that it had been established in order to cater for children with special educational needs but added:

> However, it shares the disquiet of the other Council of Europe institutions who have expressed concerns about the more basic curriculum followed in these schools and, in particular, the segregation the system causes.[120]

The question of whether such forms of segregated education violate the human rights of disabled children subjected to them thus awaits examination in a future

---

[113] *DH v Czech Republic* App No 57325/00 (13 November 2007) [184]. The Court cited, in support of this acknowledgement, its decisions in *Hugh Jordan v UK* App No 24746/94 (2001) 37 EHRR 52 [154] and *Hoogendijk v the Netherlands* Dec No 58461/00 (2005) 40 EHRR SE 22 as well as the European Community Directives 97/80/EC and 2000/43/EC.

[114] *DH v Czech Republic* App No 57325/00 (13 November 2007) [184] and [194].

[115] *Ibid*, [180] and [187]–[188].

[116] *Ibid*, [189].

[117] *Ibid*, [196].

[118] *Ibid*, [190]–[194].

[119] *Ibid*, [199]–[201].

[120] *Ibid*, [198].

case.[121] In any such case, Article 24 of the CRPD may well have some influence. The ECtHR, while stressing the distinctive character of the ECHR,[122] has also recognised the importance of interpreting that Convention consistently with relevant principles of international human rights law.[123] Interestingly, the *DH* judgment is peppered with frequent references to relevant UN instruments. Although the CRPD was not referred to in *DH*, its profile is likely to increase once it has come into force.

Article 24 of the CRPD recognises the right of disabled people to an education and obliges States to provide an 'inclusive system of education and of life-long learning'. This requires them to ensure that disabled people are able to access an inclusive and good quality primary and secondary education, in their own communities, on an equal basis with others.[124] Disabled people receiving such education must be provided with appropriate support[125] and, at all levels of education, their needs must be accommodated wherever that would be reasonable. The emphasis of Article 24 is thus very firmly on the goal of fully supported educational inclusion.[126]

DH, then, represents a clear recognition of the fact that Article 14 may be violated on the basis of indirect discrimination. To date, however, there has been no explicit acknowledgement that it also embraces principles of reasonable adjustment or accommodation. Nevertheless, the ECtHR has recognised the need to treat differently people whose material circumstances differ. In *Thlimmenos v Greece*,[127] Article 14 was held to have been violated where a State failed without justification to treat people differently from others despite the fact that their religion made a material difference to their circumstances. The potential of such reasoning for the development of a notion of reasonable accommodation is self-evident. To date, however, this potential has not been exploited by the ECtHR.[128] It is possible that the CRPD will hasten developments in this area. Its

---

[121] For discussion of the relationship between segregation and direct discrimination, see M Bell, 'Direct Discrimination' in D Schiek, L Waddington and M Bell (eds), *Cases, Materials and Text on National, Supranational and International Non-Discrimination Law* (Oxford, Hart Publishing, 2007) 257–69.

[122] See eg *Loizidou v Turkey* App No 15318/89 (1995) 20 EHRR 99 [93]; *Bankovic v Belgium* App No 52207/99 ECHR 2001-XII [80].

[123] *Al-Adsani v United Kingdom* App No 35763/97 (2002) 34 EHRR 11 [55]. See generally L Wildhaber, 'The European Convention on Human Rights and International Law' (2007) 56 *International and Comparative Law Quarterly* 217.

[124] CRPD Art 24(2)(a) and (b).

[125] *Ibid*, Art 24(2)(d).

[126] Although the provision which is made in Art 24(3) for the education of children with sensory impairments in the most appropriate modes and settings may, on occasion, authorise their education alongside others with similar impairments rather than in mainstream settings.

[127] *Thlimmenos v Greece* App No 34369/97 (2001) 31 EHRR 15. See also *Kosteski v Former Yugoslav Republic of Macedonia* App No 55170/00 [2006] ECHR 403 in which it was held that no violation of Art 9 could be established because the employee had not provided proof to his employer that he was in fact a Muslim and therefore entitled to be absent from work on relevant holy days.

[128] See, however, the British case of *Copsey v W Devon Clays* [2005] EWCA Civ 932 (discussed in ch 4, fnn 211–16 below and accompanying text), which concerned the dismissal of an employee

insistence that the concept of non-discrimination includes a principle of reasonable accommodation may well prove impossible for the ECtHR to ignore.

Article 14 and Protocol 12 undoubtedly provide the most obvious site for the development of a concept of reasonable adjustment under the ECHR. It would, however, be dangerous to confine any consideration of reasonable adjustment-related ECHR developments to these provisions. It is entirely possible to interpret the substantive ECHR rights in such a way as to incorporate some notion of reasonable adjustment. The extent to which this approach has been adopted, both by the ECtHR and by domestic courts in the United Kingdom, will now be considered.

4.2.3 Substantive Provisions

The issue of reasonable adjustment or accommodation, although not generally articulated as such, has arisen in a number of cases brought by disabled people claiming violations of Convention rights. The judicial response has varied from highly restrictive to warmly enthusiastic. Before any attempt can be made to identify possible trends or rationales which might help to explain such variation, attention must be turned to the case law itself. The articles which have generated the most obviously relevant cases are Articles 3, 8 and 6. These will now be considered in turn.

The right to be free from inhuman and degrading treatment or punishment, protected by Article 3 of the ECHR, is an absolute right to which there are no exceptions or limitations. The ECtHR has consequently set a high threshold for entry into its realms. Suffering must reach a certain minimum level before it can amount to an Article 3 violation. In assessing whether this level has been attained, a court must take into account all the circumstances of the case, including the health, age and sex of the victim.[129] This stress on the circumstances of the particular victim has been used by judges, at least in cases concerning the treatment of prisoners, to require States to pay due regard to the impairments of a disabled person in deciding whether Article 3 has been violated.[130]

---

because of his refusal, for religious reasons, to agree to an alteration in his employment contract which required him to work on Sundays. Rix LJ, having referred to the Canadian law demanding reasonable accommodation on grounds of religion, acknowledged that 'the concept of reasonable accommodation is not foreign to either Convention jurisprudence or English law' and went on to suggest that employers were obliged to make reasonable efforts to accommodate the religious needs of their employees—[67]–[69].

[129] *Ireland v UK* App No 5310/71 (1978) Series A no 25 [162].

[130] Some of the ideas considered here are further developed in A Lawson, 'Disability, Degradation and Dignity: The Role of Article 3 of the European Convention on Human Rights' (2006) 56 *Northern Ireland Legal Quarterly* 462.

In *Price v United Kingdom*,[131] which is perhaps the most important Article 3 case concerning disabled people, the ECtHR ruled that the United Kingdom had inflicted degrading treatment on Ms Price by its failure to accommodate the particular needs arising from her impairment. As a result of thalidomide, all four of her limbs were foreshortened and she had a number of associated health difficulties, including kidney problems. Her refusal to answer questions in County Court debt recovery proceedings resulted in her spending three nights in prison. She was refused permission to take the battery charger for her wheelchair to prison; she had to spend the first night in a cell which was dangerously cold for her and contained a bed she was unable to use; she had to be assisted in using the toilet by male staff (having been left sitting on the toilet for three hours on one occasion until she gave up hope of being assisted by a woman); and, at the end of her sentence, she required catheterisation due to lack of fluid and to urine retention caused by difficulties in using the toilet facilities.

The ECtHR found that Ms Price's Article 3 rights had been violated, observing:

> There is no evidence in this case of any positive intention to humiliate or debase the applicant. However, the Court considers that to detain a severely disabled person in conditions where she is dangerously cold, risks developing sores because her bed is too hard or unreachable, and is unable to go to the toilet or keep clean without the greatest of difficulty, constitutes degrading treatment.[132]

Judge Greve, who delivered a separate concurring opinion, added:

> In a civilised country like the United Kingdom, society considers it not only appropriate but a basic humane concern to try to ameliorate and compensate for the disabilities faced by a person in the applicant's situation … The applicant's disabilities are not hidden or easily overlooked. It requires no special qualification, only a minimum of ordinary human empathy, to appreciate her situation and to understand that to avoid unnecessary hardship—that is, hardship not implicit in the imprisonment of an able-bodied person—she has to be treated differently from other people because her situation is significantly different.[133]

Price thus demonstrates clearly that in order to comply with Article 3, States may have to adapt or alter mainstream conditions or regimes in order to accommodate the needs of disabled prisoners. According to other ECtHR Article 3 cases, the illness or impairment of a prisoner may, on occasion, require that they be removed from the mainstream prison environment, either by being released or by being transferred into other conditions (such as those of a hospital). Thus, in *Mouisel v France*,[134] the ECtHR held that Article 3 had been violated by the

---

[131] *Price v UK* App No 33394/96 (2001) 34 EHRR 1285. For a similar decision in the UN context, see *Hamilton v Jamaica* communication No 616/1995, Views adopted by the Human Rights Committee on 28 July 1999 (CCPR/C/66/D/616/1995) (discussed at n 46 above and accompanying text).

[132] *Price v UK* (n 131 above) [30].

[133] *Ibid.*

[134] *Mouisel v France* App No 67263/01 [2002] ECHR 740.

continued detention of a prisoner suffering from leukaemia and undergoing chemotherapy. On his frequent trips to the hospital for treatment he was chained and handcuffed.

Similarly, in the domestic Scottish case of *Napier v Scottish Ministers*,[135] Lord Bonomy ruled that the detention of a prisoner who had eczema in the conditions which then existed in the mainstream prison environment constituted degrading treatment. Robert Napier had been required to spend between 20 and 23 hours a day in his cell and to share that cell with a series of cellmates even though it was designed for only one. In addition, and most significantly, he had been granted extremely limited access to washing and toilet facilities. The 'slopping out' regime to which Napier was subjected meant using a bucket or bottle in the cell instead of a toilet, emptying these receptacles alongside other prisoners in chaotic conditions, and having extremely limited opportunities to wash—so limited that it was impossible for Napier to take adequate care of his skin, which consequently became infected, ulcerated and flaky.

Interestingly, although Lord Bonomy regarded the existence of Napier's eczema as 'crucial'[136] to the success of his Article 3 claim, he never described him as 'disabled' and made no reference to the *Price* decision. This illustrates the ability of Article 3 to respond to the particular circumstances of disabled people without imposing on them any threshold requirement in the form of a specific definition of 'disability'. It thus stands in refreshing contrast to the Disability Discrimination Act 1995, under which failure to satisfy the definition of disability has shipwrecked more cases than has any other reason.[137]

In all these cases the courts have recognised that Article 3 requires States to take into account the difference in circumstance created by an individual's impairment and to provide them with correspondingly different treatment. They thus demonstrate the operation of some form of reasonable adjustment or accommodation duty in the implementation of the fundamental and absolute right to be free from inhuman and degrading treatment.

The ambit of Article 3, however, is extremely narrow. As has been seen, it requires suffering to reach a minimum level of severity before the treatment that has caused or exacerbated it can be classified as degrading. The fact that such suffering has been endured in a prison—an institution in which the individual is under the complete control of the State—has played an important part in assessments of this minimum level. It may therefore be extremely difficult to establish the required minimum level of severity in cases falling outside the confines of an institution. An extremely cautious approach to non-institutional

---

[135] *Napier v Scottish Ministers* [2004] *Scottish Law Times* 555. See, for further discussion of this case, A Lawson and A Mukherjee, 'Slopping Out in Scotland: The Limits of Degradation and Respect' [2004] *European Human Rights Law Review* 645.

[136] *Ibid*, [76].

[137] S Leverton, *Monitoring the Disability Discrimination Act 1995 (Phase 2)* (London, Stationary Office, 2002) 14. See further, the discussion in ch 6, fnn 134–42 below and accompanying text.

cases, in which there is no deliberate intention to humiliate or debase, has certainly been adopted in the United Kingdom. This is illustrated by the case of *R (Bernard) v Enfield London Borough Council*,[138] where it was held that the minimum level of severity had not been established despite the fact that, due to the Council's failure to provide Mrs Bernard with suitable accommodation, she had lived for 20 months in an inaccessible house in which she had been unable to use her wheelchair. Neither had she been able to use the kitchen or the bathroom, or to answer the door. According to Sullivan J, however, cases such as *Price* must be treated "with great caution outside the prison gates"[139] and Mrs Bernard's Article 3 claim accordingly failed.

Article 8, although subject to a form of justification defence, is much broader in scope than Article 3. It is therefore sometimes possible, as in *Bernard*, to establish a violation of the former but not the latter. Article 8 protects the right to respect for one's private and family life, one's home and correspondence. The ECtHR has given the concept of private life a wide interpretation. According to *Botta v Italy*,[140] it embraces the 'physical and psychological integrity' of an individual and the 'development, without outside interference, of the personality of each individual in his relations with other human beings'.[141] Unsurprisingly, this rich notion of 'private life' has generated a number of cases, both at the ECtHR and at the domestic level, in which disabled people have claimed that their Article 8 rights have been violated by the failure of a State to remove access barriers or to provide them with facilitative aids and devices.[142]

The leading case on this issue is *Botta* itself. Mr Botta (a wheelchair user) claimed that, in failing adequately to enforce laws requiring private beaches to provide physical access for disabled people, the State had not complied with its obligation to respect his private life and to allow him to develop his personality. The physical barriers to accessing the beaches in question rendered him unable to enjoy a 'normal social life' and 'to participate in the life of the community'.[143] The ECtHR accepted that compliance with Article 8 would sometimes require a state to adopt 'measures designed to secure respect for private life even in the sphere of the relations of individuals between themselves'.[144] Such an obligation, however, would arise only where there was a 'direct and immediate link between the measures sought by an applicant and the latter's private and/or family life'.[145]

---

[138]   *R (Bernard) v Enfield LBC* [2002] EWHC (Admin) 2282.

[139]   *Ibid*, [28].

[140]   *Botta v Italy* App No 21439/93 (1998) 26 EHRR 241. See also *Niemietz v Germany* App No 13710/88 (1992) 16 EHRR 97.

[141]   *Botta v Italy* (n 140 above) [32].

[142]   For a recent example of the powerful role of Art 8 in relation to other disability-related issues, see *Shtukaturov v Russia* App No 44009/05 (27 March 2008) [86]–[96] in which the Russian guardianship system was held to violate Art 8 because the total and indefinite loss of decision-making power it entailed was, in that case, disproportionate to the aims it sought to achieve.

[143]   *Botta v Italy* (n 140 above) [27].

[144]   *Ibid*, [33].

[145]   *Ibid*, [34].

There was no such direct and immediate link in *Botta*—the right claimed there concerning 'interpersonal relations of such broad and indeterminate scope that there [could] be no conceivable direct link'.[146]

Similar reasoning was applied in *Zehnalova and Zehnal v Czech Republic*,[147] where a disabled person challenged the failure of the State to enforce laws requiring public buildings (including the post office, swimming pool and police station) to be made accessible. Although the buildings housed essential facilities in the town in which the applicant lived, the ECtHR considered that there was insufficient evidence as to their everyday use by the applicant to establish the necessary direct and immediate link. Failure to take positive steps to make the buildings accessible could not therefore constitute an Article 8 violation.

In two other disability-related cases, however, the ECtHR has accepted the presence of a direct and immediate link sufficient to raise the possibility that the State would be required to take positive steps to protect the Applicants' private life. In both, however, the claim failed for other reasons, as will be explained below.[148] In the first of these, Mr Marzari challenged the Italian authorities' failure to provide him with housing suitable for somebody with his particular form of physical impairment.[149] In the second, Mr Sentges challenged the Dutch authorities' refusal to supply him with a robotic arm, which would have significantly reduced his otherwise total dependence on assistance from carers and thereby given him some degree of privacy and independence.[150] Thus, whereas in *Botta* and *Zehnalova* the measures sought related to general access to public places, the measures sought in *Marzari* and *Sentges* were highly specific and personal in nature. Further, the effect of the measures in the latter two cases (where the necessary direct and immediate link was established) would extend to all aspects of the lives of the applicants and be felt on a relatively permanent basis rather than only on visits to public facilities.

The role of reasonable accommodation within the Article 8 jurisprudence has been fully explored by Olivier De Schutter.[151] He suggests that the ECtHR's introduction of the 'direct and immediate link' requirement in *Botta* represents an attempt to set the process of identifying Article 8 positive obligations on an objective basis and to distinguish that process clearly from the process of determining whether an alleged violation is or is not justified. He describes this as an attempt to tame the notion of positive obligations. If allowed to run wild, that notion

---

[146] *Ibid*, [55].
[147] *Zehlanova and Zehnal v Czech Republic* App No 38621/97 (14 May 2002).
[148] See nn 154–5 below and accompanying text.
[149] *Marzari v Italy* App No 36448/97 (1999) 28 EHRR CD 175.
[150] *Sentges v The Netherlands* App No 27677/02 (8 July 2003).
[151] O De Schutter, 'Reasonable Accommodations and Positive Obligations in the European Convention on Human Rights' in Lawson and Gooding (eds), *Disability Rights in Europe* (n 16 above).

could have led to the imposition of a requirement to undertake wide-scale restructuring of the environment wherever such restructuring could contribute, at a reasonable cost, to facilitating the self-fulfilment of disabled individuals.[152]

The result, however, is morally questionable as well as unduly restrictive. Turning again to the words of De Schutter:

> [T]he *Botta* line of cases confronts us with an implicit view that certain activities in life (eg travelling, going on vacation, having the choice of which chemist to visit) are less worthy of protection, because they are less essential to the fulfilment of one's personality. Perhaps we should question this hierarchy. Perhaps we should challenge both the practicability of such a distinction—as if housing or employment, for instance, can be distinguished from public transportation or access to services of general interest—and, especially, the underlying idea that it would be compatible with the requirement of autonomy to oblige a person to restrict him/herself to his or her immediate surroundings and deny him/her the opportunity of moving beyond them.[153]

Even in cases where a direct and immediate link can be established, there will be no violation of the Convention if the State is able to raise a defence under Article 8(2). This paragraph provides that an interference with an Article 8 right will be justified if it is 'in accordance with the law and is necessary in a democratic society'. This requires the ECtHR to weigh the interests of the individual against those of the community as a whole. The claims in both *Marzari* and *Sentges* foundered on this defence, with the result that in neither case did the applicant succeed. Allowing Sentges his robotic arm would have had serious financial implications for the rest of the community.[154] Allowing the claim in *Marzari* would have had considerable repercussions on social housing policies. In addition, that claim was ruled to be ill-founded, as the authorities had offered Marzari what an expert committee had judged to be suitable accommodation and had expressed willingness to make adaptations to his allocated apartment.[155]

Thus, although Article 8 holds promise as a source of positive obligations to take steps which would facilitate the inclusion and participation of disabled people in mainstream society (obligations in the nature of reasonable adjustment duties), that promise has not yet been realised. Its reach is tightly circumscribed by the direct and immediate link requirement and no relevant ECtHR cases have, to date, proved successful. At the domestic level, however, disabled litigants have enjoyed more success.

In the British Human Rights Act cases of both *Bernard* and *Napier*, the facts of which have already been described, the essence of the claim was that the State should have taken positive steps to ensure that the claimants were not exposed to unacceptable living conditions. In both cases it was held that the State's inaction

---

[152] *Ibid*, 45.
[153] *Ibid*, 61.
[154] *Sentges v The Netherlands* App No 27677/02 (8 July 2003).
[155] *Marzari v Italy* App No 36448/97 (1999) 28 EHRR CD 175.

did indeed violate the rights of the claimants to respect for their physical integrity and their private life. Thus, on the authority of *Marzari*, it would not have been difficult to establish the *Botta* 'direct and immediate link' in either case. In neither *Bernard* nor *Napier*, however, was this point even addressed. This may indicate that the British courts might be prepared to adopt a more expansive approach to the direct and immediate link requirement than that adopted by the ECtHR. On the other hand, the silence of the British courts on this issue in *Bernard* and *Napier* may have been due simply to the fact that they regarded the existence of the required link as obvious on the facts before them.

The case of *R (A and B) v East Sussex County Council*,[156] although not strictly concerned with the provision of reasonable accommodation measures, is also worthy of mention. It involved a challenge to the Council's blanket ban on the manual lifting of disabled people and raised questions about the role of Article 8 in protecting their dignity and independence. A and B were two sisters in their twenties who lived at home with their parents and who received significant support from the Council. They had physical impairments which meant that they had to be lifted (eg in and out of bed or the bath). Without any manual lifting whatsoever, the sisters were likely to be subjected to distressing and sometimes dangerous situations in the event, for instance, of the malfunction of equipment within their home. Further, they would have been unable to engage in activities outside the house which they enjoyed (such as shopping, swimming and horse-riding) because of the lack of reliable lifting facilities in relevant public places.

Interestingly, Article 8 was again held to be engaged, although the question of a direct and immediate link was not expressly addressed. According to Munby J, the sisters' Article 8 rights had been engaged for two reasons.[157] First, the Article would operate so as to protect their dignity against some of the effects of a blanket ban on manual lifting (such as being required to sit on the toilet or in soiled clothes for lengthy periods of time when mechanical lifting devices were unavailable). Second, it would operate to protect

> their right to participate in the life of the community and to have access to an appropriate range of recreational and cultural activities.[158]

In short, there appears to have been much more enthusiasm for developing Article 8's potential to assist disabled people at the domestic level than there has been at the European level. This may be due in part to a greater willingness of British judges to hold domestic public authorities to account for failing adequately to implement agreed policies or legal obligations. The reluctance of the ECtHR to engage in such an exercise, at least in this context,[159] is illustrated

---

[156] *R (A and B) v East Sussex CC* [2003] EWHC (Admin) 167.
[157] *Ibid*, [114].
[158] *Ibid*.
[159] See De Schutter, 'Reasonable Accommodations and Positive Obligations under the European Convention on Human Rights' (n 151 above) 49–50.

by its refusal to intervene in either *Botta* or *Zehnalova*, both of which arose from the inadequate implementation of relevant domestic legislation.[160]

Article 6 protects the right to a fair trial. Although its potential scope is much narrower than that of Article 8, it has generated a number of interesting cases in which the central issue has in effect been the entitlement of a disabled litigant to reasonable adjustment. The approach which emerges from the Strasbourg cases is, however, disappointingly restrictive.

Malone v United Kingdom[161] concerned the accessibility of court facilities to an Applicant who had rheumatoid arthritis and used a wheelchair. Ms Malone complained that, in connection with a housing dispute, she had been required to attend an inaccessible court in London, which was some 500 km away from where she lived. The long journey, which began at 4.30 am, caused her so much pain that she had to spend the next four days in bed. Because the building was inaccessible, she had to be carried by court officials up the steps into, and also inside, the court building. She suffered extreme discomfort as a result of the inaccessible toilet facilities—a problem intensified by the fact that, on one occasion, she had had to wait for nearly six hours before her case was heard. The case, she argued, should have been transferred to an accessible court in her home town, and the State's failure to do this amounted to a violation of her Article 6 rights.

Ms Malone's case was held to be inadmissible because she had failed to take adequate steps to bring her requirements to the attention of the court. She had not applied for a transfer until the case had been listed for London.

Malone is, as Clements and Read observe, 'an unsatisfactory decision'.[162] While disabled people should be expected to inform relevant authorities of their requirements, this should not absolve those authorities of all responsibility when, as in *Malone*, the disability is known to them and the consequences of failure to act will be serious for the disabled person. 'Equal treatment', they comment, 'is not a special dispensation available only if booked in advance'.[163]

Another disappointing Strasbourg decision is *Stanford v United Kingdom*.[164] There, the applicant, who had a severe hearing impairment, had been tried for rape. He had been unable to hear the testimony of the victim. He had complained about this to his prison guard and also to his solicitor but his lawyers did not mention this to the judge. When he challenged the proceedings under Article 6, it

---

[160] But see, for an example of a case in which the ECtHR was prepared to take a more expansive approach to Art 8 than the domestic courts, *Wainwright v UK* App No 12350/04 (26 September 2006)—a case which concerned strip searches of relatives (one of whom had mental and physical impairments which increased the stress of the process) in connection with a visit to a convicted prisoner. The prison authorities' failure to comply with their own procedures (which included giving the visitors the relevant consent forms for the searches only after they had been carried out) was thought not to violate Art 8 by the House of Lords but held to do so by the ECtHR.

[161] *Malone v UK* App No 25290/94 (28 February 1996).

[162] Clements and Read, *Disabled People and European Human Rights* (n 16 above) 45.

[163] *Ibid.*

[164] *Stanford v UK* App No 16757/90 (1994) Series A no 282-A.

was accepted that the right of an accused to participate effectively in a trial conferred by that article included, 'not only his right to be present, but also to hear and follow the proceedings'.[165] According to the ECtHR, however, Article 6 had not been infringed because the applicant had not brought his hearing difficulty to the attention of the trial judge. Although he had mentioned it to his guard and his solicitor, they were not court officials and therefore the court itself was not at fault. Like *Malone*, this case appears to require a disabled applicant to discharge a heavy burden (one which may indeed have been impossible for Stanford to discharge) before any form of reasonable adjustment duties will be triggered.

The more recent case of *Young v United Kingdom*[166] also concerned a disabled prisoner. Ms Young, who had cerebral palsy, had been unable to provide a urine sample when required to do so for purposes of a drugs test. The authorities treated this as a deliberate refusal to co-operate and added three days to her sentence as a penalty. Ms Young challenged the fairness of these proceedings on a number of grounds, some of which were disability-related. She claimed that she had been unable to provide the sample because of the physical symptoms of her cerebral palsy and that the authorities had, both at that point and in the subsequent disciplinary proceedings, taken insufficient account of the linguistic and communication-related aspects of her impairment. A Chamber of the Court's Fourth Section found that the relevant disciplinary proceedings had violated Article 6 for reasons unrelated to Ms Young's impairment. It did not therefore need to address the disability-related arguments and chose not to do so. Disappointingly, therefore, *Young* does not expand the somewhat restrictive approach of the ECtHR to the notion of reasonable accommodation in the Article 6 context.

At the domestic level the outlook has been more positive. Article 6 came to the assistance of a disabled person in *R v Isleworth Crown Court (ex parte King)*.[167] There, Mr King sought judicial review of a decision to reject his appeal against a conviction for an offence under the Housing Act 1985. A stroke three years before the appeal had rendered him unable to walk, talk or write. Although he had slowly recovered these functions, his concentration, memory and clarity of thought and expression were still significantly impaired, particularly when he was tired or stressed. Mr King was tired by the time his case was heard, it having been delayed for five hours, and his stress and anxiety when presenting his argument had been exacerbated by the evident irritation and impatience with which he was treated by the judge. In quashing the decision, the High Court emphasised the importance of complying with the guidance as to the treatment of disabled people which had been issued by the Judicial Studies Board, albeit after the challenged proceedings. According to that guidance, steps should be taken to

---

[165] *Ibid*, [26].
[166] *Young v UK* App No 60682/00 [2007] ECHR 48.
[167] *R v Isleworth Crown Court (ex p King)* [2001] Administrative Court Digest 289.

minimise the ordeal associated with court appearances for disabled people such as Mr King. The guidance was based on the requirements of Article 6, and the fact that it had not been issued at the time of Mr King's case did not absolve the court of responsibility for failing to protect his right to a fair trial.[168]

To conclude, the Article 3 jurisprudence contains clear and powerful recognition of the need to take steps to accommodate the needs of disabled people—at least if they are confined in institutions—in order to ensure that the way in which they are treated does not cause them disproportionate hardship. This is the case both at the level of the ECtHR and of domestic courts. The ECtHR approach to the issue of disability-related accommodations under Articles 6 and 8 has, to date, been somewhat disappointing. A more expansive approach appears to be evident in domestic jurisprudence. Although it is tempting to attribute this difference in approach to needless caution on the part of the ECtHR, it should be remembered that the more expansive British decisions tend to be of much more recent origin than their ECtHR counterparts. In a field which has been developing as rapidly as that of disability law, time is undoubtedly a significant factor. The well-recognised (but uncomfortable) fact that surprisingly few disability-related cases reach the ECtHR[169] means that there are relatively few opportunities to demonstrate a more confident and positive approach to the issue of disability-related accommodation duties. It is, perhaps, no accident that *Price v United Kingdom*[170] is one of the most recent of the ECtHR cases considered here and that it is also the one in which such duties were most warmly embraced. Nevertheless, the most recent case is *Young* and it suggests that the Court is not prepared to take advantage of every available opportunity to develop human rights law in a disability-sensitive manner.

It would certainly be unrealistically optimistic to attribute the apparent reluctance of the ECtHR to develop reasonable-adjustment-type positive obligations entirely to the scarcity of recent cases raising such issues. The potentially obstructive fact remains that, unlike the ESC, the primary aim of the ECHR is not to confer positive rights. Such positive obligations as there are 'emerge in the afterglow of essentially negative rights'.[171] Nevertheless, it is to be hoped that the clarification of the link between reasonable accommodation and the effective enjoyment of human rights provided by the CRPD will act as a catalyst to the ECtHR in this regard.[172]

---

[168] *Ibid*, [291].

[169] See eg Clements and Read, 'The Dog that Didn't Bark' (n 16 above).

[170] *Price v UK* App No 33394/96 (2001) 34 EHRR 1285.

[171] G Quinn, 'The European Social Charter and EU Anti-Discrimination Law in the Field of Disability: Two Gravitational Fields with One Common Purpose' in G de Burca and B de Witte (eds), *Social Rights in Europe* (Oxford, Oxford University Press, 2005) 298.

[172] A Lawson, 'The United Nations Convention on the Rights of Persons with Disabilities and European Disability Law: A Catalyst for Cohesion?' in Arnardottir and Quinn (eds), *The UN Convention on the Rights of Persons with Disabilities* (n 48 above).

4.3   Reasonable Adjustment and the European Social Charter

As has been indicated above, the ESC 1961 is the sister instrument of the ECHR and is designed to protect social, cultural and economic rights. According to Part 1, its aim is to attain conditions in which the rights set out in a number of specified principles may be effectively realised. These principles refer to rights such as the opportunity to earn a living in a freely-chosen occupation[173]; the right to just working conditions[174]; and the right to benefit from measures designed to secure the highest possible standard of health.[175] The effective realisation of such rights by disabled people will, for the reasons explained at the beginning of this chapter, necessarily entail some notion of reasonable accommodation. As might be expected of an instrument of its time, however, the concept of reasonable adjustment or accommodation is not explicitly mentioned.

Indeed, the emphasis of Article 15, which deals specifically with disability, is firmly on notions of rehabilitation and the making of adaptations to a disabled individual rather than to his or her environment. According to it, States undertake to provide training facilities for disabled people, including by means of 'specialized institutions', and to facilitate the placing of disabled people in employment by, for example, 'specialized placing services, facilities for sheltered employment and measures to encourage employers to admit disabled persons to employment'.

Under the Revised European Social Charter 1996, however, the emphasis of Article 15 is very different. Although reference continues to be made to 'specialized institutions' and 'sheltered employment', a much higher profile is given to principles of mainstreaming and integration—principles which depend upon the notion of reasonable accommodation for their practical realisation. Further, its scope is extended beyond training and employment to 'independence, social integration and participation' in the life of mainstream society more generally. Unsurprisingly, concepts of reasonable accommodation are clearly (if implicitly) drawn upon. Reference is made, for instance, to the need to 'adjust the working conditions to the needs of the disabled' and, more generally, to 'promote their full social integration and participation in the life of the community in particular through measures, including technical aids, aiming to overcome barriers to communication and mobility and enabling access to transport, housing, cultural activities and leisure'.

Gerard Quinn has succinctly encapsulated the shift in emphasis between the 1961 and the 1996 versions of Article 15 as one from 'rehabilitation with a nod toward equality' to 'equality with a nod toward rehabilitation'.[176] The heightened

---

[173]   European Social Charter, Principle 1.
[174]   *Ibid*, Principle 2.
[175]   *Ibid*, Principle 11.
[176]   Quinn, 'The European Social Charter and EU Anti-Discrimination Law in the Field of Disability' (n 171 above).

profile of equality is not confined to Article 15. In the 1961 version of the Charter, the principle of non-discrimination is mentioned only in the preamble. In the 1996 version, however, a non-discrimination requirement (very similar to that contained in Article 14 of the ECHR) is set out in Article E.

The European Committee of Social Rights, charged with the responsibility of overseeing the implementation of the ESC, has made some extremely valuable disability-related contributions.[177] From 2003 onwards, its interpretations of the requirements of even the 1961 version of Article 15 prioritise the creation of opportunity to participate in mainstream society. Indeed, in that year, it concluded negatively against Denmark in relation to the original Article 15 because it did not have legislation prohibiting disability discrimination in the employment sphere.[178] Although not stated expressly, the Committee appears to have regarded a reasonable accommodation duty as an essential element of such legislation.

Similarly, in the context of Article 15 of the revised Charter, the Committee concluded negatively against France for its failure to adopt legislation prohibiting disability discrimination in education[179] and asked it to provide further information as to the nature of any reasonable accommodation duties in its existing equality law.[180] Also worthy of note is the decision of the Committee in *Autisme-Europe v France*.[181] This case was brought under the collective complaints protocol and challenged the level of educational provision made for autistic people both within the French mainstream and special education sectors. The Committee upheld this challenge and again drew attention to the importance of non-discrimination principles.[182] After referring to the decision of the ECtHR in *Thlimmenos v Greece*,[183] the Committee stressed that the application of these principles necessarily involved the recognition and accommodation of difference. In its words,

> [h]uman difference in a democratic society should not only be viewed positively but should be responded to with discernment in order to ensure real and effective equality.[184]

Thus, the disability-specific language of the original ESC, to which the United Kingdom is a party, appears to leave little room for the concept of reasonable accommodation. Nevertheless, it has been expansively interpreted by the European Committee of Social Rights so as to require anti-discrimination legislation which includes reasonable accommodation duties. The scope of the revised

---

[177]   See further Quinn, *ibid*, 287.
[178]   Conclusions XVI-2, vol 1 (2003) para 229.
[179]   *Ibid*, para 158.
[180]   *Ibid*, para 168.
[181]   Decision of the European Committee of Social Rights, Collective Complaint 13 (2003).
[182]   See further '*Autisme-Europe v France*: Collective Complaint No 13/2002', Resolution (2004), (875th meeting of the Minister's Deputies).
[183]   *Thlimmenos v Greece* [2000] ECHR 161 (6 April 2000).
[184]   Decision of the European Committee of Social Rights, Collective Complaint 13 (2003) at para 52.

Charter is wider and its obligations clearer. Reasonable accommodation thus emerges plainly as an integral element of the effective enjoyment of social human rights by disabled people.

5. Reasonable Adjustment and Human Rights Within the European Union

The origins of the European Union lie in the furtherance of principles, not of human rights, but of market economy. Nevertheless, the past decade has witnessed a considerable strengthening of the profile of human rights concerns.[185] In the context of equality, the view that allowing all citizens the opportunity to fulfill their potential and contribute to the life of their societies free from irrational discrimination has gained increasing prevalence. Equality accordingly features large in both the Charter of Fundamental Rights and in the Treaty of Amsterdam and its ensuing Directives.[186]

The Charter of Fundamental Rights of the European Union was initially proclaimed on 7 December 2000 and then again, after amendments, on 12 December 2007.[187] It draws on instruments such as the ECHR and the ESC and aims to set out all the civil, political, economic and social rights to which European citizens and residents are entitled. Article 21 of the Charter lists disability as one of the grounds on which discrimination must be prohibited. The sphere of operation of this Article is wide. It is not restricted either to a particular context (such as employment) or to the enjoyment of the rights conferred by the

---

[185] See generally G More, 'The Principle of Equal Treatment: From Market Unifier to Fundamental Right?' in P Craig and G de Burca (eds), *The Evolution of EU Law* (Oxford, Oxford University Press, 1999); P Alston (ed), *The EU and Human Rights* (Oxford, Oxford University Press, 1999); S Prechal, 'Equal Treatment, Non-Discrimination and Social Policy: Achievement in Three Themes' (2004) 41 *Common Market Law Review* 533; P Craig and G de Burca, *EU Law: Text, Cases, and Materials* (Oxford, Oxford University Press, 2007) 379–427; and C McCrudden and H Kountouros, 'Human Rights and European Equality Law' in H Meenan (ed), *Equality Law in an Enlarged European Union: Understanding the Article 13 Directives* (Cambridge, Cambridge University Press, 2007).

[186] See generally M Bell, *Anti-Discrimination Law and the European Union* (Oxford, Oxford University Press, 2002); C Costello and E Barry (eds), *Equality in Diversity* (Dublin/Oxford, Irish Centre for European Law, 2003); E Ellis, *EU Anti-Discrimination Law* (Oxford, Oxford University Press, 2005); Meenan (ed), *Equality Law in an Enlarged European Union* (n 185 above); and Schiek, Waddington and Bell (eds), *Cases, Materials and Text on National, Supranational and International Non-Discrimination Law* (n 121 above).

[187] OJ C364, 18 December 2000; and OJ C303, 14 December 2007 respectively. See generally S Fredman, C McCrudden and M Freedland, 'An EU Charter of Fundamental Rights' [2007] *Public Law* 178; B Hepple, 'The EU Charter of Fundamental Rights' (2001) 30 *Industrial Law Journal* 225; T Hervey and J Kenner (eds), *Economic and Social Rights under the EU Charter of Fundamental Rights* (Oxford, Hart Publishing, 2003); B Bercusson, 'Episodes on the Path Towards the European Social Model: The EU Charter of Fundamental Rights and the Convention on the Future of Europe' in C Barnard, S Deakin and GS Morris (eds), *The Future of Labour Law* (Oxford, Hart Publishing, 2004); P Alston and O De Schutter (eds), *Monitoring Fundamental Rights in the EU: The Contribution of the Fundamental Rights Agency* (Oxford, Hart Publishing, 2005); and S Fredman, 'Transformation or Dilution: Fundamental Rights in the EU Social Space' (2006) 12 *European Law Journal* 41.

Charter. Although reasonable accommodation duties are not specifically mentioned, they will clearly be required by this Article if they are classified as a form of non-discrimination measure. After the CRPD, such a classification seems inevitable despite the fact that the Employment Equality Directive has generated some uncertainty on the point.[188]

Article 26 is also of considerable importance. According to this,

> [t]he Union recognises and respects the right of persons with disabilities to benefit from measures designed to ensure their independence, social and occupational integration and participation in the life of the community.

It is entirely arguable that reasonable accommodation obligations should number amongst these measures.

The Charter would have been incorporated by reference into the draft EU Constitution, which was rejected by 'No' votes in referenda in France and The Netherlands in 2005. It remains an integral part of the proposals for EU reform now contained in the Treaty of Lisbon. That treaty was signed by government representatives of all the Member States on 13 December 2007.[189] It will accordingly enter into force if it is ratified by all the Member States in accordance with their own domestic constitutions—an eventuality thrown into some doubt by the rejection of the Treaty in the Irish referendum.[190] If adopted, the Lisbon Treaty would have the effect of making the Charter's provisions binding on all the institutions of the EU and also on all but two of the Member States in their implementation of EU law. It would amend Article 6(1) of the Treaty on European Union so as to require the provisions of the Charter to be recognised and to be given the same 'legal value' as the treaties themselves.

The Charter of Fundamental Rights has proved particularly controversial in the United Kingdom and also in Poland. This is largely because of the rights contained in Part IV, which relate to employment and social security. Accordingly, the Lisbon Treaty contains a Protocol on the Application of the Charter of Fundamental Rights of the European Union to Poland and to the United Kingdom. This effectively exempts the United Kingdom and Poland from the provisions of the Charter. The Charter will thus not have binding legal effect in this country even if the Lisbon Treaty comes into force. Nevertheless, it will inevitably prove highly influential in the development of EU law and policy and thus seems likely to operate indirectly to influence British law.[191]

Finally, on the Lisbon Treaty, it should be noted that it makes provision for the accession of the European Union to the European Convention on Human

---

[188] See nn 202–3 below and accompanying text.

[189] OJ C306.50, 17 December 2007.

[190] 13 June 2008. See generally H McDonald, 'Irish Voters Reject EU Treaty' *The Guardian*, 13 June 2008.

[191] See generally P Craig and G de Burca, *EU Law: Text, Cases, and Materials* (Oxford, Oxford University Press, 2007) 379–80. See also Case C-540/03 *EP v Council and Commission* [2006] ECR I-5769 (ECJ, 27 June 2006).

Rights.[192] Disappointingly, however, it does not provide for accession to the Revised European Social Charter.[193] Nevertheless, the practical implications of this omission in the disability context are likely to be minimal given the plans of the European Commission to ratify the CRPD.[194]

The implications for British law of the non-discrimination provisions of the Treaty of Amsterdam[195] are much more obvious than are the implications for it of the Charter of Fundamental Rights. Indeed, this is an issue which will be revisited in chapter 4 below. Given its significance, however, some awareness of its nature and scope is helpful at this stage.

It should be acknowledged at the outset that, as in Britain, the development of EC non-discrimination law and policy did not occur with the exclusive purpose of furthering principles of human rights. Nevertheless, and again as in Britain, the overlap between the concerns of the EC non-discrimination and human rights agendas is becoming increasingly apparent. This is well illustrated by the clear overlap between Article 21 of the Charter of Fundamental Rights, considered above, and the Employment Equality Directive, to which attention will now be turned.[196]

The Amsterdam Treaty inserted a new Article 13 into the consolidated EC Treaty which authorised 'the Council, acting unanimously on a proposal from the Commission and after consulting the European Parliament', to take appropriate action 'to combat discrimination based on sex, racial or ethnic origin, religion or belief, disability, age or sexual orientation'. The inclusion of disability in the list of Article 13 grounds was a highly significant development in EC disability policy. For the first time, an EU treaty acknowledged the existence of disabled people as

---

[192] By virtue of its amendments to Art 6(2) of the Treaty on European Union.

[193] O de Schutter, 'Anchoring the European Union to the European Social Charter: The Case for Accession' in de Burca and de Witte (eds), *Social Rights in Europe* (n 171 above).

[194] European Commission, 'Situation of Disabled People in the European Union: The European Action Plan 2008–2009' Communication from the Commission to the Council, the European Parliament, The European Economic and Social Committee and the Committee of the Regions, COM (2007) 738 final, 26 November 2007. See generally L Waddington, 'Breaking New Ground: The Implications of the UN Convention on the Rights of Persons with Disabilities for the European Community' in Arnardottir and Quinn (eds), *The UN Convention on the Rights of Persons with Disabilities* (n 48 above).

[195] OJ C340, 10 November 1997, Art 6A. See further, M Bell, 'The New Article 13 EC Treaty: A Sound Basis for European Anti-Discrimination Law?' (1999) 6 *Maastricht Journal of European Law* 5; R Whittle, 'Disability Discrimination and the Amsterdam Treaty' (1998) 23 *European Law Review* 50; L Waddington, 'Article 13 EC: Setting Priorities in the Proposal for a Horizontal Employment Directive' (2000) 29 *Industrial Law Journal* 176; and R Allen, 'Article 13 EC: Evolution and Current Contexts' in H Meenan (ed), *Equality Law in an Enlarged European Union* (n 185 above).

[196] See also Case C-144/04 *Mangold v Helm* [2005] ECR I-9981 (discussed in D Schiek, 'The ECJ Decision in Mangold: A Further Twist on Effects of Directives and Constitutional Relevance of Community Equality Legislation' (2006) 35 *Industrial Law Journal* 329), in which the ECJ observed that the prohibition of age discrimination was a fundamental and general principle of Community law which had effect independently of the Employment Equality Directive. No such observations were made in the much more restrictive ruling of the ECJ in the disability case of Case C-13/05 *Chacón Navas v Eurest Colectividades SA* [2006] ECR I-6467, however.

a group liable to experience discrimination and inequality.[197] The heavy emphasis given by the European Commission to principles of equality and non-discrimination in its current disability policy is evident in its Disability Action Plan 2003–2010.[198]

Action on the new Article 13 provisions was taken promptly and manifested itself in the Employment Equality Directive 2000.[199] This Directive, which applies to employment and occupation, requires Member States to take steps to prohibit discrimination on a number of grounds including disability. Article 2 makes it clear that the discrimination to be prohibited includes both direct and indirect discrimination. Article 5 imposes a specific obligation to take reasonable steps to accommodate the needs of disabled people. According to it,

> [i]n order to guarantee compliance with the principle of equal treatment in relation to persons with disabilities, reasonable accommodation shall be provided. This means that employers shall take appropriate measures, where needed in a particular case, to enable a person with a disability to have access to, participate in, or advance in employment, or to undergo training, unless such measures would impose a disproportionate burden on the employer. This burden shall not be disproportionate when it is sufficiently remedied by measures existing within the framework of the disability policy of the Member State concerned.[200]

According to Recital 20, 'appropriate measures' means 'effective and practical measures to adapt the workplace to the disability' including adaptations to premises and equipment, to work patterns and task distribution, and the provision of training.

Although Article 5 couches the reasonable accommodation obligation clearly within the equal treatment principle, that duty is nowhere explicitly categorised as a non-discrimination measure. In the version of the Directive which was originally proposed, the reasonable accommodation obligation was set out in Article 2(4).[201] Had this version been adopted, reasonable accommodation would clearly have acquired the status of a non-discrimination measure. It was moved from Article 2 into Article 5 for technical drafting reasons. These reasons were

[197] See generally, on the development of EC disability law and policy, L Waddington, *From Rome to Nice in a Wheelchair: The Development of a European Disability Policy* (Groningen, Europa Publishing, 2006); and, on the invisibility of disabled people within the EU treaty system prior to Amsterdam, T Degener et al, *Invisible Citizens: Disabled Persons' Status in the European Treaties* (Brussels, European Parliament, 1995); and L Waddington, *Disability, Employment and the European Community* (Appledoorn, Maklu, 1995).

[198] Equal Opportunities for People with Disabilities: a European Action Plan, COM/2003/650 final.

[199] Directive 2000/78/EC establishing a general framework for equal treatment in employment and occupation, [2000] OJ L 303/16.

[200] For criticism of the drafting of this article, see L Waddington, 'Reasonable Accommodation' in Schiek, Waddington and Bell (eds), *Cases, Materials and Text on National, Supranational and International Non-Discrimination Law* (n 121 above) 665–6.

[201] 'Proposal for a Council Directive Establishing a General Framework for Equal Treatment in Employment and Occupation' COM (1999) 565 final.

unrelated to the question of whether a failure to provide reasonable accommodation should be categorised as a form of unlawful discrimination. Nevertheless, the effect of the relocation to Article 5 has been to create uncertainty on this point.[202] What is clear is that, on the basis of the language of the Directive (unlike that of the CRPD), there is no explicit requirement to consider a failure to provide reasonable accommodation to be a form of unlawful discrimination. Nevertheless, there are encouraging indications that the European Commission does regard reasonable accommodation as falling clearly within the category of non-discrimination measures.[203]

The introduction of the Article 5 reasonable accommodation obligation is highly significant. Not only has it required an expansion of the domestic laws of the vast majority of Member States[204] but it also represents an important expansion of European Community equality law. For the first time at EC level, it gives binding legal force to the concept of reasonable accommodation. This represents an important deepening and enriching of the principle of equal treatment which underlies EC equality law.

The practical benefit of the Employment Equality Directive is nonetheless severely limited by the fact that its material scope is confined to employment and occupation. Thus, while it operates in both the public and private sectors, it applies only to employment, self-employment, occupation, vocational guidance and training (which covers a substantial proportion of post-16 education), examinations institutes, trade unions and professional bodies.[205] As will be apparent, this limited material scope is highly problematic. The provision of meaningful equality in the workplace is of little value if one is prevented from attaining the necessary qualifications by discriminatory education systems; from travelling to work by inaccessible transport; or from living near it by the unavailability of accessible housing.

For this reason the European Disability Forum (EDF) has long campaigned for an additional disability-specific Directive which would extend the prohibition of discrimination and the obligation to make reasonable accommodation beyond employment to areas such as education, transport, housing and goods and

---

[202] See generally G Quinn, 'Disability Discrimination Law in the European Union' in Meenan (ed), *Equality Law in an Enlarged European Union* (n 185 above) 257–9. See also Waddington, 'Reasonable Accommodation' (n 200 above) section 6.1.2 and, for an account of the variety of approaches which have been adopted to this issue at the domestic level in different Member States, section 6.5.

[203] See eg European Commission, Disability Mainstreaming in the European Employment Strategy, EMCO/11/290605 (Brussels, European Commission, 2005) p 3, where it is stated that: 'Reasonable accommodation is not a positive action left to the discretion of public or private operators, but an obligation whose failure can constitute unfair discrimination'.

[204] Prior to it the only European countries to have introduced reasonable accommodation obligations were Britain (under its DDA), Ireland (under s 16 of its Employment Equality Act 1998 and s 4 of its Equal Status Act 2000) and Sweden (under s 6 of its Disability Discrimination Act 1999). For discussion of the amendments of the British obligation, required by the Directive, see ch 3 below.

[205] Art 3. See further, R Whittle, 'The Framework Directive for Equal Treatment in Employment and Occupation: An Analysis from a Disability Rights Perspective' [2002] *European Law Review* 303 at 320–21.

services. Prompted by the pace of recent developments (particularly those associated with the CRPD), the EDF has recently published a revised version of its shadow directive containing what it regards as model provisions to be included in a new instrument.[206] A reasonable accommodation requirement is included in the article dealing with discrimination.[207] Interestingly, in addition to imposing the conventional duties to make reasonable adjustments in response to the circumstances of a particular disabled individual, this provision also carries an anticipatory element, requiring the barriers facing disabled people to be anticipated and appropriate adjustments to be made in advance of the appearance of a particular disabled customer, pupil or client. The British anticipatory reasonable adjustment duty (to be explained in the next chapter) is expressly acknowledged to have provided the inspiration for this approach. In addition, the EDF's Shadow Directive contains three Articles specifically devoted to increasing accessibility.[208]

Article 13 of the Amsterdam Treaty would clearly found an expansion of the material scope of the Employment Equality Directive, as is illustrated by the wider material scope of Directives relating to race and gender.[209] The European Commission has commissioned research into the extent of protection from discrimination currently available to disabled people at national level in the non-employment context.[210] This revealed significant variation. Following various expressions of commitment to addressing the issue through Community legislation,[211] the European Commission proposed a new Directive on 2 July 2008.[212]

The draft Directive proposed by the Commission differs from the model established by the EDF in a number of important respects. Perhaps the most fundamental of these is that, unlike the EDF's Shadow Directive, it is not disability-specific in nature but also extends to the grounds of age, sexual orientation and religion and belief. This is consistent with the approach of the

---

[206] EDF, *Proposal by the European Disability Forum for a Comprehensive Directive to Combat Discrimination Against Persons with Disabilities*, Doc EDF/0108, Brussels, February 2008.

[207] *Ibid*, Art 2(2)(c).

[208] *Ibid*, Art 4 (dealing with access to information and procedures); Art 5 (dealing with access to buildings and other public spaces, telecommunications, transport); and Art 6 (dealing with access to education).

[209] Directive 2000/43/EC implementing the principle of equal treatment between persons irrespective of racial or ethnic origin, [2000] OJ L 180/22; and Directive 2004/113/EC implementing the principle of equal treatment between men and women in the access to and supply of goods and services, [2004] OJ L 373/37.

[210] Mapping Study on Existing National Legislative Measures and their Impact in Tackling Discrimination, Outside the Field of Employment and Occupation, on the Grounds of Sex, Religion or Belief, Disability, Age and Sexual Orientation, available at: http://ec.europa.eu/employment_social/fundamental_rights/public/pubst_en.htm#stud (last accessed 29 April 2008).

[211] European Commission, 'Situation of Disabled People in the European Union: The European Action Plan 2008–2009' COM (2007) 738 final, 26 November 2007. See also European Commission, 'Commission Legislative and Work Programme 2008' COM (2007) 640 final, 23 October 2007.

[212] 'Proposal for a Council Directive on Implementing the Principle of Equal Treatment Between Persons Irrespective of Religion or Belief, Disability, Age or Sexual Orientation' COM (2008) 426.

Employment Equality Directive and has the merit of drawing attention to the similarities which exist between disability discrimination and other forms of discrimination. Nevertheless, the effective tackling of disability discrimination does require attention to be given to issues which are likely to have less significance in the context of other grounds. The constraints of a multiple-ground instrument therefore create additional challenges for the drafting of a law which adequately addresses these disability-specific issues.[213] There are concerns that, in relation to insurance and financial services[214] and also to education,[215] the terms of the draft Directive are disappointingly weak and risk failing to afford disabled people effective protection.[216]

Encouragingly, the draft Directive follows the lead of the CRPD in categorising a failure to comply with a reasonable accommodation duty as a form of discrimination.[217] A reasonable accommodation duty, similar to that contained in Article 5 of the Employment Equality Directive, is set out in Article 4(1)(b). For the purposes of assessments of 'disproportionate burden' in the context of this duty, Article 4(2) requires attention to be given to 'the size and resources of the organisation, its nature, the estimated cost, the life cycle of the goods and services, and the possible benefits of increased access for persons with disabilities' as well as to the existence of State funding to assist with the costs of relevant adjustments. While the appearance in this list of the benefits associated with improved access is refreshing, the reference to the life cycle of the goods and services is slightly puzzling and a potential cause for concern.

In addition to the familiar form of reasonable accommodation obligation set out in Article 4(1)(b), the draft Directive introduces a new duty which is anticipatory in nature. According to Art 4(1)(a),

[t]he measures necessary to enable persons with disabilities to have effective nondiscriminatory access to social protection, social advantages, health care, education and access to and supply of goods and services which are available to the public, including housing and transport, shall be provided by anticipation, including through appropriate modifications or adjustments. Such measures should not impose a disproportionate burden, nor require fundamental alteration of the social protection, social advantages, health care, education, or goods and services in question or require the provision of alternatives thereto.

The European Commission is undoubtedly to be congratulated on its willingness, as demonstrated by this provision, to include a form of anticipatory reasonable accommodation duty in the new Directive. The formulation of that

---

[213] See further EDF, *Promoting Equality and Combating Discrimination: The Need for a Disability Specific Non-Discrimination Directive Going Beyond Employment*, EDF Position Paper, Brussels, October 2007.

[214] Draft Directive (n 212 above) Art 2(7).

[215] *Ibid*, Art 3(3).

[216] EDF, 'Draft Non-Discrimination Directive Fails to Protect Disabled People' press release, Brussels, 2 July 2008.

[217] Draft Directive (n 212 above) Art 2(5).

duty is disappointing, however. Its language is somewhat obscure and thus carries the risk that it will not be clearly understood and effectively implemented by Member States. The proviso that it will not 'require fundamental alteration of the social protection, social advantages, health care, education, or goods and services in question or require the provision of alternatives thereto' also seems to confer on States an uncomfortably wide latitude in the implementation process. The following formulation, used in the EDF's Shadow Directive appears to be preferable:

> the failure to make a reasonable accommodation where this cannot be objectively justified shall be regarded as a form of discrimination.
>
> This means that the persons, including public bodies, referred to in Article 3, shall take appropriate measures, whenever possible in an anticipatory way, to enable a person or persons with disabilities to have equal access to the activities in the areas referred to in Article 3, unless such measures would impose a disproportionate burden on the provider or supplier.[218]

Accordingly, it is to be hoped that aspects of the draft Directive will be revised and strengthened before its text is finalised. Indeed, it is still to be hoped that the Commission will succumb to the demands of EDF and others in the disability movement and take the opportunity to elaborate a disability-specific instrument. Nevertheless, the emergence of a Directive which will require all EU Member States to prohibit disability discrimination (including failures to make reasonable adjustments) outside employment now seems inevitable. It is a development which is to be warmly welcomed. It also seems inevitable that this new instrument will include some form of anticipatory reasonable adjustment duty—a development which is likely to increase the interest in and scrutiny of the operation of this type of duty in Britain.

6. Conclusion

This chapter has drawn attention to the role of reasonable adjustment or accommodation principles in human rights law. At the international level, the significance of this role has been acknowledged for several decades. Its reiteration and clarification in the CRPD, however, has given it renewed energy and additional prominence. Particularly significant is the CRPD's positioning of reasonable adjustment obligations squarely within the domain of non-discrimination.

At the European level, reasonable adjustment duties have been recognised as an integral aspect of economic and social human rights in the context of the ESC. They have also been included in the package of employment-related equal

---

[218] Shadow Directive (n 206 above) Art 2(2)(c).

treatment measures which EC Directives require Member States to implement. In the context of civil and political rights, however, some ambiguity continues to cloud the exact nature and extent of their role. Nevertheless, relevant ECtHR case law does demonstrate an almost entirely unarticulated awareness of the need to make reasonable adjustments in order to ensure that the human rights of disabled individuals are not violated. Recent developments on the issue of indirect discrimination provide grounds for hope that the ECtHR may, in time, also openly accept and articulate the concept of reasonable adjustment or accommodation.

As yet it is unclear what impact the CRPD will have on European human rights law. Nevertheless, an expectation that it will strengthen and reinforce awareness of the centrality of the notion of reasonable adjustment in the area of disability non-discrimination law would not seem unrealistic. International law undoubtedly plays a powerful role in the shaping of European human rights law.[219]

The CRPD clearly demonstrates the dynamism of the relationship between European and international law. The EC, for instance, played an active role in the drafting of the Convention and many aspects of its disability law and policy have shaped the instrument. The CRPD will be the first human rights treaty to be ratified by the EC and will therefore, in its turn, inevitably exert a powerful influence over the future development of EC disability law and policy.[220]

The focus of this chapter has been human rights law. It would be impossible to tackle this subject without devoting careful attention to developments at the international and European levels. These developments are likely to have significant repercussions at the domestic level. Britain has already been required to amend the DDA in order to comply with EC Directives. Its Human Rights Act 1998 heightens the degree of scrutiny given to developments in the ECtHR by domestic actors. The Government has signed, and promise to ratify, the potentially extremely powerful CRPD.

It is therefore likely to become increasingly important for British judges, legislators and policy-makers to have regard to the underlying reasonable adjustment obligation imposed by human rights law. This obligation, although now expressly articulated in instruments such as the CRPD and the Framework Directive, is firmly rooted in fundamental principles of equality and individual dignity. Reference to it in the development and application of domestic law should therefore result in an expansive and purposive approach to the interpretation of the DDA—an approach which is free from unnecessarily restrictive

---

[219] See further eg, L Wildhaber, 'The European Convention on Human Rights and International Law' (2007) 56 *International and Comparative Law Quarterly* 217.

[220] See further eg, Waddington, 'Breaking New Ground' (n 194 above).

rulings based on linguistic technicalities.[221] Human rights law constitutes the essential, although generally unacknowledged, context within which the DDA reasonable adjustment duties operate.

---

[221] For criticism of the obstructiveness sometimes displayed to discrimination law principles by the judiciary, see A McColgan, 'Discrimination Law and the Human Rights Act 1998' in T Campbell, KD Ewing and A Tomkins (eds), *Sceptical Essays on Human Rights* (Oxford, Oxford University Press, 2001).

3

Reasonable Adjustment Obligations under the Disability Discrimination Act 1995

1. Introduction

THE CONCEPT OF 'reasonable adjustment' appeared explicitly in British law for the first time in the Disability Discrimination Act 1995 (DDA). It was not given a single unitary form but was crafted differently in different parts of the statute. The resulting complexity has been exacerbated by developments and amendments effected by subsequent legislation and case law.

The task of this chapter is to outline and evaluate the concept of reasonable adjustment as it is currently manifested in British disability non-discrimination law. Given the complexity of that law, the task is by no means a straightforward one. The standard structure adopted by guides to the DDA reflects that adopted by the legislation itself and is based on the different subject areas covered (employment, goods and services, transport etc).[1] Here, however, the aim is not to provide a reference manual on the Act for practitioners or students, nor to provide a detailed and comprehensive analysis of the entire legislation. It is, rather, to probe the conceptual boundaries of the notion of reasonable adjustment. For the purposes of this chapter, a three-fold categorisation of the DDA reasonable adjustment duties will therefore be adopted.

The first category embraces those duties which are entirely individualised and reactive in nature, simply requiring duty-bearers to take reasonable steps to accommodate the needs of a particular disabled person with whom they are confronted. The second concerns those duties which contain an anticipatory element, requiring duty-bearers not only to react to the obstacles their operations present for actual disabled employees, customers, pupils and others but also to

---

[1] See eg B Doyle, *Disability Discrimination: Law and Practice* (Bristol, Jordan Publishing, 2008); and K Monaghan, *Blackstone's Guide to the Disability Discrimination Legislation* (Oxford, Oxford University Press, 2005)—where such structuring is used within chapters.

anticipate what barriers such people are likely to encounter and to take reasonable steps to remove them in advance. These anticipatory reasonable adjustment duties have a definite group dimension and are well placed to tackle structural barriers. They are distinctively British in nature, as they do not yet seem to have appeared in this form in any other jurisdiction. As indicated in the previous chapter,[2] however, it seems likely that some form of anticipatory reasonable adjustment duty will feature in the proposed new EC Directive covering goods and services and that it may not therefore be too long before such duties play a role in the law of all Member States. The third category consists not of duties to make reasonable adjustments as such but of duties to refrain from withholding consent unreasonably to steps which others wish to take in order to facilitate access. These three categories of reasonable adjustment duty will be examined in Sections 2, 3 and 4 respectively. Because of the length and complexity of Sections 2 and 3, 'Overview' and 'Summary' sections will be included in order to assist readers unfamiliar with this area of law.

2. Reactive Reasonable Adjustment Duties

2.1 Overview

This discussion will be divided into five main parts. First, in Section 2.2, the sphere of operation of the reactive reasonable adjustment duties will be considered. These duties currently operate in two main areas—let premises and employment—and a few words will therefore be devoted to each. Second, in Section 2.3, some consideration will be given to the conditions which must be satisfied before a reactive duty will come into being. In Section 2.4 attention will shift to the actual content of the reactive reasonable adjustment duty and to the nature of the obligation it imposes on duty-bearers. In Section 2.5 a few words will be devoted to the extent to which a failure to comply with a reactive reasonable adjustment duty can be justified. Finally, in Section 2.6, issues relevant to the enforcement of these duties will be addressed.

2.2 Context and Scope

The entirely reactive reasonable adjustment duties imposed by the DDA arise in the contexts of let premises and of employment. In relation to let premises,[3] the 1995 Act originally imposed no reasonable adjustment duties at all. Such duties

---

[2] Ch 2, fnn 212–18 above and accompanying text.
[3] Let premises here includes property which is subleased and which is held under a contractual licence to occupy—DDA s 24A(4).

were inserted into the premises provisions by the DDA 2005.[4] They require people who are managing or letting premises to take reasonable steps to accommodate the needs of disabled occupiers, both by adjusting their policies, practices, procedures and the terms of leases, and by providing disabled occupiers with auxiliary aids and services.[5] These duties are reactive in nature because they are triggered only when a disabled occupier requests assistance. There is no obligation on controllers of let premises to anticipate difficulties and take steps to remove potential barriers before receiving this form of specific request.

Although these reasonable adjustment duties were primarily intended to address difficulties experienced by disabled tenants in connection with housing, they apply to commercial as well as residential lettings. Unlike the reasonable adjustment duties created elsewhere in the DDA, however, the duties imposed on managers and controllers of let premises do not extend to the making of adjustments to physical features of the premises. Provision is made, however, to prohibit landlords from unreasonably preventing disabled tenants from effecting access-related physical alterations. These will be considered further in Section 4 below.

The reasonable adjustment duties applying to let premises, like those applying to employment, are reactive in nature. This, however, is the only significant attribute they share. In all other respects the let premises duties resemble the duties imposed on service providers which will be considered in Section 3 below. In order to avoid repetition, their workings will not therefore be detailed here.

In the context of employment, the DDA imposes reasonable adjustment duties in a wide range of circumstances broadly connected with employment. Thus, under Part 2 of the Act, reasonable adjustment duties are imposed on employers in relation to employees[6]; on principals in relation to contract workers[7]; on those responsible for making, controlling and terminating appointments to non-elected public offices or posts in relation to office or post-holders[8]; on local councils (including London borough councils, county, district, parish and community councils) in relation to councillors[9]; on managers or trustees of occupational pension schemes in relation to scheme membership[10]; on firms in relation to partnerships[11]; on barristers and their clerks in relation to pupillages and tenancies[12]; on advocates in relation to their pupils[13]; on trade organisations in

---

[4] Following recommendations to this effect by the Disability Rights Task Force, *From Exclusion to Inclusion* (London, Department for Education and Employment, 1999) recommendations 6.25 and 6.26.

[5] DDA ss 24D and 24C respectively.

[6] DDA s 4A.

[7] DDA s 4B(4), (5) and (6).

[8] DDA s 4E. See also s 21B(8).

[9] DDA s 15C (inserted by DDA 2005 s 1).

[10] DDA s 4H.

[11] DDA s 6B.

[12] DDA s 7B.

[13] DDA s 7D.

relation to membership[14]; on qualifications bodies in relation to the conferral of trade or professional qualifications[15]; and on placement providers in relation to work placements.[16] These duties are expressed in virtually identical language and, for the sake of simplicity, references in the following discussion will generally be confined to those concerned directly with the employer/employee relationship.

The provisions of Part 2 of the DDA were completely reformulated by the DDA 1995 (Amendment) Regulations 2003.[17] These were introduced under section 2 of the European Communities Act 1972 in an attempt to ensure compliance with the Employment Equality Directive 2000.[18] Amongst the significant changes which they effected was the removal of the previous exemption of small employers from the scope of the DDA.[19] Thus, from 1 October 2004, with the exception of the armed forces,[20] all employers have been exposed to potential liability to make reasonable adjustments in respect of disabled applicants and employees.

The reasonable adjustments duty, previously set out in section 6, is now governed by ss 4A and 18B. As will be explained below, it emerged from the 2003 reformulation process somewhat tidier and more streamlined than it had been in its original incarnation. Because the Directive related only to employment and occupation, however, the earlier more 'unkempt' version of the duty is still to be found in other areas of the DDA. Further, despite its remoulding, doubts remain as to whether the new employment-related reasonable adjustments duty goes sufficiently far to satisfy the demands of the Directive—particularly in the light of the decision of the House of Lords in *Mayor and Burgesses of the London Borough of Lewisham v Malcolm*.[21]

2.3 Triggering the Duty

2.3.1 The Disabled Person Concerned

According to section 4A(1), an employer will have a duty to make reasonable adjustments when:

(a) a provision, criterion or practice applied by or on behalf of an employer, or
(b) any physical feature of premises occupied by the employer

---

[14] DDA s 14.
[15] DDA s 14B. The DDA 2005 inserted a new s 31AD into the 1995 Act and this imposes a similar reasonable adjustment duty on general qualifications bodies.
[16] DDA s 14D.
[17] Disability Discrimination Act 1995 (Amendment) Regulations 2003 (SI 2003/1673).
[18] Directive 2000/78/EC establishing a general framework for equal treatment in employment and occupation, [2000] OJ L 303/16.
[19] DDA s 7.
[20] DDA s 64(7).
[21] *Mayor and Burgesses of the London Borough of Lewisham v Malcolm* [2008] UKHL 43 (discussed in ch 4 below).

places the disabled person concerned at a substantial disadvantage in comparison with persons who are not disabled.

The duty will thus arise only when 'the disabled person concerned' is substantially disadvantaged by some aspect of the employer's operations. It is because the duty is not triggered until this point that it is reactive, rather than proactive, in nature. It is a duty only to react to the case of the particular disabled person concerned—the person with whom they have been confronted—and not to anticipate and remove potential barriers in advance.

For the purposes of determining to whom employment should be offered, the 'disabled person concerned' is defined as 'any disabled person who is, or has notified the employer that he may be, an applicant for that employment'.[22] For other purposes, the 'disabled person concerned' is defined as a disabled person who is '(i) an applicant , or (ii) an employee'.[23] Thus, unless a disabled person encounters an employer in one of these capacities, no duty to adjust will arise.

2.3.2 Substantial Disadvantage

The disabled person concerned must, according to section 4A(1), be placed at a 'substantial disadvantage' as compared with a non-disabled person by some aspect of the employer's operations. The focus is on the disadvantage caused to the particular disabled person and the impact of the relevant practice or measure on disabled people in general is therefore irrelevant.[24]

'Substantial' here (as elsewhere in the DDA[25]) means simply 'more than minor or trivial'.[26] It has been the cause of little controversy to date. As in other areas of non-discrimination law,[27] however, the element of comparison required by 'relative disadvantage' has proved somewhat troublesome.

It is clear that, for the purposes of section 4A(1), there is no need for a claimant to identify an actual (as opposed to a hypothetical) non-disabled comparator against whom to measure the relevant disadvantage. Other aspects of this comparator requirement have proved less straightforward, however. This is well illustrated by the range of views expressed on the matter in the leading reasonable adjustment case of *Archibald v Fife Council*.[28]

---

[22] DDA s 4A(2)(a).

[23] DDA s 4A(2)(b).

[24] *Lincolnshire Police v Weaver* [2008] UKEAT 0622.07.1903 [54] (Elias P). See also Disability Rights Commission, *DDA 1995 Code of Practice: Employment and Occupation* (London, Stationery Office, 2004) para 5.4. Contrast, however, the approach of the Employment Appeal Tribunal in *Paul v National Probation Service* [2004] IRLR 190 [23].

[25] See eg, in the context of justification for less favourable treatment of employees, *Jones v Post Office* [2001] EWCA Civ 558; and *HJ Heinz Co Ltd v Kenrick* [2000] IRLR 144 (EAT).

[26] DRC, *DDA 1995 Code of Practice: Employment and Occupation* (n 24 above) para 5.11. See also *Cave v Goodwin* [2001] EWCA Civ 391.

[27] For thought-provoking discussion of comparator requirements, see A McColgan, 'Cracking the Comparator Problem: Discrimination, "Equal" Treatment and the Role of Comparisons' [2006] *European Human Rights Law Review* 650.

[28] *Archibald v Fife Council* [2004] UKHL 32, [2004] IRLR 197.

Lord Hamilton, in the Inner House of the Scottish Court of Session, asserted that relevant comparators must be 'persons already employed in, or applicants or potential applicants for, a particular post' and not 'persons at large or persons employed in any capacity whatsoever by the employer in question'.[29] On appeal, however, Baroness Hale stressed that the comparator group must not be confined to non-disabled people performing the same job as the disabled claimant. Such an approach, in her view, would prevent consideration of possible adjustments external to the specific job (such as a transfer to an alternative position).[30] Lord Rodger, on the other hand, warned that Baroness Hale's approach might be insufficiently precise. Reference to non-disabled people generally would render the test meaningless. The limits of the relevant comparator group would, in his view, depend on the particular situation in which the discrimination was alleged to have occurred and may, for instance, include all the non-disabled people competing for a particular post or all the non-disabled people employed in differing capacities by a particular employer.[31]

The identification of the appropriate comparator group formed the central issue in *Smith v Churchill Stairlifts*.[32] Delivering its decision weeks before that of the House of Lords in *Archibald*, the Employment Appeal Tribunal had held (by a majority) that the appropriate group was non-disabled people generally. It consequently ruled that the claimant's inability to carry full-sized radiator cabinets (as required for participation in the employer's selection process) did not subject the claimant to a substantial disadvantage, as the non-disabled public would experience similar difficulties in lifting such items. In light of the House of Lords ruling in *Archibald*, this decision was reversed by the Court of Appeal. In its view, the appropriate comparators were the non-disabled applicants who were able to carry the radiators and who were therefore permitted to continue in the selection programme. According to Maurice Kay LJ, the effect of the various *Archibald* judgments on this issue was to indicate that 'the proper comparator is readily identified by reference to the disadvantage caused by the relevant arrangements'.[33] This would suggest that the relevant arrangements (or provisions, criteria or practices[34]) should be identified before the comparator group is selected.

Another question which has arisen, particularly in the context of sick pay entitlements, is that of whether a disabled person can be found to have experienced a substantial disadvantage through the operation of a general policy or practice which has universal application.[35] In *London Clubs Management Ltd v*

---

[29] *Ibid*, [24].
[30] *Ibid*, [64].
[31] *Ibid*, [35]–[39].
[32] *Smith v Churchill Stairlifts* [2005] EWCA Civ 1220.
[33] *Ibid*, [39].
[34] See section 2.3.3 below for further discussion of the meaning and relevance of 'arrangements' and 'provisions, criteria and practices'.
[35] See generally S Khoja, 'Off Work' (2006) 150 *Solicitors Journal* 1142.

Hood,[36] the Employment Appeal Tribunal expressed some scepticism as to whether a sick pay policy that applied to all employees could be regarded as putting a disabled employee at a substantial disadvantage. In *Nottinghamshire County Council v Meikle*,[37] however, the Court of Appeal had little difficulty in finding that a disabled employee, whose absence from work had been caused by the employer's failure to provide her with appropriate job-related adjustments, had been substantially disadvantaged by the application to her of the standard sick pay policy. According to that policy, a cut in sick pay was imposed after an absence of 100 days. In *O'Hanlon v Commissioners of HM Revenue and Customs*, the Employment Appeal Tribunal refreshingly declared (in a passage subsequently approved by the Court of Appeal):

> It is plainly no answer to a claim of this kind to assert that the same rules apply to all. The whole premise of this provision is that the disabled employee may be disadvantaged by the application of common rules. Unlike other forms of discrimination, the employer may be obliged to take positive steps ... to remove or alleviate the consequences of the disability.[38]

Nevertheless, granting a disabled person more sick pay than that available to a non-disabled person is likely to amount to a reasonable adjustment only in 'a very rare case indeed'.[39] Requiring such a step will generally do little to further the statute's 'important and laudable aims'.[40] This is because, in the words of the EAT,

> [t]he Act is designed to recognise the dignity of the disabled and to require modifications which will enable them to play a full part in the world of work ... It is not to treat them as objects of charity which, as the Tribunal pointed out, may in fact sometimes and for some people tend to act as a positive disincentive to return to work.[41]

2.3.3 Cause of the Substantial Disadvantage

(a) The Causal Link   In order to trigger the reasonable adjustments duty, the substantial disadvantage must be caused by either:

(a) a provision, criterion or practice applied by or on behalf of an employer, or
(b) any physical feature of premises occupied by the employer.[42]

---

[36] *London Clubs Management Ltd v Hood* [2001] IRLR 719 (EAT) [21]. See also *Paul v National Probation Service* [2004] IRLR 190 (EAT) [23] (Cox J) for a similar approach to the general application of making job offers subject to satisfactory occupational health reports.
[37] *Nottinghamshire CC v Meikle* [2004] IRLR 703 (CA).
[38] *O'Hanlon v Commissioners of HM Revenue and Customs* [2006] IRLR 840 (EAT) [56]. Approved by the Court of Appeal at [2007] EWCA Civ 283 [86].
[39] *Ibid* (EAT) [67].
[40] *Ibid* (EAT) [69].
[41] *Ibid* (EAT) [69]. See also *O'Hanlon v Commissioners of Revenue and Customs* [2007] EWCA Civ 283 [50]; and *Fowler v Waltham Forest LBC* [2007] UKEAT 0116 (6 September 2002).
[42] DDA s 4A(1).

Employers will therefore not be placed under a duty to make reasonable adjustments unless a claimant is disadvantaged by one of their provisions, criteria, practices or features. As will be discussed further below, the term 'provision, criterion or practice' was introduced into the statute by the 2003 Regulations and replaced the original reference to 'arrangements'.[43]

In *NTL Group Ltd v Difolco*[44] Ms Difolco's claim failed because her disadvantage could not be attributed to any such cause. At the time of her case the original statutory wording operated, requiring her disadvantage to have been caused by 'arrangements' of the employer rather than by any of its 'provisions, criteria or practices'. Ms Difolco, a disabled woman whose impairments made it difficult for her to work full-time, was made redundant in circumstances unrelated to her impairment. She was invited to apply for another full-time position which was then being advertised and told that, if she was offered the job, it might be possible for her to take it on a part-time basis. She did not apply because she did not wish to be pressurised into working full-time.

The Employment Appeal Tribunal identified Ms Difolco's inability to work full-time as a 'substantial disadvantage' for the purposes of the Act. It went on to hold that the employer should have adjusted its recruiting practices and offered her the post on a part-time basis without opening it to competition. According to the Court of Appeal, however, the mere fact of advertising a job on a full-time basis could not constitute a relevant arrangement and, since her dismissal had been unrelated to her disability, no other relevant arrangement could be identified. This undermined the finding of 'substantial disadvantage' because, according to the statute, the disadvantage must result from the relevant arrangement.[45]

In contrast with the type of scrutiny associated with the DDA's threshold requirement of being 'disabled',[46] the focus in reasonable adjustment disputes is on the negative impact of factors external to a disabled person and not on medical assessments of their particular impairment-related limitations. Nevertheless, the disadvantage caused by the offending provision, criterion, practice or physical feature must be, in some way, connected with the claimant's impairment. Thus, in *Bruce v Chamberlain*,[47] the Court of Appeal held that a prospective employer was under no obligation to adjust a job specification because the disabled applicant lacked the degree of legal expertise which had been specified. The demand for a higher degree of expertise than he possessed was insufficiently related to his impairment to trigger a reasonable adjustment duty.

The decision in *Bruce* is of particular interest because, unlike the US Americans With Disabilities Act 1990 (ADA) and many other disability non-discrimination laws, the DDA does not explicitly specify that a disabled person

---

[43] See section 2.3.3(b) below.
[44] *NTL Group Ltd v Difolco* [2006] EWCA Civ 1508.
[45] *Ibid*, [20]. See also *Smith v Churchill Stairlifts* [2005] EWCA Civ 1220, [33] (Maurice Kay LJ).
[46] See further ch 6, fnn 134–42 below and accompanying text.
[47] *Bruce v Chamberlain* [2004] EWCA Civ 1047.

must be able to perform the 'essential functions' of a job (whether with or without reasonable adjustment) in order to gain the protection of the statute.[48] Lisa Waddington has attributed this tendency to insist on an ability to perform essential functions to the fact that the aim of reasonable adjustment duties is the promotion of equality and non-discrimination as opposed to the fostering of positive action or more favourable treatment.[49] Insistence on this requirement ensures that no duty will be imposed on employers in favour of people incapable of performing the job.

British law appears to achieve a similar result to that attained by the essential functions requirement but by different means. As demonstrated by *Bruce*, there will be no issue of disability discrimination if a disabled person, even after reasonable adjustments are made in their favour, would be incapable of performing a particular job for reasons unconnected with their disability. The importance attached in this process to the effect that reasonable adjustments might have had on the claimant's ability to carry out the relevant job is illustrated by the case of *Paul v National Probation Service*.[50]

In that case, a position was offered to Mr Paul subject to his passing an occupational health assessment. The offer was withdrawn when the employer received a report from its occupational health officer stating that Mr Paul's history of depression rendered him unfit for the post. That report had been based on a letter from Mr Paul's general practitioner, who had not treated him for the condition and did not know him well. The employer took no steps to investigate its accuracy (by, for instance, insisting that the occupational health officer should interview Mr Paul or seek advice from his psychiatric consultant). Neither did it consider adjustments (such as lengthening his induction period or giving him additional mentoring support) that might have been made in order to reduce the stress that the post might otherwise have placed on Mr Paul. The employer was therefore held to have failed to comply with its duty to make reasonable adjustments.

(b) Provisions, Criteria or Practices   The phrase 'provision, criterion or practice' was introduced by the DDA (Amendment) Regulations 2003 and replaced the original section 6 reference to 'arrangements made by or on behalf of an employer'. These Regulations, as has already been explained, were introduced in order to bring British law into line with the requirements of the Employment

---

[48] Americans With Disabilities Act 1990, 42 USC s 12111(8), on which see generally W Gray, 'The Essential Functions Limitation on the Civil Rights of People with Disabilities and John Rawls' Concept of Social Justice' (1992) 22 *New Mexico Law Review* 295; and DA Snyder, 'Qualified Individuals with Disabilities: Defining the ADA's Protected Class' (1993) 44 *Labor Law Journal* 101. See also Directive 2000/78/EC establishing a general framework for equal treatment in employment and occupation, [2000] OJ L 303/16, recital 17; and L Waddington, 'Reasonable Accommodation' in D Schiek, L Waddington and M Bell (eds), *Cases, Materials and Texts on National, Supranational and International Non-Discrimination Law* (Oxford, Hart Publishing, 2007) 702–5.
[49] Waddington, 'Reasonable Accommodation' (n 48 above) 702–3.
[50] *Paul v National Probation Service* [2004] IRLR 190 (EAT).

Equality Directive 2000.[51] The phrase 'provision, criterion or practice' is not defined in the Directive and has not, to date, been the subject of scrutiny by the European Court of Justice. It is not exhaustively defined in the DDA but section 18D states that it includes the formerly used notion of 'arrangements'.[52] It is therefore worth considering some of the discussions which have taken place about the limits of the term 'arrangements', while bearing in mind the likelihood that the concept of 'provision, criterion or practice' will be interpreted much more generously.

The meaning of 'arrangements', for the purposes of the now repealed section 6, was restricted by section 6(2) to

(a) arrangements for determining to whom employment should be offered; [and]

(b) any term, condition or arrangements on which employment, promotion, a transfer, training or any other benefit is offered or afforded.

The precise limits of the notion of 'arrangements' proved to be a complex issue, which generated a not inconsiderable body of case law. Some of the most significant judicial explorations of these limits will now be outlined.

Before the Disability Discrimination Act 1995 (Amendment) Regulations 2003, disadvantages caused by certain forms of scheme or arrangement were specifically excluded from the scope of the employment reasonable adjustment provisions by the now repealed section 6(11). According to that subsection, the rest of section 6 (which set out the reasonable adjustment duty) would not apply to

any benefit under an occupational pension scheme or any other benefit payable in money or money's worth under a scheme or arrangement for the benefit of employees in respect of ...

(c) accident, injury, sickness or invalidity.

Arguments that employers were therefore not obliged to make adjustments to their contractual sick pay arrangements were, however, rejected by the Court of Appeal in *Nottinghamshire County Council v Meikle*.[53] The purpose of section 6(11), it was held, was to exclude third party insurance schemes over which employers did not have control. Contractual sick pay terms, on the other hand, fell into the ambit of 'arrangements', which might trigger a reasonable adjustment duty. Any lingering uncertainty on this point was removed by the 2003 Regulations, which do not include an equivalent of the former section 6(11) exclusion in the new section 4A.

---

[51] See nn 18–20 above and accompanying text.

[52] See also DRC, *DDA 1995 Code of Practice: Employment and Occupation* (n 24 above) para 5.8.

[53] *Nottinghamshire County Council v Meikle* [2004] IRLR 703 (CA), following *London Clubs Management v Hood* [2001] IRLR 719 (EAT). See also, more recently, *O'Hanlon v Commissioners of Revenue and Customs* [2007] EWCA Civ 283.

In *Clark v Novacold*,[54] the Court of Appeal held that dismissals were not relevant arrangements for the purposes of section 6. A dismissal, according to their Lordships, was neither an arrangement 'for determining to whom employment should be offered' nor a 'term, condition or arrangement on which employment, promotion, a transfer, training or any other benefit is offered or afforded'. It therefore fell outside the scope of section 6(2) with the result that no duty to make adjustments would arise in relation to the actual act of a dismissal. The significance of this exclusion, however, was minimal because all pre-dismissal arrangements (such as disciplinary meetings[55] and redundancy criteria[56]) would fall clearly within the scope of section 6(2). The exclusion of dismissals was thus based on statutory language which has now disappeared. With the appearance of the new reference to provisions, criteria and practices, dismissals would now appear to be covered.

Another limit on the meaning of 'arrangements' was imposed in the case of *Kenny v Hampshire Constabulary*.[57] This case concerned a graduate in information technology who had been offered a computing job because he was the best-qualified applicant. The offer was withdrawn when it emerged that, because of his cerebral palsy, he would need personal assistance with urinating.

The Employment Appeal Tribunal in *Kenny* held that arrangements relating to the provision of personal care were not relevant arrangements within the meaning of section 6(2) and that, consequently, they could never trigger a duty to make reasonable adjustments. On this view then, even where the post in question is in an establishment such as a hospital where there are plenty of staff willing and able to provide such assistance, the employer will be under no duty to take steps to provide it. According to the Employment Appeal Tribunal, 'a line [had] to be drawn' somewhere.[58]

In drawing its distinction between measures which are job-related and those which relate to personal care, the Employment Appeal Tribunal in *Kenny* drew upon the US approach for support.[59] The solidity of that support is, however, far from clear. Relevant guidance on the Americans with Disabilities Act 1990, issued by the Equal Employment Opportunity Commission, provides that:

> An employer does not have to provide as reasonable accommodations personal use items needed in accomplishing daily activities both on and off the job. Thus, an employer is not required to provide an employee with a prosthetic limb, a wheelchair, eyeglasses, hearing aids, or similar devices if they are also needed off the job. Furthermore, an employer is not required to provide personal use amenities, such as a hot pot or refrigerator, if those items are not provided to employees without disabilities.

---

[54] *Clark v Novacold* [1999] IRLR 318 (CA).
[55] See eg *Taylor v OCS Group* [2006] IRLR 613 (CA), concerning the provision of sign language interpretation to a deaf employee in order to ensure full participation in a disciplinary hearing.
[56] See eg *Tarbuck v Sainsbury's Supermarkets* [2006] IRLR 664 (EAT).
[57] *Kenny v Hampshire Constabulary* [1999] ICR 27 (EAT).
[58] *Ibid*, [37].
[59] *Ibid*, [34].

However, items that might otherwise be considered personal may be required as reasonable accommodations where they are specifically designed or required to meet job-related rather than personal needs.[60]

The distinction being made here relates to the provision of items which are required specifically for work and ones which are required for day-to-day living.[61] The dispute in *Kenny* did not concern this distinction, however, as it related to the provision of assistance (albeit of a type which he required and which was already available to him outside work) during the working day and within work premises.

In *Kenny*, as in *Novacold*, the court was heavily influenced by the wording of section 6(2). It attached considerable weight to the fact that that sub-section purported to be describing the 'only' types of arrangement which would trigger duties to make adjustments. Further, according to it, the types of arrangement it described were all job-related.

Kenny thus assumes a distinction between employment-related arrangements, which may trigger the reasonable adjustments duty, and personal needs, which—although having a fundamental impact on ability to perform a job—will never require an employer to provide support. Such a distinction is unfortunate. It cannot be drawn with clarity and has the potential to be developed to create an undesirable exemption from the scope of the reasonable adjustment obligation. The problem would have been avoided had it been accepted that, although such a duty might arise, it may not have been reasonable in the particular circumstances of the case for the employer to have arranged toileting assistance. The concept of reasonableness should, it is suggested, be allowed to determine the issue on a case-by-case basis. It is to be hoped that the disappearance of the section 6(2) wording will facilitate a fresh judicial examination of this issue should a similar case arise in the future. Interestingly, in the context of education, the Court of Appeal has been prepared to assume that catering for the cleaning and changing of an incontinent child might fall within the scope of a reasonable adjustment duty although, in that case, it would not have been reasonable for the school to have provided such a service.[62]

Another restrictive judicial interpretation of 'arrangements' is to be found in the decision of the Employment Appeal Tribunal in *Mills v Hillingdon London Borough Council*.[63] 'Arrangements' was there held to entail

---

[60] Equal Employment Opportunity Commission, *Enforcement Guidance: Reasonable Accommodation and Undue Hardship Under the Americans with Disabilities Act* (EEOC, 2002), available at http://www.eeoc.gov/policy/docs/accommodation.html#N_15_ (last accessed 15 March 2008); 29 CFR pt 1630.9 (1997).

[61] See Waddington, 'Reasonable Accommodation' (n 48 above) 647 where it is suggested that this distinction is to be found 'explicitly or implicitly' in all reasonable accommodation laws on employment.

[62] *K v X Grammar School Governors* [2007] EWCA Civ 165 [48].

[63] *Mills v Hillingdon LBC* (2001) EAT/0954/00.

some positive steps taken by an employer whether by a scheme of work or instructions as to how work should be performed.[64]

Under such an approach it appears that omissions by an employer are unlikely to qualify as 'arrangements' and therefore to trigger reasonable adjustment duties. This possibility attracted the attention of the Disability Rights Commission (DRC), which criticised the *Mills* interpretation and called for its reversal.[65] Although the matter has not been explicitly addressed in subsequent legislation, the reference to 'practice' in the new phraseology would seem to be sufficiently broad to include omissions and hence to allay concerns about the potential of *Mills* to limit the operation of reasonable adjustment duties.

Important though these developments are, the most significant case to have considered the meaning of 'arrangements' is undoubtedly *Archibald v Fife Council*—a case in which an expansive interpretation was adopted.[66] In that case the claimant, formerly employed as a road sweeper by Fife Council, became physically unable to perform the essential functions of the job due to the onset of a serious medical condition. The House of Lords was required to decide whether any arrangement causing her a substantial disadvantage might be identified. Their Lordships firmly rejected the temptation to hold that any disadvantage she experienced was the result of her medical condition and not of an employment-related arrangement.[67] They also rejected the view of the Scottish Inner House in that case that 'arrangements' could not include the fundamental essence of the job.[68] They ruled instead that it was an implied condition, or 'arrangement' of Ms Archibald's employment contract that she should be physically fit and another that she was liable to dismissal if she should cease to be physically fit. Accordingly, the relevant 'arrangements' were to be found in 'the terms, conditions and arrangements relating to the essential functions of the disabled person's employment'.[69] Once she had become disabled, these arrangements placed her at a substantial disadvantage as compared with her physically fit colleagues who were still able to carry out the essential functions of the job. A reasonable adjustment duty was therefore triggered.

Thus, under British law, the essential functions of a job may themselves constitute the provision, criterion or practice which triggers a reasonable adjustment duty. Where a disabled person is unable to perform those essential functions, attention should first be given to whether that inability is closely

---

[64] *Ibid*, [8].

[65] DRC, *Disability Equality: Making it Happen* (London, DRC, 2003) para 8.

[66] *Archibald v Fife Council* [2004] UKHL 32, [2004] IRLR 197 (discussed in P Hughs, 'Equality of Outcome' (2004) 148 *Solicitors Journal* 1012).

[67] A viewpoint for which Lord McCluskey had thought there was 'a strong argument' in the Inner House of the Court of Session—*ibid*, [43].

[68] *Ibid*, [35]–[37] (Lord McFadyen). See also [25] and [44] (Lords Hamilton and McCluskey respectively).

[69] *Ibid*, [40]–[41] (Lord Rodger). See also [64] (Baroness Hale).

related to their impairment.[70] If it is, attention should then be given to whether the making of reasonable adjustments might enable the disabled person to carry out the essential functions.[71] If no reasonable adjustments would enable them to do so then attention may need to be given to whether it would be reasonable to transfer them (possibly on a non-competitive basis) to another post.[72]

(c) Physical Features   The reasonable adjustment duty, it will be remembered, may be triggered when a substantial disadvantage is caused to the disabled person concerned either by a provision, criterion or practice of the employer or by a 'physical feature of premises' occupied by the employer. The term 'physical feature' is relatively unproblematic. Guidance as to its meaning is provided by section 18D(2)[73] according to which it includes:

(a) any feature arising from the design or construction of a building on the premises,
(b) any feature on the premises of any approach to, exit from or access to such a building,
(c) any fixtures, fittings, furnishings, furniture, equipment or material in or on the premises,
(d) any other physical element or quality of any land comprised in the premises.

It is perhaps worth stressing, in this connection, that physical features would include those not directly related to performance of the job, such as parking or toilet facilities. It may therefore be possible for a disabled person, unable to use an employer's toilet facilities unassisted, to argue that the reasonable adjustment duty is triggered by the difficulty created by the toilets as a physical feature even though, as in *Kenny*,[74] they may be prevented from arguing that it is triggered by the absence of assistance in their use. Once triggered, however, the reasonableness of providing assistance to a disabled person in the use of toilet facilities which present physical barriers may well need to be assessed. This possibility provides further grounds for a reassessment of the logic behind the decision in *Kenny*.

2.3.4 The Knowledge Requirement

According to section 4A(3), no reasonable adjustments duty will arise if an employer does not know and could not reasonably be expected to know:

(a) in the case of an applicant or potential applicant, that the disabled person concerned is, or may be, an applicant for the employment; or
(b) in any case, that that person has a disability and is likely to be affected in the way mentioned in subsection (1).

---

[70] *Bruce v Chamberlain* [2004] EWCA Civ 1047. See nn 47–49 above and accompanying text.
[71] *Paul v National Probation Service* [2004] IRLR 190. See n 50 above and accompanying text.
[72] *Archibald v Fife Council* (n 66 above).
[73] See also DRC, *DDA 1995 Code of Practice: Employment and Occupation* (n 24 above) paras 5.9–5.10.
[74] *Kenny v Hampshire Constabulary* [1999] ICR 27 (EAT); see nn 57–62 above and accompanying text.

This requirement thus reinforces the reactive nature of the reasonable adjustment duty in the employment context. Employers are placed under no obligation to consider adjustments until they are confronted either by an applicant or employee whom they know—or ought to know—to be disabled and to be exposed to a substantial disadvantage as a result of their provisions, criteria, practices or physical features.

It is thus clear that no duty will arise if the employer has not been made aware, and has no means of discovering, that an employee or applicant is disabled.[75] The determination of when an employer ought reasonably to have known either that an employee or applicant was disabled, or that one known to be disabled was substantially disadvantaged, has, however, proved to be a complex and controversial issue, reminiscent of debates surrounding the level of inquiry appropriate for purchasers of land under the traditional (and now largely defunct) doctrine of notice. Although the matter has not yet received attention from a court of high authority,[76] such decisions as there have been reveal considerable judicial concern to avoid placing employers under too heavy a burden of inquiry. Such concern appears to be based on the fear of requiring intrusive and burdensome inquiries which would be unpleasant to employers and disabled people alike.

In *Davies v Toys'R'Us*,[77] an Industrial Tribunal was confronted with the question of whether an employer ought reasonably to have known that an employee it knew to be disabled was placed at a substantial disadvantage by reason of its arrangements or physical features. The employee in question used an artificial arm and had been required to climb a ladder and to handle goods. Following his dismissal it was argued that the employer had failed to comply with its duty to make reasonable adjustments in order to accommodate his needs. This argument was rejected on the ground that no such duty had arisen because the employer could not reasonably have been expected to know that the employee in question had been placed at a substantial disadvantage. On several occasions it had asked him whether he was experiencing any difficulties connected with his impairment and he had replied in the negative.

It was held in *Ridout v TC Group*,[78] as in *Davies*, that an employer was under no duty to make reasonable adjustments because it could not reasonably be expected to know that the disabled applicant would be placed at a substantial disadvantage by its interview arrangements. Ms Ridout had informed it, before her interview, that she had medically controlled photosensitive epilepsy but it had

---

[75] See eg *Callaghan v Glasgow City Council* [2001] IRLR 724.

[76] But see ch 4, fnn 39–50 below and accompanying text for discussion of a similar issue in the context of disability-related discrimination and its treatment by the House of Lords in *Lewisham LBC v Malcolm* [2008] UKHL 43.

[77] *Davies v Toys'R'Us* (1998) ET/1900286/98. See generally Equal Opportunities Review, 'Interpreting the Disability Discrimination Act—Part 2: Discrimination, Justification and Adjustment' (2001) 98 *Equal Opportunities Review* 12.

[78] *Ridout v TC Group* [1998] IRLR 628. See generally C Pigott, 'Knowledge and the Employer's Duty to Make Reasonable Adjustments' (2002) 152 *New Law Journal* 1656.

not inquired as to the implications of this for the arrangements it would need to make in order to ensure that she was not placed at a substantial disadvantage. When she entered the interview room she indicated that the bright fluorescent lighting might place her at a disadvantage. The employer, however, treated this merely as an explanation of the fact that she was carrying sunglasses and made no inquiry as to whether appropriate adjustments might be made. According to the Employment Appeal Tribunal, Ms Ridout had been insufficiently explicit as to the nature of the potential disadvantage and the steps required to overcome it. The employer's duty to make reasonable adjustments in her favour had therefore not been triggered.

Thus, unlike the employer in *Davies*, the employer in *Ridout* made no attempt to inquire whether the disabled person concerned might be experiencing difficulties as a result of its arrangements or physical features. Further, although Ms Ridout had not stated explicitly what adjustments should be made, she did indicate that she had a condition which made her photosensitive and also that the particular lighting to which she was exposed by the employer was problematic. Given these facts, the ruling that the employer could not reasonably have been expected to know that Ms Ridout might be subjected to a substantial disadvantage by its lighting appears to have allowed the concern to avoid intrusive inquiries to go a considerable way towards curtailing the scope of the reasonable adjustments duty, thereby undermining the purpose of the legislation.[79]

2.4 Discharging the Duty

2.4.1 Employer's Responsibility to Assess

Some uncertainty has clouded the question of whether the DDA reasonable adjustment obligations impose a specific obligation on employers to assess the needs and circumstances of the disabled person in question. Schwab and Willborn[80] (two prominent US commentators) refer to obligations to carry out such assessments as the 'procedural component' of reasonable accommodation. Although its importance is often overshadowed by the 'substantive component' of reasonable accommodation, they stress the crucial nature of its role and draw particular attention to its insistence on interaction and dialogue between employer and employee.

In *Mid Staffordshire NHS Trust v Cambridge*,[81] the EAT suggested that the carrying out of such an assessment was 'a necessary pre-condition' to the

---

[79] For the argument that *Ridout* would not be consistent with the requirements of the Employment Equality Directive—which does not explicitly require an employer's knowledge to trigger the reasonable adjustment duty—see Monaghan, *Blackstone's Guide to the Disability Discrimination Legislation* (n 1 above) 112.

[80] SJ Schwab and SL Willborn, 'Reasonable Accommodation of Workplace Disabilities' (2003) 44 *William and Mary Law Review* 1197 at 1258–64.

[81] *Mid Staffordshire NHS Trust v Cambridge* [2003] IRLR 566 (EAT).

fulfilment of a reasonable adjustment duty.[82] Failure to carry one out would therefore inevitably constitute a breach of a reasonable adjustment obligation.

In *Tarbuck v Sainsbury's Supermarkets*,[83] however, the EAT indicated that a failure to assess would not of itself necessarily amount to such a breach. Nevertheless, it stressed that such a failure would be unwise and potentially jeopardise the employer's legal position. A consensus based upon this approach now appears to be emerging.[84] Its application, and the continuing importance of carrying out thorough and individualised assessments, is well illustrated by the case of *Project Management Institute v Latif*.[85]

Ms Latif, who was registered blind, challenged PMI under section 14 of the DDA for its failure to provide her with reasonable adjustments in connection with the manner in which she took a professional exam. Her request to take the exam on a computer equipped with her speech-synthesis software was rejected and she was provided with a reader and additional time instead. This decision was influenced, not by a considered response to Ms Latif's individual needs, but by reference to PMI's standard approach to making provision for blind candidates.

The EAT upheld the complaint. It was heavily influenced by the finding that, had PMI consulted with and listened to Ms Latif, an appropriate and affordable adjustment which suited her particular circumstances would have emerged. According to Elias P, the case represented 'a good example' of the type of situation, envisaged in *Tarbuck*, in which

> a failure to carry out a proper assessment ... may well result in a respondent failing to make adjustments which he ought reasonably to make.[86]

He went on to observe:

> A respondent, be it an employer or qualifying body, cannot rely on that omission as a shield to justify a failure to make a reasonable adjustment which a proper assessment would have identified.[87]

It is worth stressing that, once confronted with a potential reasonable adjustment, the burden of showing that that adjustment would not in fact have been reasonable passes to the defendant.[88] This will occur even if details of that adjustment are suggested once the parties are in dispute. Indeed, it may occur (as in *Latif*) when a suggestion is made by the plaintiff's legal representative in the course of legal proceedings or even when it is made by the tribunal itself.[89] It is

---

[82] *Ibid*, [17].

[83] *Tarbuck v Sainsbury's Supermarkets* [2006] IRLR 664 (EAT) [77]–[78].

[84] See eg *Hay v Surrey CC* [2007] EWCA Civ 93; *HM Prison Service v Johnson* [2007] IRLR 951 (EAT) [86]; and *Scottish and Southern Energy v Mackay* [2007] UK EATS/0075/06/MT [42].

[85] *Project Management Institute v Latif* [2007] IRLR 579 (EAT) [11].

[86] *Ibid*, [35].

[87] *Ibid*.

[88] *Ibid*, [53]–[57].

[89] *Ibid*, [57].

therefore entirely possible that an employer will be held liable for a failure to make an adjustment which was never specifically requested by the relevant disabled person.[90] Accordingly, while it now appears that employers and others cannot be made liable simply on the basis of a failure to address the question of reasonable adjustments,[91] they would certainly be well advised to carry out a thorough assessment and to consider all possible solutions without confining their attention to those adjustments which are expressly suggested to them.

2.4.2 Possible Adjustments

The DDA and the relevant Code of Practice provide guidance as to the range of steps which should be considered by a person under a duty to make reasonable adjustments in the employment sphere. This guidance is set out in section 18B of the Act and in paras 5.18–5.23 of the Code. Section 18B(2) gives the following as examples of possible steps:

(a) making adjustments to premises;
(b) allocating some of the disabled person's duties to another person;
(c) transferring him to fill an existing vacancy;
(d) altering his hours of working or training;
(e) assigning him to a different place of work or training;
(f) allowing him to be absent during working or training hours for rehabilitation, assessment or treatment;
(g) giving, or arranging for, training or mentoring (whether for the disabled person or any other person);[92]
(h) acquiring or modifying equipment;
(i) modifying instructions or reference manuals;
(j) modifying procedures for testing or assessment;
(k) providing a reader or interpreter;
(l) providing supervision or other support.

In addition to providing practical examples to supplement each of these paragraphs, the Code stresses that more than one type of adjustment may need to be made in any particular case.[93] It also indicates that the section 18B(2) list is not exhaustive and provides examples of additional steps which may be required of an employer. These include:

---

[90] As was the case in *Latif* and also in *Cosgrove v Caesar and Howie* [2001] IRLR 653 (EAT).

[91] According to Elias P in *Project Management Institute v Latif* [2007] IRLR 579 (EAT) [56], in so far as *Cosgrove v Caesar and Howie* [2001] IRLR 653 (EAT) suggested this, it no longer represented good law. See also *HM Prison Service v Johnson* [2007] IRLR 951 (EAT) [86].

[92] This explicit reference to the training of people other than the disabled person was not contained in the original version of the list (set out in the now repealed s 6(3) DDA) but was added as a result of the DDA 1995 (Amendment) Regulations 2003. See further *Simpson v West Lothian Council* (2004) EATS/0049/04 on the possibility of organising awareness training for the colleagues of a deaf employee as a form of reasonable adjustment.

[93] DRC, *DDA 1995 Code of Practice: Employment and Occupation* (n 24 above) para 5.18.

conducting a proper assessment of what reasonable adjustments may be required

permitting flexible working

allowing a disabled employee to take a period of disability leave ...

participating in supported employment schemes, such as Workstep ...

employing a support worker to assist a disabled employee ...

modifying disciplinary or grievance procedures ...

adjusting redundancy selection criteria ...

modifying performance-related pay arrangements.[94]

Although this is not the place for an exhaustive analysis of each of these potential steps, a few words will be devoted to the issue of job transfers, which has enjoyed a particularly high profile in reported cases to date and which, in many ways, tests the boundaries of the notion of reasonable adjustment more directly than other forms of adjustment.[95]

As indicated above, section 18B(2)(c) lists the transfer of a disabled person to an existing vacancy as one of the steps to be considered by an employer under a reasonable adjustment duty. In *Archibald v Fife Council*[96] it was argued that the Council should have discharged its duty to make reasonable adjustments by transferring Ms Archibald from her road-sweeping job—which her inability to walk made impossible for her to perform—to a sedentary, office-based position. The only such positions were at a higher grade than Ms Archibald's original position, however, and the Council generally required those applying for higher grades to go through a competitive interview selection process. Ms Archibald argued that this requirement should have been waived in her case and that she should have been transferred to a post for which she was qualified although not necessarily judged to be the best person. Although the Scottish Inner House held that no reasonable adjustments duty arose, their Lordships indicated obiter that, had it done so, it would not have required the Council to make any such transfer. According to Lord Hamilton, section 18B(2)(c)[97] might be relied upon where the transfer was to 'another job of the same category' but would not extend to a case such as *Archibald* where the result would be that the claimant acquired 'a completely different job'. The House of Lords, however, took a different view and accepted Ms Archibald's argument.

After *Archibald*, then, it is clear that a reasonable adjustment duty may require employers to transfer a disabled person to a different position, even one of a higher grade, without subjecting them to a competitive selection process. The limits of this obligation were explored by the Court of Appeal in *NTL Group Ltd*

---

[94] DRC, *DDA 1995 Code of Practice: Employment and Occupation* (n 24 above) para 5.20.

[95] Research indicates that this form of adjustment, by a substantial margin, featured more than any other in the early DDA cases—see eg S Leverton, *Monitoring the Disability Discrimination Act 1995: Phase 2, Department for Work and Pensions In-House Report 91* (London, Department for Work and Pensions, 2002).

[96] *Archibald v Fife Council* [2004] UKHL 32, [2004] IRLR 197.

[97] Formerly s 6(3)(c).

v Difolco.[98] According to Laws LJ, with whom Waller and Leveson LJJ agreed, this *Archibald* duty would arise only where the person concerned had been dismissed (or become liable to dismissal) for a reason related to their disability. In cases where a disabled person was liable to be dismissed for entirely different reasons, no such duty would arise.[99]

Finally, on this issue, it is interesting to note that the DDA approach to transfers, as interpreted in *Archibald*, appears to be considerably more generous than the US approach. This is illustrated by the case of *United States Airways v Barnett*,[100] which concerned the claim of an employee who became disabled due to a work-related injury. He argued that reassigning him to an available, less physically demanding position (for which he was qualified and to which he had already been transferred on a temporary basis) would have constituted a reasonable accommodation. He relied on the fact that the ADA 1990 specifically refers to the reassignment of a disabled employee to a vacant position as an example of a reasonable accommodation.[101] Nevertheless, his claim failed and it was held that the employer had been entitled to give preference to the more senior non-disabled employees who had applied for the post in question. The fact that the claimant had consequently been forced out of work did not therefore amount to unlawful discrimination. According to the Supreme Court, an accommodation which conflicted with an established seniority system would be regarded as reasonable only in a very rare case.[102]

2.4.3 Reasonableness

Guidance as to the meaning of reasonableness is provided in the DDA itself as well as in the relevant code of practice. The DDA indeed provides a level of detail on this issue which, as Lisa Waddington has observed, 'contrasts starkly' with the brevity of comparable provisions in other European countries.[103] Before turning to this guidance, however, it should be stressed that the notion of 'reasonableness' is objective in nature. It is therefore to be assessed not by reference to what the particular employer genuinely believed to be the case but by reference to objectively demonstrable facts and circumstances.[104]

According to section 18B(1), in assessing whether it is reasonable for a person under an employment-related reasonable adjustment duty to have to take a particular step, regard must be had to a number of factors. The first of these is the extent to which the step in question would remove the substantial disadvantage

---

[98] *NTL Group Ltd v Difolco* [2006] EWCA Civ 1508.
[99] *Ibid*, [18].
[100] *US Airways v Barnett*, 535 US 391 (2002).
[101] Americans with Disabilities Act 1990, 42 USC s 12111(9)(b).
[102] *US Airways v Barnett*, 535 US 391 at 394 (2002).
[103] Waddington, 'Reasonable Accommodation' (n 48 above) 668.
[104] See eg *Collins v Royal National Theatre* [2004] IRLR 395 (CA) [20] (Sedley LJ); *Smith v Churchill Stairlifts* [2005] EWCA Civ 1220 [44]–[45] (Maurice Kay LJ); and *O'Hanlon v Commissioners of Revenue and Customs* [2006] IRLR 840 (EAT) [28]–[29] (Elias P).

which caused the duty to arise. This consideration thus focuses attention squarely on the impact of the adjustment on the disabled person. In this respect it stands apart from all the other specified considerations because they each focus on some aspect of the impact of making the adjustment on the employer. Accordingly, because of its solitary claimant-orientated focus, this first consideration is particularly important.

In assessing the extent to which a particular adjustment would remove a relevant disadvantage, regard is obviously to be had to the question of its effectiveness. Clearly, a step which will totally remove the relevant disadvantage is likely to be judged to be a reasonable one, provided, of course, that it does not entail burdensome costs or other difficulties. The fact, however, that there is some uncertainty about the likely effectiveness of the proposed step will not necessarily prevent it being regarded as a reasonable measure and thereby absolve the employer from the need to take it.[105] Neither will the fact that taking a proposed step would result in a disabled person being treated more favourably than others necessarily render that step unreasonable if, as in *Archibald*, it is required in order to remove the relevant disadvantage.

Section 18B(1)(b) refers to the practicability of taking a particular step. Although considerations of practicality will often be closely linked to those of financial expense, the fact that they appear in separate paragraphs emphasises that, on occasion, factors not directly related to expenditure may make it difficult to carry out a particular adjustment. The example given in the Code concerns the physical alteration of an entrance which is likely to take longer than the employer is able conveniently to wait for the services of the particular employee.[106]

Paragraphs (c) and (d) of section 18B(1) relate to the burden which would be imposed on the employer by taking the step. Paragraph (c) refers to the cost of the step (in terms of issues such as staffing as well as direct finances[107]) and the extent to which it would disrupt the employer's activities. The Code indicates that, in assessing cost for these purposes, account must be taken of expenses the employer would otherwise have to undertake (eg those associated with advertising for a new employee) and that it might be reasonable to expect employers to carry a higher burden of cost and disruption where the employee in question has a considerable degree of experience or expertise.[108] Although not mentioned in the Code, it appears that it may sometimes be permissible to have regard to the cost, not only of making the particular adjustment in question, but also to its wider financial implications. In *O'Hanlon v Commissioners of HM Revenue and Customs*,[109] for instance, the Employment Appeal Tribunal, in ruling that it would not be reasonable for an employer to have increased the level of sick pay

---

[105] *Beart v HM Prison Service* [2003] EWCA Civ 119.
[106] DRC, *DDA 1995 Code of Practice: Employment and Occupation* (n 24 above) para 5.30.
[107] *Ibid*, para 5.31.
[108] *Ibid*, paras 5.31–5.34.
[109] *O'Hanlon v Commissioners of HM Revenue and Customs* [2006] IRLR 840 (EAT).

the claimant received in respect of disability-related absence, was mindful of the significant financial and administrative burden which a contrary decision might have imposed. Such a ruling might have placed a heavy burden, not only on the particular employer in question, but also on employers more generally.

Paragraph (d) refers to the extent of the employer's resources. This indicates that it is likely to be reasonable for employers with significant resources at their disposal to have to carry out more costly adjustments than would be the case for poorer employers.

According to paragraph (e), reference must be made to any financial or other assistance which may be available to the employer in carrying out a particular step. Of great significance in this regard is the funding provided to assist with the costs of making adjustments for disabled employees by the Access to Work scheme.[110] This provides a mechanism through which the State contributes towards the funding of the costs of employment-related adjustments. Under this scheme, employers are expected to provide the cost of adjustments up to a specified modest sum (currently £300). There is then provision for costs exceeding that amount to be shared between the employer and the State, with the former contributing at least 20 per cent, and for costs exceeding another specified larger amount (currently £10,000) to be paid entirely by the State. There is no upper limit on the amount of Access to Work funding which may be awarded in any particular case.

Under the British system, the availability of Access to Work funding is a significant factor in assessments of reasonableness. Because of it, adjustments which would otherwise impose unfeasible financial burdens on employers become reasonable and thereby obligatory. This system might appear to impose significant demands on the public purse.[111] Nevertheless, it should not be forgotten that money spent on Access to Work may allow a disabled person to obtain or retain work (thereby reducing the amount spent on unemployment benefits). It is also likely to confer employment on others (whether directly, in roles such as support worker or communicator, or indirectly, through the generation of additional work associated with the provision of physical access or specialist equipment).[112]

The interplay between State and employer funding adopted in the Access to Work scheme differs from the model which has been adopted at the federal level

---

[110] See generally Department for Work and Pensions, *Public Consultation. Helping People Achieve their Full Potential: Improving Specialist Disability Employment Services* (London, Department for Work and Pensions, 2007) ch 5; and Cabinet Office Strategy Unit, *Improving the Life Chances of Disabled People* (London, Stationery Office, 2005) Section 7.4.

[111] The Government anticipates that the Access to Work budget for 2008 will amount to some £66,000,000—DWP, *Helping People Achieve their Full Potential* (n 110 above) para 5.8.

[112] See generally, on economic arguments for devoting public funds to pay for disability-related workplace adjustments, SA Moss and DA Malin, 'Public Funding for Disability Accommodations: A Rational Solution to Rational Discrimination and the Disabilities of the ADA' (1998) 33 *Harvard Civil Rights and Civil Liberties Law Review* 197.

in the United States.[113] There, under a number of different tax credit schemes, public funding may be available to organisations which need to make adjustments in order to accommodate disabled employees. Under the Disabled Access Credit scheme,[114] small businesses are entitled to recover half of the amount they spend on making disability-related adjustments for an employee in any year up to a maximum of US$5,000.[115] In addition, businesses providing services to the public may be able to recover up to US$15,000 a year under the Barrier Removal Deduction scheme.[116] This applies to money spent on the removal of architectural or transport-related barriers.[117]

Thus, under the US system, the subsidies which are available in respect of the costs of making adjustments for disabled employees are subject to a relatively modest upper limit. Indeed, larger businesses are likely to receive no subsidy at all for adjustments which do not concern the removal of physical barriers. This contrasts sharply with the British approach, according to which Access to Work has no upper limit and is currently available to all employers apart from Government ministerial departments (which were withdrawn from the scheme in October 2006). Another important distinction is that, because the US financial assistance takes the form of tax credits, it is available on a retrospective basis. Access to Work funding, on the other hand, is generally available at the point at which the adjustment is being purchased.

Michael Stein,[118] an eminent American disability law scholar, has probed the relationship between the reasonableness of an adjustment and the availability of public subsidies. He suggests that the reasonableness of a proposed adjustment should be considered without regard to the question of State support and that employers should be required to bear the entire cost of adjustments deemed to be reasonable. State funding may then be devoted to paying for what might be regarded as unreasonable adjustments—measures which it would not otherwise

---

[113] See generally L Nelsestuen and M Reid, 'Coordination of Tax Incentives Associated with Compliance with the Americans with Disabilities Act' (2003) 81 *Taxes* 37; and MA Stein, 'The Law and Economics of Disability Accommodations' (2003) 53 *Duke Law Journal* 79 at 124–6.

[114] Disabled Access Credit, 26 USC s 44 (2000). See further http://www.irs.gov/businesses/small/article/0,,id=106480,00.html (last accessed 15 March 2008).

[115] *Ibid*, s 44(a).

[116] Barrier Removal Deduction, 26 USC s 190 (2000). See further http://www.irs.gov/pub/irs-pdf/p535.pdf (last accessed 15 March 2008).

[117] Another tax credit scheme which is sometimes mentioned in connection with costs arising under the ADA is the Work Opportunity Tax Credit (26 USC s 51 (2000)). It allows employers to recover up to US$9,000 a year of the wages paid to any employee who is a member of one of the specified target groups (which include veterans, ex-felons, young people from deprived areas and people in receipt of certain benefits). While many disabled people are likely to fall within one or more of these groups, the aim is not to help with the costs of adjustments but to encourage employers to recruit people from disadvantaged backgrounds. The duration of the scheme was extended, by the Small Business and Work Opportunity Tax Credit Act 2007, until September 2011.

[118] Stein, 'The Law and Economics of Disability Accommodations' (n 113 above) 124–6. See also MA Stein, 'Empirical Implications of Title I' (2000) 85 *Iowa Law Review* 1671.

be reasonable to require of employers.[119] This approach, he argues, would uphold the principle that equality requires employers to pay for reasonable adjustments in the same way as it requires them to pay for expenses associated with the operation of a working environment free from direct and indirect discrimination.

Thought-provoking though Stein's argument is, it is unlikely to appeal to disability equality proponents in Britain.[120] The British approach of factoring the availability of Access to Work funding into assessments of reasonableness has an attractive simplicity. It avoids the potentially confusing need, associated with Stein's approach, to refer to obligations to make (if not to pay for) unreasonable adjustments. Its effect is not dissimilar, however, as under both approaches State funding is used to make affordable—and therefore achievable—adjustments which would otherwise have been classified as unreasonable. The British approach is certainly a great deal closer to Stein's model than is the current US funding strategy. The implications of these different approaches to subsidising the costs of reasonable adjustments will be explored further in chapter six below.[121]

Returning to the DDA Code of Practice on Employment, another finance-related point which it stresses is that disabled people themselves are not required to contribute towards the cost of adjustments made in their favour.[122] Thus, the fact that the employee in question may be relatively wealthy is not a factor which employers will be able to take into account in deciding whether or not a particular measure is reasonable. Any other approach would risk diluting the message that the obligation to make adjustments is placed on employers rather than on disabled people themselves.

Paragraphs (f) and (g) of section 18B(1) were added by the DDA 1995 (Amendment) Regulations 2003 and were linked to the withdrawal of the previous DDA exemption for small employers. Paragraph (f) refers to the employer's size and the nature of its activities. Although there is likely to be a large overlap between the size of an organisation and its wealth (a consideration covered in paragraph (d)), the reasonableness of a particular adjustment may

---

[119] A similar division between State and employer funding for adjustments which are 'site-specific' (in that they effect physical or structural changes likely to benefit people other than the specific disabled employee in question) is suggested in SA Krenek, 'Beyond Reasonable Accommodation' (1994) 72 *Texas Law Review* 1969 at 2009–13. For adjustments which are 'employee-specific' (in that they benefit only the specific disabled employee in question), however, Krenek argues that the State should bear the entire cost. For the argument that the State should bear the entire cost for all adjustments, see Moss and Malin, 'Public Funding for Disability Accommodations' (n 112 above).

[120] The Access to Work scheme is generally popular with, and regarded as effective by, those who use it—A Corden and P Thornton, *Employment Programmes for Disabled People: Lessons from Research Evaluation* (London, Department for Work and Pensions, 2000); and was recently described by the Government as 'one of our most popular and successful labour market programmes'—DWP, *Helping People Achieve their Full Potential* (n 110 above) para 5.0.

[121] Ch 6, fnn 81–92 below and accompanying text.

[122] DRC, *DDA 1995 Code of Practice: Employment and Occupation* (n 24 above) para 5.39.

sometimes be affected by size-related considerations which have no obvious connection with financial resources. The examples provided in the Code relate to situations in which the small scale of an undertaking means that an employer does not have a more sedentary position to offer an employee who has acquired a physical impairment; or that an employer does not have adequate staff coverage to release an employee with mental health difficulties to attend weekly psycho-therapy appointments.[123]

The final paragraph of section 18B(1)—paragraph (g)—relates to adjustments in favour of people working in private households. According to it, regard must be had in such cases to the extent to which the adjustment would disrupt the household or disturb any of its residents. Thus, while it might be reasonable to have to communicate with a deaf cleaner through writing, the Code suggests that it would probably not be reasonable to have to ensure a dust-free environment for a nanny with a dust allergy.[124] Similar formulations of a less demanding approach for employment in private households are to be found elsewhere in British non-discrimination law. They represent a compromise between the demands of equality and those of private and family life.[125]

Like the section 18B(2) list of steps to which an employer must have regard, the section 18B(1) list of factors relevant to reasonableness is not exhaustive. Other factors are mentioned in the Code and include the effect of the proposed adjustment on other employees, and the number of other disabled employees who would benefit from the same adjustment—eg improved physical access.[126]

It should also be noted here that the UK approach to reasonableness in this context is unusual. Under the approach outlined here, an assessment of reasonableness will require the consideration of factors relating to the effectiveness of the adjustment in removing the barriers encountered by the disabled person as well as the consideration of factors relating to the burden which such an adjustment might place on the employer. By contrast, in the vast majority of legal systems which have introduced reasonable adjustment duties, there is an additional reference to the defence of 'undue hardship' or 'disproportionate burden'.[127] This facilitates a two-stage approach to the question of whether a particular measure would be required by a relevant duty. It allows factors relating to that measure's

---

[123] *Ibid*, para 5.40.

[124] *Ibid*, para 5.41.

[125] See generally, M Bell, 'Direct Discrimination' in Schiek, Waddington and Bell (eds), *Cases, Materials and Text on National, Supranational and International Non-Discrimination Law* (n 48 above) 290–93.

[126] DRC, *DDA 1995 Code of Practice: Employment and Occupation* (n 24 above) para 5.42. See also *Lincolnshire Police v Weaver* [2008] UKEAT 0622.07.1903 [51] and [52] (Elias P) where the Employment Tribunal's failure to have regard to the impact of an adjustment on other employees was severely criticised.

[127] See, for an excellent account of the varying approaches within the EU, Waddington, 'Reasonable Accommodation' (n 48 above) 634–70; and, for a critical analysis of this requirement under US law, S Epstein, 'In Search of a Bright Line: Determining When an Employer's Financial Hardship Becomes "Undue" Under the Americans with Disabilities Act' (1995) 48 *Vanderbilt Law Review* 391.

effectiveness to be considered in assessments of reasonableness and factors relating to the cost to be considered in connection with undue hardship or disproportionate burden. In the United States, however, it has been held that there is no such clear-cut division between the Americans with Disabilities Act concepts of 'reasonableness' and 'undue hardship'.[128] The burden of a proposed adjustment will be relevant both to assessments of reasonableness and also to attempts to establish undue hardship.

The British approach has the advantage of avoiding an apparent dichotomy between the interests of disabled people on the one hand and those of employers on the other.[129] Nevertheless, the use of an 'undue hardship' defence has the advantage of emphasising that the relevant test is

> a test which goes far beyond concerns about business inconvenience, and which clearly contemplates that required accommodations can impose some degree of hardship on an employer or other respondent.[130]

Because this is not made explicit in the DDA, additional vigilance is required in order to ensure that adjustments are not too easily regarded as unreasonable.

2.4.4 Reasonableness Considerations Specific to Physical Alterations

In addition to the issues relating to the assessment of reasonableness already considered, several others, which are specific to the making of physical alterations, must be addressed. For present purposes, these will be divided into two main groups—those relating to the guidance provided by building codes and regulations and those relating to legal obstacles in the way of making alterations, notably the need to obtain consent from a third party.

Basic access standards, set out in various building regulations, must be complied with whenever a new building is constructed or an existing one is materially altered.[131] Compliance with these, however, does not exempt the employer from making additional adjustments to the building or its physical features in order to remove the disadvantage which would otherwise be experienced by a particular disabled employee.[132] Whilst not negating the obligation to assess the needs of every disabled person individually, the Code of Practice[133] suggests that it is unlikely to be regarded as reasonable for an employer to have to adjust physical features of their building if it complies with the more rigorous

---

[128] *US Airways v Barnett* 535 US 391 (2002).

[129] See generally K Wells, 'The Impact of the Framework Employment Directive on UK Disability Discrimination Law' [2003] *Industrial Law Journal* 253 at 264.

[130] D Lepofsky, 'The Duty to Accommodate: A Purposive Approach' (1992) *Canadian Labour Law Journal* 1 at 2.

[131] In the case of England and Wales, the Building Regulations 2000 (SI 2000/2531) Schedule 1 Part M; and, in the case of Scotland, the Building (Scotland) Regulations 2004.

[132] DRC, *DDA 1995 Code of Practice: Employment and Occupation* (n 24 above) paras 12.7 and 12.8.

[133] *Ibid,* paras 12.9 and 12.10.

standards set out in either the British Standards[134] or in the most up-to-date version of the guidance accompanying the relevant part of the Building Regulations.[135]

The DDA contains specific provisions relating to three types of case in which, without the consent of a third party, an employer will not be able to carry out the physical alterations required to discharge their reasonable adjustment obligations. First, the fact that they wish to make the change in order to effect a reasonable adjustment does not exempt them from the need to obtain various statutorily regulated consents (such as planning permission, building regulations approval, building warrants and listed building consent).[136] According to the Code of Practice, it may be reasonable for employers in these circumstances to make alternative interim adjustments for a disabled employee pending the granting of such consent and, in some cases, the reasonable adjustment duty may oblige them to appeal against an initial refusal of consent.[137]

The second type of case in which third party consent to a physical adjustment is required is governed by section 18B(3). This applies to cases in which the employer is required to obtain the consent of another person to the making of physical alterations by virtue of any legal obligation (such as a charge, mortgage or restrictive covenant) other than a lease.[138] According to section 18B(3) it will always be deemed reasonable, in such cases, for the employer to take steps (falling short of applying to a court or tribunal[139]) to obtain the necessary consent and never reasonable for them to have to make the alteration without it.

The final type of case concerning the consent of a third party to a physical alteration is that of leases. Section 18A of the DDA contains provisions designed to facilitate the performance of duties to make reasonable adjustments to the physical features of premises which employers occupy under leases. Under section 18A(2), unless there is an express term to the same effect, a term will be implied into such leases according to which the employer will be permitted to apply to the landlord for consent to the carrying out of disability-related physical alterations. According to section 18A(2)(c) and (d) respectively, landlords will be prohibited from withholding consent unreasonably but may make their consent subject to reasonable conditions. Questions relating to the reasonableness of such consents will be addressed in Section 4 below.

---

[134] 'Design of Buildings and their Approaches to Meet the Needs of Disabled People', British Standard 8300:2001—Code of Practice.

[135] Approved Document M—Access to and Use of Buildings (May 2006).

[136] DDA s 59.

[137] DRC, *DDA 1995 Code of Practice: Employment and Occupation* (n 24 above) paras 12.4 and 12.5.

[138] See also *ibid*, para 12.12 and DDA s 18B(5).

[139] DDA s 18B(4).

2.5 Justification Defence

When initially enacted, the DDA contained a justification defence, which operated where an employer had failed to make a reasonable adjustment. In view of its possible inconsistency with the Employment Equality Directive, this defence was removed by the DDA 1995 (Amendment) Regulations 2003. Thus, in the context of employment, liability will turn on the reasonableness of disputed adjustments and not on whether a failure to make one that was reasonable might be justified.

In relation to let premises, it is still possible to justify a failure to make a reasonable adjustment. This defence is identical to that laid down for service providers, details of which are provided in Section 3 below.

2.6 Enforcement

Disputes arising under the employment-related provisions of the DDA may be brought before Employment Tribunals. From these, there is the possibility of an appeal to the Employment Appeal Tribunal and from there to the Court of Appeal and the conventional court system. The burden of proving that a disabled employee was placed at a substantial disadvantage by an employer's provision, criterion, practice or physical feature falls on the disabled person. The burden of proving that the reasonable adjustment duty was properly discharged falls upon the employer, but only after it has been shown (whether by the claimant, their legal representative or the tribunal itself) that there was some adjustment which it appears might have been reasonable for the employer to have made.[140]

Employment Tribunals may order the reinstatement or re-engagement of an employee who has been unfairly dismissed but have no power to do so on the basis of a finding of unlawful discrimination alone. These remedies are therefore unavailable to employees who have not worked for the one-year minimum qualifying period required for unfair dismissal actions. Neither do Employment Tribunals have the power to order an employer to appoint a person to whom, on the basis of unlawful discrimination, they refused a position. The authors of the Hepple Report, and others, have recommended that these rules be altered and tribunals permitted to order engagement, re-engagement or reinstatement subject to the limits of reasonable practicability.[141]

Another issue which has been the cause of concern is the limited extent to which Tribunals are permitted to make recommendations to defendants found to have engaged in unlawful discrimination. Currently, they are permitted to make

---

[140] *Project Management Institute v Latif* [2007] IRLR 579 (EAT) [53]–[57]; and *HM Prison Service v Johnson* [2007] IRLR 951 (EAT) [89]–[91]. See generally, on the burden of proof in discrimination cases, *Igen v Wong* [2005] EWCA Civ 142; and *Madarassy v Nomura* [2007] EWCA Civ 33.

[141] B Hepple, M Coussey and T Choudhury, *Equality: A New Framework* (Oxford, Hart Publishing, 2000) recommendation 51.

recommendations as to how discriminatory practices might be avoided only if those recommendations would directly benefit the claimant. In the vast majority of employment cases, however, the claimant will no longer work with the defendant and will therefore not be in a position to benefit from any recommendation made to that defendant. Nevertheless, recommendations clearly have the potential to benefit others and to promote good equality practice. The Government has therefore announced its intention to widen the range of situations in which Tribunals will be permitted to make them.[142]

2.7 Summary

The employment-related reactive reasonable adjustment duties have been the site of considerable legal development since their birth in 1995. Legislative amendments, initiated by the Employment Equality Directive, have strengthened them considerably. They have ensured that reasonable adjustment entitlements will no longer be out of the reach of disabled people applying to or working for small employers. They have widened the scope of what must have caused the disabled person to be put at a substantial disadvantage, from employers' 'arrangements' to employers' 'provisions, criteria or practices'. They have removed the justification defence which was previously available to employers who had failed to discharge reasonable adjustment duties.

There has also been considerable judicial activity in this area. Some clarity now seems to be emerging on troublesome issues such as 'substantial disadvantage' and assessments of needs. The term 'arrangements' has generated many cases. Although a worryingly restrictive approach to this term seemed to be emerging from some of the early cases, the House of Lords in *Archibald* adopted a refreshingly expansive view. The substitution of the phrase 'provision, criterion or practice' for that of 'arrangements' will inevitably encourage the trend towards expansiveness in this area.

Outside the employment area, entirely reactive reasonable adjustment duties also operate in the context of let premises. These are relatively new duties, having been created by the Disability Discrimination Act 2005 (DDA 2005). They have not, therefore, yet been the site of significant subsequent legal activity. Despite the fact that they are reactive in nature, they share many features with the anticipatory duties which will be considered in the next section.

---

[142] Government Equalities Office, *The Equality Bill: Government Response to the Consultation* (London, Stationery Office, 21 July 2008) paras 6.2–6.19.

3. Anticipatory Reasonable Adjustment Duties

3.1 Overview

This discussion of the DDA's anticipatory reasonable adjustment duties will be structured along the same lines as the discussion of reactive duties in the previous Section. This, it is hoped, will facilitate comparison between the two forms of duty.

This Section, like Section 2, will consist of five substantive parts. The first, Section 3.2, will be concerned with the sphere of operation of anticipatory reasonable adjustment duties. A few words will also be devoted to the way in which these duties emerged from the soil of unpromising statutory language. Section 3.3 will focus on the conditions which must be satisfied before an anticipatory duty will come into being. Section 3.4 will deal with the actual content of the anticipatory reasonable adjustment duty and the nature of the obligation it imposes. The justification defences available to duty-bearers who have failed to comply with relevant duties will be outlined in Section 3.5. Finally, Section 3.6 will address issues relevant to the enforcement of these anticipatory duties.

3.2 Context and Scope

The DDA imposes a number of reasonable adjustment duties which require duty-bearers to anticipate barriers which their operations might present to disabled people and to take steps to remove or reduce those obstacles. Unlike the purely reactive duties relating to employment and premises, these anticipatory duties require adjustments to be made in advance of the appearance of a particular disabled person wishing to make use of the operation in question. The fact that they contain a strong anticipatory element, however, does not preclude the possibility that duty-bearers will, in addition, be required to react to the circumstances of a particular case by implementing reasonable adjustments to accommodate the needs of a specific disabled individual.

The history of these anticipatory duties is an interesting one. The DDA itself does not state explicitly that they should operate in an anticipatory manner. Neither was there any significant reference to this dimension of reasonable adjustment in the parliamentary debates leading to its enactment. The statutory language, in which the anticipatory element of these duties is rooted, consists simply of the use of the term 'disabled persons' in the plural as opposed to that of 'a disabled person' in the singular.

Members of the National Disability Council clearly regarded the fact that these reasonable adjustment duties were to be triggered when 'disabled persons' as a group experienced a specified level of disadvantage as highly significant.[143] That Council, which was established by the DDA and subsequently replaced by the much more powerful Disability Rights Commission in 2000, was charged with the responsibility of drawing up the first Codes of Practice. Since 1999, when the relevant duties first came into force, the Codes of Practice have consistently asserted that those duties impose an obligation on duty-bearers to take reasonable steps to remove or alter disabling barriers in advance of the appearance of a particular disabled person.[144] These Codes have undoubtedly proved highly influential in the development of the anticipatory duties.[145] Their interpretation of the mechanics of the duties has now been accepted and further clarified by Sedley LJ's very powerful judgment in *Roads v Central Trains*.[146]

The anticipatory reasonable adjustment duties arise in a variety of contexts which, broadly conceived, may be regarded as relating to the provision of services. Although some were contained in the DDA as originally enacted, many others have been added by subsequent legislation. The original duties placed on service providers by section 21 provided a template for subsequent ones but, particularly in the context of pre-16 education, there are some significant differences in approach.

The original anticipatory reasonable adjustment duties were imposed by section 21 of the DDA on providers of services to the public. Section 19 set out the limits of the services to be covered, indicating that the provision of services included the provision of goods and facilities, and that whether or not they were provided in exchange for a fee was irrelevant.[147] In sub-section (3), it listed the following as examples of services which were covered:

(a) access to and use of any place which members of the public are permitted to enter;
(b) access to and use of means of communication;
(c) access to and use of information services;
(d) accommodation in a hotel, boarding house or other similar establishment;
(e) facilities by way of banking or insurance or for grants, loans, credit or finance;

---

[143] See generally the account of these duties provided by Jenny White (a member of that body) in 'DDA: Service Providers' Duty to Make Reasonable Adjustments' (1999) 88 *Equal Opportunities Review* 33. For discussion of the history of the advisory and enforcement bodies associated with the DDA, see above ch 1, section 4.

[144] Department for Education and Employment, *DDA 1995 Code of Practice: Rights of Access— Goods, Facilities, Services and Premises* (London, Stationery Office, 1999) para 4.7; DRC, *DDA 1995 Code of Practice: Rights of Access—Goods, Facilities, Services and Premises* (London, Stationery Office, 2002) para 4.14; and DRC, *DDA 1995 Code of Practice: Rights of Access—Services to the Public, Public Authority Functions, Private Clubs and Premises* (London, Stationery Office, 2006) para 6.16.

[145] See, for interesting discussions of these anticipatory duties by people heavily involved in the drafting of the various Part 3 Codes of Practice, B Doyle, *Disability Discrimination Law and Practice* (Bristol, Jordan Publishing, 2008) 147–53; White, 'DDA: Service Providers' Duties to Make Reasonable Adjustments' (n 143 above); and C Gooding and C Casserley, 'Open for All: Disability Discrimination Laws in Europe on Goods and Services' in A Lawson and C Gooding (eds), *Disability Rights in Europe: From Theory to Practice* (Oxford, Hart Publishing, 2005) 152–4.

[146] *Roads v Central Trains* [2004] EWCA Civ 1541. See nn 165–170 below and accompanying text.

[147] DDA s 19(2).

(f) facilities for entertainment, recreation or refreshment;

(g) facilities provided by employment agencies or under section 2 of the Employment and Training Act 1973;

(h) the services of any profession or trade, or any local or other public authority.

The section 21 duty contains three main elements, which will be considered in more detail below. First it requires duty-bearers to take reasonable steps to adjust their practices, policies and procedures. Second, it requires them to provide assistive auxiliary aids and services. Finally, it requires them to take reasonable steps to overcome obstacles created by their physical features.

Before considering the ways in which the coverage of sections 19–21 has been extended, particularly by the DDA 2005, a few words will be devoted to employment services. These are defined in section 21A(1) to mean 'services providing assistance with recruitment or retention or vocational guidance or training'. Although they fall clearly within the scope of section 19, being services provided to the public, their employment focus brings them within the ambit of the Employment Equality Directive. In order to ensure compliance, section 21A was introduced by the 2003 Regulations. It alters the standard section 21 reasonable adjustment duties in their application to employment services. The result is a complex hybrid, made up of elements of the reasonable adjustment duty that generally applies to service providers and elements of the duty that applies to employers. Some of its peculiarities will be identified at relevant points in the discussion which follows.

As originally drafted, the legislation contained two highly controversial exemptions from the scope of the section 21 duties.[148] First, education was very largely excluded.[149] This significant gap in the protection afforded by the DDA was plugged by the Special Educational Needs and Disability Act 2001, which inserted a new Part 4 into the DDA.[150] Part 4 is divided into two chapters which deal with schools (or pre-16 education) and with further and higher education (post-16 education). From the outset, the reasonable adjustment duties relating to pre-16 education contained a number of significant departures from the section 21 template. The duties relating to post-16 education, on the other hand, began life in almost identical terms to the section 21 duties. However, they have since been considerably modified by the Disability Discrimination Act 1995 (Amendment) (Further and Higher Education) Regulations 2006, which were introduced to give effect to the Employment Equality Directive. As a result, the post-16 duties now bear a much closer resemblance to the employment duties—apart from the important fact that, unlike the latter, they possess a strong anticipatory element.

---

[148] DDA s 19(5).

[149] DDA s 19(5)(a).

[150] See generally M Davies, 'The Special Educational Needs and Disability Act: Implications for Higher Education' (2003) 15 *Education and the Law* 19; and A Blair and A Lawson, 'Disability Discrimination Reforms in Education: Could do Better?' (2003) 15 *Child and Family Law Quarterly* 41.

The second much-criticised exemption related to transport. This excluded 'any service so far as it consist[ed] of the use of any means of transport'. Confusingly, however, aspects of transport services which did not involve the use of a means of transport (eg the facilities provided at a train station, bus stop or airport) were subject to sections 19–21. Further, Part 5 of the original version of the DDA set out technical standards for the design of taxis, and of public service and rail vehicles. It also required taxis to carry guide or hearing dogs without charging an additional fee.[151] Similar obligations were placed on private hire vehicles following the Private Hire Vehicles (Carriage of Guide Dogs etc) Act 2002.

Despite the fact that some aspects of transport provision were covered by the original version of the DDA, the exclusion of those aspects which involved the use of a means of transport was by no means insignificant. It meant that drivers were largely free to refuse to take a disabled passenger on the basis of no valid reason whatsoever. The following is an example of a case, reported to the Disability Rights Commission, in which the DDA offered no redress:

> A man who uses a wheelchair found that, despite the availability of accessible buses, drivers refused to stop. On one occasion when the bus did stop, the driver was abusive, pushed his chair back off the footplate and drove away.[152]

Provision was made in the DDA 2005 for the removal of the partial exemption of transport services from the scope of sections 19–21 of the 1995 Act. According to the new section 21ZA(3), Regulations may be introduced by the Secretary of State with the effect of lifting (or partially lifting) the pre-existing exemption. Such Regulations have been introduced and are now in force.[153] With the exception of ships and aircraft,[154] these Regulations lift the exemption for virtually all types of vehicle in which the public might be expected to travel.[155]

The reasonable adjustment duties which apply to such vehicles are accordingly those laid down in section 21.[156] Obstacles created by physical features, however, are dealt with through the technical standards set out in Part 5 of the DDA and not by means of reasonable adjustment duties.

The services of 'any local or public authority' are included in the list of examples of services covered by sections 19–21.[157] Nevertheless, there was

---

[151] DDA s 37.
[152] DRC, *An Initial Briefing on the New Disability Discrimination Act 2005* (London, DRC, 2005).
[153] Disability Discrimination (Transport Vehicles) Regulations 2005 (SI 2005/3190). See also DRC, *DDA 1995 Code of Practice: Provision and Use of Transport* (London, Stationery Office, 2006).
[154] For criticism of the continued exemption of air travel, see DRC, 'DRC Says Voluntary Airline Code not Working' press release 4 August 2006, in which it is noted that over a third of transport-related calls to the DRC's Helpline concern the treatment of disabled passengers by airlines. This is a problem which is not confined to Britain and which has attracted concern at European Community level. It has resulted in the adoption of the important Regulation EC 1107/2006 concerning the rights of disabled persons and persons with reduced mobility when travelling by air, [2006] OJ L 204/1, which requires that disabled passengers must be provided with assistance of a prescribed standard.
[155] Disability Discrimination (Transport Vehicles) Regulations 2005 (SI 2005/3190) reg 3.
[156] *Ibid*, reg 4.
[157] DDA s 19(3)(h).

concern that these might be interpreted restrictively so as not to cover public functions such as planning, highways, fostering and adoption, immigration control, and aspects of law enforcement and the prison system.[158] The DDA 2005 therefore inserted sections 21B–21E into the 1995 Act. These sections ensure that, subject to specified exceptions, public authorities will fall within the ambit of the DDA when exercising their public functions. Section 21E places them under a similar, though not identical, reasonable adjustment duty to that imposed on providers of services by section 21.

The final area to which the 2005 Act extended the coverage of the DDA is that of private clubs. It inserted sections 21F–21J into the 1995 Act. These prohibit private clubs (such as sports clubs) with more than 25 members from discriminating against disabled people. Although they do not spell out the details of a reasonable adjustment duty, section 21H confers a power on the Secretary of State to introduce such a duty through regulations. The Disability Discrimination (Private Clubs etc) Regulations 2005[159] were accordingly drawn up and impose reasonable adjustment duties almost identical to those set out in section 21.

3.3 Triggering the Duties

3.3.1 Disabled Persons

The section 21 duty will arise only if 'disabled persons' would otherwise find it impossible or unreasonably difficult to use the service in question or if their use of it would be enabled or facilitated by the provision of an auxiliary aid or service. This reference to 'disabled persons' is replicated in all the other anticipatory reasonable adjustment provisions mentioned above.[160] It stands in sharp contrast with the reference, in the employment context, to 'the disabled person concerned', and it is from it that the anticipatory nature of these reasonable adjustment duties springs.

Essentially, then, the duties are triggered whenever disabled people would encounter the required degree of difficulty in using a relevant service. It therefore falls to service providers to gauge, on an on-going basis, how easily disabled people will be able to use their services. Although it would be impossible for them to anticipate all the particular needs of every single disabled individual who might wish to use their service, they will be required to give thought to removing

---

[158] These concerns arose from restrictive interpretations as to the scope of the goods and services provisions in the Sex Discrimination Act 1975 and the Race Relations Act 1976—see in particular *R v Immigration Appeal Tribunal ex parte Kassam* [1980] 1 WLR 1037; and *Re Amin* [1983] 2 AC 818 (HL).

[159] Disability Discrimination (Private Clubs etc) Regulations 2005 (SI 2005/3258).

[160] In relation to post-16 education, s 28T(1) and (1C) impose anticipatory duties and refer to 'disabled persons'. These broadly concern duties towards students. Section 28T(1A), (1B) and (1D) and s 28UA(5), however, refer to a particular disabled person experiencing the relevant disadvantage and are therefore more reactive in nature. They apply to the conferral and holding of qualifications and to relevant relationships which have come to an end.

the types of barrier which will generally create difficulties for broad groups of disabled people, such as those with physical, mental or sensory impairments.[161]

Crucially, although the imposition of these anticipatory reasonable adjustment duties is not dependent on the materialisation of a specific disabled person wishing to use the relevant service, the enforcement of these duties is dependent on the appearance of such an individual. According to section 21(10), the section 21 duties are enforceable, not in their own right, but only as part of a discrimination claim. Such a claim may be brought only by a disabled individual who, as a result of a service provider's failure to comply with a reasonable adjustment duty,[162] has found it impossible or unreasonably difficult to access the service in question.[163]

The question of whether a particular service was impossible or unreasonably difficult to use therefore arises at two stages. First, in order to trigger the duty, it must be shown that it was impossible or unreasonably difficult for 'disabled persons' to use the service and second, in order to enforce it, it must be shown that it was impossible or unreasonably difficult for the particular claimant to use it.[164] There is thus both what may be termed a group disadvantage requirement and also a claimant disadvantage requirement.

The Court of Appeal, in *Roads v Central Trains*,[165] rejected the argument that the first of these requirements (the group disadvantage requirement) could be overlooked in cases where it was clear that the second (the claimant disadvantage requirement) had been established. Regardless of the level of difficulty that may be experienced by the particular claimant, the duty will not arise unless 'disabled persons' generally would have experienced the required level of difficulty. *Roads* thus accepts that group disadvantage is an essential element of anticipatory reasonable adjustment claims. Unsurprisingly, therefore, it also provides some guidance on the nature of this requirement.

In order to establish that 'disabled persons' would have been sufficiently inconvenienced, according to Sedley LJ,[166] it is not necessary to show that 'all or most disabled persons' would have been so affected. A demonstration that there would have been 'any significant impact on, say, wheelchair users as a class' would, he suggested, suffice.[167] He also warned that reliance on statistical

---

[161] See eg *Roads v Central Trains* [2004] EWCA Civ 1540 [11] (Sedley LJ); and DRC, *DDA 1995 Code of Practice: Rights of Access—Services to the Public, Public Authority Functions, Private Clubs and Premises* (n 144 above) para 6.15.

[162] DDA s 20(2).

[163] DDA s 19(1)(b). Some of the anticipatory duties define the required level of disadvantage differently—see below section 3.3.2.

[164] See generally White, 'DDA: Service Providers' Duty to Make Reasonable Adjustments' (n 143 above).

[165] *Roads v Central Trains* [2004] EWCA Civ 1540.

[166] *Ibid*, [26].

[167] *Ibid*, [26].

evidence on this issue may prove 'invidious or arbitrary', and recommended that judges should instead rely on their own appraisal of the situation with the help of expert evidence where appropriate.[168]

The Court of Appeal's recognition of the importance of the group disadvantage requirement in anticipatory reasonable adjustment duties is to be welcomed. It reinforces the group dimension of these duties and draws attention to their role in breaking down structural barriers. The pragmatic approach taken to the question of how group disadvantage should be proved is also helpful. It ensures that establishing group disadvantage will generally not be a complex and expensive task requiring the collection and analysis of swathes of statistics. It is unclear, however, whether the group disadvantage requirement will or should be applied in all contexts as strictly as it was in *Roads*.

It should be stressed that, although these reasonable adjustment duties are anticipatory in that they require service providers to anticipate and remove potential barriers, they will also sometimes require service providers to respond to the needs of a particular disabled person. This reactive element of the duty is likely to arise if the service provider has become aware of an individual disabled customer and the specific difficulty they face in accessing the service.[169] It is thus particularly likely to arise in the context of education, where relationships between service-providers and disabled individuals are likely to be relatively long-lasting and close.

The reasonable adjustment duties which are placed on education-providers, as has already been mentioned, are triggered when 'disabled persons' would otherwise be subjected to a substantial disadvantage. They are thus anticipatory in nature. In view of the proximity and duration of the connection between education-provider and student, however, it is likely to be reasonable for them to have to go to greater lengths to provide individualised adjustments in response to needs of which they have become aware than it would be for other types of service provider. So strong is this reactive element of the duty on education-providers that strict insistence on group disadvantage may sometimes prove problematic. This type of scenario is well illustrated by the following example, set out in the Code of Practice on post-16 education:

> A university anticipates that some deaf students will require the use of [British Sign Language] BSL interpreters and ensures it has access to BSL interpreters at short notice. However, a student who arrives at the university uses American Sign Language (ASL) and had not previously notified the university of this. As soon as the university is aware of this it should make the necessary reasonable adjustment by seeking an ASL

---

[168] *Ibid*, [26].

[169] DRC, *DDA 1995 Code of Practice: Rights of Access—Services to the Public, Public Authority Functions, Private Clubs and Premises* (n 144 above) para 6.21.

interpreter, even though it may not have been reasonable to have arrangements with an ASL interpreter before the student arrives.[170]

It is clearly possible to argue that group disadvantage is demonstrated in a case such as this—the University should have anticipated that deaf students would be placed at a substantial disadvantage unless steps were taken to make oral information accessible to them. On the other hand, it is also possible to imagine the opposite view being taken—the University could not have anticipated that deaf students would be placed at a substantial disadvantage, given the provisions it had already made for ensuring the availability of BSL interpreters. Insistence on the demonstration of group disadvantage in all cases would lay questions such as this open to the courts, not all of which are likely to be as sensitive to the interests at stake as was the Court of Appeal in *Roads*.

In short, *Roads* holds that no reasonable adjustment duty will arise under section 21 of the DDA unless it can be shown that the challenged policy, practice, procedure or feature caused the required level of group disadvantage. While this approach is generally to be welcomed, its application to reasonable adjustment duties in the education context may cause some difficulty. Because the relevant statutory language in the education context is identical to that in section 21, it is likely that *Roads* will indeed be applied in that sphere. An ideal solution would be a statutory amendment whereby entirely reactive duties, not requiring group disadvantage (along the lines of those currently operating in relation to employment), were introduced to run alongside the existing educational anticipatory duties. In the absence of such a development, however, hope must instead be attached to judicial sensitivity. An insensitive application of the group disadvantage requirement in education cases has the potential to place a dangerous stranglehold on educational reasonable adjustment duties and thereby to cause serious damage.

3.3.2 Impossibility, Difficulty or Disadvantage

(a) 'Impossible or Unreasonably Difficult'   As may already have become clear, the section 21 duty to adjust practices, policies and procedures will be imposed on service providers only if those practices, policies or procedures would otherwise make it impossible or unreasonably difficult for disabled people to use the service in question.[171] This same trigger of impossibility or unreasonable difficulty is used in relation to the duty to make reasonable adjustments to overcome physical features.[172]

---

[170] DRC, *DDA 1995 Code of Practice: Post-16 Education* (London, Stationery Office, 2006) para 5.14.

[171] DDA s 21(1).

[172] DDA s 21(2). The duty came into force on 1 October 2004, nearly a decade after the passage of the Act, in order to allow service providers time to implement necessary changes.

The same trigger of impossibility and unreasonable difficulty, with an important addition, also appears in the context of the duties of public authorities to make adjustments to their policies, practices, procedures and physical features in discharging public functions.[173] The addition consists of the phrase 'unreasonably adverse' and, according to the Code of Practice, is intended to cover cases in which the effect of the relevant public function on the person concerned is adverse rather than beneficial (eg being arrested or subjected to immigration control).[174] Although there has not yet been any litigation on the issue, it is likely that 'unreasonably adverse' will be interpreted as requiring a similar degree of disproportionate impact on disabled people as 'unreasonably difficult'.[175]

The DDA provides no definition of 'impossible', 'unreasonably difficult' or 'unreasonably adverse'. Although the meaning of 'impossible' is unlikely to be contentious, opinions may differ markedly about the degree of difficulty or adversity which should be accepted as reasonable and therefore as failing to trigger relevant reasonable adjustment duties. Much practical guidance as to what might be regarded as unreasonably difficult, supported by hypothetical examples, is provided in the relevant codes of practice. In particular, the DDA Part 3 Code urges that, in assessing whether the experience of a disabled person is unreasonably difficult or adverse, service providers and public authorities should have regard to whether

> the time, inconvenience, effort, discomfort, anxiety or loss of dignity entailed in using the service would be considered unreasonable by other people if they had to endure similar difficulties.[176]

Such considerations are also relevant to the earlier assessment of whether the required degree of difficulty would be encountered by disabled people generally. In addition, at that stage, the fact that other disabled people with similar impairments are able to negotiate the disputed barrier is likely to be a relevant (though not conclusive) factor.[177]

Early, and slightly worrying, county court cases on the standard of unreasonable difficulty include *Baggley v Kingston-upon-Hull Council*[178] and *Appleby v Department for Work and Pensions*.[179] In *Baggley*, it was suggested that the required level of unreasonable difficulty had not been reached where a wheelchair user was obliged to sit at the back of a concert hall. His level of difficulty in accessing the service was considered to be reasonable despite the fact that he was

---

[173] DDA s 21E(1) and (3).

[174] DRC, *DDA 1995 Code of Practice: Rights of Access—Services to the Public, Public Authority Functions, Private Clubs and Premises* (n 144 above) para 11.38.

[175] This point is certainly assumed in the Code—see eg *ibid*, paras 6.35, 7.6 and 11.39.

[176] *Ibid*, para 6.36.

[177] See eg *Roads v Central Trains* [2004] EWCA Civ 1540.

[178] Kingston upon Hull County Court, Claim No KH101929 (discussed in Gooding and Casserley, 'Open for All?' (n 145 above) 152).

[179] Lambeth County Court, Claim No LB001649 (discussed in Gooding and Casserley, 'Open for All?' (n 145 above)).

unable to see the performer (Sporty Spice) because other concertgoers were standing and blocking his view. The standard was assumed to be similarly high in *Appleby*. This case concerned the queuing system adopted by a benefits agency when its standard procedure of indicating whose turn it was through a visual display monitor and an audible tannoy system were out of action. The claimant, who had a severe hearing impairment, had asked if a member of staff would let him know when it was his turn but been told that this would not be possible and that he should instead seek assistance from a member of the public. The unavailability of staff help in such circumstances was held not to make it unreasonably difficult for him to use the service and therefore not to trigger the reasonable adjustment duty.

Encouragingly, however, the required level of difficulty was held to have been demonstrated in the two Court of Appeal cases of *Ross v Ryanair and Stansted Airport*[180] and *Roads v Central Trains*.[181] In *Ross* it was held, with little difficulty, that the long distance between the check-in desk and the departure gate at Stansted Airport made it unreasonably difficult for disabled people (and for the particular claimant who had cerebral palsy) to make use of the airport.[182] In *Roads*, it was held that it was unreasonably difficult for wheelchair users to have to travel half a mile along a pot-holed and partially unpaved lane in order to change from one railway platform to another in the same station. Interestingly, much weight was placed on the nature of the road and it is therefore possible that the decision might have been different had the road been well surfaced.

Concern has been expressed that the language of 'impossibility' and 'unreasonable difficulty or adversity' allows the trigger to be placed unacceptably high, with the effect that reasonable adjustment duties will arise too infrequently.[183] It certainly appears to set a higher standard than that required to establish a 'substantial disadvantage' in the employment context. This difference may be intended to reflect the fact that service providers tend to have much more fleeting relationships with their customers than do employers with their employees and should therefore be placed under less burdensome reasonable adjustment duties than are employers. This difference, however, is adequately addressed by the fact that service providers are not required to anticipate and provide for all the specific requirements of a particular individual. Further, the concept of reasonableness is sufficiently flexible to take this difference into account and require less onerous steps of service providers than employers in specific cases. It is therefore by no means clear that there are sufficiently strong reasons for the use of the different, and higher, trigger for the reasonable adjustment duties of service providers. The Disability Rights Commission's recommendation, accepted by the

---

180 *Ross v Ryanair* [2004] EWCA Civ 1751.
181 *Roads v Central Trains* [2004] EWCA Civ 1540.
182 See, in particular, *Ross v Ryanair* (n 180 above) [31].
183 See eg Gooding and Casserley, 'Open for All?' (n 145 above) 152.

Discrimination Law Review, of applying the single trigger of 'substantial disadvantage' throughout the Act therefore has much to recommend it.[184] The Government's decision to include provisions to this effect in its forthcoming Equality Bill is therefore to be warmly welcomed.[185]

(b) Enablement or Facilitation   As has been seen, the trigger of impossibility or unreasonable difficulty/adversity operates in relation to the duty to adjust practices, policies and procedures and the duty to overcome physical features. The trigger for the duty to take reasonable steps to provide auxiliary aids and services is set much lower.

According to section 21(4)(a) of the DDA,[186] such a duty will arise where the provision of such an aid or service would 'enable' disabled persons to use the service. The inability of particular groups to use the service without such assistance is implicit. Consequently, this element of the trigger broadly equates to that of 'impossibility' discussed above. Under section 21(4)(b),[187] the auxiliary aids and services duty will also be triggered if the provision of such assistance would 'facilitate' disabled people in their use of the service. The emphasis is thus on facilitating disabled people's use, regardless of the degree of difficulty they would otherwise have experienced. There is accordingly no threshold requirement of 'unreasonable difficulty' in this context.

The anticipatory duty to provide auxiliary aids and services is thus triggered more easily than other forms of reasonable adjustment duty. However, as with the other forms of duty, it will be enforceable only by a disabled individual who is able to show that the service provider's failure to comply with it had the effect of making it impossible or unreasonably difficult for them to use the service.[188]

(c) Substantial Disadvantage   Unlike the majority of other anticipatory reasonable adjustment duties, those relating to education are triggered by reference to the concept of 'substantial disadvantage'.[189] This phrase has already been considered in some depth in the employment context. In that context, the focus was on the disadvantage caused to a particular disabled employee or applicant. In the

---

[184]   DRC, *Disability Equality: Making it Happen* (n 65 above) para 16; Department for Communities and Local Government, *Discrimination Law Review—A Framework for Fairness: Proposals for a Single Equality Bill for Great Britain* (London, Stationery Office, 2007) paras 1.58–1.59.

[185]   Government Equalities Office, *The Equality Bill* (n 142 above) paras 11.31–11.44.

[186]   See also DDA s 21E(6)(a) in the context of public authorities (which covers both the enabling and facilitating of the use of a service) and Disability Discrimination (Private Clubs etc) Regulations 2005 (SI 2005/3258) reg 6(3)(a).

[187]   See also DDA s 21E(6)(b) in the context of public authorities, (which refers to the reduction of adversity) and Disability Discrimination (Private Clubs etc) Regulations 2005 (SI 2005/3258) reg 6(3)(b).

[188]   DDA ss 19(1)(b) and 20(2).

[189]   DDA s 28C, for pre-16 education, and s 28T(1) and (1C) and s 28UA(5), for post-16 education.

education context, however, the focus is on the substantial disadvantage experienced by disabled persons generally, with the result that the duties are anticipatory in nature.

In relation to employment services, too, substantial disadvantage is adopted as the trigger for the duty to adjust practices, policies and procedures.[190] As in relation to education, the disadvantage required must be suffered by disabled persons generally and not by a specific individual. Confusingly, however, the employment services provisions retain the trigger of impossibility or unreasonable difficulty for the physical features duty. This differentiation between the triggers for the different reasonable adjustment duties applying to employment services was effected by the DDA 1995 (Amendment) Regulations 2003 and accordingly appears to be based on an interpretation of the requirements of the Employment Equality Directive. There is, however, nothing in the latter to support such a distinction.

3.3.3 Cause of the Impossibility, Difficulty or Disadvantage

(a) Practices, Policies or Procedures   As will now be apparent, in most contexts service providers will be subjected to an anticipatory duty to make reasonable adjustments to such of their practices, policies or procedures as would make it unduly difficult for disabled people to use their services. There is no comprehensive definition of a 'practice, policy or procedure' but, according to section 21(1A), it includes a 'provision or criterion'. This paragraph was inserted into the DDA by the DDA 1995 (Amendment) Regulations 2003 with the primary purpose not of clarifying the meaning of the phrase but of ensuring that the scope of the reasonable adjustment duty for employment services was sufficiently wide to comply with the Employment Equality Directive.

The Code of Practice suggests that a practice may be regarded as 'what a service provider actually does', a policy as 'what a service provider intends to do' and a procedure as 'how a service provider plans to go about it'.[191] It warns, however, that the terms overlap and that it may not therefore always be sensible to treat them as separate concepts.[192]

(b) Physical Features   Under section 21(2) of the DDA,[193] where a physical feature makes the use of a service impossible or unreasonably difficult for disabled people, service providers have a duty to take reasonable steps to:

(a) remove the feature;

---

[190]   DDA s 21A(6).

[191]   DRC, *DDA 1995 Code of Practice: Rights of Access—Services to the Public, Public Authority Functions, Private Clubs and Premises* (n 144 above) para 7.7.

[192]   *Ibid*, para 7.8.

[193]   See also s 21E(3) and (4), for public authorities; s 21E(1C), for further and higher education; and the Disability Discrimination (Private Clubs etc) Regulations 2005 (SI 2005/3258) reg 6(2), for private clubs.

(b) alter it so that it no longer has that effect;

(c) provide a reasonable means of avoiding the feature; or

(d) provide a reasonable alternative method of making the service in question available to disabled persons.

The term 'physical feature' is given a meaning which mirrors that given to it in the employment sphere.[194]

The various ways of discharging the duty to overcome troublesome physical features set out in paragraphs (a) to (d) of section 21(2) are not explicitly ranked in order of priority. Thus, it is not clear that there is an obligation on a service provider to remove or alter the physical barrier in preference to making the service available to disabled people through alternative means. There is, however, very clear guidance on this issue in the Code of Practice. The Code draws attention to the fact that the policy of the Act is to 'approximate the access enjoyed by disabled persons to that enjoyed by the rest of the public'[195]; to the value of an 'inclusive approach' which enables disabled and non-disabled people to participate in the same way[196]; and to the greater respect demonstrated by such an approach for the dignity of disabled people and its potential long-term economic benefits.[197] It then goes on to recommend that:

a service provider should first consider whether any physical features that create a barrier for disabled people can be removed or altered

if that is not reasonable, a service provider should then consider providing a reasonable means of avoiding the physical feature

if that is also not reasonable, the service provider should then consider providing a reasonable alternative method of making the service available to disabled people.[198]

This prioritisation of possible adjustments was endorsed by Sedley LJ in *Roads v Central Trains*.[199] He insisted that, in assessments of the reasonableness of adjustments, regard should be had to the fact that the policy of the Act is

to provide access to a service as close as it is reasonably possible to get to the standard normally offered to the public at large.[200]

---

[194] See section 2.3.3(c) above. See also, Disability Discrimination (Services and Premises) Regulations 1999 (SI 1999/1191) reg 3.

[195] DRC, *DDA 1995 Code of Practice: Rights of Access—Services to the Public, Public Authority Functions, Private Clubs and Premises* (n 144 above) para 7.36.

[196] *Ibid*, para 7.38.

[197] *Ibid*, para 7.39.

[198] *Ibid*, para 7.40.

[199] *Roads v Central Trains* [2004] EWCA Civ 1540 [13].

[200] *Ibid*, quoting from Myners Ch in *Re Holy Cross, Pershore* [2002] Fam 1 [105] (Worcester Consistory Ct).

The duty to make reasonable adjustments to physical features does not extend to schools or to transport vehicles.[201] In relation to schools, a duty is instead placed on each local education authority to draw up, review and implement accessibility strategies covering all the schools for which it is the responsible body.[202] Such strategies are required to detail the steps which will be taken, within a specified period, to improve the physical environment of the schools so as to increase the extent to which disabled pupils can take advantage of the 'education and associated services' provided or offered by the schools.[203] These plans, which may involve maximising resources by focusing on improving the physical access of particular (but not all) schools in the area, must be available for inspection.[204] The Secretary of State (or other appropriate authority) is given power to issue directions if a responsible body is behaving unreasonably in relation to an accessibility strategy.[205] Physical access is thus a matter falling within the general purview of school inspection procedures, and a failure to remove a physical obstacle will not be enforceable by an aggrieved individual as a discrimination claim.

In relation to the vast majority of transport vehicles,[206] there is no duty to make reasonable adjustments in order to overcome physical features.[207] Instead, Part 5 of the DDA provides for the issuing of Regulations detailing technical standards relating to the construction, use and maintenance of such vehicles. While non-compliance with the standards specified may affect licences and result in financial penalties, it cannot found an action for discrimination by an affected individual.

The Disability Rights Commission drew attention to the need to review the operation of the DDA reasonable adjustment duties in relation to transport.[208] It expressed particular concern about the absence of any clear duty on transport operators to provide a service through reasonable alternative means. A train operator, for instance, would appear to have no obvious obligation to return a disabled passenger to the station at which they intended to alight when, because that station had ceased to be staffed, the passenger had been forced to remain on the train until they reached a station where assistance was available.

In relation to both schools and transport vehicles, the use of access standards and strategies is to be welcomed. Nevertheless, it is not obvious that such standards and strategies should have excluded the physical feature reasonable

---

[201] DDA s 28C(2)(a) and Disability Discrimination (Transport Vehicles) Regulations 2005 (SI 2005/3190) reg 4 respectively.

[202] DDA s 28D(1). The responsible bodies of maintained, independent and special schools are also covered—s 28D(7)–(12).

[203] DDA s 28D(2)(b).

[204] DDA s 21E.

[205] DDA s 28M.

[206] With the exception of breakdown recovery vehicles and certain hire vehicles—Disability Discrimination (Transport Vehicles) Regulations 2005 (SI 2005/3190) regs 5 and 6 respectively.

[207] *Ibid*, reg 4.

[208] DRC, *Initial Submission to the Discrimination Law Review* (London, DRC, 2006) para 2.4.

adjustment duty. Retaining such a duty in these contexts would have given individuals the opportunity to sue under discrimination law should they be disadvantaged by inadequate attempts to provide physical access. Such an approach would thus have introduced a useful supplementary enforcement mechanism. It would also have achieved greater consistency with other parts of the DDA and constituted an acknowledgement of the significance of the serious impact which inadequate access frequently has upon the lives of disabled individuals. Were it to be adopted, the important role of technical standards and strategies might be emphasised by a rule that compliance with relevant technical standards, or with the terms of an approved access strategy, should constitute irrebuttable evidence of reasonableness.[209]

(c) Auxiliary Aids and Services   The duty to provide such auxiliary aids and services as would be reasonable is imposed on service providers by section 21(4) of the DDA, and on public authorities and private clubs by analogous provisions.[210] In the post-16 education context, although the reasonable adjustment duties do extend to the provision of auxiliary aids and services,[211] the relevant statutory provisions make no explicit reference to them.

In the pre-16 education context, by contrast, the provision of auxiliary aids and services is expressly excluded from the scope of the reasonable adjustment duty.[212] This exclusion was grounded on the view that such assistance should be provided instead through the pre-existing 'statementing' procedure. That procedure makes Local Education Authorities responsible for drawing up statements of the special educational needs (SEN) of pupils and for providing them with the support required to meet those needs.[213] This gap in the coverage of the DDA reasonable adjustment duties would appear to make it important to identify the precise boundaries of the concept of auxiliary aids and services.

The DDA does not define the term 'auxiliary aids and services'.[214] By way of example of an auxiliary aid, however, section 21(4) refers to the provision of

---

[209]   See, eg, the role of 'action plans' in the Australian Disability Discrimination Act 1992, Part 3.

[210]   DDA s 21E(6) and (7); and Disability Discrimination (Private Clubs etc) Regulations 2005 (SI 2005/3258) regs 6(3), 7(2), 8(2) and 9(2) respectively.

[211]   A point made in DRC, *DDA 1995 Code of Practice: Post-16 Education* (n 170 above) para 5.62.

[212]   DDA s 28C(2)(b).

[213]   Education Act 1996, Part 4. For an overview of the SEN system and recommendations leading to the introduction of the DDA education provisions, see generally Disability Rights Task Force, *From Exclusion to Inclusion* (n 4 above) ch 4. See also A Blair, 'Rights, Duties and Resources: The Case of Special Educational Needs' (2000) 12 *Education and the Law* 177; and C O'Mahony, 'Constitutionalism and Legislation in Special Educational Needs Law: An Anglo-Irish Perspective' [2008] *Public Law* 125.

[214]   In the context of transport vehicles, reg 7 of the Disability Discrimination (Transport Vehicles) Regulations 2005 (SI 2005/3190) specifies that devices, structures or equipment which necessitate a permanent change to the fabric of the vehicle should not be classified as auxiliary aids or services. Under reg 4 of the Disability Discrimination (Services and Premises) Regulations 1999 (SI 1999/1191), various physical additions and adaptations were deemed not to be auxiliary aids. This,

information on audiotape and, by way of example of an auxiliary service, it mentions the provision of a sign language interpreter. Further non-educational examples of auxiliary aids used in the DDA Part 3 Code of Practice include the provision of adapted supermarket baskets and trolleys for use by people with mobility impairments; the provision of an electronic barcode reader for use by people with visual impairments; the installation of induction loop facilities; and the availability of a portable ramp.[215] The Code stresses that auxiliary services may take the form of additional staff assistance, such as ensuring that a member of staff will be available to assist a visually impaired customer to find items in a supermarket.[216]

In the context of education the Code of Practice for Schools gives, as an example of an auxiliary aid, the provision of a radio system to a child with a hearing impairment in mainstream education, and, as an example of an auxiliary service, the support provided to such a child through a peripatetic teacher of the deaf.[217] Given the lack of a precise definition of auxiliary services, and indications that the provision of additional staff support should be so classified, there is a risk that schools will regard the provision of such support to disabled pupils as an auxiliary service for which they are not therefore responsible. In *McAuley Catholic High School v CC and Others*,[218] however, it was held that the provision of additional pastoral support, to help an autistic child to manage unstructured time and the transition from one year to the next, was a responsibility which fell to the school under section 28C of the DDA. Its failure to make this provision was the result of inadequate organisation and planning rather than the result of inadequate finances. Although the auxiliary service exemption was not explicitly addressed, it is clearly implicit in this decision that the pastoral support in question did not fall within the auxiliary aids and services exemption.

In *K v X Grammar School Governors*,[219] the Court of Appeal again chose not to search too closely for the exact boundaries of an 'auxiliary' aid or service. In that case, the mother of an incontinent disabled child argued that the school's refusal to clean and change him amounted to a failure to discharge a reasonable adjustment duty. Wall LJ, unlike the judges in the lower courts, did not dismiss this argument on the ground that such a service was 'auxiliary' and therefore outside the scope of the section 28C duty. He was instead prepared to assume,

---

however, was designed simply to ease the burden of the duty to make physical alterations imposed on service providers and, once the duty to make physical alterations came into force (on 1 October 2004), this regulation ceased to have effect.

[215] DRC, *DDA 1995 Code of Practice: Rights of Access—Services to the Public, Public Authority Functions, Private Clubs and Premises* (n 144 above) paras 7.13–7.16.

[216] *Ibid*, para 7.14.

[217] DRC, *DDA 1995 Part 4: Code of Practice for Schools* (London, Stationery Office, 2002) para 6.20.

[218] *McAuley Catholic High School v CC and Others* [2004] ICR 1563. See also *R (T) v Independent Appeal Panel for Devon CC* [2007] EWHC (Admin) 763, which concerned the exclusion of a pupil with Asperger's Syndrome from school.

[219] *K v X Grammar School Governors* [2007] EWCA Civ 165.

without deciding, that failure to provide such a service might, in some circumstances, represent a breach of that duty. The fact that the school had approached the Local Education Authority with a request for help in providing relevant support through the SEN system was a significant factor in his decision that the school had, in this case, taken all reasonable steps to remove the disadvantage caused to the disabled child by having to be sent home for cleaning and changing.[220] There was, in his view, 'no sharp dichotomy or barrier' between the duties imposed by the DDA and by the SEN framework.[221]

The interrelationship of the SEN and DDA systems is further illustrated by the decision of the Special Educational Needs and Disability Tribunal in *Buniak v Jenny Hammond Primary School*.[222] A school was there held liable for disability-related discrimination against a disabled boy. His statement of special educational needs made provision for the funding of a full-time learning support assistant but, due to the school's failure to appoint such a person, he had been able to attend his class for only two hours a day. Thus, although the auxiliary service was to be funded through the SEN system, the school's failure to ensure that that service was effectively installed amounted to unjustified less favourable treatment of the disabled child.

(d) Provisions, Criteria and Practices   Although the three archetypal sites for the DDA's anticipatory reasonable adjustment duties are: first, practices, policies and procedures; second, physical features; and third, auxiliary aids and services, a number of others exist. In the context of post-16 education, for instance, the two key sites of such duties are: first, physical features; and second, provisions, criteria and practices. The latter phrase was adopted in order to ensure compliance with the Employment Equality Directive. According to the relevant Code of Practice, provisions, criteria and practices are broad terms, which cover all of an education provider's 'arrangements, policies, procedures and activities'.[223] Under section 28T, however, the duty to make adjustments applies only to those provisions, criteria and practices which relate to admission arrangements and student services[224]; those which concern the conferment of qualifications[225]; and others which would disadvantage a disabled person who applies for, or already holds, a qualification conferred by the education provider.[226]

The terms used in the first of these categories—arrangements relating to admissions and student services—are very similar to those used in the reasonable

---

[220]   *Ibid*, [48]–[49].

[221]   *Ibid*, [50].

[222]   Special Educational Needs and Disability Tribunal 03–50019 (discussed in S Enright, 'Special Educational Needs: Failure to Comply with SEN Statement' (2004) 154 *New Law Journal* 730).

[223]   DRC, *DDA 1995 Code of Practice: Post-16 Education* (n 170 above) para 5.29. See also the discussion of provisions, criteria and practices above section 2.3.3(b).

[224]   DDA s 28T(1).

[225]   DDA s 28T(1A).

[226]   DDA s 28T(1B).

adjustment duties relating to pre-16 education. It is to the pre-16 education context that attention will now be turned.

(e) Admission Arrangements and Education and Associated Services

Section 28C(1), which imposes reasonable adjustment duties on the bodies responsible for schools, uses none of the phrases considered thus far in this Section. Instead it requires such bodies to adjust the 'arrangements it makes for determining the admission of pupils to the school' and matters relating to 'education and associated services provided for, or offered to, pupils at the school'. Admission arrangements are not defined in the Act but, according to the Code of Practice for Schools, would include 'any criteria for deciding who will be admitted to the school when it is over-subscribed'; 'the operation of those criteria'; the terms on which admission is offered; and the refusal or deliberate omission of an application for admission.[227] 'Education and associated services', according to the Code, 'is a broad term that covers all aspects of school life' affecting pupils and prospective pupils.[228] As has already been seen, the schools' reasonable adjustment duty does not extend to the provision of auxiliary aids and services or the alteration of physical features. The line between the adjustment of an educational or associated service and the provision of an auxiliary service is, however, not entirely clear.[229]

3.3.4 The Knowledge Requirement

The anticipatory nature of the duties under consideration here requires those subjected to them to make reasonable adjustments to various aspects of their operations in advance of the appearance of a particular disabled person. To allow them to escape liability for a failure to make such adjustments, on the ground that they were unaware that the claimant was disabled, would therefore appear to be a nonsense. Unsurprisingly, therefore, there is no such defence in the vast majority of the contexts in which these anticipatory duties operate. In relation to education, however, there is such a defence.

The apparent oddity of such a defence in the context of anticipatory duties is lessened when regard is had to the fact that these duties also contain a reactive element. As well as anticipating and removing likely obstacles, service providers may well have to react to the circumstances of an actual disabled customer, particularly when that customer has requested reasonable alterations which would facilitate their use of the service. Education providers are likely to have closer and more enduring relationships with their disabled 'customers' than are other types of service provider. As a result, the lengths to which they are expected to go in accommodating the particular needs of a disabled pupil or student are likely to be greater than those expected of other service providers.

---

[227] DRC, *DDA 1995 Part 4: Code of Practice for Schools* (n 217 above) para 4.22.
[228] *Ibid*, para 4.23.
[229] See nn 216–218 above and accompanying text.

In relation to both pre and post-16 education, the relevant knowledge require-ment reads as follows:

> In relation to a failure to take a particular step, a responsible body does not discriminate against a person if it shows—
>
> (a) that, at the time in question, it did not know and could not reasonably have been expected to know, that he was disabled; and
> (b) that its failure to take the step was attributable to that lack of knowledge.[230]

Although this terminology is not dissimilar to the analogous defence in the employment context, the existence of the anticipatory element of the reasonable adjustment duty in this context is likely to result in a more expansive construc-tion of what education providers ought to have known. They will, for example, be expected to take steps to create an open, welcoming and supportive atmosphere in order to encourage disclosures of disability and to invite such disclosures on an on-going basis.[231]

3.4 Discharging the Duty

3.4.1 Duty to Keep Services under Review

The anticipatory element of the reasonable adjustments duty necessarily imposes upon duty-bearers a responsibility to keep the accessibility of their services under continual review.[232] The potential benefits of involving disabled people and their organisations in review processes is stressed by the Code.[233] A one-off assessment will not suffice, as the introduction of new systems and technologies may create both fresh obstacles for disabled people and fresh means of overcoming them. In circumstances where it is important to tailor adjustments to the specific needs of a particular disabled person (such as in relation to education), however, assess-ments of individual needs are also likely to be required.

3.4.2 Possible Adjustments

The DDA provisions dealing with these anticipatory duties, unlike those dealing with employment, provide no guidance as to the types of steps which it might be appropriate for duty-bearers to take. The Codes of Practice contain numerous examples, however, some of which have been drawn upon in the preceding text. Although these undoubtedly constitute a valuable source of information and inspiration, they will not be set out in detail here.

---

[230] DDA ss 28B(3) and 28S(3).

[231] DRC, *DDA 1995 Part 4: Code of Practice for Schools* (n 217 above) para 7.9; DRC, *DDA 1995 Code of Practice: Post-16 Education* (n 170 above) paras 8.37–8.38.

[232] DRC, *DDA 1995 Code of Practice: Rights of Access—Services to the Public, Public Authority Functions, Private Clubs and Premises* (n 144 above) para 6.22.

[233] *Ibid*, para 6.11.

As is stressed in the DDA Part 3 Code,[234] staff training has an extremely significant role to play in relation to reasonable adjustment duties. General disability awareness training may enable staff to interact more easily with disabled people, and training in the workings of auxiliary aids would enable them to assist disabled people to maximise the benefits of such devices. It should also be stressed that the anticipatory reasonable adjustment duties require thought to be given to the access requirements of people with all types of impairment and that making adjustments to accommodate some disabled people (eg people with hearing impairments) will not constitute a defence to a failure to consider the needs of others (eg people with mobility impairments or learning difficulties).[235]

3.4.3 Reasonableness

The Act itself sets out no list of factors to be taken into account in assessing what steps would be reasonable for an anticipatory duty-bearer to have to take.[236] The following non-exhaustive list appears in the Part 3 Code, however:

> whether taking any particular steps would be effective in overcoming the difficulty that disabled people face in accessing the services in question;
>
> the extent to which it is practicable for the service provider to take the steps;
>
> the financial and other costs of making the adjustment;
>
> the extent of any disruption which taking the steps would cause;
>
> the extent of the service provider's financial and other resources;
>
> the amount of any resources already spent on making adjustments; and
>
> the availability of financial or other assistance.[237]

These are similar to the factors which have already been considered in the employment context, making detailed elaboration of their implications unnecessary here. Importantly, however, the Code also states that the policy of the Act is not 'a minimalist policy of simply ensuring that some access is available to disabled people'.[238] The purpose of the reasonable adjustment duties is rather

> to provide access to a service as close as it is reasonably possible to get to the standard normally offered, to the public at large.[239]

---

[234] *Ibid*, paras 6.12 and 6.18.

[235] *Ibid*, para 6.27.

[236] For criticism of this omission, see DRC, *Disability Equality: Making it Happen* (n 65 above) para 14.

[237] DRC, *DDA 1995 Code of Practice: Rights of Access—Services to the Public, Public Authority Functions, Private Clubs and Premises* (n 144 above) para 6.25. See also DRC, *DDA 1995 Code of Practice: Provision and Use of Transport* (n 153 above) para 5.29, which is virtually identical.

[238] DRC, *DDA 1995 Code of Practice: Rights of Access—Services to the Public, Public Authority Functions, Private Clubs and Premises* (n 144 above) para 6.4.

[239] *Ibid*.

In the event that there are various possible adjustments that might be made, service providers would be well-advised to have regard to this policy and consider which of the options would further it most effectively.[240]

Section 21(6) in effect imposes an express limit on what may be regarded as a reasonable adjustment under that section. According to it, a service provider will not be required to take any steps which would 'fundamentally alter the nature of the service ... or the nature of his trade, profession or business'. Thus, according to the Code, a restaurant which has no home delivery service would be unlikely to have to deliver a meal to the home of a disabled person; and a nightclub would be unlikely to have to install brighter lighting in order to assist people with visual impairments.[241]

On the issue of cost, section 21(8) provides for the introduction of Regulations specifying a prescribed maximum expenditure which service providers would not be expected to exceed in effecting reasonable adjustments.[242] No such Regulations have been introduced to date and it is to be hoped that they will not prove to be necessary. Sensitivity to the extent of the resources of a particular service provider is an important factor in the assessment of reasonableness.[243] There is a risk that the introduction of absolute figures would distort the essentially relative nature of this exercise.

As in relation to employment, disabled people are not expected to contribute towards the cost of adjustments and requiring them to do so is expressly prohibited.[244] This issue arose in *Ross v Ryanair and Stansted Airport Ltd*,[245] which concerned Ryanair's policy of charging disabled customers £18 for the use of a wheelchair in Stansted Airport. The provision of wheelchair assistance for passengers with mobility impairments was held to be a reasonable adjustment. The costs of providing such assistance could not therefore be passed on to the customer and had to be borne by the service provider instead.

In relation to education, slightly different considerations apply, although again no guidance is provided in the statute itself. According to the Code of Practice for Schools, any assessment of the reasonableness of possible adjustments should be made with the clear aim of maximising the participation of disabled children in every aspect of school life.[246] The following factors are suggested as having relevance to such assessments:

the need to maintain academic, musical, sporting and other standards;

the financial resources available to the responsible body;

---

[240] See also *Roads v Central Trains* [2004] EWCA Civ 1540 [13] (Sedley LJ).
[241] DRC, *DDA 1995 Code of Practice: Rights of Access—Services to the Public, Public Authority Functions, Private Clubs and Premises* (n 144 above) para 10.39.
[242] DDA s 21(7).
[243] DRC, *DDA 1995 Code of Practice: Rights of Access—Services to the Public, Public Authority Functions, Private Clubs and Premises* (n 144 above) para 6.26.
[244] See eg DDA ss 20(5) and 21G(4).
[245] *Ross v Ryanair and Stansted Airport Ltd* [2005] 1 WLR 2447 (CA).
[246] DRC, *DDA 1995 Part 4: Code of Practice for Schools* (n 217 above) para 6.29.

the cost of taking a particular step;

the extent to which it is practicable to take a particular step;

the extent to which aids and services will be provided to disabled pupils at the school under Part IV of the Education Act 1996 or Sections 60–65G of the Education (Scotland) Act 1980;

health and safety requirements;

the interests of other pupils and persons who may be admitted to the school as pupils.[247]

A similar non-exhaustive list of relevant factors is set out in the code of practice relating to post-16 education providers.[248] In that list, however, the maintenance of standards does not appear. This is because the post-16 educational provisions craft the reasonable adjustments duties in such a way as to ensure that they will not apply to 'competence standards'. There is therefore never any obligation to adjust such standards in order to accommodate the requirements of a disabled person.

Finally, in this context, it is worth again drawing attention to the significance of the fact that the duties under consideration have an anticipatory element. Although this aspect of the duty is not directly enforceable, failure to plan and implement adjustments in advance of the arrival of a particular disabled customer, pupil or student, may well result in liability should that person encounter difficulties in using the service. A delay in providing them with appropriate assistance, which would not have occurred had adequate steps been taken in advance, may well be regarded as unreasonable and as constituting a breach of the duty.[249] Further, it is entirely possible that service providers will be held to have failed to discharge the duty if they could have removed a barrier in the past—through the purchase of access-related equipment for instance—but cannot now do so because of a decline in their finances or because the equipment in question is no longer available.

3.4.4 Reasonableness Considerations Specific to Physical Alterations

As regards building regulations and design standards, providers of post-16 education are in a very similar position to that of employers. While compliance with such regulations and standards is likely to protect them against claims that it would be reasonable to make physical adjustments, there is no guarantee of such protection.[250] Service providers (including public authorities and private clubs) are in a stronger position in this respect. Under Regulation 3(3) of the Disability

---

[247] *Ibid*, para 6.30.

[248] DRC, *DDA 1995 Code of Practice: Post-16 Education* (n 170 above) para 5.37.

[249] See eg DRC, *DDA 1995 Code of Practice: Rights of Access—Services to the Public, Public Authority Functions, Private Clubs and Premises* (n 144 above) para 6.16; DRC, *DDA 1995 Part 4: Code of Practice for Schools* (n 217 above) para 6.12; and DRC, *DDA 1995 Code of Practice: Post-16 Education* (n 170 above) para 2.10.

[250] See eg DRC, *DDA 1995 Code of Practice: Post-16 Education* (n 170 above) para 12.7.

Discrimination (Providers of Services) (Adjustment of Premises) Regulations 2001,[251] service providers will be exempt from altering physical features of their buildings if those features comply with standards laid down in Approved Document M—Access to and Use of Buildings (or, in Scotland, the Technical Standards) and less than 10 years have elapsed since the installation of the feature or the completion of the work. The exemption, however, may not spare service providers from the need to provide reasonable means of avoiding the feature or of making the service available in an alternative way.[252]

In relation to the obtaining of consents for the making of physical adjustments to property, there is no significant difference between the position of service providers (including providers of post-16 education) and that of employers. Thus, they too are required to obtain necessary statutory consents (such as planning permission) and may be obliged to carry out interim adjustments pending the outcome of the application. Like employers, if they are bound to obtain the consent of a third party under some form of legal obligation (such as a mortgage or restrictive covenant), it will always be reasonable for them to take steps to obtain the necessary consent and never reasonable for them to have to make the alteration without it.[253] Finally, if a service provider occupies the premises under a lease the terms of which prohibit alterations, the DDA alters its terms so as to permit alterations subject to the landlord's consent, and prevents that consent being unreasonably withheld.[254]

3.5 Justifying Failures to Take Reasonable Steps

3.5.1 Absence of a Justification Defence

As initially enacted, the DDA allowed any failure to make a reasonable adjustment to be justified in certain circumstances. In situations covered by the Regulations implementing the Employment Equality Directive, however, this justification defence has been removed. Thus, in the contexts of employment and post-16 education, the failure of a duty-bearer to take reasonable steps to make relevant adjustments will render them liable for disability discrimination without any possible resort to a justification defence. In these situations liability will therefore turn exclusively on the reasonableness of any steps taken. It is to be

---

[251] Disability Discrimination (Providers of Services) (Adjustment of Premises) Regulations 2001 (SI No 2001/3253). See also the Disability Discrimination (Service Providers and Public Authorities Carrying out Functions) Regulations 2005 (SI 2005/2901) reg 11; and the Disability Discrimination (Private Clubs etc) Regulations 2005 (SI 2005/3258) reg 12.

[252] See DRC, *DDA 1995 Code of Practice: Rights of Access—Services to the Public, Public Authority Functions, Private Clubs and Premises* (n 144 above) Appendix para 23.

[253] Disability Discrimination (Providers of Services) (Adjustment of Premises) Regulations 2001 (SI 2001/3253) reg 3(2); Disability Discrimination (Service Providers and Public Authorities Carrying out Functions) Regulations 2005 (SI 2005/2901) reg 10; and Disability Discrimination (Private Clubs etc) Regulations 2005 (SI 2005/3258) reg 11.

[254] DDA s 27(2) and s 28W(2).

hoped that the Government's resolve to extend this approach throughout the Act remains unshaken by the parliamentary process and that all the remaining justification defences for failures to make reasonable adjustments (explained below) will shortly be abolished.[255]

3.5.2 The Material and Substantial Justification Defence

The justification defence that formerly existed in relation to employment and post-16 education required the reason for the failure to take reasonable steps to be both 'material to the circumstances of the particular case and substantial'.[256] Although this defence no longer applies in those contexts, it continues to exist in relation to pre-16 education.[257] The leading case on the construction of this defence arose in relation to employment, just before the implementing Regulations took effect.

The central issue for the Court of Appeal in *Collins v Royal National Theatre Board*[258] was the extent of the role, if any, that was left to the justification defence once it had been decided that reasonable steps had not been taken. This matter had to be considered in the light of the interpretation given to the identically worded justification defence for disability-related discrimination by the Court of Appeal in *Jones v The Post Office*.[259] According to *Jones*, 'material' required the existence of a 'reasonably strong connection' between the employer's reason for failing to take the steps and the facts of the particular case.[260] 'Substantial' was held to mean that the reason must simply be 'more than trivial or minor'.[261] A reason could be regarded as material and substantial even if it was based on a misunderstanding which a reasonable employer would not have formed. It would fail to be so considered only if it was one which no reasonable employer could have accepted. The justification defence would thus succeed as long as the reason could be shown to fall within the range of reasonable responses to the known facts.

The *Jones* interpretation has been criticised for setting the threshold of the justification defence for disability-related discrimination unacceptably low.[262] In *Collins*, the Court of Appeal recognised that applying that same threshold to the justification defence for a failure to make a reasonable adjustment risked undermining the DDA's purpose. This was because the threshold required for an adjustment to qualify as reasonable was higher than that of the *Jones* justification standard. Applying *Jones* to reasonable adjustments might therefore allow the arguments of a defendant, insufficient to convince a tribunal that the steps taken

---

255   *The Equality Bill* (n 142 above) paras 11.29–11.30.
256   Former DDA s 5(4) and s 28S(2)(b) and (8) respectively.
257   DDA s 28B(2)(b) and (7).
258   *Collins v Royal National Theatre Board Ltd* [2004] EWCA Civ 144.
259   *Jones v The Post Office* [2001] EWCA Civ 558.
260   *Ibid*, [37].
261   *Ibid*, [21]
262   See further ch 4, section 2.1.4 below.

had been reasonable, to succeed in justifying their failure to do more. It would, in other words, risk allowing duty-bearers to escape liability for failures to make reasonable adjustments on the ground that those failures were justified.

These difficulties led their Lordships in *Collins* to a piece of statutory construction which they acknowledged might be regarded as 'extraordinary'.[263] They held that the two identically worded justification defences should be interpreted differently. For attempts to justify less favourable treatment, the test of 'material' and 'substantial' applied to all factors. For attempts to justify a failure to take reasonable steps, however, only those factors irrelevant to the assessment of reasonableness should be subjected to that test. In the words of Sedley LJ,

> what is material and substantial for the purposes of justifying an established failure to take such steps as are reasonable ... cannot, consistently with the statutory scheme, include elements which have already been, or could already have been, evaluated in establishing that failure.[264]

Collins thus has the effect of restricting the scope of the 'material' and 'substantial' justification defence for failures to make reasonable adjustments virtually to vanishing point. It is extremely difficult to envisage cases in which there will be factors which are relevant to the justification issue but not to the assessment of reasonableness. Consequently, although the defence remains on the books in relation to pre-16 education, it has little, if any, practical effect. Its continued existence merely introduces unnecessary complexity into the statute, which would benefit greatly from its removal.[265] The concept of reasonableness is sufficiently broad and flexible to be the sole determinant of the necessity or otherwise of taking a particular step. The fact that the Discrimination Law Review did not recommend the abolition of this justification defence was extremely disappointing.[266] Thankfully, however, such a recommendation did appear in the Government's response to the consultation which followed the Discrimination Law Review.[267]

3.5.3 The Specific Belief Justification Defence

The justification defence for the failure of service providers (including private clubs and public authorities) to make reasonable adjustments is laid out differently. The defence is the same as that which applies in less favourable treatment claims brought against service providers. In order to establish it, service providers

---

[263] *Collins v Royal National Theatre* [2004] EWCA Civ 144 [33] (Sedley LJ).

[264] *Ibid*, [32] (Sedley LJ).

[265] For recommendations to this effect, see Disability Rights Task Force, *From Exclusion to Inclusion* (n 4 above) recommendations 5.2 and 6.7; and DRC, *Disability Equality: Making it Happen* (n 65 above) para 17.

[266] Department for Communities and Local Government, *Discrimination Law Review* (n 184 above) para 1.52, recommending instead that it be replaced with an objective justification defence based on the need to establish that the failure to make the adjustment constituted a proportionate means of achieving a legitimate aim.

[267] Government Equalities Office, *The Equality Bill* (n 142 above) paras 11.29–11.30.

must show first that, in their opinion, one or more of a number of specified conditions was satisfied and, second, that it was reasonable, in all the circumstances of the case, for them to hold that opinion.[268]

The specified conditions envisage certain reasons which may have motivated the disputed 'treatment'. Although references to 'treatment' are designed to embrace cases of failure to make reasonable adjustment,[269] substituting the latter phrase for the former makes the conditions appear somewhat confusing and convoluted. Nevertheless, because the justification of failures to make reasonable adjustments is the subject at issue here, this form of substitution will be made in the discussion of the specified conditions below.

Two of the specified conditions apply to service providers, public authorities and private clubs. According to these, the alleged discriminator must have believed, either that refraining from taking the reasonable steps in question was

necessary in order not to endanger the health or safety of any person (which may include that of the disabled person),[270]

or that failing to take the reasonable step was reasonable because the disabled person was

incapable of entering into an enforceable agreement, or of giving an informed consent.[271]

Other specified conditions apply specifically to service providers, to public authorities or to private clubs. Only one of these, however, relates unequivocally to a failure to make a reasonable adjustment as well as to less favourable treatment. This concerns a failure by a public authority to make a reasonable adjustment. It justifies such a failure if the authority can demonstrate that it reasonably believed a refusal to make the adjustment in favour of a disabled person was necessary in order to protect the rights and freedoms of others.[272]

This justification defence thus consists of two elements. The first—a demonstration of a belief in the existence of one or more of the specified conditions—is entirely subjective in nature. The second—a demonstration that that belief was reasonably held—is objective. It concerns, not the reasonableness of the belief itself, but the reasonableness of the holding of that belief by the particular service provider in the particular circumstances of the case. This test was intended to be more lenient than the 'material and substantial' defence, originally laid down for

---

[268] DDA s 20(3), s 21D(3) and s 21G(2).
[269] DDA s 20(9).
[270] DDA s 20(4)(a), s 21D(4)(a), s 21G(3)(a); and the Disability Discrimination (Private Clubs etc) Regulations 2005 (SI 2005/3258) reg 13(2)(a).
[271] DDA s 20(4)(b), s 21D(4)(b), s 21G(3)(b); and the Disability Discrimination (Private Clubs etc) Regulations 2005 (SI 2005/3258) reg 13(2)(b).
[272] DDA s 21D(4)(d).

employment and education, in recognition of the more transient nature of the relationship between service providers and their customers and the associated need for quick decisions.[273]

It therefore appears that, in this context, the threshold of the justification defence is set much lower than is the threshold of the reasonableness of an adjustment. This would appear to raise similar difficulties to those identified in *Collins v Royal National Theatre*.[274] A safety concern, for instance, may be considered insufficient to render it unreasonable to take a particular step and yet be strong enough to found a justification defence for failing to make that very reasonable adjustment. Although it is tempting to extend the *Collins* approach to this form of justification defence, the possible impact of significant differences in the statutory language used in the two forms of justification defence should not be overlooked.

The 'specific belief' justification defence, unlike the 'material and substantial' justification defence, operates only in relation to three specific considerations: health and safety; lack of capacity to contract or consent; and, in relation to public authorities, the rights and freedoms of others. These considerations, particularly the first and last, would seem to be highly relevant to any assessment of the reasonableness of an adjustment. Applying *Collins*, however, would mean that if they were indeed so regarded, they could not be considered again at the justification stage. The specificity of the opinion-based justification defence may present additional obstacles for such an interpretation in this context.

As has already been suggested, this justification defence, as applied to a failure to make a reasonable adjustment, is liable to cause confusion. It is difficult to conceive of any realistic situation in which such a defence could be relied upon to good effect and, interestingly, the Code does not provide any. In any workable system of reasonable adjustments, it is suggested, there is no place for this justification defence for a failure to make a reasonable adjustment. The concept of 'reasonableness' itself should determine liability. Encouragingly, the Government has now decided to abandon the Discrimination Law Review's proposal to replace this justification defence with an objective one (based on the notion of a proportionate means of achieving a legitimate aim) in favour of abolishing it altogether.[275]

3.5.4 The Objective Justification Defence

An additional form of justification defence was inserted into the DDA by the DDA 2005 to apply specifically to public authorities. Under the new section 21D(5), a public authority will be able to justify a failure to make a reasonable

---

[273] Hansard, 18 July 1995, HL Debates, vol 566, col 119.

[274] *Collins v Royal National Theatre* [2004] EWCA Civ 144.

[275] Department for Communities and Local Government, *Discrimination Law Review* (n 184 above) para 1.52; and Government Equalities Office, *The Equality Bill* (n 142 above) para 11.29–11.30.

adjustment if it can show that doing so was a proportionate means of achieving a legitimate aim. In order to establish this, it must be demonstrated that:

there is a pressing policy need that supports the aim which the treatment is designed to achieve, and it is therefore a 'legitimate' aim; and

the authority's action is causally related to achieving that aim; and

there was no other way to achieve the aim that had a less detrimental impact on the rights of disabled people.[276]

There is undoubtedly a need to protect public authorities from liability in such circumstances. Nevertheless, the required degree of protection would also appear to be achieved by reliance on the notion of reasonableness which lies at the very heart of reasonable adjustment duties.

3.6   Enforcement

With the exception of disputes relating to pre-16 education, DDA cases which do not concern employment are heard, in the first instance, by county courts in England and Wales and sheriff courts in Scotland. Consequently, cases tend to be more expensive and subject to longer delays than those brought before Employment Tribunals.[277] Factors such as these may help to explain why so few DDA goods and services cases have emerged.[278] Concern has also been expressed as to the relative unfamiliarity of the judges in county and sheriff courts with discrimination law concepts and principles.[279] Those sitting in Employment Tribunals are likely to have had a much greater exposure to discrimination law, as the vast majority of discrimination cases are brought in the employment context. Consequently, it has been suggested that non-employment DDA cases (together with equivalent cases under other non-discrimination legislation) should be heard by Employment or 'Equality' Tribunals instead of county and sheriff courts.[280]

---

[276] DRC, *DDA 1995 Code of Practice: Rights of Access—Services to the Public, Public Authority Functions, Private Clubs and Premises* (n 144 above) para 11.56.

[277] See eg N Meagre et al, *Monitoring the Disability Discrimination Act 1995* (London, Department for Education and Employment, 1999) para 7.5; Hepple, Coussey and Choudhury, *Equality: A New Framework* (n 141 above) paras 4.12–4.17; and Royal National Institute of the Blind, *The Price of Justice* (London, RNIB, 2000).

[278] Leverton, *Monitoring the Disability Discrimination Act 1995 (Phase 2)* (n 95 above) 140–41.

[279] See eg DRC, *Disability Equality: Making it Happen* (n 65 above) para 18.

[280] *Ibid.* See also Hepple, Coussey and Choudhury, *Equality: A New Framework* (n 141 above) recommendation 41.

This proposal was rejected by the Discrimination Law Review on the ground that it would overburden Employment Tribunals and create jurisdictional difficulties.[281] It was also rejected by the Government in its response to the Discrimination Law review consultation process.[282] The Government, however, accepted the need to increase equality expertise within the county and sheriff courts and proposed that this should occur through expanded programmes for training judges in discrimination law and the increased use of expert assessors in relevant cases.[283] While such measures are likely to prove helpful, it is not obvious that they will go far enough. In particular, it is to be hoped that the narrow emphasis on training in 'discrimination law', which is evident in the Government's response, is not reflected in the training itself. An understanding of the relevant law is likely to be unhelpful unless accompanied by a broad awareness of underlying equality issues.

Finally, there is some concern as to the effectiveness of the remedies available to the county and sheriff courts. Although they have the power to grant injunctions (or interdicts) to require defendants to carry out reasonable adjustment obligations, in practice these remedies are used very rarely—emphasis being placed instead on the awarding of damages. Potential difficulties are associated with the need for such orders to be extremely specific in nature (which may make ordering the carrying out of physical alterations problematic), and for them to relate specifically to the conduct complained of (which may prevent the ordering of more general measures, such as disability equality training).[284]

These difficulties connected with remedies for breach of the goods and services provisions of the DDA may be contrasted with difficulties connected with the remedies for breach of equivalent provisions in the US Americans with Disabilities Act 1990. Under Title III of that Act, only injunctive relief is available in suits brought by private individuals.[285] The absence of a power to award damages to disabled claimants under this Title has been identified as a considerable weakness in the machinery of the Act and as a major disincentive to the bringing of relevant cases.[286]

---

[281] Department for Communities and Local Government, *Discrimination Law Review* (n 184 above) paras 7.23–7.24.

[282] Government Equalities Office, *The Equality Bill* (n 142 above) paras 6.66–6.74.

[283] *Ibid*, paras 6.88–6.90.

[284] DRC, *Initial Submission to the Discrimination Law Review* (n 208 above) para 2.3.2.

[285] Americans with Disabilities Act 1990, 42 USC s 12188(a)(2). Under 42 USC s 12188(b), however, fines may be imposed in cases brought by the Attorney-General.

[286] See eg R Colker, 'ADA Title III: A Fragile Compromise' in L Pickering Francis and A Silvers (eds), *Americans with Disabilities: Exploring Implications of the Law for Individuals and Institutions* (New York, Routledge, 2000).

3.7 Summary

It would be surprising if the overriding impression left by this discussion of anticipatory reasonable adjustment duties were not one of complexity and confusion. Although section 21 provides a template, there are many departures from it. An already complex statutory scheme is still further complicated by the existence of a variety of justification defences for failures to make reasonable adjustments—defences which, it has been argued, are unnecessary and unhelpful.

Nevertheless, it must be remembered that out of the morass of these statutory provisions has arisen a reasonable adjustment duty unlike any other. It has been moulded by statutory codes of practice and by Court of Appeal judgments. Its distinctiveness lies in its group dimension and in its anticipatory nature. These characteristics will receive further attention in the next chapter when this anticipatory duty is compared with the concept, more familiar to British equality lawyers, of indirect discrimination.

The significance of the anticipatory group-based nature of this reasonable adjustment duty cannot be over-stated. It stands in marked contrast with a tendency, evident in connection with the employment provisions of both the DDA and the US Americans with Disabilities Act, to regard the concept of reasonable adjustment or accommodation as entailing an entirely individualised process. Although the identification of individual solutions is clearly important, there is a risk that an exclusive focus on it will obscure the underlying group dimension of the exclusionary barriers concerned. This, according to Professors Stein and Waterstone, has had the result that in the United States reasonable accommodation claims have developed as 'the antithesis of collective action'.[287]

4. Duties Not To Withhold Consent Unreasonably to the Making Of Adjustments

Reference has already been made to the various situations in which the DDA overrides the terms of leases in order to facilitate the execution of access-related physical alterations to rented premises. In such circumstances, landlords are prohibited from withholding their consent unreasonably to the making of such alterations but are permitted to attach reasonable conditions to the granting of

---

[287] MA Stein and ME Waterstone, 'Disability, Disparate Impact and Class Actions' (2006) 56 *Duke Law Journal* 861 at 879. See also A Asch, 'Critical Race Theory, Feminism, and Disability: Reflections on Social Justice and Personal Identity' (2001) 62 *Ohio State Law Journal* 391; M Kelman, 'Does Disability Status Matter?' in Pickering Francis and Silvers (eds), *Americans with Disabilities* (n 287 above); S Day and G Brodsky, 'The Duty to Accommodate: Who will Benefit?' (1996) 75 *Canadian Bar Review* 433 at 462; and L Waddington and A Hendriks, 'The Expanding Concept of Employment Discrimination in Europe: From Direct and Indirect Discrimination to Reasonable Accommodation Discrimination' (2002) 18 *International Journal of Comparative Labour Law and Industrial Relations* 403 at 415–17.

consent. These obligations not to withhold consent unreasonably to the making of physical alterations fall into two main categories. The first concerns cases in which the tenant wishing to carry out the improvements is an employer, a service provider or a post-16 educational establishment, attempting to discharge their own responsibilities to make reasonable adjustments under the DDA. The second category concerns cases in which the property in question is residential and the tenant needs to make a physical alteration because they are, or a member of their household is, disabled and experiencing difficulty in accessing their home.

Neither of these forms of duty is a reasonable adjustment duty as such. Their relationship with reasonable adjustments, however, is sufficiently close to entitle them to some coverage here. The duty which operates in the non-residential sector facilitates others in the execution of reasonable adjustments. The duty which operates in the residential sector shares the same policy goal as that of reasonable adjustment duties. Like them, its concern is to promote the independence of disabled people and their inclusion and participation in the life of mainstream society. Further, like reasonable adjustment duties, these consent-based duties are essentially obligations to do what is reasonable in order to facilitate the removal of unnecessary barriers in the way of disabled people.

Non-residential consent-based duties were included in the DDA from the outset. Guidance as to the meaning of reasonableness for the purposes of these duties is now to be found in the various Codes of Practice as well as in Regulations issued under the Act. According to this, although it will not be reasonable to refuse to consent to an alteration on the grounds of a trivial or arbitrary reason, it may be reasonable to do so if the alteration is likely to result in a permanent and substantial reduction in the value of the property or if it is likely to cause significant disruption or inconvenience to other tenants.[288] Examples of conditions which may be regarded as reasonable for landlords to attach to the granting of consent include permitting the landlord a reasonable opportunity to inspect the work; reimbursing any reasonable expenses incurred by the landlord in connection with the granting of consent; and, where it would otherwise have been reasonable to withhold consent, requiring the premises to be reinstated to their original condition at the end of the lease.[289] Further, landlords will be taken to have withheld consent if they fail to reply to relevant requests within a specified time or to attempt to obtain any necessary consents from other parties

---

[288] DRC, *DDA 1995 Code of Practice: Employment and Occupation* (n 24 above) paras 12.22 and 12.23; and DRC, *DDA 1995 Code of Practice: Rights of Access—Services to the Public, Public Authority Functions, Private Clubs and Premises* (n 144 above) Appendix B paras 45 and 46.

[289] Disability Discrimination (Employment Field) (Leasehold Premises) Regulations 2004 (SI 2004/153) reg 7. See also Disability Discrimination (Educational Institutions) (Alteration of Lease-hold Premises) Regulations 2005 (SI 2005/1070) reg 6; and Disability Discrimination (Providers of Services) (Adjustment of Premises) Regulations 2001 (SI 2001/3253) reg 8—but note that the reinstatement example is not included in these last two sets of regulations.

in a prompt and effective manner.[290] While landlords of service providers (including providers of post-16 education) may be challenged directly for unreasonably withholding consent or making it subject to unreasonable conditions, landlords of employers may be challenged only if they are joined as parties in disability discrimination proceedings brought against their tenants.

The residential consent-based duty was introduced into the DDA by the DDA 2005.[291] Under the new section 24D,[292] landlords are likely to have to adjust terms prohibiting the making of alterations so as to permit those required by a disabled person in order to facilitate access.

The new section 49G applies to leases (other than protected and statutory tenancies which are covered by the Housing Act 1980 and secure tenancies which are covered by the Housing Act 1985) which allow physical alterations subject to the landlord's consent.[293] It requires that consent not to be unreasonably withheld but permits it to be granted subject to reasonable conditions. The Housing Acts imply similar provisions into protected, statutory and secure tenancies.

The factors identified in the Housing Acts as potentially relevant to the reasonableness of withholding consent to a proposed alteration are the likely impact of the alteration on the safety of occupiers, on the expenditure of the landlord and on the value of the property or the rent which may be charged for it. Although no such factors are identified explicitly in the DDA, the DDA Part 3 Code suggests that the same considerations are likely to prove relevant in assessments of reasonableness under section 49G.[294] The Code also lists the following additional factors, which may be relevant for the purposes of both section 49G and the Housing Acts[295]:

consent;

the ability of the tenant to pay for the improvement;

the scale of the proposed adaptations;

---

[290] In relation to service providers and educational establishments, the period is 42 days—(SI 2001/3253) reg 5 and (SI 2005/1070) reg 3 respectively. In relation to employers, the period is 21 days—(SI 2004/153) reg 4.

[291] Following the recommendations of the Disability Rights Task Force, *From Exclusion to Inclusion* (n 4 above) recommendations 6.27 and 6.28; and the report of the Parliamentary Joint Committee on the Draft Disability Discrimination Bill (London, Stationery Office, 2004) ch 8. Slightly different provisions apply in Scotland, although they are to the same effect. The present discussion is confined to the law applying in England and Wales. See generally A Lawson, 'Landlords, Disabled Tenants and the Rising Tide of Equality Law' in M Dixon and G Griffiths (eds), *Contemporary Perspectives on Property, Equity and Trusts Law* (Oxford, Oxford University Press, 2007).

[292] Supplemented by the Disability Discrimination (Premises) Regulations 2006 (SI 2006/887) reg 7.

[293] The Landlord and Tenant Act 1927 s 19(2) also performs this function but, for various reasons, was not relied on by disabled tenants. Because its operation is not excluded by s 49G, there is an overlap between the two sections.

[294] DRC, *DDA 1995 Code of Practice: Rights of Access—Services to the Public, Public Authority Functions, Private Clubs and Premises* (n 144 above) para 18.24.

[295] According to para 18.37, these factors would also be relevant to cases brought by disabled people under the Landlord and Tenant Act 1927.

the feasibility of the works;

the length of the term remaining under the letting;

the nature of the tenancy (eg the type and length);

the nature of the premises (eg their type, design, age and quality);

the extent of any disruption and the effect on other occupiers of adjoining premises;

the effect of, and compliance with, planning and Building Regulations requirements; and

the desirability or practicability of reinstatement of the premises at the end of the lease.[296]

It stresses that landlords must give 'due weight', in particular, to the needs of the disabled person in question.[297] On the issue of conditions that are likely to be reasonable to attach to the granting of consent, the Code gives similar examples to those provided in the non-residential context. In relation to re-instatement, however, it suggests that it is likely to require this only if the alteration would substantially reduce the value of the property.[298]

The addition of this consent-based duty and the elaboration of it (together with the analogous duties imposed by mainstream property law statutes) in the Code of Practice is extremely welcome. It should go some way towards removing the barriers which thousands of disabled tenants have traditionally encountered in making their homes more useable and accessible. Some indication of the size of the problem is provided by the English Housing Survey 2001–2002, according to which nine per cent of disabled tenants (some 18,000 people) were living in unsuitable, inaccessible conditions because their landlords had refused to allow them to make physical adaptations to their homes.[299] Nevertheless, the duty as currently framed does not go far enough. It extends only to the premises included in the letting and does not therefore extend to communal areas or external approaches. The consequent difficulties are well illustrated by the case of *Williams v Richmond Court.*[300]

Mrs Williams was 81 and had mobility impairments. She was the tenant of a third floor flat and wished to install a stair-lift, at her own expense, in order to facilitate access to her home. The landlord refused to grant consent to this because of a contrary vote by the other tenants and the inconvenience it would cause them, because it would not be aesthetically pleasing and because of the potential cost of repair. The Court of Appeal held that this refusal did not

---

[296] DRC, *DDA 1995 Code of Practice: Rights of Access—Services to the Public, Public Authority Functions, Private Clubs and Premises* (n 144 above) para 18.25.

[297] *Ibid*, para 18.22.

[298] *Ibid*, paras 18.28 and 18.29.

[299] Office of the Deputy Prime Minister, *Housing in England 2001/2: A Report on the 2001/02 Survey of English Housing* (London, Stationery Office, 2003). See also report of the Parliamentary Joint Committee on the Draft Disability Discrimination Bill 2003 (n 291 above) para 313.

[300] *Williams v Richmond Court* [2006] EWCA Civ 1719 (discussed in S Murdoch, 'A Stairlift Fraught with Problems' [2007] *Estates Gazette* 201).

contravene the DDA because the Act imposed no obligation on landlords either to make reasonable adjustments or to refrain from withholding consent unreasonably in relation to the physical features of the common parts of buildings.

The omission of common parts from the DDA 2005 was criticised by the Joint Committee on the draft Disability Discrimination Bill.[301] Reference was made in Parliament to the illogicality of the current position (which forbids the unreasonable refusal of consent to disability-related alterations if they happen to be needed inside the home but not if they are needed in order to reach it) as well as to its injustice. Lord Morris observed that,

> a totally accessible flat may be of little use to a person who needs to but cannot negotiate even a short flight of steps to enter it.[302]

The Government refused to amend the Bill[303] but accepted the need for action and set up the Review Group on Common Parts to review the problem and recommend possible reforms.[304]

The Review Group published its report on 23 December 2005.[305] It recommended that the Government should, without delay, introduce non-legislative measures to provide clarity and assistance to those involved in relevant disputes. These recommendations were received favourably and have been largely implemented.[306] The Review Group also recommended that the Government should consult further on the appropriateness of extending a duty, similar to that imposed by section 49G of the DDA, to the common parts of let premises.[307] Chapter 13 of the Discrimination Law Review sets out such proposals. These would extend obligations, analogous to those currently applying only to let premises, to common parts, and are therefore to be warmly welcomed.[308]

In cases which are currently covered by the legislation, if a landlord withholds consent unreasonably or grants it subject to unreasonable conditions, the tenant will be entitled to proceed as if consent had been given. However, because of uncertainty as to what a court may consider reasonable in a particular case, tenants would be well advised to obtain a judicial declaration of the landlord's

---

[301] *Report of the Parliamentary Joint Committee on the Draft Disability Discrimination Bill* (n 291 above) paras 322–5.

[302] Hansard, 20 February 2005, HL Debates, col 314.

[303] Department for Work and Pensions, *The Government's Response to the Report of the Joint Committee on the Draft Disability Discrimination Bill* (London, Stationery Office, 2004) response 57.

[304] See eg House of Lords, Hansard, 20 January 2005, col 320 (Baroness Hollis, echoing earlier sentiments expressed by Lord Rooker in debates on the Housing Bill (House of Commons, Hansard, 3 November 2004, col 370)).

[305] *A Review of the Current Position in Relation to Adjustments to the Common Parts of Let Residential Premises and Recommendations for Change* (London, Department for Work and Pensions, 2005).

[306] Hansard, 13 July 2006, cols 79WS–80WS (Ann McGuire (Minister for Disabled People)).

[307] *A Review of the Current Position in Relation to Adjustments to the Common Parts of Let Residential Premises and Recommendations for Change* (n 305 above) ch 6.

[308] See also Government Equalities Office, *The Equality Bill* (n 142 above) paras 11.60–11.70 where commitment to these proposals is reaffirmed.

unreasonableness before altering the property. Further, such disputes may be referred to the Equality and Human Rights Commission for conciliation, regardless of whether they arose under section 49G[309] or the Housing Acts.[310]

5. Conclusion

In conclusion, the DDA sets out an extremely complex scheme to regulate reasonable adjustment duties. It is a scheme which dates back to the early days of the Act but to which additions and alterations have been made, on a somewhat ad hoc basis, over the intervening years. Accordingly, while its coverage is now reasonably comprehensive, its navigability is impeded by a daunting level of intricacy and inconsistency.

In line with its objectives of simplifying and harmonising equality legislation, the Government (both in the Discrimination Law Review and in its response to the consultation which followed it) has made a number of recommendations which would reduce the complexity currently surrounding reasonable adjustments. Particularly welcome are the proposals that all reasonable adjustment duties should be subject to the single trigger of 'substantial disadvantage' and that all the justification defences for failures to make reasonable adjustments should be removed.

An analysis of the bare statutory language of British reasonable adjustments may not therefore be very inspiring. Despite their relatively unpromising legislative base, however, the duties have acquired a surprising energy and vibrancy. This has been breathed into them by the statutory codes of practice which accompany the DDA and also by a number of powerful appellate decisions. The decision of the House of Lords in *Archibald v Fife Council*[311] and of the Court of Appeal in *Roads v Central Trains*[312] are particularly worthy of note in this regard.

One of the most innovative aspects of British reasonable adjustment law has been the development of the notion of a group-based anticipatory duty. Regrettably, however, this does not currently operate in the employment sphere. Reasonable adjustment duties do not therefore oblige employers to anticipate and to take steps to remove or reduce disabling barriers. This is a great pity.

The addition of an anticipatory element to the employment reasonable adjustment duties would significantly enhance British equality law. It would require employers to take access issues into account when making relevant plans and decisions, whether or not they currently had any disabled employees. It might thus require thought to be given to accessibility issues in the context of decisions as to which new intranet system should be purchased. The installation

---

[309] Or, indeed, s 19(2) of the Landlord and Tenant Act 1927.
[310] DDA s 49H(1).
[311] *Archibald v Fife Council* [2004] UKHL 32, [2004] IRLR 197.
[312] *Roads v Central Trains* [2004] EWCA Civ 1540.

of an accessible system might then make a significant difference to the career prospects of a future visually impaired employee. Similarly, such an anticipatory duty might require consideration to be given to the needs of people with mobility impairments, in decisions relating to the purchase of new premises, even though there were currently no employees with such impairments. It would, in other words, require employers to take a much more pro-active role to the question of disability and oblige them to take reasonable steps to ensure that disabling environments are not created from the outset.

The possibility of extending anticipatory reasonable adjustment duties into the employment context was not considered by the Discrimination Law Review. Indeed, its Consultation Paper makes no mention at all of the concept of anticipatory reasonable adjustment. Given the centrality of this concept to the DDA, its neglect by the Discrimination Law Review is distinctly alarming.

Reassuringly, the Government's response to the Discrimination Law Review did acknowledge the existence of anticipatory reasonable adjustment duties.[313] It also acknowledged the existence of pressure, from some quarters, to extend these duties into the employment arena. Unfortunately, however, it rejected such an extension on the ground that the employment relationship is generally a long-term one in which it is particularly important that adjustments should be tailored to the specific circumstances of the individual disabled person. Accordingly, in its view:

> There is a risk that introducing a legal anticipatory requirement could lead employers to spend money on adjustments which turned out to be unsuited to disabled people they subsequently employed. And having spent money on these anticipatory measures, they might have insufficient remaining resources to make adequate individual adjustments.[314]

This argument, however, overlooks the role of the concept of 'reasonableness' in limiting the extent of any additional investment which such duties would require of employers. It also overlooks the considerable reduction in the costs of making adjustments for a particular individual which are likely to be encountered in many cases where the general environment has been designed from the outset with accessibility in mind.

Public sector employers, as will be explained in chapter five, now have a positive duty to promote disability equality. This will require them to adopt the type of pro-active approach outlined above. Its existence, however, does not remove the need to extend the anticipatory element of reasonable adjustment duties to employment. The disability equality duty does not apply to private sector employers. Neither does it allow individuals to sue for discrimination if a relevant body fails to take reasonable steps to anticipate and remove disabling barriers.

---

[313] Government Equalities Office, *The Equality Bill* (n 142 above) paras 11.48–11.50.
[314] *Ibid*, para 11.50.

A group-based anticipatory element should therefore be added to employment reasonable adjustment duties. Care should be taken, however, to ensure that this operates as a genuine addition to the current reactive duties and not as a substitution for them. The current anticipatory duties appear to require group disadvantage to be established in all cases, regardless of the degree of disadvantage which might be experienced by the individual claimant. Room must be left in the employment context, and also in that of education, for reasonable adjustment duties to be triggered on a purely individual and reactive basis in circumstances where the demonstration of group disadvantage might be problematic.

In sum, the DDA reasonable adjustment duties have existed for little more than a decade. They have nevertheless already taken a form which is distinctive and original. Not only do they occupy a unique position within British equality law but they also appear to do so within the broader setting of reasonable accommodation law internationally.

The relative newness and uniqueness of British reasonable adjustment duties has inevitably resulted in some confusion as to how they should be positioned within the broader framework of equality and non-discrimination law. The next two chapters will therefore be devoted to a more detailed analysis of the relationship between reasonable adjustment duties and other concepts at work in the field of equality and non-discrimination. In the next chapter, attention will focus on the relationship between reasonable adjustment and other concepts of non-discrimination. Its relationship with concepts based on the notion of positive action will then be explored in chapter five. It will be suggested that, although reasonable adjustment duties have much in common with concepts falling into the latter category, they belong firmly in the category of non-discrimination measures.

4

Reasonable Adjustment and Non-Discrimination Measures

1. Introduction

I N THE PREVIOUS chapter, the way in which British non-discrimination law has structured the concept of reasonable adjustment was outlined. In this chapter, the nature of that concept and the role it is intended to play will be further examined. The focus here will be on the relationship between the notion of reasonable adjustment and other concepts which provide the basis for discrimination claims in Britain. Although victimisation also clearly features amongst such concepts, it will not be considered here, as an analysis of it promises to throw little light on the issue of reasonable adjustment. Neither will the relationship between reasonable adjustment and other equality concepts concerned with positive action and positive duties be considered here. That will instead be explored at length in the next chapter.

The concepts selected for discussion here are disability-related discrimination, direct discrimination and indirect discrimination. The first two of these operate, alongside reasonable adjustment, within the DDA. It is therefore important to understand the extent to which they overlap with reasonable adjustment obligations and the nature of their co-existence. Indirect discrimination, on the other hand, does not appear in the DDA. Nevertheless, it occupies a prominent place both in the Employment Equality Directive and also in virtually all other British non-discrimination law. An explanation often provided for its absence from the DDA is that much of its function is performed by the concept of reasonable adjustment. Clearly, therefore, an understanding of the relationship between reasonable adjustment and indirect discrimination is important, despite the fact that the two concepts currently operate in separate spheres.

Section 2 below will explore the concept which has become known as 'disability-related discrimination'.[1] This form of discrimination will be addressed

---

[1] The use of this term has become widespread since its appearance in DRC, *DDA 1995 Code of Practice: Employment and Occupation* (London, Stationery Office, 2004) where it is explained at para 4.28.

first because, like the reasonable adjustment duty, it appeared in the DDA as it was originally enacted and, at least until recently, has played a pivotal role in disability non-discrimination law. The concept of direct discrimination, which was added to the DDA in 2004, will then be considered in Section 3. The concept of indirect discrimination will form the subject-matter of Section 4. In Section 5, attention will be turned to the question of whether reactive reasonable adjustment duties operate, or should operate, in the context of equality strands other than disability. Finally, in Section 6, the way in which reasonable adjustment claims are categorised as a form of freestanding non-discrimination measure will be considered.

2. Disability-Related Discrimination

2.1 Outline of the Concept

2.1.1 Overview

According to s 3A(1) of the DDA:

> For the purposes of this Part, a person discriminates against a disabled person if—
>
> (a) for a reason which relates to the disabled person's disability, he treats him less favourably than he treats or would treat others to whom that reason does not or would not apply, and
> (b) he cannot show that the treatment in question is justified.

Identical provisions appear in the non-employment parts of the Act with the result that this form of discrimination appears in all areas to which the DDA applies.[2] Importantly, however, the way in which the associated justification defence operates differs markedly in different parts of the Act. These differences appear to provide at least a partial explanation of the House of Lords decision in the housing case of *Lewisham London Borough Council v Malcolm*[3] to overturn the previous well-established understanding of disability-related discrimination—an understanding largely derived from employment cases. As will be seen, the effect of *Lewisham* is drastically to restrict and indeed to emasculate this form of liability for disability discrimination.

Disability-related discrimination is based on the establishment of three key elements: First, there must have been less favourable treatment; second, the reason for that treatment must have been related to the disabled person's

---

[2] For goods, facilities and services, in s 20(1); for premises, in s 24(1); for pre-16 education, in s 28B(1); for post-16 education, in s 28S(1); for public authorities, in s 21D(1); for private clubs, in s 21G(1); and for general qualifications bodies, in s 31AB(1).

[3] *Lewisham LBC v Malcolm* [2008] UKHL 43.

disability; and, third, there must have been no justification for that treatment. These three elements will now be considered in turn.

2.1.2 Less Favourable Treatment

The starting-point for any analysis of this issue is the decision of the Court of Appeal in *Clark v Novacold*.[4] This case concerned the dismissal of Mr Clark from his employment in a company which dealt with the storage and processing of frozen foods. Mr Clark's job had been a manual one and was physically demanding. Following an injury at work, Mr Clark became disabled within the meaning of the DDA and was unable to return to work for a considerable length of time. He was dismissed some five months after the accident because his absence was likely to continue for a year.

In the Court of Appeal, Mummery LJ acknowledged that the language of what is now section 3A(1) was ambiguous. Its requirement for the defendant to have treated the disabled person 'less favourably than he treats or would treat others to whom that reason does not or would not apply' could be interpreted in two ways. First, it might be construed so as to require the disabled person's treatment to be compared with the treatment which would have been received by a person who was not disabled but was otherwise similarly situated. On this view, the treatment of Mr Clark should have been compared with the treatment of a non-disabled person who had been off work for the same length of time as he had been. Such a person would also have been dismissed, and therefore, on this understanding, there would have been no less favourable treatment and consequently no disability-related discrimination.

This first possible construction of the less favourable treatment requirement was rejected by the Court of Appeal in *Novacold* in favour of the second and wider construction. According to this, the correct comparator was a person to whom the reason for the relevant treatment did not apply. The reason for Mr Clark's dismissal had been his lengthy absence from work. The essential question was therefore whether he had been treated less favourably than a person who had not had a lengthy absence from work would have been treated. A person who had not taken time off would not have been dismissed and, accordingly, Mr Clark had clearly been treated less favourably than such a person.

This second approach is considerably more expansive than the first. In favouring it, Mummery LJ claimed to be having regard to the 'context' of the ambiguous language and to the 'aim' of the statute.[5] He pointed out that, although the first approach would have been more consistent with the methods of comparator selection used in relation to direct discrimination under the Sex Discrimination Act 1975 (SDA) and the Race Relations Act 1976 (RRA), the DDA differed from those statutes in two significant respects. First, unlike them, the

---

[4] *Clark v Novacold* [1999] IRLR 318 (CA).
[5] *Ibid*, [29]–[34].

DDA did not specify that comparison must be made between the claimant and a person who fell outside the relevant group but who was otherwise in circumstances which were the same as, or not materially different from, those of the claimant. Secondly, unlike the direct discrimination parts of those Acts, the DDA's disability-related provisions contained a broad justification defence. Mummery LJ was also influenced by the observation of the Minister for Social Security and Disabled People, during the passage of the DDA, that this notion of disability-related discrimination was intended to cover indirect as well as direct discrimination and that it would consequently make it unlawful for a service provider to apply, without justification, a 'no dogs' rule to prevent a blind person entering a café with a guide dog.[6] Only the second of the two possible interpretations of the statutory language would allow instances of indirect discrimination, such as the application of a 'no dogs' rule to guide dog owners, to fall within the embrace of disability-related discrimination.

Thus, under the *Novacold* approach, it was relatively easy for claimants to establish less favourable treatment—much easier than it has conventionally been in the context of direct discrimination. As Mummery LJ recognised,[7] this approach has the effect of shifting the focus of contention in the bulk of disability-related discrimination cases from the issue of less favourable treatment to that of justification. As was recognised by their Lordships in *Lewisham*,[8] it also increases the significance of the question of whether the less favourable treatment concerned was for a reason related to the disabled person's disability.

The *Novacold* construction of less favourable treatment reigned unchallenged for nearly a decade until, on 25 June 2008, it was overthrown by the House of Lords in *Lewisham*.[9] Their Lordships were there faced with the distinctly unsympathetic claim of Mr Malcolm that the attempt by Lewisham LBC to evict him from his rented council flat amounted to disability-related discrimination. The Council had commenced possession proceedings because Mr Malcolm had sub-let and moved out of the property—conduct which was in breach of the terms of his lease and which caused him to lose his security of tenure.[10] Mr Malcolm, however, claimed that he was being treated less favourably for a reason which related to his disability, because his schizophrenia had caused him to sub-let his flat by rendering him unable to understand the consequences of his actions. Although his claim succeeded in the Court of Appeal, it failed in the House of Lords.

Under the *Novacold* approach, the treatment received by Mr Malcolm would have had to be compared with the treatment of a person who did not have schizophrenia and who would not therefore have sub-let his flat. The Council

---

[6] Hansard, 24 January 1995, HC Debates, col 150.
[7] *Clark v Novacold* [1999] IRLR 318 (CA) [95].
[8] *Lewisham LBC v Malcolm* [2008] UKHL 43, [82] (Baroness Hale) and [149] (Lord Neuberger).
[9] *Lewisham LBC v Malcolm* [2008] UKHL 43.
[10] Housing Act 1985 ss 79(1), 81 and 93(2).

would clearly not have attempted to evict such a comparator and less favourable treatment would therefore have been established. Lords Bingham, Scott, Brown and Neuberger rejected this approach. Instead, they adopted the first and much narrower of the two constructions considered in *Novacold*. According to this, the treatment received by Mr Malcolm must be compared with the treatment that would have been received by a person who had sub-let their flat despite the fact that they had no mental illness. The Council would have treated such a comparator in exactly the same way as it had treated Mr Malcolm, and his treatment could not therefore be classified as less favourable. Their Lordships' decision to overturn *Novacold* appears to have been grounded on two principal reasons.

First, considerable emphasis was placed on the fact that the interpretation favoured in *Lewisham* gave rise to a 'more natural',[11] 'commonsense'[12] and 'meaningful'[13] comparison than that required by the *Novacold* approach. Attention was also drawn to the 'pointlessness'[14] of the comparative exercise required by *Novacold*. In the words of Lord Scott,

> [w]hat is the point of asking whether a person has been treated 'less favourably than others' if the 'others' are those to whom the reason why the disabled person was subjected to the complained of treatment cannot apply? If a person has been dismissed because he is incapable of doing his job, what is the point of making the lawfulness of his dismissal depend on whether those who are capable of doing their job would have been dismissed? If a person has been dismissed because he will be absent from work for a year, what is the point of making the lawfulness of his dismissal dependant on whether those who will not be absent from work will be dismissed? If a tenant has been given notice terminating his tenancy because he has sub-let in breach of the tenancy agreement, what is the point of making the lawfulness of the action taken by his landlord dependant on whether notice to quit would have been served on tenants who had not sub-let? Parliament must surely have intended the comparison ... to be a meaningful comparison in order to distinguish between treatment that was discriminatory and treatment that was not.[15]

Second, the potential injustice which might result from the *Novacold* construction also appears to have been influential. This is particularly evident from the judgment of Lord Neuberger. He described its impact on landlords and others as 'somewhat startling',[16] potentially 'highly invasive',[17] 'extraordinary and positively penal'.[18] It should be noted, however, that the establishment of less favourable treatment is only one element of disability-related discrimination and that the

---

[11] *Lewisham LBC v Malcolm* [2008] UKHL 43, [15] (Lord Bingham) and [139] (Lord Neuberger).
[12] *Ibid*, [30] and [31] (Lord Scott).
[13] *Ibid*, [32] (Lord Scott) and [113] (Lord Brown).
[14] *Ibid*, [14] (Lord Bingham), [33] (Lord Scott), [112] (Lord Brown) and [158] (Lord Neuberger).
[15] *Ibid*, [32].
[16] *Ibid*, [142].
[17] *Ibid*, [143].
[18] *Ibid*, [148].

injustice about which Lord Neuberger was concerned would not have arisen had the relevant justification defence been differently drafted.

Their Lordships recognised that the effect of their ruling on this point would be to impose a severe constraint on the reach of the concept of disability-related discrimination.[19] It would mean, for instance, despite a rather confusing assertion to the contrary by Lord Scott,[20] that a blind person turned away from a restaurant because of his guide dog would probably no longer have been subjected to disability-related discrimination because he would not have been treated less favourably than a non-disabled person who attempted to enter with a dog. It would, in short, have the effect of dramatically reducing the scope of disability-related discrimination. The precise extent of this reduction, however, will depend upon how a question that was not directly addressed in *Lewisham* will be answered in future cases.

This question concerns the role to be played by reasonable adjustments in the comparative exercise. If the alleged discriminator was under a duty to make a reasonable adjustment in favour of the disabled person, should the effect of that adjustment on the circumstances of the disabled person (whether or not the adjustment was actually made) be factored into the comparative exercise? The issue may be illustrated by reference to a case in which a disabled employee is dismissed because of their slow typing speed despite the fact that their speed would have increased considerably had the employer fulfilled its obligation to provide them with an adapted keyboard by way of reasonable adjustment. Should the speed of the disabled person used in the comparison with the treatment of a non-disabled person be the slow speed they were able to achieve on the standard keyboard or should it be the faster speed which they would have attained had the reasonable adjustment been made?

If this question were answered so as to exclude the effect of unfulfilled reasonable adjustment obligations from the comparative exercise, the scope of disability-related discrimination would be confined to what has hitherto been the much narrower reach of direct discrimination.[21] Unlike the latter, however, disability-related discrimination is subject to a justification defence. This would restrict its sphere of operation still further. Accordingly, if this is the type of comparison required by *Lewisham*, it renders the notion of disability-related discrimination entirely redundant in those areas of the Act in which the concept of direct discrimination (which is not subject to a justification defence) operates. Outside those areas, disability-related discrimination will continue to have some relevance but is likely to be established only in very rare cases.

If, by contrast, the effect of required reasonable adjustments is factored into the comparative exercise then the shrinkage effected by *Lewisham* will be less devastating. Although less favourable treatment will be less easy to establish than

---

[19] See eg *ibid*, [15] (Lord Bingham), [114] (Lord Brown) and [141] (Lord Neuberger).
[20] *Ibid*, [35].
[21] A point explicitly recognised: *ibid*, [114] (Lord Brown).

it was under the *Novacold* approach, it will continue to be easier to establish it for the purposes of disability-related discrimination than for the purposes of direct discrimination.[22] The general tenor of the majority judgments in *Lewisham* suggests that it was not this construction that their Lordships had in mind. However, the question of reasonable adjustment was not relevant in that case and the adoption of this damage-limiting approach would therefore seem to be open to judges in future cases.

Given the potentially drastic scale of the *Lewisham* restrictions on disability-related discrimination, it is unsurprising that two of their Lordships expressed misgivings about their decision to overturn *Novacold*.[23] It enshrines an approach to comparators for disability cases which is reminiscent of the early tendency in pregnancy cases to compare pregnant women with sick men[24]—a tendency which was checked by the European Court of Justice and consequently abandoned.[25] Baroness Hale, who delivered a very powerful dissenting judgment, defended the wider construction adopted in *Novacold*. She accepted that, for the first of the reasons explained above,[26] this construction might appear to be a 'surprising' one because it did 'not fit with … normal assumptions about discrimination'.[27] Nevertheless, she insisted that on closer examination it was this construction which made the statute workable and which must have represented the intention of Parliament. She thus endorsed the reasoning of Mummery LJ in *Novacold* itself.[28]

In addition, Baroness Hale pointed out that, in the employment field, the *Novacold* approach appeared to have caused no difficulty in practice and that it represented 'the settled understanding of employment lawyers and tribunals'.[29] Further, it also appeared to represent the understanding of Parliament.[30] This was evident, not only from statements made prior to the enactment of the DDA, but also from the way in which the Employment Equality Directive[31] had been implemented. Under that Directive, as will be explained below,[32] Member States are required to prohibit direct discrimination against disabled people in the field of employment and occupation. Under the narrow construction of disability-related discrimination adopted in *Lewisham*, the direct discrimination demands of the Directive would have been satisfied by the simple abolition of the

---

[22] See section 3.1.2 below.
[23] *Lewisham LBC v Malcolm* [2008] UKHL 43, [16] (Lord Bingham) and [139] (Lord Neuberger).
[24] See eg *Hayes v Malleable Working Men's Club and Institute* [1985] ICR 703.
[25] Case C-177/88 *Dekker v Stichting Vorrningscentrum voor Jonge Volwassen (VJV-Centrum) Plus* [1990].
[26] See nn 11–15 above and accompanying text.
[27] *Lewisham LBC v Malcolm* [2008] UKHL 43, [71].
[28] See nn 5–6 above and accompanying text.
[29] *Lewisham LBC v Malcolm* [2008] UKHL 43, [81].
[30] *Ibid*, [73]–[81].
[31] Directive 2000/78/EC establishing a general framework for equal treatment in employment and occupation, [2000] OJ L 303/16.
[32] Section 3.1.1 below.

justification defence. Parliament, however, considered it necessary to introduce an entirely new form of discrimination with a differently worded comparator requirement.

The decision of the majority of their Lordships in *Lewisham* dealt the biggest judicial blow to the DDA that it has received since its enactment. Through its restrictive interpretation of the comparator requirement, it has reduced, almost to vanishing-point, a vital mechanism by which to oblige employers, service providers, landlords, public authorities and others to explain and to justify their unfavourable treatment of disabled people. Thankfully, as will be explained below, reasonable adjustment duties will continue to require such explanations to be given in many cases.[33] The impact of this annihilation of disability-related discrimination is nevertheless an issue which demands a high priority in the promised single equality legislation.[34]

2.1.3 A Reason Related to the Disabled Person's Disability

The requirement that the less favourable treatment be for 'a reason which relates to the disabled person's disability' raises a number of issues which have clustered around three main questions. The first of these concerns the meaning of a 'reason' in this context and the second concerns the extent to which such a reason requires the defendant to have knowledge of the disability in question. The third concerns the degree of connection which must be established between the reason for the treatment and the disability. These issues will now be discussed in turn.

Before attention can be turned to the question of whether a relevant reason is disability-related, it must be established that it was indeed a reason for the unfavourable treatment in question. The House of Lords affirmed, in *Lewisham*,[35] that this required the issue to be present in the mind of the defendant. In the words of Lord Bingham, courts must therefore ascertain 'the real reason for the treatment, the reason which operates on the mind of the alleged discriminator' which 'may not be the reason given' or 'the only reason'.[36] The reason for the treatment complained of in that case was generally regarded as being the fact that Mr Malcolm had sub-let and moved out of his flat.[37] Lord Bingham, however, expressed the reason in slightly broader terms, considering that

---

[33] Section 2.2 below.

[34] *Lewisham* was decided less than a month before the Government published its response to the consultation on the Discrimination Law Review. That document does not therefore include any relevant recommendations but it does state that the Government is giving serious consideration to the implications of *Lewisham*—Government Equalities Office, *The Equality Bill: Government Response to the Consultation* (London, Stationery Office, 21 July 2008) para 11.47.

[35] *Lewisham LBC v Malcolm* [2008] UKHL 43.

[36] *Ibid*, [9].

[37] *Ibid*, [26] (Lord Scott), [90] (Baroness Hale) and [149] (Lord Neuberger).

Lewisham, as a social landlord with a limited stock of housing and a heavy demand from those on its waiting list, acted as it did because it was not prepared to allow tenancies to continue where the tenant was not living in the premises demised.[38]

In accepting that a reason must be present in the mind of the defendant, the House of Lords in *Lewisham* adopted the approach of the Court of Appeal in *Taylor v OCS Group*.[39] That case concerned a deaf employee who had been dismissed for accessing the private correspondence of a colleague and who had been unable to participate effectively in the associated disciplinary process because the employer had not provided him with sign language support. The Court of Appeal held that, in order to establish this form of discrimination, a disability-related reason for the less favourable treatment must have been present in the mind of the employer.[40] Somewhat confusingly, it accepted that such a reason might be present either consciously or subconsciously.[41] In that case, however, it was found that no reason related to Mr Taylor's disability had been present in his employer's mind when the decision was made to dismiss him. Consequently, no disability-related discrimination could be established.

Taylor and *Lewisham* thus make it clear that a reason, for the purposes of disability-related discrimination, must have affected the mind of the defendant in a subjective (even if subconscious) manner. This then raises the question of whether, to be a reason 'related' to the disabled person's disability, the defendant must have been aware that the person in question was disabled and that the reason was related to their disability. This is another area in which *Lewisham* appears to have effected a significant narrowing of the previous approach.

Before *Lewisham*, despite some judicial criticism,[42] it was generally accepted that the link between the reason for the relevant treatment and the disability of the claimant was to be assessed objectively without reference to the defendant's knowledge. This point is clearly expressed in the Employment Code of Practice:

> The reason for any less favourable treatment may well relate to the disability even if the employer does not have knowledge of the disability as such, or of whether its salient features are such that it meets the definition of disability in the Act. Less favourable treatment which is not itself direct discrimination would still be unlawful (subject to justification) if, in fact, the reason for it related to the person's disability.[43]

---

[38] *Ibid*, [9].

[39] *Taylor v OCS Group* [2006] IRLR 613 (CA).

[40] *Ibid*, [72] (Smith LJ).

[41] *Ibid*. This view was approved in *S v Floyd and The Equality and Human Rights Commission* [2008] EWCA Civ 201, [57] (Mummery LJ); and *Lewisham LBC v Malcolm* [2008] UKHL 43, [37] (Lord Scott).

[42] See eg *Manchester CC v Romano* [2004] EWCA Civ 834 [121]–[122] (Brooke LJ). It should also be noted that, in the context of pre-16 education, s 28B(4) expressly provides that a person cannot be liable for disability-related discrimination unless they knew, or ought to have known, that the person concerned was disabled.

[43] DRC, *DDA 1995 Code of Practice: Employment and Occupation* (n 1 above) para 4.31.

Thus, in *Heinz Co Ltd v Kenrick*,[44] the claimant was dismissed because of his long period of absence from work due to ill health. It subsequently emerged that he had chronic fatigue syndrome and was disabled for the purposes of the DDA. It was not disputed that an employer's knowledge that an employee was disabled may have relevance to issues such as the justification defence for disability-related discrimination or liability to make reasonable adjustments. According to the Employment Appeal Tribunal, however, the employer's ignorance of the fact that the employee's ill health amounted to a disability at the time of the dismissal was irrelevant for the purposes of determining prima facie liability for disability-related discrimination. A reason might be disability-related even if the employer, and even the employee, were unaware of its connection with disability at the time of the less favourable treatment. In the words of Lindsay P,

> there is no language in section [3A(1)] that requires that the relationship between the disability and the treatment should be adjudged subjectively, through the eyes of the employer, so ... the applicable test should be the objective one of whether the relationship exists, not whether the employer knew of it. Indeed, unless the test is objective there will be difficulties with credible and honest yet ignorant or obtuse employers who fail to recognise or acknowledge the obvious.[45]

In *Lewisham*,[46] however, it was held that the knowledge of the defendant had a vital role to play in establishing that a reason was disability-related. Unless the defendant knew, or ought to have known, of the claimant's physical or mental impairment (though not necessarily that it amounted to a disability for the purposes of the DDA) the reason for the treatment could not be regarded as disability-related.[47] Thus, the reason for a restaurant-owner's refusal to agree over the telephone to a customer being accompanied by a dog would not be disability-related unless the owner had been told that the person was blind and that the dog in question was a guide dog.[48] By analogy it would appear that the reason for the dismissal of a postman with an artificial leg because of his slow pace might, contrary to the view of the Employment Appeal Tribunal in *Heinz Co Ltd v Kenrick*,[49] not be regarded as disability-related if the postman had concealed his disability from his employer. Similarly, and again contrary to the approach in *Heinz*, the reason for the dismissal of a dyslexic secretary for bad spelling may

---

[44] *Heinz Co Ltd v Kenrick* [2000] IRLR 144 (EAT). Contrast *O'Neill v Symm & Co* [1998] ICR 481 (EAT) and *Quinn v Schwarzkopf Ltd* [2002] IRLR 602 (Court of Session). See also *London Borough of Hammersmith and Fulham v Farnsworth* [2000] IRLR 691.

[45] *Heinz Co Ltd v Kenrick* [2000] IRLR 144 (EAT) [26]. It should be noted however that, in the context of pre-16 education, s 28B(4) expressly provides that a person cannot be liable for disability-related discrimination unless they knew, or ought to have known, that the person concerned was disabled.

[46] *Lewisham LBC v Malcolm* [2008] UKHL 43.

[47] See eg *ibid*, [18]–[19] (Lord Bingham), [26]–[29] (Lord Scott), [84]–[92] (Baroness Hale), [113] (Lord Brown) and [161]–[163] (Lord Neuberger).

[48] *Ibid*, [18] (Lord Bingham), [36] (Lord Scott) and [85] (Baroness Hale).

[49] *Heinz Co Ltd v Kenrick* [2000] IRLR 144, [25] (Lindsay P)

well not be regarded as disability-related if the dyslexia was at that time unbeknown to the employer and the employee.[50] It is possible, however, that these latter two examples would be distinguished from the former on the ground that, in them, what is known to the defendant (the slowness of pace and the poor spelling) is more in the nature of a symptom of the impairment than is what is known to the defendant in the first scenario (ie, the wish to take a dog into a restaurant). Such a distinction is not entirely convincing, however.

A number of the judgments in *Lewisham* appear to suggest that knowledge of the impairment may itself not be sufficient to ensure that a reason is disability-related and that it should, in addition, constitute something like a motive for the less favourable treatment. Baroness Hale, for instance, suggests that 'either the illness or a potential link with [the claimant's] behaviour' must or ought to have been 'present' to the mind of the defendant when they were deciding on the relevant treatment.[51] Although the precise implications of this are unclear, it appears to come close to requiring the disability to have played a part in the actual decision to embark on that treatment. Such a requirement emerges more clearly from Lord Scott's judgment. According to him,

> if the physical or mental condition that constitutes the disability has played no motivating part in the decision of the alleged discriminator to inflict on the disabled person the treatment complained of, the alleged discriminator's reason for that treatment cannot ... relate to the disability.[52]

Thus, in his view, the denial of entry to a person with a guide dog would not be for a reason related to the owner's blindness if it was motivated by the wish to deny access to the dog as opposed to the blind person.[53]

The net effect of *Lewisham's* insertion of this knowledge requirement into the link between the claimant's disability and the defendant's reason for the disputed treatment is not entirely clear. Lord Scott's judgment suggests that it might open an escape route from liability to the 'honest yet ignorant or obtuse' defendant who fails 'to 'recognise or acknowledge the obvious', described by Lindsay P.[54] It certainly opens up another site for legal argument—argument which would be better housed within the context of an appropriately drafted general justification defence. Unfortunately however, as will be seen in the next section, the justification defence for disability-related discrimination in the context of housing and goods and services is neither appropriately drafted nor general in nature.

The second issue which has been raised by the requirement that the reason for the relevant treatment of a disabled person must be 'related' to their disability is the question of how close the relationship between the reason and the disability is required to be. In *Novacold*, Mummery LJ suggested that this issue should be

---

[50]   *Ibid.*
[51]   *Lewisham LBC v Malcolm* [2008] UKHL 43, [91].
[52]   *Ibid,* [29].
[53]   *Ibid,* [35].
[54]   *Heinz Co Ltd v Kenrick* [2000] IRLR 144 (EAT) [26].

regarded as a question of fact requiring no comparisons to be made.[55] The question, however, is not an easy one as is illustrated by the fact that it divided their Lordships in *Lewisham London Borough Council v Malcolm*.[56] Baroness Hale explained the difficulty as follows:

> In a direct discrimination case, the reason may be the disability itself. In other cases, the reason may not be the disability, but the disability may have been the cause of the reason. But that is not necessarily enough. The connection between the disability and the reason must not be too remote. It is not easy to lay down a simple test by which to judge that remoteness. The number of links in the chain may be a pointer.[57]

Causation thus seems likely to provide a useful though not necessarily definitive guide. In Lord Neuberger's words, the link between the reason and the disability will

> always, or at least almost always, be causal, but not in the limited sense in which that term is used in other fields—eg in tort.[58]

Accordingly, in *Novacold*, the reason Mr Clark had been dismissed was his absence from work. This was held to be related to his disability because it was caused by it. In *Lewisham*, the reason Mr Malcolm was served with a notice to quit was the fact that he had sub-let and moved out of the property. Baroness Hale, Lord Brown and Lord Neuberger, influenced by the trial judge's ruling that the sub-letting had not been caused by his schizophrenia, ruled that the reason for the unfavourable treatment was not sufficiently related to Mr Malcolm's disability to fall within the ambit of disability-related discrimination.

Practical difficulties of proof are also likely to face claimants wishing to establish the required link between the reason for their treatment and their disability. It appears that medical evidence is likely to have an important role to play in many such cases. In *Edwards v Mid Suffolk District Council*,[59] for instance, Mr Edwards was dismissed because of his behaviour towards his allocated assistant with whom he found it impossible to work. Mr Edwards produced medical evidence which suggested that this behaviour might have been caused by his chronic anxiety disorder. At first instance, however, the Tribunal found that it had been caused entirely by interpersonal difficulties unrelated to Mr Edwards's disability. On appeal, the Employment Appeal Tribunal found that the Tribunal's decision was fatally flawed by its failure to address the medical evidence and to provide reasons for rejecting it.

Finally, on this issue, it is worth noting that the reason must relate to the disability of the disabled person bringing the case. Disability-related discrimination cases may not therefore be brought by a person discriminated against on the

---

[55] *Clark v Novacold* [1999] IRLR 318 (CA) [53].
[56] *Lewisham LBC v Malcolm* [2008] UKHL 43.
[57] *Ibid*, 83.
[58] *Ibid*, [169].
[59] *Edwards v Mid Suffolk DC* [2001] ICR 616 (EAT).

grounds of the disability of another person, on the grounds of a disability they are mistakenly assumed to have by the defendant, or on the grounds of their commitment to ensuring disability equality. In this respect it differs from the much wider scope of the Race Relations Act 1976 (RRA).[60]

2.1.4 Justification

It is always open to defendants in cases of disability-related discrimination to argue that their less favourable treatment of the disabled person was justified. If such arguments succeed, they will not be liable for disability discrimination. The DDA lays down three general forms of justification defence for less favourable treatment. These are drafted in identical language to that of the justification defences applying to failures to make reasonable adjustments. As these have been considered in some depth in the previous chapter, the present discussion will be brief. Before considering the three defences, however, it should be noted that, at least in relation to the first of them, it will not be possible to justify less favourable treatment on the basis of circumstances which would not have existed had relevant reasonable adjustment duties been discharged.[61] For this reason, in cases where disability-related discrimination and a failure to make a reasonable adjustment are both alleged, the latter issue must be addressed before the former.[62]

The first form of justification defence for less favourable treatment, which applies in the contexts of employment and education, may be relied on if the reason for the less favourable treatment was 'material to the circumstances of the particular case and substantial'.[63] The leading case on the construction of this defence is *Jones v The Post Office*.[64] There, Mr Jones argued that his employer had discriminated against him when it reduced the number of hours he was allowed to work as a delivery driver because he had become diabetic and dependent on insulin. The reduction in hours had been imposed in pursuance of the employer's general policy on fitness standards for drivers and was based on the belief that allowing him to work longer hours would entail risks to the safety of himself and others. On the basis of the medical evidence presented to it, however, the

---

[60] See section 3.1.3 below for discussion of this issue in the context of direct discrimination.

[61] This is made explicit in relation to the first form of justification defence by the DDA ss 3A(6) and 28B(8). Although there is no comparable provision for the second form of justification defence, guidance to the same effect is set out in DRC, *DDA 1995 Code of Practice: Rights of Access—Services to the Public, Public Authority Functions, Private Clubs and Premises* (London, Stationery Office, 2006) para 7.8.

[62] See eg *Archibald v Fife Council* [2004] UKHL 32, [2004] IRLR 197, [32] (Lord Rodger); *Nottinghamshire CC v Meikle* [2004] IRLR 703 (CA) [66] (Keene LJ); and *O'Hanlon v Commissioners of Revenue and Customs* [2007] EWCA Civ 283, [23] (Hooper LJ).

[63] DDA s 3A(3).

[64] *Jones v The Post Office* [2001] ICR 814 (CA).

Employment Tribunal found that Mr Jones's insulin dependence posed no such additional risk and that the reduction in his hours could not therefore be justified.

The Court of Appeal ruled that the less favourable treatment of Mr Jones was justified, even though the employer may have been mistaken about the risks associated with his driving long hours. The justification defence did not require the reason for the less favourable treatment to be correct or convincing. It simply required it to be 'material' to the circumstances of the case and 'substantial'. 'Material' required a reasonably close link between the reason and the particular facts and a reason would be considered to be 'substantial' as long as it was 'supportable' or based on 'credible' arguments.[65]

The *Jones* ruling makes it extremely easy to justify disability-related less favourable treatment. This is illustrated by the Employment Appeal Tribunal's decision in *Surrey Police v Marshall*.[66] It was there held that the police were justified in rejecting a job applicant with bipolar affective disorder on the basis of a recommendation from their occupational health adviser, who had neither met the candidate nor received advice from her medical practitioners!

Nevertheless, there are important cases in which the *Jones* defence has been defeated. One such case is *High Quality Lifestyles v Watts*.[67] This concerned the dismissal of a care worker who had disclosed that he was HIV+. The Employment Appeal Tribunal upheld the first instance decision that the dismissal could not be justified, as it was based on a risk assessment which was procedurally flawed and which did not relate specifically to the claimant's case.

Another such case is *Williams v J Walter Thompson Group*.[68] There, the Walter Thompson Group was found to have treated Ms Williams less favourably for reasons relating to her disability in a number of respects. It had appointed her as a computer programmer knowing that she was blind and that she would require specialist training and additional access software. The specialist equipment did not arrive until several months after Ms Williams took up her post and her employers failed to provide her with appropriate training. During this time, they also failed to provide her with work she could perform without the equipment or training. In ruling that this treatment was not justified, Mummery LJ stressed that the case was 'exceptional' because:

> JWT agreed to employ Ms Williams to do a specific job (Worldwide Software Developer) knowing that she was totally blind; that she did not know how to use Lotus Notes; and that she would need to learn and be trained how to use them in order to do the job she was employed to do in JWT. Having taken Ms Williams on in those circumstances,

---

65 *Ibid*, [42] (Arden LJ) and [25] (Pill LJ).
66 *Surrey Police v Marshall* [2002] IRLR 843 (EAT).
67 *High Quality Lifestyles v Watts* [2006] IRLR 850 (EAT).
68 *Williams v J Walter Thompson Group* [2005] EWCA Civ 133.

JWT then failed properly to investigate either before or after she started her employ-ment the cost and time that it would take fully to train an unsighted person for the job that she was employed to do.[69]

Following *Jones* then, it is clear that employers are granted 'considerable leeway ... when the issue of justification is under scrutiny'.[70] The leeway granted to service providers, managers of premises, private clubs and others by the second form of justification defence, however, is, in some respects, greater still. As already indicated, the discrepancy between these two forms of justification defence was based on the belief that service providers would frequently be required to make decisions more quickly than employers or education providers, without the benefit of familiarity with a particular disabled person and their needs and circumstances.[71]

This second form of justification defence requires a defendant to establish: first, that they held one or more of a number of specified beliefs; and, second, that it was reasonable for them to do so.[72] Significantly, the relevant belief does not itself have to be reasonable. All that is required is that it was reasonable for the particular defendant to hold it in all the circumstances of the particular case.

The relatively early case of *Rose v Bouchet*[73] suggested that this specific belief justification defence might be raised with alarming ease. A landlord's refusal to lease a flat to a blind person was there held to be justified. He was found to have genuinely believed that it would be dangerous for Mr Rose to occupy the flat because the steps leading to it were not railed. According to the Scottish Court of Sessions, it had been reasonable for him to hold this belief even though he had not consulted Mr Rose himself or any other body which might be regarded as having expertise on the issue. After *Rose*, however, the relevant Code of Practice was revised so as to stress the importance of dialogue and consultation with disabled people where possible.[74]

The prime focus of litigation in connection with the specific belief justification defence has been the claims of tenants with mental health problems to the continued enjoyment of their tenancies. In *North Devon Homes Ltd v Brazier*[75] it was held that the eviction of a tenant, whose psychiatric disorder caused her to engage in anti-social behaviour (including shouting, foul language and banging on walls), amounted to less favourable treatment for a reason related to her

---

[69] *Ibid*, [54].

[70] *O'Hanlon v Commissioners of Revenue and Customs* [2006] IRLR 840 (EAT) [43] (Elias P).

[71] See ch 3, fn 273 above and accompanying text.

[72] See eg DDA s 20(3) and (4).

[73] *Rose v Bouchet* [1999] IRLR 463 (Court of Session) (discussed in A Lawson, 'Selling, Letting and Managing Premises: New Rights for Disabled People?' [2000] *Conveyancer and Property Lawyer* 128).

[74] See now DRC, *DDA 1995 Code of Practice: Rights of Access—Services to the Public, Public Authority Functions, Private Clubs and Premises* (n 61 above) para 7.8.

[75] *North Devon Homes Ltd v Brazier* [2003] EWHC 574 (QBD) (discussed in S Collins, 'Mentally Disabled Tenants, Anti-Social Behaviour and the Disability Discrimination Act 1995' [2003] *Journal of Housing Law* 57).

disability. The landlord's attempt to justify the eviction failed because there was no evidence that it had actually held the belief that allowing her to remain would constitute a threat to the health and safety of other tenants. The landlord in *Manchester City Council v Romano*,[76] however, managed to raise this defence successfully. The Court of Appeal there stressed that 'health', for the purposes of the 'health and safety' justification defence, must be interpreted broadly so as to include general mental and emotional well-being.[77]

As has already been explained, the attempt to evict a tenant with schizophrenia came before the House of Lords in *Lewisham London Borough Council v Malcolm*.[78] In this case, however, it was accepted that none of the listed specific beliefs were applicable and that consequently no justification defence could be raised. It was this absence of a justification defence, caused by the straitjacket of the specific belief justification defence, which appears to have pushed their Lordships into reversing *Novacold* and adopting its stiflingly narrow construction of the comparator requirement.

The specific belief justification defence is thus a singularly unfortunate piece of statutory draughtsmanship. It risks being satisfied too easily in cases where one of the specified beliefs appears to be relevant—particularly in cases such as *Rose*, where the defendant is a private individual or small business. In other cases such as *Lewisham* however, where none of the specific beliefs fit the facts, significant injustice may be caused to defendants. It was in the attempt to reduce this latter possibility that the House of Lords dealt its death-blow to the concept of disability-related discrimination in *Lewisham*.[79]

The third type of justification defence requires a defendant to demonstrate that the treatment in question represents a proportionate means of achieving a legitimate aim. This defence did not appear in the DDA as originally enacted but was added later by virtue of Regulations implementing the Employment Equality Directive and by the DDA 2005. Its sphere of operation is restricted to two main contexts.

First, this proportionate means of achieving a legitimate aim defence applies to cases concerning competence standards. It applies where, for a disability-related reason, a disabled person is treated less favourably as a result of the application to them of a competence standard by a post-16 educational provider[80] or by a body

---

[76] *Manchester City Council v Romano* [2004] EWCA (Civ) 834 [69] (discussed in S Murdoch, 'Careful Who You Evict' [2004] *Estates Gazette* 141).

[77] *Ibid*, [69].

[78] *Lewisham LBC v Malcolm* [2008] UKHL 43. For the Court of Appeal decision, see [2007] EWCA Civ 763 (discussed in S Murdoch, 'Mandatory is Not Always Compulsory' [2007] *Estates Gazette* 293).

[79] Sections 2.1.2 and 2.1.3 above and accompanying text.

[80] DDA s 28S(6). In relation to pre-16 education, on the other hand, less favourable treatment is justified if it occurs under a 'permitted form of selection', for which there needs to be no demonstration of proportionality or legitimacy in the individual case—s 28B(6).

conferring either professional or trade qualifications[81] or general qualifications.[82] For the purposes of post-16 education, a competence standard is defined as

> an academic, medical or other standard applied ... for the purpose of determining whether or not a person has a particular level of competence or ability.[83]

In these cases a defendant wishing to raise the defence must show that

> (a) the standard is, or would be, applied equally to persons who do not have [the] particular disability; and
> (b) its application is a proportionate means of achieving a legitimate aim.

The second context in which this defence of a proportionate means of achieving a legitimate aim applies is that of public authorities. Under the DDA section 21D(5), a public authority may justify less favourable treatment if it can demonstrate that that treatment amounted to a proportionate means of achieving a legitimate aim. The specific belief justification defence also operates in this context, allowing public authorities the possibility of arguing either or both forms of defence.

This third defence—the proportionate means of achieving a legitimate aim—is the same as the defence for claims of indirect discrimination outside the disability context. The standard it lays down is an objective one and, in this sense, is a great deal higher than the standard laid down by the other DDA justification defences. Its sphere of operation in the context of disability-related discrimination, however, is currently extremely narrow.

The first two forms of defence—the material and substantial reason defence and the specific belief defence—have both been severely criticised as laying down too low a standard.[84] Their appearance in the DDA represents a departure from the role-model provided by the US Americans with Disabilities Act 1990. Under the latter, the emphasis is on ability to comply (with or without the benefit of reasonable accommodation) with essential occupational requirements for employment, or with essential eligibility requirements for the receipt of services, rather than on the application of a general justification defence.[85] Such defences as it does create are more tightly circumscribed, being based on considerations such as 'business necessity' and 'direct threat'.[86] The Disability Rights Task Force declined to recommend that the DDA adopt such an approach because of the

---

[81] DDA s 14A(3).
[82] DDA s 31AB(4).
[83] DDA s 28S(11).
[84] See eg Sedley LJ in *Collins v Royal National Theatre Board* [2004] EWCA Civ 144 [14]–[16] and [22]–[26]; and also in *O'Hanlon v Commissioners of Revenue and Customs* [2007] EWCA Civ 283 [98]; J Davies, 'A Cuckoo in the Nest: A "Range of Reasonable Responses", Justification and the Disability Discrimination Act 1995' (2003) 32 *Industrial Law Journal* 164; and Lawson, 'Selling, Letting and Managing Premises: New Rights for Disabled People?' (n 73 above).
[85] See, in particular, 42 USC s 12111(8) and s 12182(b)(2)(A).
[86] See eg 42 USC s 12113.

bureaucratic burden and inflexibility associated with the identification of essential requirements and criteria.[87] It did, however, find favour with the authors of the Hepple Report.[88]

The DRC suggested that the weakness of the current justification defences for disability discrimination was 'one of the most important disability-specific issues' facing the Discrimination Law Review.[89] It urged that the defences be amended so as to bring them into line with the stronger justification defence applying to indirect discrimination in other statutes.[90] As has been seen, this defence has already made an appearance (albeit a limited one) in the DDA, and for reasons of consistency and simplicity would now seem preferable to an ADA-based approach. Recommendations to replace all the DDA justification defences with this type of objective defence are indeed made by the Discrimination Law Review and are repeated in the Government's response to the consultation.[91] Sadly, however, such a change has not come in time to rescue British disability law from the restrictive approach adopted by the House of Lords in *Lewisham* – an approach which might well have been avoided had the relevant justification defence already been reformed in this way.

2.2 Relationship with Reasonable Adjustment

Disability-related discrimination and failure to discharge a reasonable adjustment duty were the two forms of discrimination contained in the first incarnation of the DDA. Both were then subject to the same justification defences and this continues to be the case outside the areas covered by the Employment Equality Directive. As was explained in the previous chapter, however, the Regulations implementing that Directive have now removed the justification defence for failures to make reasonable adjustments in the areas of employment and post-16 education.

There is no clear-cut divide between the spheres of operation of these two forms of discrimination. Under the expansive interpretation given to disability-related discrimination in *Clark v Novacold* there was a considerable overlap between them. The application of a 'no dogs' rule to a guide dog owner, for example, could have been regarded either as an instance of disability-related

---

[87] Disability Rights Task Force, *From Exclusion to Inclusion* (London, Department for Education and Employment, 1999) para 5.10.

[88] B Hepple, M Coussey and T Choudhury, *Equality: A New Framework* (Oxford, Hart Publishing, 2000) recommendation 9, para 2.45. See also DRC, *Disability Equality: Making it Happen* (London, DRC, 2003) Employment, recommendation 2.

[89] DRC, *Initial Submission to the Discrimination Law Review* (London, DRC, February 2006) para 1.1.2.

[90] *Ibid.*

[91] Department for Communities and Local Government, *Discrimination Law Review—A Framework for Fairness: Proposals for a Single Equality Bill for Great Britain* (London, Stationery Office, 2007) paras 1.46–1.53; and Government Equalities Office, *The Equality Bill* (n 34 above) paras 11.12–11.27.

discrimination or as a failure to make a reasonable adjustment.[92] After *Lewisham*,[93] however, the drastic shrinkage in the scope of disability-related discrimination has considerably reduced the extent of this overlap. Application of a 'no dogs' rule now appears to fall outside the reach of disability-related discrimination and those disadvantaged by it must therefore depend entirely on reasonable adjustment principles for redress.

In one important respect, it may be easier to bring a claim for disability-related discrimination than one for a failure to make a reasonable adjustment. While the former type of claim requires a demonstration of less favourable treatment, unlike the latter, there is no stipulation that the claimant must be placed at a substantial disadvantage or that they must find it impossible or unreasonably difficult to access a service. The degree of detriment required by less favourable treatment is not specified but, given the silence of the codes of practice and the case law on the point, the threshold would appear to be a low one.

In all other respects, however, it appears easier to bring a claim for a failure to make a reasonable adjustment than for disability-related discrimination. As was discussed in the previous chapter, the reasonableness of an adjustment is judged objectively and therefore sets a much higher standard for defendants than the standards set by the subjective justification defences for disability-related discrimination considered above. The contrast between the two approaches has been described by Elias P as 'striking'[94] and leads to the inevitable result that defendants will find it easier to justify treating a disabled person less favourably than to demonstrate that taking a particular step to accommodate their needs would have been unreasonable.[95]

This discrepancy has created difficulty in applying a justification defence to the reasonable adjustment duty itself.[96] In relation to the justification of disability-related discrimination, however, it is less problematic. Less favourable treatment can be justified by reference only to factors that would have remained relevant had the defendant effectively discharged any applicable reasonable adjustment duty. Consequently, the reasonableness of adjustments must be considered before the justification defence can be applied. In this way, the higher demands imposed by the reasonableness of an adjustment are effectively incorporated into the otherwise largely subjective issue of justification. For this reason it has been said that

---

[92] For an occasion where it was used as an example of disability-related discrimination, see n 6 above and accompanying text. For occasions where it has been used as an example of a failure to make a reasonable adjustment, see Hansard, 18 July 1995, HL Debates vol 566, cols 266–7 (Lord Mackay); and DRC, *DDA 1995 Code of Practice: Rights of Access—Services to the Public, Public Authority Functions, Private Clubs and Premises* (n 61 above) para 5.6.

[93] *Lewisham LBC v Malcolm* [2008] UKHL 43.

[94] *O'Hanlon v Commissioners of Revenue and Customs* [2006] IRLR 840 (EAT) [28].

[95] See further *Collins v Royal National Theatre* [2004] EWCA Civ 144 [20] (Sedley LJ); and *Smith v Churchill Stairlifts* [2005] EWCA Civ 1220 [44]–[45] (Maurice Kay LJ).

[96] See the discussion of *Collins v Royal National Theatre Board Ltd* [2004] EWCA Civ 144 in ch 3, fnn 258–67 above and accompanying text.

the real substance of the justification issue is to be discovered in the question whether the employer has failed to make reasonable adjustment for the person's disability[97]

Well-advised claimants will therefore be keen to identify relevant reasonable adjustment duties and avoid relying solely on claims of disability-related discrimination.

3. Direct Discrimination

3.1 Outline of the Concept

3.1.1 Overview

Although the Sex Discrimination Act 1975 (SDA) and the Race Relations Act 1976 (RRA) had long been structured around the two key concepts of direct discrimination and indirect discrimination, neither of these concepts appeared in the DDA when it was first enacted. The notion of direct discrimination was introduced into it by the Regulations implementing the Employment Equality Directive. This form of discrimination therefore currently applies only to the areas affected by that Directive—employment and occupation (including training and post-16 education). It seems likely, however, that provision will be made in the forthcoming Equality Bill to extend its operation to all areas.[98]

In the employment context, section 3A(5) of the DDA provides:

A person directly discriminates against a disabled person if, on the ground of the disabled person's disability, he treats the disabled person less favourably than he treats or would treat a person not having that particular disability whose relevant circumstances, including his abilities, are the same as, or not materially different from, those of the disabled person.[99]

In addition, section 3A(4) provides that, unlike disability-related discrimination, direct discrimination can never be justified.[100]

3.1.2 Less Favourable Treatment

In direct discrimination cases the treatment received by the disabled person must be compared with the treatment which was (or would have been) received by

---

[97] H Collins, 'Discrimination, Equality and Social Inclusion' (2003) 66 *Modern Law Review* 16 at 34.

[98] Government Equalities Office, *The Equality Bill* (n 34 above) paras 11.2–11.11.

[99] There is an identical provision in the context of post-16 education—s 28S(10).

[100] See s 28S(9) in the post-16 education context.

a person not having that particular disability whose relevant circumstances, including his abilities, are the same as, or not materially different from, those of the disabled person.[101]

A direct discrimination claim is dependent on such a comparison revealing that the treatment received by the disabled claimant was less favourable than that which was, or would have been, received by the comparator.

This approach to the identification of the comparator in direct disability discrimination claims reflects that which applies in cases of direct discrimination on other grounds[102] and which, after *Lewisham v Malcolm*,[103] also applies in disability-related discrimination cases. The focus is on identifying a comparator (real or hypothetical) who, apart from the relevant characteristic of disability, sex or race, is identically situated to the claimant for all relevant purposes.[104] Thus, in *High Quality Lifestyles v Watts*,[105] the claimant (who was HIV+) had to be compared with a hypothetical person who had the same abilities, skills and experience as he did and also some condition, other than HIV+, which carried the same risk of transmitting to others an illness of equivalent seriousness.[106] Since it had not been demonstrated that Mr Watts had been treated less favourably than such a comparator, his claim for direct discrimination failed.

In making the comparison required by section 3A(5), the disabled person's abilities must be assessed as they in fact were at the relevant time. Thus, if the disabled person's ability to perform a job has been enhanced because of a reasonable adjustment made in their favour, it is their enhanced level of performance which will be relevant. If, on the other hand, an employer has failed to make reasonable adjustments which would have improved the claimant's performance, the relevant level of ability will be the lower, unenhanced standard. This is illustrated by the following example in the Code of Practice:

> A disabled person who applies for an administrative job which includes typing is not allowed to use her own adapted keyboard (even though it would have been reasonable for the employer to allow this) and types a test document at 30 [words per minute]. Her speed with the adapted keyboard would have been 50 [words per minute]. A non-disabled candidate is given the job because her typing speed on the test was 45 [words per minute] with the same accuracy rate. This is not direct discrimination, as the comparator is a non-disabled person typing at 30 [words per minute].[107]

---

[101] DDA s 3A(5).

[102] See eg *Shamoon v Chief Constable of the Royal Ulster Constabulary* [2003] UKHL 11.

[103] *Lewisham LBC v Malcolm* [2008] UKHL 43.

[104] For the view that British law should place less emphasis on the comparator requirement, see Discrimination Law Association, *Discrimination Law Association Submissions for the Discrimination Law Review* (London, Discrimination Law Association, 2006) paras 30–33. See also A McColgan, 'Cracking the Comparator Problem: Discrimination, "Equal" Treatment and the Role of Comparisons' [2006] *European Human Rights Law Review* 650.

[105] *High Quality Lifestyles v Watts* [2006] IRLR 850 (EAT).

[106] *Ibid*, [48].

[107] DRC, *DDA 1995 Code of Practice: Employment and Occupation* (n 1 above) para 4.22.

Facts such as these would clearly have grounded a claim for disability-related discrimination prior to *Lewisham v Malcolm*.[108] Under the *Novacold* approach, the disabled person would have had no difficulty in establishing less favourable treatment. The justification defence could not be established by reference to the slow typing speed because, had the employer properly discharged their reasonable adjustment duty, the claimant's typing speed would have been faster than that of the person to whom the job was offered. After *Lewisham* however, as discussed above,[109] it is unclear whether less favourable treatment could be demonstrated in these circumstances.

3.1.3 On the Ground of the Disabled Person's Disability

Before *Lewisham*, it was generally accepted that the direct discrimination requirement that less favourable treatment be 'on the ground of' a person's disability was much more stringent than the disability-related discrimination requirement that it be 'for a reason related to' the disabled person's disability. This conventional view has not been confined to the disability context as is illustrated by the high profile case of *R (Equal Opportunities Commission) v Secretary of State for Trade and Industry*.[110] This case essentially concerned the question of whether or not there was a difference between the phrases 'on the ground of' and 'for a reason related to'.

Burton J ruled that the former was significantly narrower than the latter and that consequently the British Government had failed adequately to implement the sexual harassment provisions of the Equal Treatment Amendment Directive 2002.[111] While the Directive required 'unwanted conduct related to' sex to be prohibited, section 4A of the SDA prohibited only unwanted conduct which was 'on the ground of' the complainant's sex. The SDA formulation was held to prohibit a much narrower range of unwanted conduct than that covered by the Directive. While *Lewisham* blurs the difference between 'on the ground of' and 'for a reason related to' in the context of disability-related discrimination, it has not achieved this by changing the meaning of the former phrase.

According to the DDA employment Code of Practice and in line with equivalent sex and race legislation, treatment will generally be recognised as being on the ground of disability if, but for the disability of the claimant, it would not have

---

[108] *Lewisham LBC v Malcolm* [2008] UKHL 43.

[109] See nn 21–22 above and accompanying text.

[110] *R (EOC) v Secretary of State for Trade and Industry* [2007] EWHC 483 (Admin). See generally L Barnes, 'Constitutional and Conceptual Complexities in UK Implementation of the EU Harassment Provisions' (2007) 36 *Industrial Law Journal* 446; and Y Gallagher, 'Is the Hypothetical Man Finally Dead?' (2007) 80 *Employment Law Journal* 6.

[111] Council Directive 2002/73/EC amending Council Directive 76/207/EEC on the implementation of the principle of equal treatment for men and women as regards access to employment, vocational training and promotion and working conditions, [2002] OJ L 269/15.

happened.[112] According to the Employment Appeal Tribunal in *High Quality Lifestyles v Watts*, however, what is in issue is the disability itself and not its effects. Thus, in that case, it had to be demonstrated that the claimant had been discriminated against on the ground that he was HIV+ and not because of the risk of transmitting the disease to others.[113]

The requirement that the less favourable treatment was on the ground of the claimant's disability does not require the disability to have been the only—or even the principal—cause of the treatment.[114] Neither does it require the defendant to have had any particular motive or intention or even to have had knowledge of the fact that the person in question was disabled.[115] The Code of Practice illustrates this by referring to a case in which an employer advertises a promotion opportunity but stipulates that it would be unsuitable for people with a history of mental illness. An employee who has such a history, although unknown to the employer, and who is otherwise suitably qualified for the job may be able to bring a case for direct discrimination based on the blanket restriction on their opportunities for career advancement.[116]

Section 3A(5) specifies that the less favourable treatment must be on the grounds of 'the disabled person's disability'. This means that, as in relation to disability-related discrimination, direct discrimination claims may be brought only by the disabled person whose disability has prompted the less favourable treatment, and not by a non-disabled person discriminated against because of their association with a disabled person or because they themselves are wrongly perceived to be disabled. This stands in contrast with the less restrictive approach contained in the legislative provisions prohibiting direct discrimination in the contexts of race,[117] religion and belief[118] and sexual orientation.[119]

Further, people discriminated against because of the risk that they will become disabled in the future will not be protected.[120] Although this problem is not likely

---

[112] DRC, *DDA 1995 Code of Practice: Employment and Occupation* (n 1 above) para 4.7. See also *James v Eastleigh Borough Council* [1990] 2 AC 751 (HL); and *R v Birmingham City Council ex parte EOC* [1989] IRLR 172 (HL).

[113] *High Quality Lifestyles v Watts* [2006] IRLR 850 (EAT) [43].

[114] *Nagarajan v London Regional Transport* [2000] 1 AC 501 (HL) [14] (Lord Nicholls).

[115] DRC, *DDA 1995 Code of Practice: Employment and Occupation* (n 1 above) para 4.11.

[116] *Ibid.*

[117] RRA s 1(1)(a)—'on racial grounds'. It was applied in this expansive way in *Showboat Entertainment Centre v Owens* [1984] IRLR 7. See also the controversial decision of the Employment Appeal Tribunal in *Redfearn v Serco Ltd* [2005] IRLR 744 and the judgment of the Court of Appeal at [2006] EWCA Civ 659.

[118] Employment Equality (Religion or Belief) Regulations 2003 (SI 2003/1660) reg 3(1)—'on grounds of religion or belief'; and the Equality Act 2006 s 45(1) and (2)—'on grounds of the religion or belief of [the claimant]' including one s/he is thought to possess 'or of any other person'.

[119] Employment Equality (Sexual Orientation) Regulations 2003 (SI 2003/1661) reg 3(1)—'on grounds of sexual orientation'.

[120] The Government has rejected the idea of legislating to provide protection from discrimination against people on the grounds of genetic predisposition to illness or impairment in *The Equality Bill* (n 34 above) paras 15.14–15.25.

to prove to be an important issue for the other strands covered by non-discrimination law, it would be addressed by wording such as that currently used in the contexts of race, religion and belief, and sexual orientation. Direct age discrimination, however, like direct disability discrimination, is linked to the age of the particular claimant. However, provision is made for this to include the claimant's 'apparent age',[121] thus addressing the issue of mistaken perception in the age context.

The Employment Equality Directive requires Member States to prohibit direct discrimination on grounds of disability. Its wording does not explicitly restrict the scope of the required prohibition to people discriminated against on grounds of their own disability. Concerns that British law does not currently comply with this Directive[122] have been heightened by the decision of the European Court of Justice (ECJ) on 17 July 2008 in *Coleman v Attridge Law*—a case referred to it for a preliminary ruling by the South London Employment Tribunal.[123]

The question raised by *Coleman* related to the way in which a non-disabled woman was treated by her employer because her child was disabled. Ms Coleman argued that her requests for flexible work were rejected whereas similar requests by parents of non-disabled children were granted. She also contended that she was harassed on the ground of her child's impairments and her role as carer. As has been seen, on its natural construction, the DDA would afford Ms Coleman no protection because she herself was not, and had not been, disabled. According to the ECJ, however, such an approach would undermine the objectives of the Employment Equality Directive and deprive it of an important element of its intended effect.[124] Thus, as the Advocate General pointed out, the effect of the Directive is to exclude disability

> from the range of permissible reasons an employer may legitimately rely upon in order to treat one employee less favourably than another.[125]

Accordingly, the treatment Ms Coleman had received was 'on the ground' of disability—albeit the disability of another person—within the meaning of the Directive. This decision is likely to require changes to be made to the law as set out in the DDA and the Government has indicated that it is currently considering the implications of *Coleman* for its Equality Bill.[126]

---

[121] Employment Equality (Age) Regulations 2006 (SI 2006/1031) reg 3(3).
[122] See eg Discrimination Law Association, *Discrimination Law Association Submissions for the Discrimination Law Review* (n 104 above) paras 35–7.
[123] Case C-303/06 *Coleman v Attridge Law*, OJ C 237 (30 September 2006) p 6.
[124] *Ibid*, [48]–[51].
[125] *Ibid*, [18].
[126] Government Equalities Office, *The Equality Bill* (n 34 above) para 7.16.

The Government had previously considered the issue of extending protection from discrimination on the basis of association and perception, and recommended the retention of the current approach in all areas except one.[127] The sole change it proposed involved extending protection to people discriminated against because of their association with a transsexual person.[128] It thus recommended that, in the context of disability, protection from discrimination should be confined to people who were themselves currently disabled or who had been disabled in the past. The principal reason for this was its concern that extending protection to people who were not themselves disabled might result in reasonable adjustment duties being imposed in an extensive range of additional situations in favour of people who merely associated with a disabled person or who were wrongly perceived to be disabled.[129] Clearly, however, it would be possible to frame a law which granted no entitlement to reasonable adjustment to non-disabled people but which would offer them protection from direct discrimination on the grounds of their association with a disabled person or of having been perceived to be a disabled person. This, indeed, is the interpretation of the Directive provided by the ECJ in *Coleman*.[130]

3.1.4 Genuine Occupational Requirements and Qualifications

The concept of direct discrimination in British law has traditionally been characterised by the fact that it is subject to no general justification defence of the types applying to disability-related discrimination or indirect discrimination.[131] This, as will become evident in the next chapter, has caused some difficulty in the context of promoting positive action in favour of disadvantaged groups. Direct sex and race discrimination are made subject to a number of very specific and somewhat anomalous exceptions or justifications, which are known as 'genuine occupational qualifications'.[132] The Regulations introduced to give effect to the Employment Equality Directive in relation to religion and belief, sexual orientation and age contain similar—though more generically worded—exceptions for

---

[127] Department for Communities and Local Government, *Discrimination Law Review* (n 91 above) paras 1.19–1.25; and Government Equalities Office, *The Equality Bill* (n 34 above) paras 7.11–7.16.

[128] Government Equalities Office, *The Equality Bill* (n 34 above) paras 9.3–9.11.

[129] Department for Communities and Local Government, *Discrimination Law Review* (n 91 above) para 1.22.

[130] Case C-303/06 *Coleman v Attridge Law* (17 July 2008) [39]–[40].

[131] However, such a general defence (explicitly excluded in the context of direct disability discrimination by the DDA ss 3A(4) and 28S(9)) does exist in the context of direct age discrimination—Employment Equality (Age) Regulations 2006 (SI No 2006/1031) reg 3(1). See further J Swift, 'Justifying Age Discrimination' (2006) 35 *Industrial Law Journal* 228; and M Sargeant, 'The Employment Equality (Age) Regulations 2006: A Legitimisation of Age Discrimination in Employment' (2006) 35 *Industrial Law Journal* 209.

[132] Sex Discrimination Act 1975 s 7; Race Relations Act 1976 s 5. For a thought-provoking discussion of such requirements, see M Bell, 'Direct Discrimination' in D Schiek, L Waddington and M Bell (eds), *Cases, Materials and Texts on National, Supranational and International Non-Discrimination Law* (Oxford, Hart Publishing, 2007) 275–89.

'genuine'[133] or for 'genuine and determining'[134] occupational requirements which it is proportionate to apply in a particular case.

The Government has proposed that the exhaustive list approach, used in the SDA and the RRA, should be abandoned in favour of a more generic and flexible approach. In the employment context, this more generic approach might be based on the notion of a genuine occupational requirement.[135] It also contemplated (but subsequently rejected) the introduction of a similar generic defence based on the notion in the goods and services context.[136]

Surprisingly perhaps, the DDA sets out no exception to the operation of its direct discrimination provisions based on a genuine and determining occupational requirement. An important consideration in this regard is clearly the asymmetrical nature of the DDA, which makes it permissible to treat disabled people more favourably than non-disabled people.[137] Further, as discussed above, there will be no *direct* discrimination where a non-disabled person with greater abilities than a disabled person is selected even if the disabled person would have been the more able candidate had they received appropriate reasonable adjustments.

While there are clearly grounds for the argument that a genuine occupational requirement is unnecessary for disability, the absence of any such exception is likely to encourage judges to take an extremely restrictive approach to the limits of direct disability discrimination. The judgment of McMullen QC in *High Quality Lifestyles v Watts*[138] (the first case to have raised the issue of direct disability discrimination) reveals that the Employment Appeal Tribunal was mindful of the absence of exceptions or justifications when ruling that direct discrimination had not been established in that case.

3.2 Relationship with Reasonable Adjustment

Thus, as may be apparent, there is no overlap between the spheres of operation of direct discrimination and reasonable adjustment. Direct discrimination is confined to the broad areas of employment and post-16 education. In those contexts, there is no justification defence either to it or to a failure to make a reasonable adjustment. The key feature of the relationship between the two DDA concepts of direct discrimination and reasonable adjustment is the effective blindness of the former towards the latter. As explained above, in assessing whether a claimant has

---

[133] Employment Equality (Religion or Belief) Regulations 2003 (SI No 2003/1660) reg 7(3).

[134] *Ibid*, reg 7(2); Employment Equality (Sexual Orientation) Regulations 2003 (SI No 2003/1661) reg 7(2); and Employment Equality (Age) Regulations 2006 (SI No 2006/1031) reg 8.

[135] Department for Communities and Local Government, *Discrimination Law Review* (n 91 above) para 1.70; and Government Equalities Office, *The Equality Bill* (n 34 above) paras 8.5–8.16.

[136] *Discrimination Law Review* (n 91 above) paras 1.71–1.76; rejected in *The Equality Bill* (n 34 above) paras 8.18–8.26.

[137] Government Equalities Office, *The Equality Bill* (n 34 above) para 8.17.

[138] *High Quality Lifestyles v Watts* [2006] IRLR 850 (EAT) [49].

been the victim of direct discrimination, no regard whatsoever will be had to the existence of a reasonable adjustment duty which, had it been properly discharged, would have radically altered the claimant's position.

This may be contrasted with approaches adopted elsewhere. In the United States and in the Canadian province of Ontario, for example, a disabled person's abilities must be judged on the assumption that any accommodation of their needs, which would not impose undue hardship, has been provided.[139] The duty to accommodate the needs of otherwise marginalised groups (extending beyond disabled people) is given an additional role to play within Ontario's concept of direct discrimination. The question of whether such a duty has arisen and been properly discharged must be considered before an employer will be able to rely on the limited defence of a bona fide occupational requirement.[140] Nevertheless, given that there are no such defences in the DDA, reasonable adjustments are highly unlikely to make an appearance in the workings of British direct disability discrimination law.

In Britain, then, there is currently a stark division between the concepts of direct discrimination and reasonable adjustment. This reflects an understanding of direct discrimination as being concerned with ensuring that disabled people are treated in the same way as their non-disabled peers, and of reasonable adjustment duties as being concerned with ensuring that they are treated differently from them. Both concepts undoubtedly have important roles to play. The former is well placed to tackle blanket exclusions and the most blatant forms of discrimination. The function of the latter, however, is to ensure that participation occurs in a way that is meaningful and effective. The former, in short, is concerned with formal equality and the latter with a notion of equality which is substantive.

4. Indirect Discrimination

4.1 Outline of the Concept

4.1.1 Overview

In essence, indirect discrimination involves the unjustified application of an apparently neutral criterion, provision or practice which has a disparate impact on the relevant group and which actually disadvantages the claimant. It made its first appearance in British non-discrimination law in the SDA 1975. The British concept of indirect discrimination followed in the wake of the development of

---

[139] See, respectively, Americans with Disabilities Act 1990, 42 USC s 12111(8); and Ontario Human Rights Code 1990, ch H 19, s 17(1A). See also *Alberta Human Rights Commission v Central Alberta Dairy Pool* [1990] 2 SCR 489 at 528 (Sopinka J, with LaForest and McLachlin JJ concurring).
[140] Ontario Human Rights Code 1986, ch 64, s 18(8), (9) and (15).

the US 'disparate impact' doctrine.[141] That doctrine emerged from the 1971 case of *Griggs v Duke Power*.[142] The US Supreme Court there found that employers who made certain jobs available only to people who had a high school diploma or a good score in an IQ test (these requirements bearing no relation to job performance) amounted to racial discrimination under the Civil Rights Act 1964. The use of these requirements had the effect of disqualifying a disproportionate number of black people.

Unlike direct discrimination, therefore, indirect discrimination is concerned with provisions, criteria or practices which are apparently neutral. Such provisions, criteria and practices make no explicit reference to the prohibited ground (race, gender etc) and are applied in an identical manner to all. In the words of Baroness Hale,

> [i]t looks beyond the formal equality achieved by the prohibition of direct discrimination towards the more substantive equality of results.[143]

If it can be shown that an apparently neutral rule disproportionately disadvantages members of a relevant group, the indirect discrimination inquiry will require a demonstration of the need for that rule. If such a need cannot be demonstrated, indirect discrimination will be established.

The indirect discrimination provisions of British law have been significantly altered in recent years in response to the requirements of a number of EC Directives which, for reasons of convenience, will be referred to here as the 'non-discrimination directives'.[144] The transformation has, however, not been wholesale and there are therefore some areas in which the original and more restrictive provisions still apply.[145]

---

[141] See further RC Hunter and EW Shoben, 'Disparate Impact Discrimination: American Oddity or Internationally Accepted Concept?' (1998) 19 *Berkeley Journal of Employment and Labor Law* 108.

[142] *Griggs v Duke Power*, 401 US 424 (1971).

[143] *Rutherford v Sec of State for Trade and Industry (No 2)* [2006] UKHL 19 [71].

[144] On gender, see Council Directive 97/80/EC on the burden of proof in cases of discrimination based on sex, [1998] OJ L 14/6, Art 2(2); Council Directive 2002/73/EC amending Council Directive 76/207/EEC on the implementation of the principle of equal treatment for men and women as regards access to employment, vocational training and promotion and working conditions, [2002] OJ L 269/15; and Council Directive 2004/113/EC implementing the principle of equal treatment between men and women in the access to and supply of goods and services, [2004] OJ L 373/37–43. On race, see Council Directive 2000/43/EC implementing the principle of equal treatment between persons irrespective of racial or ethnic origin, [2000] OJ L 180/22, Art 2(2); and, on disability, age, sexual orientation and religion and belief, see Council Directive 2000/78/EC establishing a general framework for equal treatment in employment and occupation, [2000] OJ L 303/16. For full accounts of relevant EU developments see M Bell, *Anti-Discrimination Law and the European Union* (Oxford, Oxford University Press, 2002); and E Ellis, *EU Anti-Discrimination Law* (Oxford, Oxford University Press, 2005).

[145] For example, in relation to any discrimination based on colour or national origin under the RRA. This is set to change, however, as it is proposed that in the Equality Bill the new definition of indirect discrimination should totally replace the old—Government Equalities Office, *The Equality Bill* (n 34 above) paras 7.17–7.26.

The newer and more wide-reaching version of the concept is set out, in the context of race, in s 1(1A) of the RRA as follows:

> A person also discriminates against another if ... he applies to that other a provision, criterion or practice which he applies or would apply equally to persons not of the same race or ethnic or national origins as that other, but

> (a) which puts or would put persons of the same race or ethnic or national origins as that other at a particular disadvantage when compared with other persons,

> (b) which puts that other at that disadvantage, and

> (c) which he cannot show to be a proportionate means of achieving a legitimate aim.

The elements of this definition will shortly be examined further. Some reference will also be made to ways in which the new approach departs from the old—both because the old approach continues to operate in some spheres and because it sheds some light on the development of the law in this area. The purpose of this examination is not to provide a detailed and comprehensive account of British indirect discrimination law—a law which, as has already been mentioned, does not operate in the context of disability. Rather, its purpose is to provide a very basic idea of some of the key features of British indirect discrimination law and thereby to lay a foundation for the more detailed analysis of the relationship between indirect discrimination and reasonable adjustment which follows. That relationship is fascinating from a theoretical perspective. It also has significant practical ramifications, as, in many ways, it is fundamental to the controversy as to whether Britain's refusal to introduce the concept of indirect discrimination into the DDA is compatible with the demands of the Employment Equality Directive.

4.1.2 An Apparently Neutral Provision, Criterion or Practice

The original provisions of the SDA and the RRA allowed only a 'requirement' or a 'condition' to be challenged by way of a claim for indirect discrimination.[146] These terms were often interpreted restrictively. It was held, for instance, that they did not include selection criteria for a job if they fell short of essential requirements.[147] Neither were they held to include basic terms of employment (such as working on a full-time basis) if they represented the essential nature of the job.[148]

The non-discrimination directives adopt a less stringent approach to this issue than that previously taken in Britain. Domestic law has therefore been required to become more expansive in this regard with the result that its previous

---

[146] Section 1(1)(b) of both the SDA 1975 and the RRA 1976.

[147] *Perera v Civil Service Commission (No 2)* [1983] IRLR 166 (CA). For criticism, however, see *Meer v Tower Hamlets* [1988] IRLR 399 (CA) and *Falkirk Council v Whyte* [1997] IRLR 560 (EAT).

[148] *Clymo v Wandsworth LBC* [1989] ICR 250 (EAT). For criticism, see *Briggs v North Eastern Education Library Board* [1990] IRLR 181 (NICA).

reference to 'requirement or condition' has now largely been replaced by a reference to 'a provision, criterion or practice'.[149] Although there has been little judicial discussion of this phrase, it is clear that it will be interpreted more generously than its predecessor in order to ensure consistency with EC law.

4.1.3 Group Disadvantage

The second key element of an indirect discrimination claim is the disparate or disproportionate impact of the challenged provision, criterion or practice on the relevant group. Under the remoulded indirect discrimination provisions, this requires a demonstration of the fact that the provision, criterion or practice 'puts or would put' persons of the same race, age, sexual orientation or religion or belief as the claimant 'at a particular disadvantage when compared with other persons'. This departs from the former British approach in various ways.

Under the original indirect discrimination provisions of the SDA and RRA, it was necessary to show that the relevant requirement or condition was one with which a 'considerably smaller' proportion of the members of the claimant's racial or gender group could comply than could others not belonging to that group. The application of these provisions often resulted in extremely complex arguments revolving around detailed statistics. The preparation of such statistics before a case came to court was hampered by the need to anticipate correctly how the court or tribunal would identify the pool of people within which comparisons were to be made—for example, the entire working population, all graduates,[150] or all employees in the same job and on the same grade as the claimant.[151] Failure to anticipate the correct pool for comparison risked rendering one's statistical evidence entirely irrelevant.[152]

The original statutory reference to 'can comply' placed the emphasis very firmly on a demonstration of the ability of actual, rather than hypothetical, people to comply with the requirement or condition and therefore on its application in the present rather than in the future. The reference to a 'considerably smaller' proportion raised questions about how much smaller the proportion was required to be and caused particular difficulty in cases where proportions were skewed by the fact that there were very few members of a particular group within the pool for comparison[153] and where proportions were

---

[149] See eg Race Relations Act 1976 s 1(1A); Sex Discrimination Act 1975 s 1(2); Employment Equality (Religion or Belief) Regulations 2003 (SI 2003/1660) reg 3(1)(b); Equality Act 2006 s 45(3); Employment Equality (Sexual Orientation) Regulations 2003 (SI 2003/1661) reg 3(1)(b); and Employment Equality (Age) Regulations 2006 (SI 2006/1031) reg 3(1)(b). See also Department for Communities and Local Government, *Discrimination Law Review* (n 91 above) para 1.37, for the recommendation that the phrase 'provision, criterion or practice' be substituted for 'requirement or condition' throughout British indirect discrimination law.

[150] *Jones v University of Manchester* [1993] IRLR 218 (CA).

[151] *Clymo v Wandsworth LBC* [1989] ICR 250 (CA).

[152] *Pearse v City of Bradford Metropolitan Council* [1998] IRLR 379 (EAT).

[153] *London Underground v Edwards (No 2)* [1998] IRLR 364 (CA).

difficult to compare because the relevant requirement or condition excluded virtually everybody.[154] The ECJ, in its development of indirect sex discrimination law, has not escaped such difficulties—particularly those relating to the use of statistics.[155]

The new approach, as was explained above, is the result of EC Directives. In the context of indirect discrimination, a key aim of the drafters of these instruments was the reduction of the amount and complexity of statistical evidence required.[156] It should be noted, however, that statistical evidence may sometimes prove extremely helpful in establishing indirect discrimination, and that explicit provision for its use is made in the Employment Equality Directive.[157]

Under the new British approach, then, reference is made to the question of whether members of the relevant group are 'put or would be put' at 'a particular disadvantage' rather than to whether a 'considerably smaller' proportion of them 'can comply'.[158] This wording may allow British indirect discrimination law to escape from some of the worst of the technicalities in which it was previously ensnared.[159] The extent to which it *does*, however, remains to be seen. Whatever the outcome, the need for an apparently neutral provision, criterion or practice to disadvantage a relevant group will remain an essential feature of British indirect discrimination claims.

4.1.4 Claimant Disadvantage

Both the original and the new approaches to indirect discrimination require claimants to have been negatively affected by the challenged measure. Under the new approach, a claimant must have been put at the particular disadvantage found to affect the group to which they belong. This differs from the previous approach.

Under the original indirect discrimination provisions, a claimant was required to show that they had suffered a detriment 'because' they could not comply with the requirement or condition in dispute. Much judicial energy was therefore devoted to the issue of whether or not a claimant could comply with the

---

[154] *Coker v Lord Chancellor* [2002] IRLR 80 (CA).

[155] See, eg, *R v Sec of State for Employment ex parte Seymour Smith and Perez* [1999] IRLR 253 (discussed in C Barnard and B Hepple, 'Indirect Discrimination: Interpreting Seymour-Smith' (1999) 58 *Cambridge Law Journal* 399). Contrast, though, the much less statistical approach adopted by the ECJ in relation to migrant workers and free movement of persons—Case C-237/94 *O'Flynn v Adjudication Officer* [1996] ECR I-2617.

[156] See further HL Select Committee on the EU 9th Report, *EU Proposals to Combat Discrimination* (HL Paper 65 (1999–2000)) paras 79–83; C Barnard and B Hepple, 'Substantive Equality' (2000) 59 *Cambridge Law Journal* 562; and L Waddington and M Bell, 'More Equal than Others: Distinguishing European Union Equality Directives' [2001] *Common Market Law Review* 587.

[157] Employment Equality Directive Recital 15.

[158] See Department for Communities and Local Government, *Discrimination Law Review* (n 91 above) para 1.39, for a recommendation that this alteration in wording be applied throughout British indirect discrimination law.

[159] A point acknowledged in Government Equalities Office, *The Equality Bill* (n 34 above) para 7.25.

particular requirement or condition. Should a mother, for instance, be regarded as unable to comply with a requirement to work full-time when she could reduce her child-care responsibilities by employing a nanny?[160] Should a Sikh child be regarded as unable to comply with school uniform rules against the wearing of headgear when there is nothing physically to prevent him removing his turban?[161]

The new indirect discrimination provisions remove the emphasis on the claimant's ability to comply with the provision, criterion or practice. They simply require that that provision, criterion or practice put the claimant at a particular disadvantage. This language would appear comfortably to embrace cases in which the disadvantage results from having to sacrifice something, regarded as important by the claimant and the group to which they belong, in order to comply with the measure in question. It thus reduces the risk of cases failing on this somewhat technical ground.

It is unlikely that the new provisions will herald a significantly different approach to the level of disadvantage or detriment required. In the context of the old approach, it has been suggested in the Employment Appeal Tribunal[162] and the Court of Appeal[163] that the necessary detriment may be demonstrated only if it would have material and substantial physical or economic consequences for the claimant. The House of Lords, however, has favoured a less stringent approach, according to which the essential question is whether a reasonable worker in similar circumstances might regard themselves as being disadvantaged.[164] Although these cases were decided in the context of employment, they would appear to have equal relevance in other fields.

4.1.5 Justification

Under the new provisions, a defendant can justify what would otherwise amount to indirect discrimination only if they can establish that the provision, criterion or practice in question is in pursuance of a 'legitimate aim' and that it represents a 'proportionate means' of achieving that aim. This unequivocally lays down an objective test. In order to establish that the otherwise discriminatory measure has a legitimate aim, employers and other defendants are required to produce objective evidence demonstrating their need for it. If such an aim can be established, defendants must go on to demonstrate that their application of the challenged measure is a proportionate means of achieving it. This will involve a

---

[160] *Clymo v Wandsworth LBC* [1989] ICR 250 (EAT).

[161] *Mandla v Dowell Lee* [1983] 2 AC 548 (HL).

[162] *Lord Chancellor v Coker and Osamor* [2001] IRLR 116 (EAT).

[163] *Shamoon v Chief Constable of the Royal Ulster Constabulary* [2001] NICA 23.

[164] *Chief Constable of West Yorkshire Constabulary v Khan* [2001] UKHL 48; and *Shamoon v Chief Constable of Royal Ulster Constabulary* [2003] UKHL 11. Neither of these cases arose from an indirect discrimination claim but their discussion of the meaning of 'detriment' is undoubtedly highly persuasive.

consideration of the discriminatory impact of the measure, any business consid-erations underlying its application, the effectiveness of any alternative methods that might have been used and the existence of any immorality associated with its use.[165]

Although the original domestic indirect discrimination provisions laid down a justification defence, they provided no indication as to how this defence was to be applied. It therefore became a matter of some uncertainty. There were attempts to develop it in a highly subjective manner based on the defendant's motive for adopting the relevant requirement or condition.[166] Since the decision of the Court of Appeal in *Hampson v Department of Education and Science*,[167] however, these have given way (with the powerful influence of EC law on equal pay[168]) to an objective approach very similar to that required by the new provisions.[169]

Notwithstanding the adoption of the objective test laid down in *Hampson*, the justification defence appears to have been established with surprising ease in a number of cases.[170] Nevertheless, there is authority to the effect that a defendant is unlikely to be able to establish that a requirement is justified if alternative arrangements could have been introduced, at minimal cost, which would have eliminated the discriminatory effect in question.[171] Neither is the justification defence likely to be raised where a defendant failed to discuss or to consider the difficulties caused to a particular individual by a potentially discriminatory requirement.

Interestingly, in *Hardys and Hansons v Lax*,[172] the Court of Appeal held that the range of reasonable responses test, favoured in the disability-related discrimi-nation case of *Jones v The Post Office*,[173] had no role to play in this context. More was required of defendants in order to establish the justification defence for indirect discrimination. They must be able to persuade the Tribunal that the requirement or condition was reasonably necessary, taking into account the

---

[165] See, on the latter point in particular, *Allen and Others v GMB* [2008] EWCA Civ 810.

[166] See eg *Panesar v Nestlé Co* [1980] ICR 144 (CA); and *Singh v Rowntree Mackintosh* [1979] IRLR 199 (EAT). See also *Ojutiku and Oburoni v Manpower Services Commission* [1982] ICR 661 (CA).

[167] *Hampson v Department of Education and Science* [1990] 2 All ER 25 (CA). For an early authority in support of such an approach, see *Steel v Union of Post Office Workers* [1978] 2 All ER 504 (EAT).

[168] Case C-170/84 *Bilka-Kaufhaus* [1986] ECR 1607; *Rainey v Greater Glasgow Health Board* [1987] 1 AC 224 (HL).

[169] See further *Webb v EMO* [1992] 4 All ER 929 (QBD); *Barry v Midland Bank* [1999] ICR 859 (HL); and *Allonby v Accrington and Rossendale College* [2001] ICR 1189 (CA).

[170] See, eg, *Briggs v North Eastern Library Board* [1990] IRLR 181 (NICA), where the impact of the potentially discriminatory requirement on the claimant appears to have had little consideration; and *Eley v Huntleigh Diagnostics Ltd* (EAT/1441/96) and *Nelson v Chesterfield Law Centre* (EAT/1359/95), where employers were not required to produce any evidence as to the impracticability of adopting alternative methods which would not have operated to the disadvantage of the affected group.

[171] *London Underground v Edwards (No 2)* [1997] IRLR 157 (EAT).

[172] *Hardys and Hansons v Lax* [2005] EWCA Civ 846.

[173] *Jones v The Post Office* [2001] ICR 814 (CA).

employer's reasonable needs as revealed by a fair and detailed analysis of the working practices and business considerations involved.

Finally, it should be noted that the wording of the justification defence appearing in the revised indirect discrimination provisions has attracted some concern. The Discrimination Law Association, for instance, has drawn attention to the possibility that the phrase 'legitimate aim' may be interpreted as laying down a justification standard that will be too easily satisfied. In order to emphasise the strength of the relevant test, it has recommended that the phrase 'necessary and legitimate' be substituted.[174] This would more closely reflect the language of the Directives themselves, in which the phrase 'appropriate and necessary' is used. It would also bring British law closer to US law, where the governing test is that of 'business necessity'.[175] The Government, however, has firmly rejected this idea on the ground that it may be interpreted so strictly as to make it too difficult for defendants to establish the defence.[176]

4.2 Relationship with Reasonable Adjustments

4.2.1 Conceptual Ambiguities and Multiplicities

The task of analysing the relationship between the concepts of indirect discrimination and reasonable adjustment is by no means a straightforward one. The complexity arises, in large part, from the fact that neither concept takes a single unitary shape. Two principal forms of reasonable adjustment duty were outlined in the previous chapter—those which are entirely reactive in nature and those which have an anticipatory element. The latter, which appear to be peculiar to Britain, have a clear group dimension and therefore relate to indirect discrimination in a very different way from their entirely reactive and individualised siblings.

Indirect discrimination, too, may manifest itself in different ways.[177] According to Sandra Fredman, the multiplicity of definitions of indirect discrimination appearing in EC and UK law reveals 'a deep-seated set of ambiguities in the concept'.[178] Her three-fold classification of forms of indirect discrimination—all of which focus on the impact of an apparently neutral measure on an individual or group because of relevant characteristics (such as sex, race or disability)—is helpful and will therefore be repeated here.

---

[174] Discrimination Law Association, *Discrimination Law Association Submissions for the Discrimination Law Review* (n 104 above) para 38.

[175] Americans with Disabilities Act 1990, 42 USC s 2000e-2(k)(1)(A)(i). For discussion of this concept, see C Jolls, 'Antidiscrimination and Accommodation' (2001) 115 *Harvard Law Review* 642 at 665–7.

[176] Government Equalities Office, *The Equality Bill* (n 34 above) para 7.26.

[177] For a thorough account of the various approaches adopted within the EU, see D Schiek, 'Indirect Discrimination' in Schiek, Waddington and Bell (eds), *Cases, Materials and Texts on National, Supranational and International Non-Discrimination Law* (n 132 above).

[178] S Fredman, 'Equality: A New Generation?' (2001) 30 *Industrial Law Journal* 145 at 161.

In the first and most individualistic of the forms of indirect discrimination identified by Professor Fredman, the focus is on the effect of a measure on the individual rather than on the group to which they belong. Because there is no need to establish the disadvantageous impact of the measure on a group (eg people of a particular race or gender), the problem of demonstrating such disadvantageous impact through complex statistical evidence does not arise. All that is required is that the measure be shown to disadvantage an individual because of their sex, race, disability or other protected characteristic. For this reason, this formulation of the concept is favoured in the various EC non-discrimination Directives.[179] However, it has received severe criticism, not least because of the stress it places upon formal equality and its tendency to assimilate the notions of direct and indirect discrimination.[180]

Under the second approach, however, it is essential to demonstrate that the apparently neutral measure does inflict a group disadvantage. If this is established, discrimination against the relevant group will be assumed unless it can be shown that the measure in question is justified by reference to non-discriminatory considerations. In the event of such a measure being found to be justified, its disproportionately disadvantageous impact on the relevant group will be allowed to continue without censure. This approach underlies the British formulation of indirect discrimination outlined in the previous Section.

The final form of indirect discrimination set out by Professor Fredman is not currently to be found in the legal machinery of either Britain or the EC. Like the second form, it is based on the identification of a group disadvantage. Under it, however, there is no justification defence. The emphasis is thus firmly on achieving equality of results. It thus resembles laws requiring quotas of particular groups—reflecting their prevalence in the general population—to be present in the workforce, educational establishment or other relevant body.

All these conceptions of indirect discrimination contain both group and individual dimensions. Dagmar Schiek has drawn attention to the interplay of these two dimensions and to the fact that, as a result, indirect discrimination is something of a 'conceptual hybrid'.[181] In her words,

> [i]t guarantees an individual right while acknowledging that discrimination in social reality is group related. It corresponds to the concept of corrective justice, while taking wider aims of distributive justice as standard for legally acceptable behaviour. It requires remedying a specific individual situation, which results from group-related disadvantage. Above all, indirect discrimination law is linked to substantive equality, while not providing for measures to achieve this aim.[182]

---

[179] For arguments supporting such an approach, see K Lundstrom, 'Indirect Sex Discrimination in the European Court of Justice's Vision' in A Numhauser-Henning (ed), *Legal Perspectives on Equal Treatment and Non-discrimination* (The Hague, Kluwer, 2001) 143.

[180] See eg Barnard and Hepple, 'Substantive Equality' (n 156 above) 568–9.

[181] Schiek, 'Indirect Discrimination' (n 177 above) 332.

[182] *Ibid.*

It is thus clear that both the concept of reasonable adjustment and that of indirect discrimination take various forms. Any attempt to compare or contrast the two concepts will therefore require considerable care and clarity as to subject-matter. Only by making such comparisons, however, will it be possible to gain a firm understanding of the distinctiveness of the role played by reasonable adjustment duties. Such an understanding is essential to clear thinking about whether those duties could usefully be extended into other equality strands or whether, conversely, the law would be improved by wiping them off the face of the DDA and replacing them with indirect discrimination provisions analogous to those currently operating in the non-disability sphere.

Accordingly, the following two sections will consider the relationship between the British concept of indirect discrimination and, respectively, the DDA notions of anticipatory and of reactive reasonable adjustment. Finally, in Section 4.2.4, the relationship between British reasonable adjustment duties and the concept of indirect discrimination set out in the Employment Equality Directive will be considered.

4.2.2 British Indirect Discrimination and Anticipatory Reasonable Adjustment Duties

(a) Similarities and Differences   As was explained in the previous chapter, out-side the areas of employment and housing, the DDA duty to make reasonable adjustments is anticipatory in nature. This means that, in addition to the obligation to take reasonable steps to accommodate the needs of disabled individuals with whom they actually come into contact, service providers, educational establishments, private clubs and public authorities must anticipate ways in which their operations might disadvantage disabled people and take reasonable steps to remove or minimise the potential difficulty. Such an exercise should involve scrutinising physical features and apparently neutral provisions, criteria and practices in order to identify the disproportionate disadvantage they may cause to disabled people. Consideration should then be given to how potentially problematic physical features, provisions, criteria or practices might be removed, altered or avoided. There are a number of obvious similarities between this concept and that of indirect discrimination (as it is manifested in British law).

One similarity between the two concepts is that, in a claim for either indirect discrimination or for breach of an anticipatory reasonable adjustment duty, it must be shown that there was a group disadvantage. For the purposes of the latter, the central role of this requirement was emphasised by the Court of Appeal in *Roads v Central Trains*.[183] Before such a claim can succeed, it must be established that the challenged policy, procedure, practice or physical feature

---

[183]   *Roads v Central Trains* [2004] EWCA Civ 1541.

made it impossible or unreasonably difficult for broad groups of disabled people (such as those with mobility or visual impairments) to use the relevant service. The Government, however, has recommended that the stringency of this requirement should be reduced and that a demonstration of substantial disadvantage should suffice. The duty to take reasonable steps to provide an 'auxiliary aid or service' is triggered more easily—requiring only that the provision of such an aid or service would facilitate groups of disabled people in their use of the relevant service.

Under the traditional British approach to indirect discrimination, it had to be demonstrated that the proportion of people falling within the relevant group who could comply with the challenged requirement or condition was considerably smaller than the proportion of people not falling within that group. The emphasis was thus on group ability to comply rather than on group disadvantage as such. Under the new approach, however, it must be shown that the challenged provision, criterion or practice puts (or would put) members of the relevant group at a particular disadvantage. There is, as yet, little guidance on the degree of disadvantage envisaged by this requirement. It seems likely, however, that it will fall well short of the DDA requirement of 'impossibility or unreasonable difficulty' and that it may also fall short of the Discrimination Law Revue's proposed level of substantial disadvantage. It would appear to set the level of group disadvantage at a similar level to that required to trigger the anticipatory reasonable adjustment duty relating to the provision of auxiliary aids and services.

Thus, while both concepts require a demonstration of group disadvantage, the level of that disadvantage may well be greater for anticipatory reasonable adjustment than for indirect discrimination. This discrepancy is likely to be significantly, and perhaps entirely, reduced if 'substantial disadvantage' replaces 'impossibility or unreasonable difficulty' as the trigger for anticipatory reasonable adjustment duties. Until more clarity emerges about the meaning of 'particular disadvantage' in the context of indirect discrimination, any comparison will remain somewhat speculative.

Difficulties of comparison also affect the question of how the group disadvantage is to be proved. Traditional indirect discrimination cases were characterised by complex and often confusing statistical data directed at the issue of the proportions of different groups which could comply with particular requirements or conditions. Sedley LJ, in *Roads*, firmly indicated that such data had no role to play in connection with the group disadvantage element of anticipatory reasonable adjustment. The role of such data in cases concerning the new approach to indirect discrimination is also likely to be considerably smaller than its role in cases concerning the old approach. Thus, it remains unclear whether there will be any significant difference between the nature and extent of its roles in cases of indirect discrimination based on the new approach and in cases of reasonable adjustment.

A second similarity between the British concepts of indirect discrimination and anticipatory reasonable adjustment is that both require the individual claimant to have suffered some sort of disadvantage. Broadly, the degree of disadvantage required here reflects that required to establish the relevant group disadvantage. Thus, for indirect discrimination, it must be shown that the claimant was subjected to a 'particular disadvantage' and, for anticipatory reasonable adjustment, it must be shown that it was impossible or unreasonably difficult for the claimant to use the service in question. It is perhaps worth adding that, in the latter context, the standard of 'impossibility or unreasonable difficulty' is required of claimants challenging the failure of a service provider to take reasonable steps to provide an auxiliary aid or service, even though the level of group disadvantage required to trigger the relevant duty is much lower.

The various levels of disadvantage relevant here have already been considered in the context of group disadvantage. This issue will not therefore be examined further. However, the fact that both indirect discrimination and anticipatory reasonable adjustment depend on a demonstration of claimant disadvantage is an important one, the implications of which merit some consideration.

The claimant disadvantage requirement renders it impossible for indirect discrimination or reasonable adjustment claims to be brought until an individual disadvantaged by the particular provision, criteria, policy, procedure, practice or feature is willing to bring a case. Without such a disadvantaged and willing litigant, claims may not be brought no matter how clear it is that a particular practice or procedure is violating principles of indirect discrimination or anticipatory reasonable adjustment. Evidence that it is operating to disadvantage and exclude significant numbers of people from disadvantaged groups will be irrelevant unless one of those disadvantaged people is willing to bring a case. Without that, the only mechanism for tackling such discriminatory practices would be through a formal investigation launched by the Equality and Human Rights Commission.

The Hepple Report[184] recommended that such a Commission should be given a power to initiate what are often known as class or representative actions. It should be able to institute proceedings challenging unlawful discrimination, either in its own name or jointly with individuals, where there was 'a common question of fact or law affecting a number of persons, whether identified or not'.[185] This power, it suggested, might also be extended to trade unions and employment agencies.[186] Injunctive and declaratory relief, together with the possibility of damages for a defined group of people, should be available as potential remedies in such cases.

---

[184] Hepple, Coussey and Choudhury, *Equality* (n 88 above) recommendation 44.
[185] *Ibid.*
[186] *Ibid*, para 4.24. For an excellent and thought-provoking account of the use of class actions under the Americans with Disabilities Act 1990 and other US non-discrimination law, see MA Stein and ME Waterstone, 'Disability, Disparate Impact, and Class Actions' (2006) 56 *Duke Law Journal* 861.

The Hepple Report's recommendations on class actions would, for certain cases, have removed the need to identify disadvantaged individuals willing to litigate. This, as its authors indicate,[187] would have been particularly useful in cases where the challenged provision or practice deters members of particular groups from applying for a particular job or from using a particular service. The fact that disadvantaged groups have not actually engaged in the relevant employment or service reduces the chances of finding an affected individual who is willing to litigate.

These Hepple proposals would have had particular relevance to claims of indirect discrimination and anticipatory reasonable adjustment. They would have significantly strengthened the group dimension of both such claims. They clearly did not find favour with the Discrimination Law Review, however.[188] Its authors appear to have been strongly influenced by the fears of the business community that allowing such actions might encourage a litigation culture and the spawning of spurious claims. Nevertheless, the Government has since indicated that this is an issue which it is keen to investigate further and on which it may be prepared to consider proposals.[189]

A third similarity between indirect discrimination and anticipatory reasonable adjustment lies in the fact that both direct the attention of potential defendants to the discriminatory impact of their operations and require them to consider whether there might be ways in which that impact might be reduced. For indirect discrimination, such potential defendants will be safe from liability only if they can show that the challenged provision, criterion or practice represents a proportionate means of achieving a legitimate aim. For anticipatory reasonable adjustment, they will be safe only if they have taken all reasonable steps to remove the relevant discriminatory impact. Assessments of what steps will be considered reasonable—as was stressed in *Roads*[190]—must take into account the need to ensure that disabled people are put into a position which is as close as possible to that of non-disabled people as regards use of the service in question. Implicit in this approach is the need to consider whether potentially disabling policies, practices or features can be removed and replaced by ones that will be useable by disabled and non-disabled people alike and on the same basis. Where such measures would be reasonable, the taking of steps that would achieve a method or standard of service for disabled people which falls short of this fully integrated and effective ideal is unlikely to be sufficient to discharge the duty.

Consequently, both indirect discrimination and anticipatory reasonable adjustment require the discriminatory impact of apparently neutral provisions,

---

[187] Hepple, Coussey and Choudhury, *Equality: A New Framework* (n 46 above) paras 4.24–4.26.

[188] Department for Communities and Local Government, *Discrimination Law Review* (n 91 above) paras 7.28–7.30.

[189] See eg *Framework for a Fairer Future: The Equality Bill* (London, Stationery Office, June 2008) pp 32–3; and Government Equalities Office, *The Equality Bill* (n 34 above) paras 6.36–6.48.

[190] *Roads v Central Trains* [2004] EWCA Civ 1540.

criteria and practices to be scrutinised. Under both, inability to provide convincing, objectively verifiable reasons for the use of measures which disadvantage relevant groups will result in liability.

While this obligation to scrutinise and to justify apparently neutral measures is shared by indirect discrimination and anticipatory reasonable adjustment, the form it takes in the two concepts differs in three important respects.

First, in indirect discrimination, the scrutiny process focuses on the provision of reasons for the retention of the challenged provision, criterion or practice. In anticipatory reasonable adjustment, however, it focuses on the provision of reasons for not taking steps which would have removed or reduced the disadvantageous effect of the challenged measure—either by removing or amending the measure itself or by other means. As a result, whereas indirect discrimination cases often treat the identification of a solution 'almost as an afterthought', the concept of reasonable adjustment is 'solution-orientated'.[191] It places a stronger and more explicit emphasis on the need to think creatively about means by which the discriminatory impact of a provision, criterion or practice (or physical feature) might be avoided.

Second, anticipatory reasonable adjustment appears to have the capacity to place more emphasis on the needs and circumstances of the individual claimant than does indirect discrimination. In the latter, once a claimant has established that they were disadvantaged by the relevant provision, criterion or practice, their particular circumstances, difficulties and needs have traditionally played a very minimal role. In anticipatory reasonable adjustment cases on the other hand, although the primary duty is owed to a group of disabled people and relates to the dismantling of structural barriers, there is also likely to be an obligation to identify ways in which any remaining barriers might be negotiated by the claimant. The lengths to which duty-bearers will be expected to go in providing individualised solutions will vary from case to case. The nature of the service in question, the proximity of the relationship between the duty-bearer and the claimant, and the probable duration of the relationship between them are all likely to be relevant factors.

Third, anticipation is given a more prominent emphasis in anticipatory reasonable adjustment than it is in indirect discrimination. Because this reasonable adjustment duty is anticipatory, it renders duty-bearers vulnerable to liability if they fail adequately to address issues of disability equality in designing and implementing their structures and operations. It emphasises that organisations should take steps in advance of the arrival of a disabled person and that the need for such steps must be assessed on an on-going basis. It has the potential, for instance, to render a service-provider (such as a library) liable for choosing to buy inaccessible software for use by its customers when there was an equally suitable but more accessible version on the market.

---

[191] DRC, *Initial Submission to the Discrimination Law Review* (n 89 above) para 1.3.2.

This is perhaps the most important aspect of the anticipatory reasonable adjustment duty because it operates to deter duty-bearers from creating new disabling barriers and to encourage them to think creatively about ways of removing or reducing the disadvantageous effect of existing ones. It recognises that, because of the length of time often required in order to take effective steps to tackle disabling barriers, there may be very little that can be done when a disabled customer or service-user actually appears on the scene. It therefore represents a great strength of the anticipatory reasonable adjustment duties. However, it carries with it some requirement of awareness and predictability of the relevant disadvantage which is absent from indirect discrimination. Consequently, in this regard, indirect discrimination will have a wider reach than will anticipatory reasonable adjustment.

It is clear then that there is much in common between the anticipatory reasonable adjustment duty and indirect discrimination. Both require the demonstration of group disadvantage and also claimant disadvantage. The aim of both is to encourage relevant organisations to consider the potentially discriminatory impact of apparently neutral aspects of their operations and to minimise this wherever possible. Despite the important differences between them noted here, the closeness of their relationship raises the question of whether there is any need to retain both. Might the law be simplified and harmonised by removing one of these concepts and allowing the other to take its place?

(b) Harmonisation?   Given the longer history of indirect discrimination, and its operation in a greater proportion of current non-discrimination legislation, the most obvious form of substitution might appear to be one in which indirect discrimination replaced anticipatory reasonable adjustment. This would undoubtedly have the advantage of bringing the DDA more closely into line with statutes such as the SDA and RRA. The abandonment of a notion of anticipatory reasonable adjustment may also facilitate greater clarity about the notion of reactive reasonable adjustment—a notion which would need to remain firmly in place even if its anticipatory sibling were to disappear.

Arguments have frequently been made to the effect that indirect discrimination is better placed to tackle group disadvantage than is reasonable adjustment.[192] These arguments have tended to be based on a reactive conception of reasonable adjustment, however, and therefore contribute little to debate about the relationship between indirect discrimination and anticipatory reasonable adjustment.

---

[192]   See eg L Waddington and A Hendriks, 'The Expanding Concept of Employment and Discrimination in Europe: From Direct and Indirect Discrimination to Reasonable Accommodation Discrimination' (2002) 8 *International Journal of Comparative Labour Law and Industrial Relations* 403 at 415; K Wells, 'The Impact of the Framework Employment Directive on UK Disability Discrimination Law' (2003) 32 *Industrial Law Journal* 253 at 271–2; and R Whittle, 'The Framework Directive for Equal Treatment in Employment and Occupation: An Analysis from a Disability Rights Perspective' (2002) 27 *European Law Review* 303 at 310.

Indirect discrimination, however, is clearly wider in scope than anticipatory reasonable adjustment. It requires (at least at present) a lesser degree of disadvantage to be demonstrated. Unlike anticipatory reasonable adjustment, it does not require the relevant disadvantage to have been of a type which should have been foreseen by the alleged discriminator. Further, it operates comfortably in cases where it might not be possible to remove the relevant disadvantage by means of a reasonable adjustment. Until recently, the concept of disability-related discrimination played an important role in filling this gap between the outer edges of anticipatory reasonable adjustment and those of indirect discrimination. After *Lewisham London Borough Council v Malcolm*,[193] however, this will no longer be the case.

The unquestionable benefits of simplicity and harmonisation are, it is suggested, insufficient to outweigh the potential damage which might be effected by replacing anticipatory reasonable adjustment with indirect discrimination. As explained above, the former appears to be more powerful and vibrant than the latter in a number of respects. It is less encumbered by the baggage of statistical data than is the traditional version of indirect discrimination. Although the new incarnation of indirect discrimination may be less burdened than its predecessor, the extent to which its load has been lightened is as yet unclear.

Further, anticipatory reasonable adjustment is likely to require more from organisations than is indirect discrimination. A strong indirect discrimination justification defence—capable of requiring organisations to bear some cost in order to accommodate relevant needs and to effect reorganisations of structures, practices and job descriptions—would generate thinking similar to that generated by a reasonable adjustment duty.[194] Currently, however, the British indirect justification defence appears to fall short of this. It would require still further development to acquire the anticipatory and individualised dimensions of anticipatory reasonable adjustment.

Accordingly, there are strong arguments for retaining the concept of anticipatory reasonable adjustment in the DDA. These may, at least in part, explain why calls to introduce indirect discrimination into the disability context have to date been resisted.[195] Such calls were firmly rejected by the Discrimination Law

---

[193] *Lewisham LBC v Malcolm* [2008] UKHL 43.

[194] See further Jolls, 'Antidiscrimination and Accommodation' (n 175 above); Collins, 'Discrimination, Equality and Social Inclusion' (n 97 above) 37–8; and S Fredman, *Discrimination Law* (Oxford, Oxford University Press, 2002) 316–18.

[195] For examples of such calls see Discrimination Law Association, *Discrimination Law Association Submissions for the Discrimination Law Review* (n 104 above) para 41; Equality Commission for Northern Ireland, *Response to "Promoting Equality of Opportunity Implementing EU Equality Obligations in Northern Ireland" A Consultation by the Office of the First and Deputy First Minister* (Belfast, Equality Commission for Northern Ireland, 2003).

Review, for instance, (albeit on the basis of minimal and unconvincing analysis).[196] Nevertheless, *Lewisham* has opened up a serious gap in the protection from discrimination afforded to disabled people. It needs to be filled either by the reinstatement of the *Novacold* approach or by the introduction of some notion of indirect discrimination which safeguards the strengths of the current anticipatory reasonable adjustment duties.

The benefits of greater consistency and harmonisation would, of course, also be achieved by a substitution of anticipatory reasonable adjustment for indirect discrimination in the non-disability contexts. This would allow indirect discrimination to benefit from some of the distinctive characteristics of anticipatory reasonable adjustment outlined above. The level of frustration and despair which British indirect discrimination law triggered in many of the judgments in the recent case of *Rutherford v Secretary of State for Trade and Industry*[197] perhaps lends some support to arguments that it is indeed time for such an injection of vibrancy and vigour. Lord Roger bemoaned the 'battle of statistics' with which the court had been confronted[198] and Lord Walker[199] indicated that it was impossible not to have some sympathy with Mummery LJ's observation in the lower court that

> [t]he legal materials on indirect discrimination ... are increasingly voluminous and incredibly intractable. The available arguments have become more convoluted, while continuing to multiply. Separating the wheat from the chaff takes more and more time. The short snappy decisions of the early days of the industrial tribunals have long since disappeared. They have been replaced by what truly are 'extended reasons' which have to grapple with factual situations of escalating complexity and with thicker seams of domestic and EC law, as interpreted in cascades of case law from the House of Lords and the European Court of Justice.[200]

The fact that people with Mummery LJ's degree of experience and expertise in the subject are making observations such as this, as Lord Scott acknowledged, suggests that 'something has gone awry with the jurisprudence about indirect discrimination'.[201] The weary and beleaguered image of indirect discrimination conjured by such utterances contrasts sharply with the youth and freshness of the anticipatory reasonable adjustment duty.

Nevertheless, it would plainly be unrealistic to hope for a wholesale replacement of indirect discrimination by anticipatory reasonable adjustment. Although such a move would achieve consistency across all the strands protected by British

---

[196] Department for Communities and Local Government, *Discrimination Law Review* (n 91 above) paras 1.34–1.35. See also Government Equalities Office, *The Equality Bill* (n 34 above) paras 11.45–11.49; and Disability Rights Task Force, *From Exclusion to Inclusion* (n 87 above) para 5.66.

[197] *Rutherford v Secretary of State for Trade and Industry* [2006] UKHL 19 (discussed in C Barnard, 'The Aging Model of Indirect Discrimination' (2007) 66 *Cambridge Law Journal* 37).

[198] *Rutherford v Secretary of State for Trade and Industry* [2006] UKHL 19 [27].

[199] *Ibid*, [37].

[200] *Rutherford v Secretary of State for Trade and Industry* [2004] EWCA Civ 1186 [3].

[201] *Rutherford v Secretary of State for Trade and Industry* [2006] UKHL 19 [7].

non-discrimination legislation, it would inevitably result in major conceptual upheaval and confusion. It would also risk exchanging the wide scope of indirect discrimination for the somewhat narrower scope of anticipatory reasonable adjustment and thereby effecting an undesirable shrinkage in the extent of protection. The most pragmatic approach, therefore, would seem to be to retain the concept of indirect discrimination for grounds other than disability but to have regard to the concept of anticipatory reasonable adjustment when fleshing out the details of its new EC-driven incarnation.

4.2.3 British Indirect Discrimination and Reactive Reasonable Adjustment Duties

The relationship between indirect discrimination and the reactive reasonable adjustment duties, applying to employment and housing, is far less close than the relationship between it and the anticipatory reasonable adjustment duties. There is no group disadvantage requirement for reactive reasonable adjustment duties. Neither is there any need to contemplate steps which would benefit a group. The exclusive focus is on steps which it would be reasonable to take in order to remove the barriers encountered by a particular individual and to provide them with a specifically tailored package of appropriate support.

Under the DDA, neither the concept of anticipatory reasonable adjustment nor that of indirect discrimination operates in the contexts of employment and housing. Consequently, in those areas, there is no group-based non-discrimination concept at work. Employers are not placed under any obligation to consider and to avoid or remove institutional barriers against disabled people unless they are subject to the public sector disability equality duty—a duty which will be considered in depth in the next chapter.

The following passage from the DRC's review of relevant legislation in 2003 draws attention to the damaging consequences of the present highly individualised and reactive focus of current DDA employment law:

> [A] visually impaired person was away from work recuperating from an eye operation. On returning to work, she found that a new telephone system had been installed which she could no longer operate. As she was employed as an operator this made her work impossible. She had not been consulted about the change in systems. Whilst under the present law her employer is under an obligation to consider a reasonable adjustment, this may not in practice help this operator to retain her job as the costs of rectifying the situation for one person may be judged 'unreasonable'. The real solution is for the employer to be considering visually impaired employees and potential employees when purchasing a system. It is not onerous to specify that a system should be compatible with technology allowing visually impaired employees to access the system. This will benefit not only this individual but possibly others in the future.[202]

---

[202] DRC, *Disability Equality: Making it Happen* (n 88 above) Employment recommendation 1.

The absence of a group dimension to the current non-discrimination concepts at work in the employment parts of the DDA is therefore lamentable. An important part of any solution, as was argued in the last chapter and will be repeated below, is to extend anticipatory reasonable adjustment to employment under the DDA.

4.2.4 EC Indirect Discrimination and British Reasonable Adjustment Duties

Under Article 2(1) of the Employment Equality Directive, Member States are required to prohibit indirect discrimination on the basis of a number of grounds, one of which is disability. Article 2(2)(b) defines indirect discrimination, for these purposes, in the following terms:

> Indirect discrimination shall be taken to occur where an apparently neutral provision, criterion or practice would put persons having ... a particular disability ... at a particular disadvantage compared with other persons unless:

> (i) that provision, criterion or practice is objectively justified by a legitimate aim and the means of achieving that aim are appropriate and necessary,

> or

> (ii) as regards persons with a particular disability, the employer or any person or organisation to whom this Directive applies, is obliged, under national legislation, to take appropriate measures in line with the principles contained in Article 5 in order to eliminate disadvantages entailed by such provision, criterion or practice.

The first of these two exceptions, set out in sub-paragraph (i), lays down the form of justification defence which is to be found elsewhere in European Community indirect discrimination law. The second exception, set out in sub-paragraph (ii), is more complex. It permits Member States to refrain from prohibiting indirect discrimination if their own national legislation requires employers and others 'to take appropriate measures in line with the principles contained in Article 5' in order to 'eliminate' the disadvantage which would otherwise result from the provision, criterion or practice. The principles contained in Article 5 are those of reasonable accommodation or, in British terminology, reasonable adjustment.[203]

The British Government's decision not to prohibit indirect disability discrimination is based on the second of the Article 2(2)(b) exceptions. In its view, domestic law relating to reasonable adjustments does oblige employers and others to take the measures referred to in Article 2(2)(b)(ii). Consequently, in its view, the Directive did not necessitate the introduction of further legislation

---

[203] See ch 2, fnn 200–05 above and accompanying text.

prohibiting indirect discrimination against disabled people.[204] There are concerns, however, (even pre-dating *Lewisham*[205]) that this view was incorrect and that British law therefore falls short of its obligations under the Directive.[206] These issues—which concern the relationship between the specific form of indirect discrimination set out in the Directive and the British reactive reasonable adjustments concept applicable to employment—will now be considered.

First, in relation to employment, the DDA reasonable adjustment duty is entirely reactive in the sense that it will arise only if the disabled person in question is actually placed at a disadvantage by the provision, criterion, practice or physical feature. Under the Directive, however, indirect discrimination will occur where the offending provision, criterion or practice 'would put' a disabled person at a disadvantage. This suggests that, for the purposes of the Directive, indirect discrimination may occur despite the fact that a disabled person has not yet been placed at a disadvantage. In confining its scope to actual disadvantage, the DDA employment reasonable adjustment duty may therefore fall short of the Directive's demands.

Second, in relation to both employment and post-16 education, a DDA reasonable adjustment duty will arise only where the relevant disadvantage is 'substantial'. Under the Directive, the relevant disadvantage is qualified only by the word 'particular'. It is possible, though by no means certain, that 'particular disadvantage' sets a lower threshold than 'substantial disadvantage'. If this is the case, British law would again seem to fall short of the standard required by the Directive.

Third, the Directive might arguably be interpreted as permitting Member States to rely on the reasonable accommodation approach only when their legislation actually requires an employer to take steps in a particular case.[207] On this view, where an employer is not obliged to take such steps (because, for example, doing so would not be regarded as reasonable) the indirect discrimination caused by an apparently neutral measure should be prohibited unless the application of that measure could be shown to be a proportionate means of achieving a legitimate aim. Under British law, however, if an adjustment is not deemed to be reasonable, there is no need to go on to consider whether the offending measure disadvantages disabled people as a group or whether it is itself justified. Accordingly, if this interpretation were held to be correct, British law would not comply with the Directive.

---

[204] The Draft Disability Discrimination Act 1995 (Amendment) Regulations 2003—Explanatory Notes and Supplementary Questions, para 19. See generally Wells, 'The Impact of the Framework Employment Directive on UK Disability Discrimination Law' (n 192 above) 270–73.

[205] *Lewisham LBC v Malcolm* [2008] UKHL 43.

[206] See eg Wells, 'The Impact of the Framework Employment Directive on UK Disability Discrimination Law' (n 192 above) 271; and K Monaghan, *Blackstone's Guide to the Disability Discrimination Legislation* (Oxford, Oxford University Press, 2005) section 5.2.2.

[207] See eg A McColgan, *Discrimination Law: Text, Cases and Materials* (Oxford, Hart Publishing, 2005) 562–4.

A further apparent departure relates to the way in which the comparator group is to be established. Under the DDA, the reasonable adjustment duty will arise if the disabled person is substantially disadvantaged 'in comparison with persons who are not disabled'. Under the Directive, however, the required comparison is simply with 'other persons'. Thus, for the purposes of the Directive but not the DDA, other disabled people may be used as comparators provided that they do not have the particular disability in question. The practical effects of this difference in wording are likely to be minimal. It is extremely difficult to envisage any situation in which a provision, criterion or practice which is 'apparently neutral' benefits a group of disabled people sufficiently to make them a more desirable comparator group than people who are not disabled.

Thus, although the matter will necessarily be somewhat uncertain until clarified by future rulings of the European Court of Justice, it seems that the DDA reactive reasonable adjustment duty may well fail to meet the Directive's requirements on indirect discrimination. An obvious response would therefore be to extend the British indirect discrimination provisions, applicable to other grounds, to disability in the fields of employment and occupation. However, as was demonstrated in Section 4.2.2 above, the concept of anticipatory reasonable adjustment enjoys certain advantages over that of indirect discrimination. Further, while indirect discrimination would be a wholly new concept for British disability non-discrimination law, the concept of anticipatory reasonable adjustment is already at work in the DDA.

There are therefore powerful arguments for extending anticipatory reasonable adjustment, instead of indirect discrimination, to the employment regions of the DDA. The anticipatory and group-based dimension of this duty would satisfy the first and most serious of the concerns set out above. Satisfaction of the second and third of those concerns is likely to require thought to be given to the drafting of the duty. It might require, for instance, the Directive's phrase of 'particular disadvantage' to be used in place of the phrase 'substantial disadvantage'—the phrase generally favoured in the DDA employment provisions—and might require some reference to be made to 'a proportionate means of achieving a legitimate aim' in guidance as to the meaning of 'reasonableness' for the purposes of the duty. Thus, although care would undoubtedly be required, there would seem to be no reason why the indirect discrimination demands of the Directive could not be met at least in part by an extension of the concept of anticipatory reasonable adjustment to the employment parts of the DDA. However, as was explained above, the concept of anticipatory reasonable adjustment is narrower in some important respects than that of indirect discrimination. Thought should therefore also be given to reinstating the dimensions of disability-related discrimination which existed before the painful constriction effected by the House of Lords in *Lewisham London Borough Council v Malcolm*.[208]

---

[208] *Lewisham LBC v Malcolm* [2008] UKHL 43.

For these reasons, together with those outlined elsewhere in this chapter and in the previous one, the concept of anticipatory reasonable adjustment should be extended to the DDA's employment provisions without delay. Disappointingly, and despite the existence of previous recommendations to this effect by the DRC,[209] the Discrimination Law Review made no proposals to extend the sphere of application of the anticipatory duties and the Government has since explicitly rejected the idea.[210]

5. Reactive Reasonable Adjustment and Non-Disability Grounds

The relationship between anticipatory reasonable adjustment and indirect discrimination was explored in Section 4.2.2 above. These clearly related concepts operate in parallel spheres—the former being confined to certain Parts of the DDA and the latter extending to virtually all non-disability areas of non-discrimination law. It was suggested above that, for various reasons, these two concepts should both continue to exist and to function alongside one another.

The current discussion will focus on the reactive reasonable adjustment duty. This is the only legal tool in British non-discrimination law to focus explicitly on the identification of an individualised solution. Currently, legislation makes specific provision for it only in the context of disability, but the question of whether it should be extended to grounds other than disability is an important one. Before considering whether statutory provision to this effect should be made, a few words will be devoted to the issue of whether, in the context of religion, such a duty has already begun to emerge from case law.

The case which is of particular significance here is *Copsey v WBB Devon Clays Ltd*.[211] Mr Copsey, a former employee of WBB Devon Clays, had been dismissed because of his refusal to work on Sundays—a refusal which was grounded on his firmly held Christian beliefs. He argued that this dismissal had been unfair and that it failed to accord due respect to his right (under Article 9 of the European Convention on Human Rights) to manifest his religious beliefs. In the Court of Appeal Mummery, Rix and Neuberger LJJ all found in favour of the employer but their reasoning differed. It was in the judgment of Rix LJ that the concept of reasonable accommodation featured large.

Rix LJ referred to Canadian jurisprudence on an employer's obligation to reasonably accommodate the religious beliefs of employees, subject to the limit of

---

[209] *Disability Equality: Making it Happen* (n 88 above) Employment recommendation 1. See also Disability Rights Task Force, *From Exclusion to Inclusion* (n 87 above) recommendation 5.41; and Hepple, Coussey and Choudhury, *Equality* (n 88 above) recommendation 11.

[210] Ch 3, fnn 313–14 above and accompanying text.

[211] *Copsey v WBB Devon Clays Ltd* [2005] EWCA Civ 932. See generally N Addison, *Religious Discrimination and Hatred Law* (Oxford, Routledge-Cavendish, 2007) 66–70.

undue hardship, and acknowledged that the concept of 'reasonable accommoda-tion' was no stranger to English law.[212] He thought it 'possible and necessary to contemplate' that an employee's dismissal for his refusal to agree to an alteration in working hours which clashed with his religious beliefs would be unfair unless the employer had made reasonable attempts to accommodate his employee's religious needs.[213] According to his Lordship,

> if respect for the right to manifest one's religion is to have meaning in a democratic society, it is not possible to say that an employer who, in the given situation, would simply ignore any need to seek a reasonable accommodation would be acting fairly.[214]

Such a reasonable accommodation requirement would, he considered, be easily housed within the English law of unfair dismissal where, in his view, it already resided.[215] Interestingly, however, he clearly regarded it as entirely distinct and separate from 'discrimination', and made no explicit reference to the DDA reasonable adjustment obligations.[216]

Rix LJ's judgment in *Copsey* may thus mark the beginning of a more general acceptance of the view that unfair dismissal law requires employers to reasonably accommodate the religious beliefs of their employees. It is also possible that the indirect discrimination provisions of the Employment Equality (Religion and Belief) Regulations might be interpreted in such a way as to place a reduced emphasis on group disadvantage and thereby to achieve a degree of flexibility more characteristic of reactive reasonable adjustment duties than indirect dis-crimination.[217] It would clearly be premature, at this stage, to make predictions about the nature and extent of any duty to accommodate religion. It is worth noting, however, that in jurisdictions (including the United States) where such a duty operates, it has generally been held to impose less demanding obligations on duty-bearers than do disability-related reasonable accommodation duties.[218]

If accepted in the context of unfair dismissal, there is a chance that a duty to make reasonable accommodation for religious beliefs may be extended beyond the employment context to areas such as education, public functions and the provision of goods and services. Such a development, however, appears extremely

---

[212] *Ibid*, [66]–[67].

[213] *Ibid*, [70].

[214] *Ibid*, [71].

[215] *Ibid*, [70]–[72].

[216] See eg *ibid*, [66].

[217] See, for a thought-provoking discussion of this issue, L Vickers, *Religious Freedom, Religious Discrimination and the Workplace* (Oxford, Hart Publishing, 2008) 126–35 and 220–25.

[218] SB Epstein, 'In Search of a Bright Line: Determining When an Employer's Financial Hardship Becomes "Undue" Under the Americans with Disabilities Act' (1995) 48 *Vanderbilt Law Review* 391 at 424–5; and R Coker, 'Affirmative Action, Reasonable Accommodation and Capitalism: Irreconcilable Differences?' in M Hauritz, C Sampford, S Blencowe (eds), *Justice for People with Disabilities: Legal and Institutional Issues* (Sydney, The Federation Press, 1998) 51. For discussion of religious reasonable accommodation duties operating within EU countries, see L Waddington, 'Reasonable Accommoda-tion' in Schiek, Waddington and Bell (eds), *Cases, Materials and Texts on National, Supranational and International Non-Discrimination Law* (n 132 above) 722–3.

unlikely. No mention was made of reasonable accommodation by the House of Lords in the much-publicised case of *R (on the application of Begum) v Denbigh High School*,[219] in which it was held that a school uniform policy which prohibited the wearing of the jilbab did not violate the right of a Muslim girl to manifest her religion.[220] Interestingly, the nature of the inquiry evident in such Article 9 cases appears to bear a much closer resemblance to that of indirect discrimination or even of anticipatory reasonable adjustment than it does to the inquiry involved in reactive reasonable adjustment cases.

The Hepple Report recommended that a reasonable accommodation duty, subject to the limit of undue hardship, should be imposed on employers, education providers and others in respect of religious observances.[221] This view was not shared by the Discrimination Law Review, however, which did not consider it necessary to treat religion differently, in this respect, from other non-disability grounds. It is to the question of whether a reasonable adjustment duty should be extended not simply to religion but to all other grounds that attention will now be turned.

One important potential benefit of extending a reactive reasonable adjustment duty to all equality strands would of course be the message it would send that creative inclusion-orientated thinking is required across the board. It would also achieve greater consistency within non-discrimination legislation and would thereby reduce the risk of disability-related adjustments being equated with welfare or special provision. The current structure of non-discrimination law, however, presents certain challenges for the framing of a workable freestanding reactive reasonable adjustment duty along the lines of that presently applying in the disability context.

The first problematic issue relates to the symmetrical nature of most British non-discrimination law. Outside the area of disability, protection is generally granted to specific grounds in a symmetrical manner. Thus, men and women are protected equally, as are members of majority and minority ethnic groups. If this symmetry is to be preserved, a reasonable adjustment duty must potentially apply to benefit people on both sides of the relevant divide, provided that they would otherwise be subjected to the required level of disadvantage by provisions, criteria, practices and, possibly, physical features. Such a duty may require greater flexibility of thinking from those subjected to it than is required by the disability duty, which can be triggered only in favour of the traditionally disadvantaged group—disabled people.

A further challenge to the crafting of an effective reasonable adjustment duty to extend beyond the confines of disability arises from the ground-specific nature

---

[219] *R (on the application of Begum) v Denbigh High School* [2006] UKHL 15.

[220] See also *R (Playfoot) v Millais School Governing Body* [2007] EWHC 1698 (Admin), where it was found that the wish of a Christian schoolgirl to wear a chastity ring was not sufficiently closely connected to her religious beliefs to bring the case within the realms of Art 9.

[221] Hepple, Coussey and Choudhury, *Equality* (n 88 above) recommendation 21, paras 2.77–2.82.

of current British law. Restricting the duty to situations in which people would otherwise be disadvantaged on the basis of one of the prohibited grounds may result in a duty which is disappointingly limited in scope. Childcare responsibility and family status,[222] for instance, are not amongst the prohibited grounds of discrimination. A reasonable adjustment duty extending only to the current grounds would therefore impose no duty to make reasonable adjustments in favour of people with such responsibilities. This difficulty, however, could be addressed by supplementing the general duty with specific duties applying to such groups.

Another potential obstacle to the introduction of a general reasonable adjustment duty applying to all strands is the fear that such a duty might dilute the impact of the current disability duty. Arguably, disability calls for individualised solutions more strongly than does any other ground. Some barriers confronting disabled people may be anticipated and addressed on a group basis, as is reflected in the anticipatory duty applying to service providers. There will nevertheless always be the need to make adjustments which will accommodate the particular requirements of a particular disabled person. People with exactly the same type and level of impairment may require very different adjustments. One blind employee, for instance, may be a fluent Braille reader and require material to be made available in that format, whereas another may never have learned Braille, and require material to be provided electronically instead. In relation to other grounds, it is likely to be easier to address barriers on a group basis (eg by the establishment of effective flexible working schemes).[223] As an alternative to the introduction of a general reasonable adjustment duty, the DRC therefore urged the Discrimination Law Review to consider the strengthening of rights to flexible working.[224] Outside the area of disability, it argued, rules regarding working hours are likely to present most of the difficulties to relevant groups.

British law has for a number of years made specific, if relatively limited, provision for flexible working outside the context of maternity and paternity leave. A right to request flexible working (though not to receive it) was granted to parents of young and disabled children in 2003.[225] This was extended to carers for

---

[222] For the view that 'family status' (which would cover childcare responsibility) should be added as a specified ground, see Hepple, Coussey and Choudhury, *Equality* (n 88 above) recommendation 20. See also Government Equalities Office, *The Equality Bill* (n 34 above) paras 15.2–15.13 for discussion of this issue and an explanation of the Government's decision not to add 'parent' or 'carer' to the grounds on which discrimination is prohibited.

[223] For powerful arguments in favour of extending reasonable adjustment to grounds other than disability, however, see G Moon, 'From Equal Treatment to Appropriate Treatment: What Lessons can Canadian Equality Law on Dignity and on Reasonable Accommodation Teach the United Kingdom?' [2006] *European Human Rights Law Review* 695.

[224] DRC, *Initial Submission to the Discrimination Law Review* (n 89 above) para 1.3.2.

[225] Employment Rights Act 1996 s 80F. See generally C Palmer, J Wade, A Heron and K Woods, *Maternity and Parental Rights: A Guide to Parents' Legal Rights at Work* (London, Legal Action Group, 2006) ch 12.

adults by the Work and Families Act 2006[226] and is to be extended to all parents of children under 16.[227] Despite these developments, a 2007 report indicated that flexible working remained unavailable to a significant proportion of those who would benefit from it.[228]

There is therefore some concern that the right to request flexible work should be extended to all workers and that employers who refuse a request should be placed under an obligation to provide objective justification for their view that permitting it would not have been practicable.[229] Although broadly analogous to the current DDA reasonable adjustment duties, the obligations placed on employers by such rights to request flexible work are clearly neither as strong nor as solution-oriented as the DDA duties.

Flexible working schemes, even if strengthened, will not address contentious issues such as religious dress nor assist with disputes falling outside the employment arena (such as ones relating to educational timetables and students with particular religions or childcare responsibilities). In such circumstances, however, indirect discrimination and human rights law may provide an adequate mechanism for ensuring that disproportionately disadvantageous procedures and practices are kept to a minimum.[230]

Prompted again by concerns about a potential dilution of the disability reasonable adjustment duty, the Discrimination Law Association urged that, rather than developing a universal reasonable adjustment duty, consideration be given to the crafting of additional reasonable adjustment duties, targeted at specific groups.[231] Indeed, British law may already be regarded as imposing a number of duties to accommodate, which, rather than laying down a broad requirement to do what is reasonable, have more tightly prescribed parameters.[232] Provision for maternity and paternity leave are the most obvious examples.[233]

---

[226] See generally C Palmer, 'New Rights at Work for Parents and Carers from April 2007' (2007) *Legal Action* 33; and 'ACAS Advisory Leaflet—Flexible Working: the Right to Apply. A Short Guide for Employers, Working Parents and Carers', available at http://www.acas.org.uk/media/pdf/i/t/B20_1.pdf (last accessed 30 Apr 2008).

[227] Government Equalities Office, *The Equality Bill* (n 34 above) para 15.10.

[228] Equal Opportunities Commission, *Enter the Timelords: Transforming Work to Meet the Future* (Manchester, EOC, 2007).

[229] See eg DRC, *The Disability Agenda: Creating an Alternative Future—Employment* (London, DRC, 2007) para 3.2.

[230] See generally Addison, *Religious Discrimination and Hatred Law* (n 211 above); and, on indirect discrimination specifically, L Vickers, 'The Employment Equality (Religion or Belief) Regulations 2003' (2003) 32 *Industrial Law Journal* 188 at 189.

[231] Discrimination Law Association, *Discrimination Law Association Submissions for the Discrimination Law Review* (n 104 above) 45.

[232] See eg Collins, 'Discrimination, Equality and Social Inclusion' (n 97 above) 38–9.

[233] See generally G James, 'Work and Families Act 2006: Legislation to Improve Choice and Flexibility?' (2006) 35 *Industrial Law Journal* 272; G James, 'Enjoy Your Leave but "Keep in Touch": Help to Maintain Parent/Workplace Relationships' (2007) 36 *Industrial Law Journal* 315; and E Caracciolo Di Torella, 'New Labour, New Dads—The Impact of Family Friendly Legislation on Fathers' (2007) 36 *Industrial Law Journal* 318. For the view that such measures constitute a form of

The use of precisely defined, relatively discretion-free, entitlements undoubtedly carries significant advantages in terms of certainty and practicality. They should therefore be used wherever appropriate. Even where there is a more broadly defined reasonable adjustment duty, the existence of specific, more circumscribed, duties to adjust may prove helpful. This is illustrated by the current campaigns for the introduction of a legislative scheme governing disability leave.[234] Under such a scheme, entitlements of newly disabled employees to return to work on a phased basis would be set out in some detail and thus given a more precise and explicit basis than that of reasonableness.

Thus, the concept of reasonableness is well suited to play a central role in duties to respond to the infinite variety of individual impairment and circumstance amongst disabled people. In the non-disability context, however, it is not clear that such a broad and flexible concept is needed. Where the doctrine of indirect discrimination provides insufficient incentive for employers and others to respond to the needs of particular groups, consideration should be given to the introduction of carefully circumscribed schemes that would allow their needs to be met. Although such schemes would generate duties to make adjustments, they would not be reasonable adjustments as such because they would not be governed by reference only to considerations of reasonableness. This issue received disappointingly little analysis in the Discrimination Law Review. However, the Review did propose that, because of the limits imposed by the symmetrical nature of British non-discrimination law and because of the need to retain principles of indirect discrimination, the reasonable adjustment concept should not be extended beyond the sphere of disability.[235]

---

reasonable accommodation or adjustment, see L Waddington and A Hendriks, 'The Expanding Concept of Employment Discrimination Law in Europe: From Direct and Indirect Discrimination to Reasonable Accommodation Discrimination' (2002) 18 *International Journal of Comparative Labour Law and Industrial Relations* 403 at 418–19; and Moon, 'From Equal Treatment to Appropriate Treatment' (n 223 above) 712.

[234] See generally Office for Disability Issues, *Independent Living—A Cross-Government Strategy about Independent Living for Disabled People* (London, Stationery Office, 2008) para 6.2, where support is pledged for the development of a cross-government strategy aimed at helping people who become disabled to retain their jobs. On the issue of employment retention more generally, see G Mercer, 'Job Retention: A New Policy Priority for Disabled People' in A Roulstone and C Barnes (eds), *Working Futures? Disabled People, Policy and Social Inclusion* (Bristol, The Policy Press, 2005).

[235] Department for Communities and Local Government, *Discrimination Law Review* (n 91 above) paras 4.39–4.43. See also Government Equalities Office, *The Equality Bill* (n 34 above) paras 5.1 and 5.18.

6. The Classification of Reasonable Adjustment Duties as Freestanding Non-Discrimination Measures

Under the DDA, then, liability for disability discrimination may arise in a number of ways. These include direct discrimination, disability-related discrimination and failure to comply with a reasonable adjustment duty.[236] The reasonable adjustment obligation is thus freestanding in the sense that it is capable of grounding a discrimination claim in its own right. As has been discussed above, it will sometimes also play a part in the determination of liability for disability-related discrimination. It has no role to play in the context of direct discrimination, however. This classification of the liability arising from reasonable adjustment duties is by no means universal.

Duties to reasonably adjust or accommodate are sometimes categorised not as freestanding duties but as principles integral to the operation of more familiar non-discrimination concepts. Indeed, the Canadian Supreme Court, in interpreting the equality guarantee laid down by section 15 of the Canadian Constitution Act 1982, has refused to impose a rigid classification structure on the forms that might be taken by unlawful discrimination.[237] It has instead adopted a more purposive approach, which focuses on the violation of human dignity, under which it is clear that principles of reasonable accommodation to the point of undue hardship play a crucial role in relation to all the equality strands and not just in the context of disability.[238]

A failure to make a reasonable adjustment is, in a few jurisdictions, categorised as a form of direct discrimination.[239] More commonly, however, such failures are linked to the concept of disparate impact or indirect discrimination.[240] Under section 11 of the Ontario Human Rights Code,[241] the disparate impact of a requirement, qualification or factor will not be unlawful if it is 'reasonable' and 'bona fide' in all the circumstances of the case. Section 11(2), however, provides that this reasonable and bona fide defence will not be established

---

[236] The victimisation and harassment provisions may also give rise to liability but consideration of these falls outside the scope of this work.

[237] See eg *Law v Canada (Minister of Employment and Immigration)* [1999] 1 SCR 497.

[238] See eg *Andrews v Law Society of British Columbia* [1989] 1 SCR 143; *Ontario Human Rights Commission (O'Malley) v Simpson Sears* [1985] 2 SCR 536; *Central Alberta Dairy Pool v Alberta (Human Rights Commission)* [1990] 2 SCR 489; *British Columbia (Superintendent of Motor Vehicles) v British Columbia (Council of Human Rights)* [1993] 3 SCR 868; *Eldridge v British Columbia (Att-Gen)* [1997] 3 SCR 624; and *British Columbia (Public Service Employee Relations Commission) v British Columbia Government and Service Employees' Union* [1999] 3 SCR 3. See generally Moon, 'From Equal Treatment to Appropriate Treatment' (n 223 above); MD Lepofsky, 'The Canadian Judicial Approach to Equality Rights: Freedom Ride or Roller Coaster?' (1992) 55 *Law and Contemporary Problems* 167; M Berlin, 'Reasonable Accommodation: A Positive Duty to Ensure Equal Opportunity' (1985) *Canadian Human Rights Yearbook 1984–1985* 137.

[239] See eg the discussion of Sweden and Malta in Waddington, 'Reasonable Accommodation' (n 218 above) 741–2.

[240] See the discussion of Slovakia and Spain, *ibid*, 743–4.

[241] RSO 1990, ch H.19.

unless ... the needs of the group ... cannot be accommodated without undue hardship on the person responsible for accommodating those needs.

The Hepple Report recommended that this provision be used as a template for the extension of indirect discrimination to disability in Britain.[242]

Under the approach advocated by the Hepple Report, the reasonable adjustment duty would cease to be a freestanding form of discrimination. It would instead operate within the context of indirect discrimination, preventing a provision, criterion or practice being justified unless appropriate adjustments had been made to mitigate its disadvantageous effects on the person in question. Although this approach is attractively simple, its adoption in Britain would result in an inferior level of protection for disabled people. It would restrict the benefits of reasonable adjustment duties to cases in which a group disadvantage could be demonstrated. It would therefore remove the current option of bringing a claim for breach of a reactive duty, eg in the context of employment, without the need to demonstrate any group disadvantage. It would also risk undermining the strength of the anticipatory element of the current British anticipatory reasonable adjustment duty.

Olivier de Schutter has argued cogently that, while reasonable accommodation (or adjustment) and indirect discrimination are distinct concepts, the former should operate in the wake of the latter.[243]

This would entail attention being directed, in the first instance, to the indirect discrimination inquiry as to the existence of an objectively demonstrable need for the challenged measure. If no such need could be established then that measure could not be upheld. Only if the measure could be objectively justified, according to de Schutter, should the question of reasonably accommodating the needs of particular individuals or groups become relevant.

The appeal of de Schutter's argument lies in the stress it places on the dismantling of general measures, which, although apparently neutral, operate to disadvantage particular sectors of society. In the absence of such an emphasis, there is a danger that a duty to make reasonable adjustments for disabled people

> would oblige the collectivity to make certain adjustments, here and there, to do what was needed in order to avoid excluding particular disabled people; but disabled people generally would remain inhabitants of structures conceived by and made for others – structures which, by their very nature, will render them forever strangers and outsiders.[244]

---

[242] Hepple, Coussey and Choudhury, *Equality* (n 88 above) recommendation 6, para 2.33.

[243] 'Reasonable Accommodations and Positive Obligations in the European Convention on Human Rights' in A Lawson and C Gooding (eds), *Disability Rights in Europe: From Theory to Practice* (Oxford, Hart Publishing, 2005) 62–3.

[244] *Ibid.* See also Stein and Waterstone, 'Disability, Disparate Impact, and Class Actions' (n 186 above).

Nevertheless, for the reasons outlined in Section 4 above, it is suggested that this emphasis could more effectively be achieved in British disability law by reliance on the concept of anticipatory reasonable adjustment than on that of indirect discrimination.

Thus, where reasonable adjustment is categorised as a form of non-discrimination, it is sometimes regarded as a form of direct discrimination, sometimes as a form of indirect discrimination and sometimes, as in Britain, as a third and independent freestanding form of discrimination. It is not always categorised as a non-discrimination measure of any kind, however. Under the Employment Equality Directive, for instance, the relationship between reasonable accommodation and non-discrimination is ambiguous.[245] Like British law, the Directive sets out the obligation to make reasonable accommodation as a freestanding duty.[246] Fulfilment of this duty is stated to be necessary in order to comply with the Directive's core aim, the principle of equal treatment. Violation of it, however, is not included in the definitions of discrimination set out in Article 2. Under the UN Convention on the Rights of Persons with Disabilities, by contrast, reasonable accommodation is unequivocally categorised as a form of non-discrimination measure.[247]

Reasonable adjustment is sometimes distinguished from the other concepts considered in this chapter on the ground that, unlike them, it is essentially positive in nature. It is therefore sometimes set apart from non-discrimination measures and regarded as requiring something more than equality. Direct discrimination, indirect discrimination and disability-related discrimination all appear to prohibit particular forms of conduct. Reasonable adjustment obligations, on the other hand, require engagement in a process which may result in a duty to act in a particular way. From this distinction flows a tendency to regard reasonable adjustment obligations, on the one hand, as cost-intensive, and the negative prohibitions against discriminatory conduct, on the other, as cost-free.[248]

As has been powerfully demonstrated by scholars such as Jolls and Stein, however, this dichotomy is misleading.[249] The need to avoid engaging in conduct which is directly or indirectly discriminatory is rarely cost-free. It will often

---

[245] See ch 2, fnn 200–05 above and accompanying text.

[246] Employment Equality Directive Art 5.

[247] See ch 2, section 3.2 above.

[248] S Issacharoff and J Nelson, 'Discrimination with a Difference: Can Employment Discrimination Law Accommodate the Americans with Disabilities Act?' (2001) 79 *North Carolina Law Review* 307; PS Karlan and G Rutherglen, 'Disabilities, Discrimination and Reasonable Accommodation' (1996) 46 *Duke Law Journal* 1; SJ Schwab and SL Willborn, 'Reasonable Accommodation of Workplace Disabilities' (2003) 44 *William and Mary Law Review* 1197; and M Kelman, 'Market Discrimination and Groups' (2001) 53 *Stanford Law Review* 833.

[249] Jolls, 'Antidiscrimination and Accommodation' (n 175 above); and MA Stein, 'Same Struggle, Different Difference: ADA Accommodations as Antidiscrimination' (2004) 153 *University of Pennsylvania Law Review* 579. See also Collins, 'Discrimination, Equality and Social Inclusion' (n 97 above) 37–9.

require organisations to invest money in order to bring about change (such as the installation of separate women's toilets or changing facilities, or the provision of uniforms of different sizes) and to achieve an on-going level of equality awareness amongst staff (such as through the provision of relevant training).[250]

It is thus inappropriate to draw a clear distinction between reasonable adjustment and other individually enforceable non-discrimination concepts. While the former is phrased in positive terms and the latter in negative terms, the linguistic distinction does not reflect a sharp dichotomy between the underlying approaches. Reasonable adjustment duties are distinctive for the reasons explained in other sections of this chapter but they should not be regarded as fundamentally different in kind from other, more familiar, elements of non-discrimination law. As Jolls suggests, the idea that there is a significant 'gap' between requirements not to discriminate and requirements to accommodate diminishes if the mission of the former is understood in terms of tackling group disadvantage or subordination rather than simply of eradicating irrational distinctions.[251]

7. Conclusion

Reasonable adjustment is only one of the legal mechanisms through which a disabled person may be able to bring a claim for disability discrimination. It is important, therefore, to understand its relationship with the other principal mechanisms.

As has been shown above, its relationship with direct discrimination is a distant one. There is no overlap between the two and the notion of reasonable adjustment is totally irrelevant to determinations of liability for direct discrimination. The latter is concerned only with ensuring formal equality and requires a disabled person to be treated in an identical manner to a non-disabled person. The former is concerned with substantive equality and requires a disabled person to be given different treatment where that is needed in order to facilitate the goals of inclusion and participation.

The relationship between reasonable adjustment and disability-related discrimination is more complex and also, after *Lewisham London Borough Council v Malcolm*,[252] more uncertain. There is a degree of overlap between the two concepts, which would potentially permit a claim to succeed on the basis of either of them. In addition, the existence and discharge of a reasonable adjustment duty may remain a factor to which a court must have regard in decisions about whether a claim for disability-related discrimination can succeed. In view of the

---

[250] See further the discussion of the 'social engineering' function of indirect discrimination law in Schiek, 'Indirect Discrimination' (n 177 above) 324–8.
[251] Jolls, 'Antidiscrimination and Accommodation' (n 175 above) 696–7.
[252] *Lewisham LBC v Malcolm* [2008] UKHL 43.

objective nature of reasonableness and the subjective nature of the justification defence for disability-related discrimination, reasonable adjustment claims appear to offer a stronger means of challenging exclusionary practices. Both concepts, however, have important (if overlapping) roles to play. *Lewisham* has effected a worryingly severe restriction to the role of disability-related discrimination. This increases the importance of the role to be played by reasonable adjustment. Reasonable adjustment, however, cannot bear the entire weight and it is essential that the effect of *Lewisham* be substantially reversed at the earliest available opportunity.

The most complex of the relationships considered here is that between reasonable adjustment and indirect discrimination—a concept at work in non-disability regions of non-discrimination law. Both reach beyond the demands of formal equality to address the disadvantage which results from apparently neutral requirements and practices. Both require recognition of material difference and a corresponding adaptation of practice.[253] As has been seen, however, the two concepts differ in significant respects.

The concept of reactive reasonable adjustment must be allowed to continue in operation free of the need to establish a group disadvantage in the employment regions of the DDA. It provides a unique mechanism through which to ensure that individualised solutions are found for the particular circumstances of individuals with varying forms of impairment, experience and skill. Outside the area of disability, this degree of flexibility and individualisation does not seem to be required. Consideration should be given on an on-going basis, however, to supplementing indirect discrimination laws with specific schemes designed to effect adjustments in favour of particular groups of people with specific needs.

It has been argued here that the concept of anticipatory reasonable adjustment is peculiarly well placed to tackle the creation and continuance of disabling barriers. It should therefore be retained and not replaced by its closely related older cousin—indirect discrimination. Indeed, it seems likely to be able to offer useful inspiration to courts faced with the task of fleshing out the meaning of indirect discrimination under the new amended version of the relevant statutory provisions.

Neither indirect discrimination nor anticipatory reasonable adjustment currently operates in the employment parts of the DDA. This hampers the effectiveness of the DDA and also risks UK non-compliance with the Employment Equality Directive. Anticipatory reasonable adjustment should therefore be extended to all parts of the DDA as a matter of urgency.

---

[253] See further G Quinn, 'The Human Rights of People with Disabilities under EU Law' in P Alston, M Bustello and M Keenan (eds), *The EU and Human Rights* (Oxford, Oxford University Press, 1999) 290–91.

5

Reasonable Adjustment and Positive Measures

1. Introduction

THE PREVIOUS CHAPTER examined the relationship between reasonable adjustment duties and other concepts founding actions for unlawful discrimination which may be brought by individual litigants. Unlike obligations imposed by direct discrimination, indirect discrimination and disability-related discrimination, the obligation imposed by reasonable adjustment duties is expressed in positive rather than negative terms. It has already been suggested that this linguistic dichotomy should not be regarded as reflecting a sharp substantive divide according to which reasonable adjustment obligations are categorised as positive and other individually-enforceable non-discrimination concepts as negative. Nevertheless, its clear emphasis on the need to take positive steps brings the concept of reasonable adjustment into the realm of positive measures in a manner which—unlike that of the other non-discrimination concepts considered so far—is overt and clear.

The focus of this chapter will be the relationship between reasonable adjustment duties and other concepts expressly concerned with the taking of positive steps to counter disadvantage. None of these concepts give rise to actions for unlawful discrimination enforceable by individuals. Accordingly, in this respect, they differ markedly from reasonable adjustment obligations and also from the other non-discrimination concepts examined so far.

The term 'positive measures' will be used here to refer to any measure taken with the purpose of benefiting members of disadvantaged groups. Such measures may confer direct preferences upon members of targeted groups in selection processes or may operate to tackle their under-representation in some other way. The term 'positive action' is sometimes used to cover all such measures.[1] Given the tendency in Britain to regard 'positive action' as distinct from 'positive

---

[1] See eg O de Schutter, 'Positive Action' in D Schiek, L Waddington and M Bell (eds), *Cases, Materials and Text on National, Supranational and International Non-Discrimination Law* (Oxford, Hart Publishing, 2007).

discrimination', however, 'positive action' will not be used in this broad generic sense here. Instead, it will be reserved for positive measures that do not confer direct preferences and are therefore lawful throughout British non-discrimination law. The term 'positive discrimination' will be used to cover those forms of positive measure which do confer direct preferences on members of disadvantaged groups and which are therefore presently prohibited by much of British non-discrimination law. The meaning of these terms will be further explained in Sections 2 and 3 below.

Positive measures are widely acknowledged to have a vital role to play in any system of equality law that enshrines a substantive or 'rich' (rather than purely formal) notion of equality. They will be an essential component of any serious attempt to break down institutionalised forms of discrimination and entrenched patterns of disadvantage. The growing recognition of the importance of positive measures in Britain has recently resulted in the emergence of new public sector duties to promote equality. Despite the hope inspired by such developments, discontent persists about the restrictions imposed on the development of positive measures by the generally symmetrical structure of British non-discrimination law. As will be explained below, many of these constraints do not apply in the context of disability. Some appreciation of the broader landscape of the law on positive measures is, however, an unavoidable element of any attempt to gain clarity and perspective on the concept of reasonable adjustment.

This chapter will begin with a consideration of positive measures which confer direct preferences—measures described here as 'positive discrimination'. Outside the disability context, 'positive discrimination' in this sense is generally prohibited and constitutes one of the principal constraints on the development of positive measures. In addition to exploring the limits of this constraint for the non-disability grounds, attention will be drawn to the fact that positive discrimination is permitted in favour of disabled people and to the fact that, in the past, it has actually been required. The scope of 'positive action' will be outlined in Section 3. Attention will then be turned, in Section 4, to the disability equality duty—a duty placed on public sector bodies to promote disability equality by, among other things, the taking of positive measures to counter disability-related disadvantage. Finally, in Section 5, the place occupied by reasonable adjustment duties within this landscape of positive measures and duties to promote them will be addressed.

2. Positive Discrimination

2.1 The Primacy of Formal Equality and the General Prohibition of Positive Discrimination

At the heart of many non-discrimination laws, including those of Britain and the European Community, is the prohibition of treatment which discriminates against people on a number of specified grounds. The grounds selected for protection emerged from an acknowledgement of the disadvantageous and discriminatory treatment frequently experienced by certain sectors of society, such as women, members of minority racial or ethnic groups, older people, gay or bi-sexual people and disabled people. Attempts to redress imbalances created by such patterns of disadvantage, through measures designed to favour members of affected groups, are commonly described as 'positive discrimination' or 'positive action'.

There is a high degree of terminological confusion in this area. Terms such as 'positive discrimination', 'reverse discrimination', 'affirmative action' and 'positive action' are used by different people and different jurisdictions to carry a variety of different and overlapping meanings. In Britain, for instance, the terms 'positive discrimination' and 'positive action' are commonly used whereas, in the United States the terms 'reverse discrimination' and 'affirmative action' tend to be more heavily relied upon. There is no technical legal definition of either 'positive discrimination' or 'positive action' in British law and the terms are used in a variety of senses.

In this chapter, as has already been indicated, the term 'positive discrimination' will be used to reflect a distinction which plays a crucial role in much of British non-discrimination law—the distinction between conduct which is neutral as regards a relevant ground and that which is preferential. Conduct will be preferential in this sense when, instead of ignoring the relevant characteristic (race, sex, religion etc), it treats that characteristic as a relevant factor in a selection process with the result that one person is treated more favourably than another because of it. Such discrimination will be referred to as 'positive discrimination' when the preference-giving is in favour of a member of a disadvantaged group and it is motivated by the desire to counter that disadvantage.

'Positive discrimination', in the sense in which it is used here, will therefore cover two types of case, both of which fall foul of much of current British non-discrimination law. First, it will cover cases in which a member of a disadvantaged group is favoured over another person who has better qualifications than theirs, simply because of their membership of the relevant group. Second, it will cover cases in which both people are regarded as equally well qualified but the fact that one of them is a member of the disadvantaged group is taken into account as a tie-breaking factor in their favour.

189

Situations of the first type clearly violate conventional notions of what is often termed the 'merit principle', according to which positions should be awarded to those who are best qualified for them.[2] Situations of the second type, however, would not generally be regarded as doing so. 'Positive discrimination', in the sense used here, does not therefore correlate exactly with an infringement of the 'merit principle'.

It should be noted that the term 'positive discrimination' is sometimes used in a narrower sense than that used here, to refer only to cases in which the merit principle is violated. According to the Discrimination Law Review, for instance:

> Positive discrimination means explicitly treating people more favourably on the grounds of race, sex, religion or belief, etc. by, for example, appointing someone to a job just because they are male or just because they are female, irrespective of merit.[3]

This understanding of 'positive discrimination' appears to be one in which it operates 'regardless of perceived merit'. It would not seem to cover situations of the second type set out above, in which two candidates were considered to be equally well qualified. In such a case, the member of the disadvantaged group would not have been selected 'regardless of merit' but because they, along with another person, were the best qualified and because, in addition, they were a member of the disadvantaged group.

Under British non-discrimination law, the extent to which positive discrimination is permitted depends on whether or not the protection afforded to a particular ground is symmetrical. For disability, marital status and gender re-assignment, the legislative protection is asymmetrical in that it is available only to those in the disadvantaged group. Thus, in relation to disability, the DDA may offer redress to a disabled person who has been treated less favourably than another for disability-related reasons. It will not, however, protect a non-disabled person alleging that they have been treated less favourably than a disabled person. This asymmetrical protection therefore makes it possible to treat disabled people more favourably than non-disabled people without any risk of liability for unlawful discrimination.[4]

---

[2] It should be stressed, however, that the notion of 'merit' is highly contested. The sense in which it is used here falls within the third of five models identified in C McCrudden, 'Merit Principles' (1998) 18 *Oxford Journal of Legal Studies* 543 at 559–62.

[3] Department for Communities and Local Government, *Discrimination Law Review—A Framework for Fairness: Proposals for a Single Equality Bill for Great Britain*, (London, Stationery Office, 2007) Pt 2, para 7. See also Government Equalities Office, *The Equality Bill: Government Response to the Consultation* (London, Stationery Office, 21 July 2008) para 5.2 where this understanding is reaffirmed.

[4] This contrasts with the position taken in the Netherlands where a symmetrical approach has been adopted to disability, as well as to other grounds. The duty to make effective accommodations, however, is confined to the ground of disability. See L Waddington, 'Implementing the Disability Provisions of the Framework Employment Directive: Room for Exercising National Discretion' in A Lawson and C Gooding (eds), *Disability Rights in Europe: From Theory to Practice* (Oxford, Hart Publishing, 2005) 115–17.

There is an important exception to the general rule that disabled people may lawfully be treated more favourably than their non-disabled counterparts. This is laid down in section 7 of the Local Government and Housing Act 1989, according to which all appointments of local authority, parish and community council workers must be 'made on merit'. Section 7 thus enshrines and gives statutory force to the problematic merit principle and insists that a candidate may be appointed to a relevant post only if they are judged to be the best qualified person for it.

The notion of meritocracy on which section 7, and also much of British non-discrimination legislation, appears to be based is one in which past disadvantage experienced by a particular individual (in their educational opportunities for instance) is irrelevant. So too is the fact that their ancestors may have been subjected to prolonged and damaging disadvantageous treatment, which has had repercussions on the present generation. The emphasis is firmly on the present abilities of relevant individuals—those abilities generally being judged by attainments such as exam grades and professional qualifications (which are themselves unlikely to be neutral in terms of culture or impairment).[5] The understanding of merit on which this notion of meritocracy is based is thus a relatively narrow one, which focuses on measurable performance in conventional systems of education and employment.[6]

In relation to the equality strands other than disability, marital status and gender reassignment, the protection afforded by British non-discrimination law is neutral or symmetrical in approach. Its key concern is to prevent the relevant ground becoming a determining factor in decisions affecting access to employment, education, goods, services, property and other benefits. It therefore insists on the application of a strict notion of formal equality, according to which like cases should be treated alike and irrelevant factors disregarded. Grounds are selected for symmetrical protection in order to ensure that they are regarded as irrelevant in this sense rather than operating to the disadvantage of members of one particular group.[7]

Accordingly, where protection is symmetrical in nature, any person disadvantaged on the basis of a relevant ground may seek redress whether or not they are a member of the disadvantaged and under-represented group. Men as well as women may claim the protection of the Sex Discrimination Act 1975 (SDA) and people of white Anglo-Saxon origin as well as members of minority ethnic

---

[5] See generally IM Young, *Justice and the Politics of Difference* (Princeton, Princeton University Press, 1990) 200–10.

[6] See generally McCrudden, 'Merit Principles' (n 2 above); B Parekh, 'A Case for Positive Discrimination' in B Hepple and E Szyszczak (eds), *Discrimination: The Limits of Law* (London, Mansell Publishing, 1992) 273–6; and S Sturm and L Guinier, 'The Future of Affirmative Action: Reclaiming the Innovative Ideal' (1996) 84 *California Law Review* 953.

[7] For detailed discussions of the selection of grounds and the need for them, see A McColgan, 'Reconfiguring Discrimination Law' [2007] *Public Law* 74; and S Fredman, *Discrimination Law* (Oxford, Oxford University Press, 2002) 66–82.

groups may claim the protection of the Race Relations Act 1976 (RRA). Employers and others, keen to redress the balance by preferring members of underrepresented groups, therefore run the risk of direct discrimination claims. Such claims are likely to succeed unless the positive measures in question fall within the ambit of specific positive action provisions, set out in the legislation, or within the scope of a genuine occupational requirement or qualification. There is no general defence based on a positive motive such as the promotion of social justice—motive generally being regarded as irrelevant.[8]

European Community law adopts a similar approach to the issue of positive discrimination. The Employment Equality Directive, for instance, generally adopts a symmetrical approach, which places the emphasis firmly on the need to avoid treating people differently on the basis of a specified ground. Discrimination, whether in favour of or against the disadvantaged group, is therefore problematic. Article 7(1), however, does stress that, in order to ensure the practical realisation of the principle of equal treatment, Member States are not prevented from 'maintaining or adopting specific measures to prevent or compensate for disadvantages' linked to the relevant grounds.[9]

In relation to disability, the Employment Equality Directive prohibits discrimination 'on the ground' of disability. It is conceivable that this too will be interpreted to confer symmetrical protection.[10] In this event, treating a disabled person more favourably than a non-disabled person would potentially found an action for discrimination by the latter. Article 7(2), however, confers an extremely wide latitude to Member States to permit employers to treat disabled people more favourably than others. According to it,

> [w]ith regard to disabled persons, the principle of equal treatment shall be without prejudice to the right of Member States to maintain or adopt ... measures aimed at creating or maintaining provisions or facilities for safeguarding or promoting their integration into the working environment.[11]

To sum up, while there is no legal prohibition against discriminating in favour of disabled people (except in the context of local authority employment), it is

---

[8] *James v Eastleigh BC* [1990] 2 AC 751 (HL). For an interesting discussion see L Barmes, 'Promoting Diversity and the Definition of Direct Discrimination' (2003) 32 *Industrial Law Journal* 200.

[9] Analogous provisions apply to race—Art 5 of the Race Directive (Council Directive 2000/43/EC implementing the principle of equal treatment between persons irrespective of racial or ethnic origin [2000] OJ L 180/22); and to sex—Art 2(8) of Council Directive 76/207/EEC on the implementation of the principle of equal treatment for men and women as regards access to employment, vocational training and promotion, and working conditions (amended by Council Directive 2002/73/EC (2002) OJ L 269/15) and also Art 141 of the EC Treaty.

[10] Waddington, 'Implementing the Disability Provisions of the Framework Employment Directive' (n 4 above) 115.

[11] For further discussion of Art 7, see de Schutter, 'Positive Action' (n 1 above) 821–3; and G Quinn, 'Disability Discrimination Law in the European Union' in H Meenan (ed), *Equality Law in an Enlarged European Union: Understanding the Article 13 Directives* (Cambridge, Cambridge University Press, 2007) 269–73.

generally not permissible to discriminate in favour of women, members of minority ethnic, racial or religious groups, older people, or people who are gay or bi-sexual. This legal framework therefore facilitates the tackling of disability-related disadvantage to a much greater extent than it facilitates the tackling of disadvantage associated with membership of other relevant groups, where a heavy emphasis is instead placed on identical or neutral treatment.

It is perhaps no accident that disadvantage appears to play a larger role in the context of disability than it does in most other areas of British equality law. A disability non-discrimination law targeting the elimination of different treatment rather than disadvantage would plainly do little to facilitate inclusion, participation and meaningful equality. Its primary concern would be to ensure that employers, education providers and others should disregard the characteristic of disability—a concern which would not sit easily with any obligation to recognise and respond to difference through the making of appropriate adjustments. Further, there is likely to be a greater public readiness to accept that disabled people are disadvantaged, though not necessarily through discrimination, than there is in the case of other groups such as women and members of racial and ethnic minorities. Although this perception that disabled people are particularly disadvantaged may have been helpful in the construction of a law with relatively loose limits on positive discrimination, it is often uncomfortably bound up with stereotypical images of helplessness and incompetence.

Before considering the limited extent to which positive discrimination is permitted by current British law, and addressing arguments for a more permissive approach, some examples of forms of positive discrimination which have been adopted in various countries, and sometimes struck down, will be outlined. Two of these (the 'quota scheme' and the 'reserved occupation strategy'), both of which related to disability and have now been repealed, operated on a mandatory basis in Britain. Today however, even where British law permits forms of positive discrimination in favour of disabled people, it does not make them mandatory except in so far as they amount to a reasonable adjustment.

2.2 Examples of Forms of Positive Discrimination

2.2.1 Quotas

Quota schemes represent one of the most commonly used mechanisms for tackling the under-representation of disadvantaged groups in the contexts of employment and education. They take a wide variety of forms, ranging from 'rigid', 'inflexible' or 'strong' requirements to appoint members of the relevant group in order to maintain the quota—despite the fact that there are better qualified candidates—to much 'softer' or 'weaker' systems which urge a preference for a member of the relevant group only if their qualifications are equal to those of other candidates and all relevant circumstances have been taken into account.[12] The point along this sliding scale at which the preference becomes unlawful discrimination has been a hotly contested issue in European Community law.[13] Within Britain, however, any such preference is likely to amount to direct discrimination in relation to the symmetrically-protected grounds.

Quota schemes also vary greatly in their range of application. They may take the form of national systems of general application or of systems adopted by specific organisations or institutions. Enforcement mechanisms and penalties for non-compliance range from criminal sanctions through to the non-existent. Seldom, however, do they allow for enforcement through actions brought by aggrieved individuals themselves.

Employment quota schemes have characterised twentieth century European responses to problems associated with the exclusion of disabled people from the labour market.[14] They have generally applied at a national level and been sufficiently inflexible in nature to contain a (frequently flouted) requirement that disabled people should be appointed in preference to other better-qualified candidates. Although a detailed analysis of such schemes is beyond the scope of this work, the prominence of the role they have played in British disability policy (and of the role they continue to play elsewhere) entitles them to some consideration.

In many European countries, the years following the end of the First World War witnessed the introduction of quota schemes designed to improve the employment prospects of people disabled as a result of military conflict.[15] Although many such schemes were mandatory, the British five per cent quota scheme relating to former servicemen, adopted in September 1919, was entirely voluntary in nature. Fewer than 20 per cent of employers took part in the scheme and many of them withdrew their support after only a short time.[16] 25 years later, following the recommendations of the Tomlinson Report,[17] a mandatory quota scheme was introduced by the Disabled Persons (Employment) Act 1944.[18]

---

[12] See further, particularly on the issue of terminology, E Szyszczak, 'Positive action after Kalanke' (1996) 59 *Modern Law Review* 876 at 878; and C Barnard and T Hervey, 'Softening the Approach to Quotas: Positive Action after Marschall' (1998) 20 *Journal of Social Welfare and Family Law* 333.

[13] See nn 29–38 below and accompanying text.

[14] See generally L Waddington, 'Legislating to Employ People with Disabilities: The European and American Way' [1994] 1 *Maastricht Law Journal* 367; and L Waddington, 'Reassessing the Employment of People with Disabilities in Europe: From Quotas to Anti-Discrimination Laws' (1996) 18 *Comparative Labour Law Journal* 62.

[15] See further H Bolderson, 'The Origins of the Disabled Persons Employment Quota and its Symbolic Significance' (1980) 9 *Journal of Social Policy* 169; and H Bolderson, *Social Security, Disability and Rehabilitation: Conflicts in the Development of Social Policy 1914–45* (London, Kingsley, 1991).

[16] *Report from the Select Committee on Pensions 1920* (London, HMSO, 1920) paras 2, 3 and 11; and *Report from the Select Committee on Training and Employment of Disabled Ex-service Men* (London, HMSO, 1922).

[17] *Report of the Inter-Departmental Committee on the Rehabilitation and Resettlement of Disabled Persons*, Cmnd 6415 (London, HMSO, 1943).

[18] Disabled Persons (Employment) Act 1944 ss 9–11.

The 1944 quota scheme required private sector employers with 20 or more employees to ensure that at least three per cent of their workers were registered as disabled (whether or not they had become disabled as a result of injury in the War).[19] Provision was made for exemption permits to be made available to employers where there were insufficient numbers of registered disabled people to fill relevant positions.[20] Failure to comply with quota obligations, in the absence of an exemption permit, constituted an offence, rendering an employer liable to punishment by fine or imprisonment. Prosecutions, however, could be brought only with the permission of the Secretary of State.

The failings and ineffectiveness of the British quota system are well documented.[21] The complexity of the prosecution process, combined with the fear of alienating the goodwill of employers, help to explain the fact that only 10 enforcement actions were brought throughout the quota's 50-year history.[22] Exemption permits were easily obtained with little need to demonstrate the relevant grounds with care or precision.[23] Almost 60 per cent of employers subject to the scheme were granted exemption permits.[24] The system depended on people registering themselves as disabled but, due to the perception that registration carried no advantage and to a reluctance to acquire a potentially stigmatising label, many disabled people chose not to be registered. Evidence suggests that, by the late 1980s, less than 15 per cent of disabled people of working age had registered themselves as disabled.[25]

Other weaknesses in the British quota scheme may be identified—weaknesses which would not have been diminished by effective enforcement. The 1944 scheme was designed to favour disabled people in the labour market by forcing employers to offer them positions even if there were better-qualified non-disabled candidates. It thus represented a departure from a strict system of meritocracy. Although this was designed to benefit disabled people, it imposed no obligation on employers to consider the merits of disabled people themselves. In the absence of any reasonable adjustment duty, employers were not obliged to remove obstacles that would prevent a disabled person performing to the full

---

[19] Disabled Persons (Employment) Act 1944 s 1.

[20] Disabled Persons (Employment) Act 1944 s 11.

[21] See eg B Doyle, *Disability, Discrimination and Equal Opportunities: A Comparative Study of the Employment Rights of Disabled Persons* (London, Mansell Publishing, 1995) 258–68; and L Wadding-ton, *Disability, Employment and the European Community* (Appledoorn Netherlands, MAKLU, 1995) 223–9.

[22] House of Commons Employment Committee, 'The Operation of the Disabled Persons (Employment) Act 1944: Minutes of Evidence' (Session 1993–1994, HC Paper 281) para 24.

[23] Manpower Services Commission, *Review of the Quota Scheme for the Employment of Disabled People* (Sheffield, MSC, 1981).

[24] House of Commons Employment Committee, *The Operation of the Disabled Persons (Employment) Act 1944: Minutes of Evidence* (n 22 above) para 21.

[25] J Martin, A White and H Meltzer, *Disabled Adults: Services, Transport and Employment—OPCS Surveys of Disability in Great Britain, Report 4* (London, HMSO, 1989) table 7.32; P Prescott-Clarke, *Employment and Handicap* (London, Social and Community Planning Research, 1990) 74 and table 8.1.

level of their ability. Neither was there anything to prevent employers turning suitably qualified disabled candidates away from their positions of choice on the basis of ignorance, stereotypical assumptions or simple antipathy. Necessary quota requirements could be satisfied by allowing registered disabled workers to occupy an organisation's low status menial positions, despite the fact that many of them might have been capable of assuming more demanding roles. Because no distinction was made between different levels of impairment, employers were free to choose to meet their quotas by selecting only those disabled workers with relatively mild degrees of impairment. Further, the scheme focused on recruitment and was relatively silent on other important issues such as employment conditions and career progression.

The British quota system was abandoned in favour of the non-discrimination approach of the Disability Discrimination Act 1995 (DDA).[26] In various other EU countries such as Germany and France, however, quota systems persist.[27] Such schemes, unlike the British one, differentiate between levels of impairment and are designed to assist the most severely disabled. Non-compliance with a relevant quota generally attracts a levy or fine, to be paid by an employer into a fund, which is then used to facilitate the employment of disabled people through, for example, the provision of grants to employers who have exceeded their quota or to provide subsidies for the cost of reasonable adjustments.[28]

The disability quota schemes retained by many EU countries will now need to work alongside the non-discrimination measures which the Employment Equality Directive requires of all Member States. The addition of anti-disability-discrimination principles to the laws of countries operating such schemes has the potential to enhance considerably the usefulness of quotas as tools for achieving meaningful equality. The application of non-discrimination principles to quota schemes would counter objections to them based on their failure to take into account the full abilities and potential of disabled people.

Although Britain no longer operates a mandatory quota scheme, there is nothing to prevent employers (other than local authorities), education providers and others requiring a certain quota of their employees, students or clients to be disabled. In relation to other groups, however, for whom positive discrimination is generally prohibited, the adoption of such quotas is possible only in very limited circumstances. These are set out in what are sometimes referred to as the positive action provisions of the relevant Acts and will be discussed more fully in Section 2.3 below.

---

[26] DDA s 61(7)(c).
[27] See generally N Lunt and P Thornton, *Employment Policies for Disabled People: A Review of Legislation and Services in Fifteen Countries* (London, Department for Employment, 1993).
[28] For discussion of the German scheme, see Waddington, *Disability, Employment and the European Community* (n 21 above) 229–34. For discussion of the French scheme, see P Blanck, E Hill, CD Siegal and M Waterstone, *Disability Civil Rights Law and Policy* (St Paul Mn, West Group (a Thomson Business), 2004) section 23.4.

Outside the narrowly defined situations in which positive discrimination is permitted for the symmetrical grounds of discrimination, quotas are rarely used in Britain because of the high risk that they will constitute unlawful discrimination. Nevertheless, attempts have been made to use them more widely in other European countries—attempts which have generated a considerable body of litigation at Community level.[29]

The quota systems which have come before the European Court of Justice (ECJ) represent attempts to address the significant under-representation of women in various forms of public sector employment.[30] Typically, these schemes have conferred no benefit on a female applicant who is less qualified than a male competitor.[31] Their emphasis has been on situations in which a woman and a man are considered to be equally qualified. In such tie-break situations, these quota schemes have operated to confer preferences, of varying degrees of strength, on female applicants on grounds of their sex. Thus, unlike the strict British disability quota scheme, they do not appear to offend against the merit principle, according to which the best-qualified person should be selected.[32]

The ECJ has adopted a relatively narrow conception of permitted positive action, which is nevertheless more extensive than that presently to be found in British law.[33] It has struck down schemes in which the preference to be accorded to an equally qualified woman is mandatory. Such inflexible quota systems, it has been held, prevent an individual consideration of all the circumstances of the case from taking place, and therefore constitute unlawful discrimination against men.[34] Softer schemes which do not make the preference mandatory have, however, been upheld. Thus, the inclusion of a savings clause—under which all

---

[29] See further J Shaw, 'Positive Action for Women in Germany: The Use of Legally Binding Quota Systems' in Hepple and Szyszczak (eds), *Discrimination: The Limits of Law* (n 6 above).

[30] Most of these cases focussed on Art 2(4) of Council Directive 76/207/EEC (n 9 above). This paragraph provided that the Directive was 'without prejudice to measures to promote equal opportunity for men and women, in particular by removing existing inequalities which affect women's opportunities' in relation to access to employment, vocational training and promotion, and working conditions. It has now been replaced—as a result of Art 1 of Council Directive 2002/73/EC (n 9 above)—by the more generously worded Art 2(8) which, like Art 141(4) of the EC Treaty, provides:
'With a view to ensuring full equality in practice between men and women in working life, the principle of equal treatment shall not prevent any Member State from maintaining or adopting measures providing for specific advantages in order to make it easier for the under-represented sex to pursue a vocational activity or to prevent or compensate for disadvantages in professional careers'.

[31] Case C-407/98 *Abrahamsson and Anderson v Fogelqvist*, (2000) (discussed in n 38 below and accompanying text) is an example of a case which did involve the conferral of preferences.

[32] See generally D Schiek, 'Positive Action Before the European Court of Justice: New Conceptions of Equality in Community Law? From Kalanke and Marschall to Badeck' (2000) 16 *International Journal of Comparative Labour Law and Industrial Relations* 251; D Schiek, 'Sex Equality Law after Kalanke and Marschall' (1998) 4 *European Law Journal* 148; and U O' Hare, 'Positive Action Before the European Court of Justice' [1996] 2 *Web Journal of Current Legal Issues*.

[33] See generally de Schutter, 'Positive Action' (n 1 above) 801–25; and E Howard, 'The European Year of Equal Opportunities for All—2007: Is the EU Moving Away From a Formal Idea of Equality?' (2008) 14 *European Law Journal* 168.

[34] Case C-450/93 *Kalanke v Freie Hansestadt Bremen* [1995] ECR 1–3051.

the circumstances of the case, including those of the equally qualified man, must be objectively assessed and, if appropriate, allowed to tip the balance in favour of the man—will generally safeguard the validity of a scheme.[35]

The ECJ has been criticised for adopting an unnecessarily restrictive approach—an approach which has resulted in the dismantling of numerous schemes operating within Member States in an attempt to counter disadvantage.[36] Commentators have also drawn attention to the plasticity of the requirement of equivalent qualification.[37] Although the demonstration of equal qualification is a pre-requisite of positive discrimination schemes permitted by the ECJ, it is relatively easy for employers and others to avoid engaging with such schemes by determining that the qualifications of relevant candidates are not in fact equal.

2.2.2 Reduced Entry Requirements or Qualifications

A clear form of positive discrimination is the application of a policy according to which members of under-represented groups are required to demonstrate a lower standard than that demanded of others. Such schemes are closely linked to quota systems because a pre-requisite of their application is often under-representation as judged by failure to meet relevant quota requirements.

A decision of the ECJ on the legality of Swedish legislation, intended to address the fact that only 10 per cent of professors were women, provides a clear illustration of that court's insistence that less qualified candidates must not be given preference over better qualified ones. The legislation in question provided that a woman, suitably qualified for the post, must be appointed in preference to a better-qualified man as long as the difference between their qualifications was not so great as to demonstrate lack of objectivity in the appointments process. The positive discrimination inherent in this scheme was held to contravene Community law.[38]

The issue of entry requirements for educational establishments has caused considerable controversy in the United States. In *Regents of University of California v Bakke*[39] the Supreme Court struck down a quota system which guaranteed 16 per cent of medical school places to members of under-represented racial groups. Justice Powell, however, stressed the educational importance of a racially

---

[35] Case C-409/95 *Marschall Land Nordrheln-Westfalen* [1997] ECR 1–6363; Case C-158/97 *Badeck v Hessen* [2000] ECR 1–1875.

[36] See eg Barnard and Hervey, 'Softening the Approach to Quotas' (n 12 above); C Barnard, 'The Principle of Equality in the Community Context: P, Grant, Kalanke and Marschall—Four Uneasy Bedfellows?' (1998) 57 *Cambridge Law Journal* 352; and D Caruso, 'Limits of the Classic Method: Positive Action in the European Union after the New Equality Directives' (2003) 44 *Harvard International Law Journal* 331.

[37] See eg Caruso, *ibid*, 342.

[38] Case C-407/98 *Abrahamsson and Anderson v Fogelqvist* (2000) (discussed in A Numhauser-Henning, 'Swedish Sex Equality Law Before the ECJ' (2001) 30 *Industrial Law Journal* 121).

[39] *Regents of University of California v Bakke*, 438 US 265 (1978).

diverse student body, and considered it to be a compelling governmental interest. While it was not legitimate to pursue it through quotas, approval was given to admissions policies under which every application was considered on an individual basis and membership of an under-represented racial group taken into account as a positive factor of unspecified weight. Such policies were

> flexible enough to consider all pertinent elements of diversity in light of the particular qualifications of each applicant, and to place them on the same footing for consideration, although not necessarily according them the same weight.[40]

The Supreme Court again addressed the question of racial preference in university admissions policies in the twin cases of *Grutter v Bollinger*[41] and *Gratz v Bollinger*.[42] In *Grutter*, a policy which considered all applications on an individual basis was upheld despite the fact that it stressed the educational importance of having a critical mass of students from historically disadvantaged minorities, including members of under-represented racial groups. Race was accordingly taken into account, as a factor of unspecified weight, in the selection process.

In *Gratz*, on the other hand, an admissions policy which operated on a points system was struck down as unconstitutional. According to this scheme, 110 of the total 150 available points related to academic factors. The remaining 40 points related to other factors such as sporting achievement, leadership potential, geographical origin and the existence of a parent or close relative who was a graduate of the university. Membership of an under-represented racial group was allocated 20 points, giving members of such groups a considerable advantage over others. The Supreme Court held that this scheme was insufficiently tailored to its objective of achieving a diverse student body, as its inflexibility prevented an adequate consideration of applications on an individual basis.

2.2.3 Reservation of Professions

Another strategy which has been used in an attempt to favour disadvantaged groups is the reservation of particular occupations for members of the disadvantaged group in question. In Britain, indeed, the last century witnessed an attempt to use this strategy to promote the interests of disabled people. In addition to introducing the quota system, the Disabled Persons (Employment) Act 1944 provided that certain occupations, to be designated by the Secretary of State for Employment, could be reserved for employees who were registered as disabled.[43]

---

[40] *Ibid*, 317.
[41] *Grutter v Bollinger*, 539 US 306 (2003); (discussed in K Karst, 'The Revival of Forward-Looking Affirmative Action' (2004) 104 *Columbia Law Review* 60; and H Norton, 'Stepping Through Grutter's Open Doors: What the University of Michigan Affirmative Action Cases Mean for Race-Conscious Government Decision-making' (2005) 78 *Temple Law Review* 543).
[42] *Gratz v Bollinger*, 539 US 244 (2003).
[43] Disabled Persons (Employment) Act 1944 s 12. See generally Doyle, *Disability, Discrimination and Equal Opportunities* (n 21 above) 253–5.

It would then be an offence for any employer to employ a person not registered as disabled in such a capacity. The occupations of car park attendant and lift operator were so designated in 1946.[44]

The purpose of schemes such as this is to improve the employment prospects of disabled people by removing the need for them to compete with non-disabled people for certain types of job. There are indisputable risks and drawbacks, however. The occupations selected for reservation are likely to be of low status and their association with disabled people is likely to result in a further plunge in public regard and therefore also in pay and conditions. There is a risk that such schemes will effectively segregate disabled people, making it difficult for them to apply for jobs outside their reserved professions. There is also an obvious danger that such schemes will create or reinforce negative stereotypes about disabled people and their abilities.

These difficulties were recognised as early as 1956 by the Piercy Committee. According to it,

> [i]n practice, designation can be applied only to low-grade employment, and any extension of the scheme might encourage the mistaken and undesirable belief that disabled persons are only capable of that type of work.[45]

Despite the fact that there was no evidence that it actually improved their employment prospects,[46] the reserved occupation scheme was favoured by a surprising number of disabled people.[47] By the beginning of the 1980s, however, there were calls for its abolition.[48] It was finally abolished by the DDA.[49]

2.2.4 Supported Employment

Section 15 of the Disabled Persons (Employment) Act 1944 authorised the Secretary of State to supervise the establishment of schemes for the employment and training of severely disabled people who were otherwise unlikely to find work in the open labour market, to secure employment under 'special conditions'. This section has been used to develop schemes of supported employment

---

[44] Disabled Persons (Designated Employments) Order 1946 (SI No 1257/1946).

[45] *Report of the Committee on the Rehabilitation, Training and Resettlement of Disabled Persons,* Cmnd 9883 (London, HMSO, 1956) para 177.

[46] Department of Employment, *The Quota Scheme for Disabled People: Consultative Document* (London, Department of Employment, 1973) para 102.

[47] Research Surveys of Great Britain Ltd, *Attitudes of the Disabled to Employment Legislation: Main Report* (London, Manpower Services Commission, 1978) tables 8.5.1 and 8.5.2—90% of disabled people supported the scheme before being told which occupations were reserved and 70% supported it after being given this information.

[48] See eg House of Commons Employment Committee, *The Manpower Services Commission's Review of the Quota Scheme for the Employment of Disabled People, 2nd Report, Session 1981–1982,* HC Paper 27 (London, HMSO, 1981) para 27; and S Lonsdale and A Walker, *A Right to Work: Disability and Employment,* Low Pay Unit Pamphlet No 32 (London, Disability Alliance/Low Pay Unit, 1984) 26.

[49] DDA s 61(7)(d).

as well as of sheltered employment. Supported employment is generally understood to refer to schemes which support (through funding and also through various forms of practical assistance) the employment of disabled people in mainstream employment settings.[50] Its focus on the mainstream differentiates it from what is often referred to as 'sheltered employment', where the focus is instead on finding disabled people work in segregated settings.[51] Its aim is to enhance the skills and confidence of disabled people by providing them, in effect, with relevant training and experience whilst performing a job and receiving appropriate remuneration. It is also designed to increase employers' awareness of the potential benefits of employing disabled people and to encourage them to offer disabled workers (whether introduced to them through supported employment schemes or otherwise) non-subsidised posts in the future.

Despite the existence of numerous British supported employment schemes, evidence suggests that they have tended to be little used.[52] There appears to have been a surprising lack of awareness of them amongst disabled people.[53] Further, those who do know about such opportunities have frequently declined to take them up because of fear of stigma or because of the very real worry that participation will jeopardise benefits and other entitlements. There is also evidence of dissatisfaction with the support provided by such schemes amongst those who have taken them up.[54]

Nevertheless, if implemented in conjunction with an effective benefits system[55] and in a manner which fully involves disabled people and is highly responsive to their particular needs and circumstances,[56] supported employment schemes would appear to have a vital role to play in improving the employment prospects of disabled people. Clearly, however, the number of disabled people able to secure

---

[50]   See eg the Job Introduction Scheme, according to which a subsidy of £75 a week may be paid to an employer for the first 13 weeks in which they employ a disabled person.

[51]   See generally Lunt and Thornton, *Employment Policies for Disabled People* (n 27 above); and N Lunt and P Thornton, 'Disability and Employment: Towards an Understanding of Discourse and Policy' (1994) 9 *Disability and Society* 223.

[52]   See generally A O'Bryan, K Simons, S Beyer and B Grove, *A Framework for Supported Employment* (York, Joseph Rowntree Foundation, 2000); and I Murray, 'Supported Employment Programme' (1994) 55 *Working Brief* 3.

[53]   J Morrell, *The Employment of People with Disabilities: Research into the Policies and Practices of Employers*, Research Paper No 77 (London, Department of Employment, 1990).

[54]   M Hyde, 'Fifty Years of Failure: Employment Services for Disabled People in the UK' (1996) 10 *Work, Employment & Society* 683.

[55]   For details of current government strategy on this issue, see Department for Work and Pensions, *Ready for Work: Full Employment in our Generation* (London, Stationery Office, 2007). See also Department for Work and Pensions, *Green Paper—A New Deal for Welfare: Empowering People to Work* (London, Stationery Office, 2006); the Welfare Reform Act 2007; the Employment and Support Allowance Regulations 2008; and, for discussion (particularly of the controversial conditionality involved in this regime), K Puttick, 'Empowering the Incapacitated Worker? The Employment and Support Allowance and Pathways to Work' (2007) 36 *Industrial Law Journal* 388; and A Paz-Fuchs, *Welfare to Work* (Oxford, Oxford University Press, 2008).

[56]   A point the importance of which emerges clearly from the essays in A Roulstone and C Barnes (eds), *Working Futures? Disabled People, Policy and Social Inclusion* (Bristol, Policy Press, 2005).

and retain mainstream employment will be significantly affected by the nature and quality of State-funded advice and support services.[57]

According to section 18C(2) of the DDA, providers of supported employment should not be prevented from 'treating members of a particular group of disabled persons more favourably than other persons in providing such employment'. This section may appear unnecessary in view of the fact that disability is not a symmetrical ground and that there is therefore no general prohibition against treating disabled people more favourably than others. Its inclusion, however, ensures that local authorities will also be able to participate in such schemes without risk of infringing the rule that appointments made by them must be on the basis of merit alone.[58]

2.3 The Scope of Permitted Positive Discrimination

As has already been seen, outside the context of local government employment, British non-discrimination law imposes no limits on positive discrimination in favour of disabled people. For the symmetrical grounds the position is generally very different. In a tightly circumscribed range of situations, however, positive discrimination will be permitted even on these grounds.

Discrimination on the basis of a symmetrical ground, whether it is 'positive' or 'negative' in nature, will be permitted if the case can be brought within the scope of a genuine occupational qualification or requirement. These qualifications and requirements were considered in chapter four and need no further elaboration here.

Positive discrimination, in the sense of preferential treatment, is also expressly authorised by the 'positive action' provisions of the sex and race legislation. Under these, employers and other trade or professional bodies are permitted to discriminate in favour of members of under-represented groups (including through the imposition of quotas) in the context of access to facilities for training designed to fit them for particular work.[59] Section 47 of the SDA,[60] for instance, allows training providers to favour one sex in the provision of such access if it reasonably appears that in Britain or a part of it, at any time in the preceding year, either no members of the relevant sex or a comparatively small number of them were performing the work to which the training relates. Section 48 makes similar provision for access to training facilities for existing employees and may

---

[57] For discussion of proposals to reform many such services, see Department for Work and Pensions, *Public Consultation—Helping People Achieve their Full Potential: Improving Specialist Disability Employment Services* (London, Stationery Office, 2007).

[58] Local Government and Housing Act 1989 s 7.

[59] Training connected with the application process for work (such as through apprenticeships) is, however, excluded by s 47(4).

[60] See also RRA s 37; Employment Equality (Sexual Orientation) Regulations 2003 (SI 2003/1661) reg 26; and Employment Equality (Religion and Belief) Regulations 2003 (SI 2003/1660) reg 25.

therefore be used to facilitate promotion and career progression.[61] The meaning of 'considerably smaller' is unclear and undefined—a factor which is unlikely to encourage organisations to take advantage of these sections.[62] In addition, section 47 permits preferential access to training to be given to those who are 'in special need' of such training as a result of having been out of full-time employment in order to discharge domestic or family responsibilities.

Interestingly, the Discrimination Law Review took the view that the granting of preferences in the context of training, as opposed to the contexts of recruitment or promotion, could not amount to positive discrimination.[63] On this view, the direct preferences authorised by these provisions would not constitute 'positive discrimination' because they operate only within the context of training.

The other context in which the positive action provisions permit the granting of direct preferences (in forms such as quotas) to under-represented groups is that of representation on elected bodies. Section 49 of the SDA applies to trade unions and allows them to make provision for a reasonable minimum number of seats to be taken by members of one sex. This might occur through the reservation of seats for members of that sex or through the creation of additional seats to be filled by, for example, election or co-option. The relatively new section 42A applies to political parties and, until at least 2015,[64] allows them to make arrangements for reducing inequality between the numbers of men and women elected as candidates in local, regional, national and European Community elections.[65] One such measure is the use of women-only shortlists of those who might stand for the party in question in a particular seat.

2.4   A More Expansive Approach to Positive Discrimination?[66]

Disability non-discrimination law thus stands apart from the bulk of British non-discrimination law in that its asymmetrical structure permits positive discrimination in favour of disabled people. The fact that the DDA permits this more generous approach to positive measures, however, appears to be overlooked by many employers and others.[67] The adoption of a more expansive approach in

---

[61]   See also RRA s 38.

[62]   V Sacks, 'Tackling Discrimination Positively in Britain' in Hepple and Szyszczak (eds), *Discrimination: The Limits of Law* (n 6 above).

[63]   Department for Communities and Local Government, *Discrimination Law Review* (n 3 above) para 4.17.

[64]   The Government proposes to extend the date from 2015 to 2030—see Government Equalities Office, *The Equality Bill* (n 3 above) para 5.34.

[65]   See generally N Bushy, 'Sex Equality in Political Candidature: Supply and Demand Factors and the Role of the Law' (2003) 66 *Modern Law Review* 245. See also, in the context of race, s 35 RRA which permits the provision of facilities and services to a particular racial group if they are intended to address any special needs which members of that group might have in accessing education, health, welfare or related benefits.

[66]   See generally Fredman, *Discrimination Law* (n 7 above) ch 5.

[67]   See n 96 below and accompanying text.

relation to other grounds covered by non-discrimination law may therefore result in a greater willingness to discriminate positively in favour of disabled people. Debate about a move towards such an approach is therefore of some practical importance in this context. Familiarity with it will also prove helpful in connection with the analysis of the relationship between reasonable adjustment and positive discrimination set out in Section 5 below.

Much of the restrictiveness of the British approach to positive discrimination results from its attachment to the notion of formal equality. Its prime aim is the eradication of difference in the way in which individuals are treated because of what it considers to be irrelevant characteristics. Too much emphasis, it has been argued, is placed on the eradication of different treatment and not enough on the eradication of group disadvantage.[68] A greater emphasis on the latter would result in a more welcoming approach to positive discrimination than is demonstrated by current British law.

There are considerable limitations on a legal approach to non-discrimination that aims to tackle inequality simply by requiring decision-makers to ignore factors such as sex and race. Such laws, though requiring equal treatment, do little to address pre-existing disadvantage. They can therefore generate only a very slow pace of progress towards a more equal and inclusive society. The frustration engendered by the slow speed of change resulting from an identical treatment based approach has prompted calls for more pro-active measures. This sentiment is powerfully expressed in the following words of two American writers:

> The only remedy for racial subordination based on systematic establishment of structures, institutions, and ideologies is the systemic disestablishment of those structures, institutions, and ideologies. Radical affirmative action goes beyond the remedy of simply declaring that discrimination is illegal and pretending that our culture is color blind. It is not enough for the discriminator to remove his boot from the victim's throat and call it equal opportunity.[69]

---

[68] See eg C MacKinnon, 'Reflections on Sex Equality Under Law' (1991) 100 *Yale Law Journal* 1281; N Lacey, 'From Individual to Group?' in Hepple and Szyszczak (eds), *Discrimination: The Limits of Law* (n 6 above); Barnard and Hervey, 'Softening the Approach to Quotas' (n 12 above); Barmes, 'Promoting Diversity and the Definition of Direct Discrimination' (n 8 above); A McColgan, 'Cracking the Comparator Problem: Discrimination, "Equal" Treatment and the Role of Comparisons' [2006] *European Human Rights Law Review* 650; and McColgan, 'Reconfiguring Discrimination Law' (n 7 above). For a discussion of some of the dangers of an approach which places so much emphasis on group membership that it becomes oblivious to the complexity of individual circumstance (which may entail membership of more than one relevant group), see D Schiek, 'Broadening the Scope and the Norms of EU Gender Equality Law: Towards a Multidimensional Conception of Equality Law' (2005) 12 *Maastricht Journal of European and Comparative Law* 427; and, for discussion of the fluidity of groups, see Young, *Justice and the Politics of Difference* (n 5 above) 171–2.

[69] C Lawrence and M Matsuda, *We Won't Go Back: Making the Case for Affirmative Action* (Boston and New York, Houghton Mifflin Co, 1997) 26. See also M Minow, *Not Only for Myself: Identity Politics and the Law* (New York, New Press, 1997) 153–4.

The British Equalities Review reported a high level of dissatisfaction with the current legal constraints on positive measures.[70] Discontent had been expressed to it, for instance, by employers who 'for sound business reasons' had wanted to increase the number of women or ethnic minority staff; by a national arts body which had wished to encourage young writers from particular groups by limiting a competition to them; and by a major media organisation which had wanted to set up a journalism traineeship scheme for women and members of ethnic minority groups. In addition, the security services had indicated that current non-discrimination law was hampering their efforts to appoint and integrate the diverse range of operatives needed to gain intelligence and combat terrorism as effectively as possible. The Metropolitan Police had pointed out that, on current projections, its ethnic and gender profile would not match that of the London population until the middle of the next century and that, despite the operational importance of increasing its diversity more quickly than this, non-discrimination law had already forced it to abandon a scheme designed to accelerate the recruitment of well-qualified female and ethnic minority candidates. Accordingly, the Equalities Review concluded:

> We fully appreciate that anti-discrimination law should be applicable in all situations; but it is increasingly clear that, if applied too rigidly, it may itself become the enemy of security, equality and community cohesion.[71]

Canada provides an inspiring example of a system in which notions of positive discrimination appear to have been widely embraced as a means of tackling the disadvantage frequently experienced by relevant groups. Thus, while section 15(1) of the Canadian Charter prohibits discrimination on grounds of 'race, national or ethnic origin, colour, religion, sex, age or mental or physical disability', section 15(2) goes on to state that such prohibited discrimination does not include 'any law, program or activity that has as its object the amelioration of conditions of disadvantaged individuals or groups'. The judiciary has stressed the importance of recognising and tackling disadvantage[72] and has even been prepared to impose quota schemes on organisations as a means of redressing long-standing discriminatory practices. In *Action Travail des Femmes v Canadian National Railway*,[73] for instance, the Supreme Court famously ordered a company (which for many years had relied on criteria which discriminated against women by placing undue weight on physical qualities such as strength) to ensure that a quarter of newly-appointed employees were women until the imbalance in their numbers was removed.

---

[70] Equalities Review, *Fairness and Freedom* (London, Stationery Office, 2007) 102–3. See also Government Equalities Office, *The Equality Bill* (n 3 above) paras 5.8–5.17 where it is reported that similar concerns were expressed in many of the responses made to the Discrimination Law Review.

[71] *Ibid*, 103.

[72] See eg *Andrews v British Columbia* [1989] 1 SCR 143; and *Turpin v The Queen* [1989] 1 SCR 1296.

[73] *Action Travail des Femmes v Canadian National Railway* [1987] SCR 1114.

Other jurisdictions, too, have put positive discrimination to work in an attempt to redress social inequality. A number have enshrined quotas or reservations (particularly in the context of race) in their constitutions with varying degrees of success.[74] In the United States, schemes which favour under-represented racial groups may be held to comply with the Equal Protection clause of the 14th Amendment to the US Constitution,[75] provided that they can survive the increasingly strict scrutiny to which they are subjected by the judiciary—a level of scrutiny equivalent to that received by schemes which would disadvantage minority racial groups.[76] It must be shown that the measure in question is narrowly tailored to address a compelling governmental interest. Outside the educational context—where student diversity is itself regarded as a compelling governmental interest—this has required proponents of affirmative action schemes to convince judges that their scheme is narrowly tailored to redress a proven history of specific discrimination.[77]

Interestingly, in the United States,

> [t]he clear trend in decisions regarding affirmative action shows an increasing judicial scepticism toward the proposition that differential treatment of minority groups may be necessary to establish equal opportunity and equal access.[78]

This scepticism sometimes appears to border on full-blown hostility, as is demonstrated by the following words of Thomas J:

> There can be no doubt that racial paternalism and its unintended consequences can be as poisonous and pernicious as any other form of discrimination. So-called 'benign' discrimination teaches many that, because of chronic and apparently immutable handicaps, minorities cannot compete with them without their patronizing indulgence. Inevitably, such programs engender attitudes of superiority or, alternatively, provoke resentment among those who believe that they have been wronged by the government's use of race. These programs stamp minorities with a badge of inferiority and may cause them to develop dependencies or to adopt an attitude that they are 'entitled' to preferences … In my mind, government-sponsored racial discrimination based on benign prejudice is just as noxious as discrimination inspired by malicious prejudice. In each instance, it is racial discrimination, plain and simple.[79]

---

[74] E Phillips, 'Positive Discrimination in Malaysia: A Cautionary Tale for the United Kingdom' and W Menski, 'The Indian Experience and its Lessons for Britain', both in Hepple and Szyszczak (eds), *Discrimination: The Limits of Law* (n 6 above).

[75] See also Title VII of the American Civil Rights Act 1964 (s 703(a) 42 USC s 2000e-2(a)) (discussed in Barnard and Hervey, 'Softening the Approach to Quotas' (n 12 above) 342–5).

[76] *Richmond v JA Croson Co*, 488 US 469 (1989); *Adarand Constructors Inc v Pena*, 515 US 200 (1995); *Gratz v Bollinger*, 539 US 224 (2003); and *Grutter v Bollinger*, 539 US 306 (2003).

[77] *Richmond v JA Croson Co*, 488 US 469 at 500–06 (1989).

[78] M Diller, 'Judicial Backlash, the ADA and the Civil Rights Model' (2000) 21 *Berkeley Journal of Employment and Labor* 19 at 46. See also M Adams, 'The Last Wave of Affirmative Action' (1998) *Wisconson Law Review* 1395.

[79] *Adarand Constructors v Pena Inc*, 515 US 200 at 240–41 (1995). For a discussion of the negative impact which affirmative action schemes may have on the esteem of their recipients, see GC Loury, 'Why Should We Care About Group Inequality?' (1987) 5 *Social Philosophy and Policy* 249; and for

These words, though uttered in the context of race, have particular resonance for disability. They express exactly the concerns which resulted in the repeal of the British quota and reserved occupation schemes, and serve as an important reminder of the potential danger of some positive discrimination measures.

The British Government, however, seems to be in little need of such reminders, at least in the non-disability context. The Discrimination Law Review reported that, having considered alternative models for tackling disadvantage (such as the Canadian constitutional equality guarantee), there were 'no real gains to be made from' departing from the British model but 'considerable risks' associated with doing so.[80] In its words,

> [w]hat we have is tried and tested, results in legal certainty and is easily adaptable to reflect changing circumstances in society. It is also compatible with European law. A different model would lead to legal uncertainty and consequential burdens on business and the courts. It would mean a transfer of power from Parliament to the courts and (having regard to the framework of European law within which it would need to operate) most likely result in undesired outcomes.[81]

The authors of the Discrimination Law Review thus insisted that they did not believe that positive discrimination 'provide[d] an answer to the persistent inequality experienced by some groups'[82] and emphatically refused to recommend that the current laws be changed to permit it. It should be remembered, however, that the sense in which the Discrimination Law Review used the term 'positive discrimination' appears to have been significantly narrower than the sense in which it has been used in this chapter. The Government's opposition to a more relaxed approach to positive discrimination is thus confined to situations in which direct preferences are conferred on disadvantaged groups in violation of the merit principle—situations in which a less qualified member of a disadvantaged group is given preference over a better qualified competitor.[83] It has adopted a very different approach to the tie-break situation in which there are two people who are judged to be equally well qualified.

A few months before the Discrimination Law Review was published, the Equalities Review had accepted that there was 'a case for introducing time-limited, proportionate, balancing measures of a type not currently permissible under British law'.[84] It therefore urged the Discrimination Law Review to propose the removal of the current limits on the scope of permitted positive action and

---

general criticism of affirmative action measures made by a member of the early civil rights movement, see M Abram, 'Affirmative Action: Fair Shakers and Social Engineers' (1986) 99 *Harvard Law Review* 1312.

[80] Department for Communities and Local Government, *Discrimination Law Review* (n 3 above) Pt 2 Intro, para 10.

[81] *Ibid.*

[82] *Ibid*, para 4.5.

[83] See eg *ibid*, para 4.17.

[84] Equalities Review, *Fairness and Freedom* (n 70 above) 119–21.

the inclusion, in new legislation, of 'balancing measures' consistent with the limits of positive action permitted under EC law.[85]

The Discrimination Law Review responded positively to such entreaties and recommended a significant expansion of the scope of positive action permitted under British law.[86] This recommendation, which would involve permitting what it termed 'positive action' to the full extent permitted by EC law, also appeared in the proposals set out in the Government's response to the Discrimination Law Review consultation. In its words,

> [t]his will allow all protected groups to benefit from measures to meet their special needs. It will also enable employers, where they feel it is appropriate, and where there is a choice between two or more equally qualified candidates, to take under-representation into account when making recruitment or promotion decisions, provided there is not an automatic rule favouring those with any particular protected characteristic. Positive action measures will remain strictly voluntary and the principle of selection on merit will be retained.

EC law, as indicated above, has been criticised for its failure to adopt a more radical, permissive approach to measures designed to counter disadvantage and under-representation. Nevertheless, it goes considerably further than does current British non-discrimination law relating to the symmetrical grounds. Implementation of the Government's recommendations on this point would therefore represent a considerable step forward. It would also help to bring the law relating to those grounds a little more closely into line with the law relating to disability—which, as has been seen, imposes no limits at all on positive discrimination except in the context of local authority employment.

Finally, it is worth reiterating the fact that, in the Equalities Review, the Discrimination Law Review and also the Government's response to the consultation on the latter, considerable emphasis was placed on the fact that what was being recommended was an expansion of positive action and not the legitimisation of positive discrimination. The driving force behind this repeated and heavy emphasis appears to be political in nature. As was recognised by the Equalities Review, there is no 'public appetite for what is seen as unfair favouring or special treatment of specific groups of people'.[87] Because the concept of positive discrimination is often linked to such forms of treatment, any suggestion that the proposals were to legitimise positive discrimination would risk shipwrecking them against the rock of public opinion. The term clearly tends to trigger political antagonism and is therefore understandably avoided by those arguing for a more expansive approach.

---

[85] *Ibid.*

[86] Department for Communities and Local Government, *Discrimination Law Review* (n 3 above) para 4.46.

[87] Equalities Review, *Fairness and Freedom* (n 70 above) 119–21. See also Department for Communities and Local Government, *Discrimination Law Review* (n 3 above) para 4.36.

The Government's proposals would undoubtedly herald a more permissive approach to positive discrimination in the sense that that term has been used in this chapter. They would permit membership of a disadvantaged group to be acknowledged, and to confer preference in tie-break situations where candidates were equally well qualified. They would, however, not permit direct preference to be given to members of such groups over better-qualified competitors. Accordingly, they would not permit positive discrimination in its narrower sense of an apparent infringement of the merit principle.

3. Positive Action

Like 'positive discrimination', the term 'positive action' has no precise definition. As mentioned at the beginning of this chapter, it is a term which is sometimes used to describe all measures designed to tackle under-representation and disadvantage, including those which confer direct preferences. It is also sometimes used to refer only to those positive measures which are lawful—either because they fall short of positive discrimination or because they are expressly authorised by statute—despite the fact that they confer direct preferences. Here, however, it will be used to refer to positive measures which do not confer such preferences.

The 'positive action' provisions of the sex and race legislation have already been mentioned. As was explained in Section 2.3 above, they authorise the conferral of direct preferences on members of under-represented groups in the contexts of training and of seats on elected bodies. This authorisation of direct preference-giving brings them within the scope of positive discrimination for the purposes of this chapter.

In addition, the positive action provisions expressly authorise other forms of measure designed to redress under-representation, which would confer no direct preference on members of relevant groups. Thus, section 47 of the SDA authorises the encouragement of women only (or men only) to take advantage of opportunities 'for doing [particular] work' provided that there has been a considerable under-representation of the targeted sex in that work in the past year.[88] Similar provision is made for the encouragement of existing employees in situations where one of the sexes is under-represented in a particular post or at a particular level within an organisation.[89]

There are also numerous forms of positive measure, which, although not expressly mentioned in the statutes, would not amount to discrimination. These include ensuring that advertisements for vacancies are worded so as to welcome

---

[88] SDA s 47(1)(b) and (2)(b).
[89] See eg SDA s 48. For a discussion of the implications of these provisions for the lawfulness of other forms of positive action, see Barmes, 'Promoting Diversity and the Definition of Direct Discrimination' (n 8 above) 201–2.

applications from under-represented groups and that such advertisements are placed in sources likely to be read by members of those groups. Attention may also be given to ways in which potential barriers might be removed. This might result in the provision of additional facilities (such as convenient and affordable childcare, a prayer room for use by members of different religions, and the installation of ramps and better lighting). It may also result in the revision of policies and procedures (such as those relating to flexible working and to the provision of information in formats other than print).

Despite the range of positive action measures permitted by non-discrimination law, evidence suggests that their use has been sparing and inconsistent.[90] Vera Sacks reported that the legislation's positive action provisions were 'little known, misunderstood, and minimally used'.[91] Given the vagueness of the boundary between prohibited discrimination and permitted positive action, this is unsurprising. The vigilance with which this boundary has been patrolled by the judiciary—illustrated by cases such as *ACAS v Taylor*[92]—makes the tendency to shrink away from it still more understandable.

ACAS concerned a national promotion exercise within the organisation to the rank of senior executive officer. Mr Taylor's application failed and he argued that this was the result of sex discrimination. ACAS had issued guidance to regional managers, who were responsible for assessing candidates in their area. This included the following passage:

> Please remember that more needs to be done to ensure the reality of the claim that ACAS is an equal opportunity employer. For example women make up only 17% of those at Senior Executive Officer level at present and ethnic minorities staff less than 1%. All staff should be considered on their merits as individuals. Where you have any doubts about the fairness of the Annual Reports you should not hesitate to take appropriate action.

The Employment Appeal Tribunal upheld the first instance ruling, finding that direct sex discrimination had been established. The inclusion in the guidance of the reminder that 'more needs to be done to ensure ... that ACAS is an equal opportunity employer' was particularly problematic. According to Morrison J, this wording was 'capable of being misconstrued' and of 'leading the unwary into positive discrimination'.[93] The guidance should, he suggested, have simply

---

[90] See eg Sacks, 'Tackling Discrimination Positively in Britain' (n 62 above) 357; C Welsh, J Knox and M Brett, *Acting Positively: Positive Action Under the Race Relations Act 1976* (Sheffield, Employment Department, 1994); and B Hepple, M Coussey and T Choudhury, *Equality: A New Framework* (Oxford, Hart Publishing, 2000) Appendix 1. See also the responses made to the Discrimination Law Review—Government Equalities Office, *The Equality Bill* (n 3 above) paras 5.5–5.17.

[91] Sacks, 'Tackling Discrimination Positively in Britain' (n 62 above) 380. See also Department for Communities and Local Government, *Discrimination Law Review* (n 3 above) paras 4.36–4.38.

[92] *ACAS v Taylor* EAT/788/97, set out in M Connolly, *Townshend-Smith on Discrimination Law: Text, Cases and Materials* (London, Cavendish, 2004) 580–81. See also *Hughes v Hackney LBC* [1988] IRLR 55 (IT); and *Lambeth LBC v Commission for Racial Equality* [1990] ICR 768 (CA).

[93] *ACAS v Taylor* EAT/788/97.

reminded regional managers that ACAS was an equal opportunity employer and that women and members of ethnic minorities were under-represented at senior executive level.

Presented in this way, it is clear that the line between direct discrimination and lawful positive action will appear to many employers and others to be dangerously thin. Evidence suggests that the diversity strategies of many employers might actually extend beyond this line into the forbidden territory of discrimination, albeit positive discrimination.[94] The potential risk of engaging in unlawful conduct is obviously likely to operate as a disincentive for many who might otherwise be keen to increase the diversity of their organisations through positive action measures. This disincentive extends beyond the realms of sex and race into that of disability where, as has been seen, the asymmetrical approach of the DDA permits a much more generous approach to positive measures. In the words of the Discrimination Law Association,

> [t]he present weakness and opacity of the positive action regime means that employers are often confused about the extent to which they can use positive action and, in the case of disability, are so nervous about scope for positive action that they fail to appreciate that positive action in the case of disability is not—other than in local government—unlawful.[95]

The Government has accepted that confusion as to the law has reduced the extent to which positive action measures are used. In addition to recommending that the scope of permitted positive action be increased, it therefore also recommended that the Equality and Human Rights Commission should issue clear guidance as to the purposes for which relevant balancing measures might be used.[96] Such guidance would have the added benefit of increasing the general regard for such balancing measures by reducing the common perception that they amounted to undesirable positive discrimination.[97]

Before the advent of the positive duties to promote equality there was little in non-discrimination law to counteract the disincentive against the use of positive action created by the risk of liability for unlawful positive discrimination. Commentators have frequently drawn attention to the link between the under use of positive action and the entirely permissive, rather than mandatory, nature of such action.[98] In the absence of any definite obligation to do anything more to

---

[94] L Barmes and S Ashtiany, 'The Diversity Approach to Achieving Equality: Potential and Pitfalls' (2003) 32 *Industrial Law Journal* 274–96.

[95] DRC, *Initial Submission to the Discrimination Law Review* (London, DRC, 2006) para 76. See also Office of Public Management, *Equality and Diversity in Local Government*, (London, ODPM, 2003); and ACAS, *Back to Basics—ACAS Experience of Equality and Diversity in the Workplace*, ACAS policy discussion paper (London, ACAS, 2006).

[96] Department for Communities and Local Government, *Discrimination Law Review* (n 3 above) paras 4.46 and 4.50.

[97] *Ibid*, para 4.36. See also, Government Equalities Office, *The Equality Bill* (n 3 above) para 5.21.

[98] Sacks, 'Tackling Discrimination Positively in Britain' (n 62 above) 380–81.

further equality and diversity than to ensure that forms of prohibited discrimination are avoided, there is an obvious temptation to do very little.

In recent years the Government has attempted to encourage the use of positive action in the public sector by adopting a 'goals and timetables' approach.[99] This involves the setting of specific goals relating to the representation of particular minority groups (which may include women and disabled people) and the laying down of timetables for their achievement. These goals are, however, not mandatory in nature. Neither are they accompanied by the authorisation of preferential treatment, even in tie-break situations. The Government has been at pains to stress that they do not amount to strict quotas and that they do not authorise positive discrimination.[100]

Outside mainstream non-discrimination law, legislation as fundamental as the Constitutional Reform Act 2005 has enshrined the need to have regard to the value of diversity in relation to the issue of judicial appointments.[101] The key legislative means by which the Government has sought to encourage the use of positive action measures in Britain, however, is that of the new positive duties imposed on public sector bodies to promote equality. These will now be considered in a little more depth.

4. Positive Duties to Promote Equality

The last decade has witnessed the emergence of what is often referred to as a 'fourth generation' of equality law.[102] This has taken the form of explicit statutory duties placed on public bodies across Britain, not simply to avoid engaging in unlawful discrimination, but to take positive steps to promote equality. Such duties are pro-active in nature and are clearly not fault-based. They require organisations to take positive steps to break down structural and institutional barriers. Their purpose is to achieve wide-reaching organisational change and not simply to provide compensation to individual victims of discrimination.[103]

---

[99] See eg *Modernising Government*, Cm 4310 (London, Stationery Office, 1999) paras 6.23–6.28. For general discussion of this approach see A McColgan, *Discrimination Law: Text, Cases and Materials* (Oxford, Hart Publishing, 2005) 151–5.

[100] Hansard 19 January 2000, HC Debates, col 847 (Jack Straw, Home Secretary).

[101] Constitutional Reform Act 2005 s 64. See further R Allen, 'Dealing with Difference in Equality Law: How Should we Address Diversity in Equality Law?', a paper delivered at the Equality and Diversity Forum Seminar Series, Seminar 3, 9 January 2006, paras 8–12; K Underwood, 'Sinners and Judges' (2007) 151 *Solicitors Journal* 446; and E Rackley, 'Judicial Diversity, the Woman Judge and Fairy Tale Endings' [2007] *Legal Studies* 74.

[102] See eg Hepple, Coussey and Choudhury, *Equality: A New Framework* (n 90 above) para 1.6.

[103] See further S Fredman, 'Equality: A New Generation?' (2001) 30 *Industrial Law Journal* 145; and S Fredman, 'Changing the Norm: Positive Duties in Equal Treatment Legislation' (2005) 12 *Maastricht Journal of European and Comparative Law* 369.

The emergence of such duties has led Sandra Fredman to identify two models for the achievement of equality.[104] The first is 'complaints-led' and focused on the rights of individuals. It is grounded in traditional conceptions of human rights. The second is pro-active in nature. It is not 'complaints-led' and therefore has the potential to be less adversarial and to trigger less defensive responses from those to whom it applies. Participation of relevant disadvantaged groups—both in the processes associated with discharging pro-active duties and in society more generally—is regarded as of central importance in this second model.

Legislation in 1998 imposed a duty on the newly created Welsh Assembly to ensure that its functions were exercised 'with due regard to the principle that there should be equality of opportunity for all people'.[105] A similar obligation was imposed on the Greater London Authority in 1999.[106] In addition, the Scottish Executive has been granted the power to impose a similar duty on office-holders.[107]

The first UK Act to impose positive equality duties on public authorities generally was the Northern Ireland Act 1998 (NIA).[108] Section 75(1) requires a broad range of public authorities, identified in an annex, to have 'due regard to the need to promote equality of opportunity'. Unlike the public authority duties that have since been created in Britain, the duty created by the Northern Ireland Act applies to a broad range of equality grounds. Regard must be had to the need to ensure equality of opportunity between people with different religious beliefs and political opinions; between members of different racial groups; between people of different ages, different marital status and different sexual orientations; between men and women; between people with and without dependents; and between disabled and non-disabled people. An additional duty to promote good relations is created by section 75(2) but this applies only in the contexts of religion, political belief and race. Relevant public authorities are required to produce equality schemes—on which representatives of those likely to be affected must be consulted—for approval by the Equality Commission of Northern Ireland.[109] Such schemes must be revised every five years.

---

[104] Fredman, 'Changing the Norm' (n 103 above). See also C McCrudden, 'Review of Issues Concerning the Operation of the Equality Duty' in E McLaughlin and N Faris (eds), *Section 75 Equality Review—An Operational Review* (Belfast, 2004); C McCrudden, 'Mainstreaming Equality in the Governance of Northern Ireland' in C Harvey (ed), *Human Rights, Equality and Democratic Renewal in Northern Ireland* (Oxford, Hart Publishing, 2001); C O'Cinneide, 'A New Generation of Equality Legislation? Positive Duties and Disability Rights' in Lawson and Gooding (eds), *Disability Rights in Europe* (n 4 above); and S Fredman, 'Transformation or Dilution: Fundamental Rights in the EU Social Space' (2006) 12 *European Law Journal* 41.

[105] Government of Wales Act 1998 s 120. For discussion of the impact of this duty, see P Chaney and R Fevre, *An Absolute Duty* (Cardiff, Institute of Welsh Affairs, 2002).

[106] Greater London Authority Act 1999 s 33.

[107] Scotland Act 1998 sch 5.

[108] See further McCrudden, 'Review of Issues Concerning the Operation of the Equality Duty' (n 104 above).

[109] Northern Ireland Act 1998 sch 9.

The need for similar duties in Britain became evident after the exposure, by the MacPherson Report into the death of Stephen Lawrence, of the extent of institutional discrimination in the police force.[110] Accordingly, the Race Relations (Amendment) Act 2000 inserted a new section 71 into the RRA. This imposes a general duty on the extensive list of public authorities set out in Schedule 1A to have 'due regard' to the need to eliminate unlawful discrimination and to promote equality of opportunity and good relations between persons of different racial groups.

It also provides for the imposition of specific duties on particular types of public authority to be laid down in statutory instruments. The purpose of these specific duties is to enhance the performance of the general duty by compliance with a number of detailed requirements, including ethnic monitoring and the production and publication of race equality schemes.[111] These schemes must set out the functions and policies which are regarded by an authority as relevant to its performance of its section 71 duties. They must also set out an authority's arrangements (including those relating to consultation) for assessing the impact of its proposed policies on race equality; for monitoring any adverse impact of its policies on race equality; for publicising relevant assessments and reports; and for relevant staff training.

The general section 71 duty is enforceable through judicial review proceedings by any person with sufficient locus standi to bring the case. In addition, the Equality Act 2006[112] granted the Equality and Human Rights Commission the power to assess the level to which a public authority has complied with this general duty; to make recommendations as to improvements; and to issue a compliance notice if the authority fails to respond adequately to such recommendations. The failure of an authority to respond appropriately to such a notice entitles the Commission to apply to the courts for an order requiring compliance. The specific duties may also be enforced by means of compliance notices, to be issued originally by the Commission for Racial Equality and now by the Equality and Human Rights Commission.[113] The option of judicial review is, however, not available in relation to them.

Public authorities were placed under a general disability equality duty by section 49A of the DDA, as a result of the DDA 2005. This requires that:

(1) Every public authority shall in carrying out its functions have due regard to—

(a) the need to eliminate discrimination that is unlawful under this Act;

(b) the need to eliminate harassment of disabled persons that is related to their

---

[110] Home Office, *The Stephen Lawrence Inquiry: Report of an Inquiry by Sir William Macpherson of Cluny* (1999), available at http://www.archive.official-documents.co.uk/document/cm42/4262/4262. htm (last accessed 30 April 2008).

[111] See further the Race Relations Act 1976 (Statutory Duties) Order 2001 (SI 2001/3458). See also the Race Relations Act 1976 (Statutory Duties) (Scotland) Order 2002 (SI No 2002/62).

[112] Equality Act 2006 ss 31 and 32.

[113] RRA s 71D.

disabilities;

(c) the need to promote equality of opportunity between disabled persons and other persons;

(d) the need to take steps to take account of disabled persons' disabilities, even where that involves treating disabled persons more favourably than other persons;

(e) the need to promote positive attitudes towards disabled persons; and

(f) the need to encourage participation by disabled persons in public life.

While paragraphs (b)–(f) represent welcome additions to what is contained in the RRA, section 49A does not impose a duty on public authorities to promote good relations between disabled and non-disabled people. The omission of such an obligation caused some concern in the early stages of the Bill—particularly because such a duty would have had the potential to tackle disability-based hate crime and the harassment of disabled people outside the context of employment (the only area in which harassment is currently prohibited by the DDA 1995).[114] The Parliamentary Joint Committee set up to scrutinise the draft Disability Discrimination Bill therefore recommended that a duty to promote good relations should be included. The Government, however, declined to include a reference to the promotion of good relations, taking the view that relevant concerns were adequately addressed by the pre-existing paragraphs and that adding a duty to promote good relations would introduce additional undesirable complexity.[115] Under recent Government proposals, however, a reformulated public sector duty would require public bodies to address the issue of good relations for disability as well as all the other equality strands.[116] Unlike the NIA and the RRA, the DDA does not attempt to list the public authorities to which the duty applies. Instead, the relevant authorities are defined in more generic terms in section 49B and various exceptions are set out in section 49C.

As in relation to race, provision is made for the introduction of supplementary specific disability equality duties by means of statutory instrument. The Disability Discrimination (Public Authorities) (Statutory Duties) Regulations 2005 imposed a specific duty on public authorities to draw up disability equality schemes and to publish them by 4 December 2006. The requirements for such schemes bear a close resemblance to those relating to race. Unlike the latter, however, the former include a stipulation that disability equality schemes must be drawn up with the involvement of disabled people who have an interest in the authority's performance of its functions, and that the schemes must explain how

---

[114] *Report of the Parliamentary Joint Committee on the Draft Disability Discrimination Bill* (London, Stationery Office, 2004) ch 5, paras 229–41. But see Government Equalities Office, *The Equality Bill* (n 3 above) para 13.4, where it is stated that the Government is considering the extension of this protection to non-employment contexts.

[115] Department for Work and Pensions, *The Government's Response to the Report of the Joint Committee on the Draft Disability Discrimination Bill* (London, Stationery Office, 2004) response 40.

[116] Government Equalities Office, *The Equality Bill* (n 3 above) para 2.25.

that involvement was achieved.[117] The general and specific disability equality duties are enforceable by way of judicial review and compliance notices respectively in the same way as are the general and specific race equality duties.

In *R (Chavda) v Harrow London Borough Council*[118] the disability equality duty was relied upon in a challenge brought against a local authority by way of judicial review. It was argued that its decision to withdraw care services from disabled people whose needs were classified as 'substantial' rather than as 'critical' had been made without 'due regard' to the need to promote disability equality. This challenge succeeded with the result that the Council was required to revisit the issue.

The gender equality duty was introduced by the Equality Act 2006, which inserted a new section 76A into the SDA. According to sub-section (1), this duty requires public authorities to have due regard to the need:

(a) to eliminate unlawful discrimination and harassment, and
(b) to promote equality of opportunity between men and women.

Its elaboration thus lacks the specificity of the disability equality duty. In its definition of public authorities, however, it adopts a similar approach to the DDA and, in its authorisation of the imposition of specific duties through statutory instrument, it follows the pattern of the race and disability duties. Public authorities subject to specific gender equality duties were accordingly required to produce gender equality schemes by 30 April 2007.

The gender equality duty differs from the race and disability duties in one important respect. Unlike the two earlier duties, the gender duty requires public authorities to identify gender equality objectives, to explain what steps they propose to take in order to address them and to consider the relevance of these objectives to the authority's efforts to tackle any gender pay gap. The addition of this requirement was intended to strengthen the emphasis on the need for the equality duty to achieve practical outcomes.

Both the Equalities Review and the Discrimination Law Review acknowledged the great potential of these positive equality duties to effect change. They recommended, however, that instead of the current ground-specific approach there should be a single integrated public sector duty covering all equality strands[119]—a recommendation retained in the July 2008 report.[120] Such an approach would thus bring sexual orientation, religion and belief and age within

---

[117] Disability Discrimination (Public Authorities) (Statutory Duties) Regulations 2005 (SI 2966/2005) reg 2(2) and (3). For discussion of the value of consultation and participation, see eg Fredman, *Discrimination Law* (n 7 above) 153–6; and, for early indications of its effectiveness in the disability context, see Office for Public Management, *Involvement for Real Equality: The Benefits for Public Services of Involving Disabled People* (London, Disability Rights Commission, 2007).

[118] *R (Chavda) v Harrow LBC* [2007] EWHC 3064 (Admin).

[119] Equalities Review, *Fairness and Freedom* (n 70 above) ch 5, step 6; and Department for Communities and Local Government, *Discrimination Law Review* (n 3 above) paras 5.23–5.24.

[120] Government Equalities Office, *The Equality Bill* (n 3 above) paras 2.13–2.14 and 2.59.

the ambit of a positive equality duty. In order to assist authorities with the practical implementation of such a duty, the Discrimination Law Review recommended that they should be provided with a clear statement of its purposes.[121] In its response to that consultation, however, the Government indicated that it planned to achieve this, not by the inclusion of a purpose clause, but by ensuring that the statute explained what was meant by 'advancing equality of opportunity' for purposes of the duty and that detailed guidance was made available to public bodies through statutory codes of practice.[122]

Influential on both the Equalities Review and the Discrimination Law Review were indications that the effectiveness of the race equality duty may have been hampered by its tendency to focus the attention of public authorities on the need to comply with a particular bureaucratic process rather than on achieving outcomes.[123] This is a tendency which, according to Professor Fredman, plagues pro-active duties of this type. In her words,

> proactive models frequently confuse the strategy with the aims, so that tools, such as monitoring and … impact assessments, are treated as if they were ends in themselves rather than means to achieve an end. Thus far more attention needs to be paid to what the strategy hopes to achieve.[124]

In response to such concerns it was argued that the phrase 'have due regard', in the formulation of the duties, should be replaced with stronger and more outcome-oriented language, such as 'shall take steps'.[125] Instead, however, the Discrimination Law Review proposed that the requirement to 'have due regard' to the equality impact of all aspects of their operation be replaced with a requirement to take action in a limited number of priority areas. These areas would be identified by authorities themselves through the setting of priority equality objectives, which would be reviewed every three years.[126] This proposal thus followed the model of the current gender equality objectives. Unlike them, however, it would require equality objectives to operate *instead of*, rather than in addition to, a duty to have due regard to equality in all aspects of an authority's functioning.

---

[121] Department for Communities and Local Government, *Discrimination Law Review* (n 3 above) paras 5.28–5.30.

[122] Government Equalities Office, *The Equality Bill* (n 3 above) para 2.25.

[123] Equalities Review, *Fairness and Freedom* (n 70 above) ch 4 and Department for Communities and Local Government, *Discrimination Law Review* (n 3 above) paras 5.14–5.15.

[124] Fredman, 'Changing the Norm' (n 103 above) 375.

[125] See eg S Fredman and S Spencer, 'Delivering Equality: Towards an Outcome-Focused Positive Duty' Submission to the Cabinet Office Equalities Review and to the Discrimination Law Review (June 2006) 9–10, available at http://www.edf.org.uk/news/Delivering%20equality%20submission%20030606-final.pdf (last accessed 30 April 2008); and Discrimination Law Association, *Discrimination Law Association Submissions for the Discrimination Law Review* (London, Discrimination Law Association, 2006) para 66.

[126] Department for Communities and Local Government, *Discrimination Law Review* (n 3 above) paras 5.31–5.33 and 5.40.

The proposal to remove the general duty on public bodies to 'have due regar to equality in relation to all their functions was greeted with alarm and host ity.[127] Without such an obligation, public bodies would be able to ignore th equality-related impact of various aspects of their operation and equality consi erations would thus no longer have to be mainstreamed into their gener operations. In the words of the DRC,

> [w]e oppose this break with the mainstreaming principle which is the heart of the du If this were removed, it would represent an enormous setback.[128]

More colourfully, Bert Massey (the Chair of the DRC) warned that this propos 'does to disability rights what a bulldozer does to a building' and that, implemented, it would 'do enormous damage to disabled people and ... unravel lot of successes of the last 10 years'.[129]

The Discrimination Law Review also recommended that the detail and pr scriptiveness of the current specific equality duties should be significant reduced. Instead of laying down specific requirements, the duties should identi key underlying principles and allow authorities a considerable degree autonomy and flexibility as to the manner in which they translated tho principles into action and developed their plans for achieving their priori equality objectives.[130] There would have been no specific requirement to produ equality schemes or to monitor workforce representation.

The aim of these proposals was to reduce the bureaucratic burden imposed c public authorities by the equality duties. It seems likely however that they wou have created considerable confusion and uncertainty, reduced transparency ar made the duty more difficult to enforce.[131] They would have entailed an enti restructuring of the current equality duties and risked making them mu narrower and weaker.[132]

The Discrimination Law Review's proposals were significantly remoulded the Government's response to the consultation on that Review. The Governme has now rejected the idea that the distinction between the general duty to ha due regard and its more specific supporting duties should be abandoned.[1] While it retained the idea that national governments should set strategic equali objectives, these would now operate in addition to the general duty to have d regard rather than in its place.[134] These changes in approach are extrem welcome.

---

[127] See eg T Branigan, 'Watchdogs Criticise Equality Reform Plans', *The Guardian*, 16 July 2007
[128] DRC, *Briefing—Discrimination Law Review: A Framework for Fairness* (London, DRC, 200 para 2(a).
[129] Quoted in Branigan, 'Watchdogs Criticise Equality Reform Plans' (n 127 above).
[130] Department for Communities and Local Government, *Discrimination Law Review* (n 3 abo paras 5.43–5.46.
[131] DRC, *Briefing—Discrimination Law Review: A Framework for Fairness* (n 128 above) para 2(
[132] *Ibid*, para 2.
[133] Government Equalities Office, *The Equality Bill* (n 3 above) para 2.38.
[134] *Ibid*, para 2.40.

It has been argued that some sort of positive equality duty, though not necessarily as onerous as that applying in the public sector, should be extended to private sector bodies.[135] This is a particularly important issue in view of the increasing trend of contracting out the performance of various services and functions to the private sector. The Discrimination Law Association has suggested that such a duty might require employers to monitor the composition of their workforce; to review and report on the potential impact of their employment policies and practices on equality of opportunity; to attempt to eliminate any actual or potential adverse impact of those policies and practices; and to make reasonable adjustments where necessary.[136]

Both the Equalities Review and the Discrimination Law Review rejected the extension of any form of monitoring obligation or positive equality duty to the private sector.[137] Such a duty, they considered, would impose unnecessarily burdensome obligations on private sector organisations, particularly small or medium-sized firms, and would be unlikely to attract sufficient support. Instead, the Government has recommended the development of a voluntary equality 'kite-mark' scheme to be used by private sector employers.[138]

Procurement provides a mechanism through which the public sector may be able to exert an extremely powerful influence over private and voluntary sector bodies. To date, however, the potential of this mechanism to promote equality in these other sectors has not been fully exploited.[139] The importance of procurement was recognised by the Equalities Review, which observed:

> This is an area where Government leadership is absolutely essential, and one in which Government should be seen to set an example. The Panel believes that public agencies should require suppliers to adopt the same principles under which they themselves are required to operate.[140]

In its view, however, Government had hitherto 'failed to do enough'[141] in this regard.

---

[135] See eg O'Cinneide, 'A New Generation of Equality Legislation?' (n 104 above) 239–42; and Discrimination Law Association, *Discrimination Law Association Submissions for the Discrimination Law Review* (n 125 above) paras 68–71; Hepple, Coussey and Choudhury, *Equality: a New Framework* (n 90 above) paras 3.38–4.42; and DRC, *Initial Submission to the Discrimination Law Review* (n 95 above) para 1.4.4.

[136] Discrimination Law Association, *Discrimination Law Association Submissions for the Discrimination Law Review* (n 125 above) para 69.

[137] See Equalities Review, *Fairness and Freedom* (n 70 above) ch 5, step 4; and Department for Communities and Local Government, *Discrimination Law Review* (n 3 above) paras 6.11 and 6.13.

[138] Government Equalities Office, *The Equality Bill* (n 3 above) paras 4.40–4.41. See also Department for Communities and Local Government, *Discrimination Law Review* (n 3 above) paras 6.7–6.10.

[139] For detailed consideration of this issue, see C McCrudden, *Buying Social Justice: Equality, Government Procurement, and Legal Change* (Oxford, Oxford University Press, 2007).

[140] Equalities Review, *Fairness and Freedom* (n 70 above) ch 5, step 8.

[141] *Ibid*, ch 4.

The Equalities Review recommended that the public sector equality dutie should make specific reference to the obligation to incorporate equality consic erations into the procurement policies and practices of public authorities.[142] Th approach was rejected by the Discrimination Law Review on the ground tha procurement already fell within the ambit of the duties and that specific referen to it was liable to cause confusion and complication.[143] While such a view was n rejected by the Government in its response to the Discrimination Law Revie consultation, the power of procurement as a lever for change was stressed.[144] S too was the need for public bodies to consider their procurement policies i order to discharge their positive equality duties.[145]

Finally, it is worth noting that there is some indication that the effectiveness a positive equality duty is inextricably linked to the underlying structure non-discrimination law. The effectiveness of the Northern Irish duty to promot equality of opportunity between Catholics and Protestants under the Fa Employment legislation is, at least in part, due to the breadth of positive actio measures that may be required of employers who appear to be failing to fulfi their obligations.[146] The possibility that the symmetrical approach adopted b the bulk of British anti-discrimination legislation may have a stultifying effect o relevant positive equality duties should not, therefore, be ignored. As has alread been explained, the asymmetrical approach adopted in the context of disabili permits a wide range of positive action measures to be adopted, including on which would generally be considered to violate the merit principle. In the absenc of a softening of the symmetrical approach for the other grounds, then, th disability equality duty would appear to enjoy a not-insignificant advantage ov its sibling equality duties.[147]

Attention will now be turned to the issue which is of central importance to th chapter—the relationship between the concept of reasonable adjustment and th concepts of positive discrimination, positive action and the positive equalit duties. The relationship between the reasonable adjustment duty and the disabi ity equality duty will be considered first. The question of whether reasonab adjustments should be regarded either as a form of positive discrimination or a form of positive action will then be addressed.

---

[142]   *Ibid*, ch 5, step 8.
[143]   Department for Communities and Local Government, *Discrimination Law Review* (n 3 abov paras 5.91–5.100.
[144]   Government Equalities Office, *The Equality Bill* (n 3 above) paras 4.14–4.15.
[145]   *Ibid*, para 4.16.
[146]   See further B Osborne and I Shuttleworth (eds), *Fair Employment in Northern Ireland: Generation On* (Belfast, Blackstaff Press, 2004); and C McCrudden, DR Ford and A Heath, 'Leg Regulation of Affirmative Action in Northern Ireland: An Empirical Assessment' (2004) *Oxfo Journal of Legal Studies* 24. For similar indications based on the US experience, see eg J Leonard, 'Wh Promises are Worth: The Impact of Affirmative Action Goals' (1985) 20 *Journal of Human Resources* and J Leonard, 'The Impact of Affirmative Action Regulation and Equal Employment Law on Bla Employment' (1990) 4 *Journal Of Economic Perspectives* 47.
[147]   DRC, *Initial Submission to the Discrimination Law Review* (n 95 above) para 1.4.5.

5. Reasonable Adjustment Obligations

5.1 Relationship with the Disability Equality Duty

There are important similarities between the disability equality duty and the anticipatory reasonable adjustment duty. They are both legally enforceable obligations imposing pro-active duties on organisations to take positive measures in order to facilitate disability equality. They are both concerned with the pro-active removal of disadvantages to which disabled people would otherwise be subject; with the promotion of respect for their equal dignity and worth; and with the affirmation and accommodation of their differences.[148] Nevertheless, there are also a number of important differences between the two types of duty.

The first difference between the disability equality duty and the anticipatory reasonable adjustment duty is to be found in the emphasis placed by each of them on the need for disabled people to participate in their operation. In the disability equality duty, as has been seen, public authorities are required to involve disabled people in the preparation of their disability equality schemes and ensure that those schemes explain how that involvement was achieved.[149] In anticipatory reasonable adjustment duties, on the other hand, there is no such requirement. However, the Code of Practice does urge that, in discharging such duties, considerable value is likely to be gained from consulting and involving disabled people.[150]

According to Fredman, the participation of disadvantaged groups in the process of norm setting is 'one of the key distinguishing features of pro-active models' of equality.[151] Under traditional 'complaints-led',[152] individual rights-based approaches to equality, 'norms are set and implemented through established structures based on representative democracy'[153] without the direct involvement of the disadvantaged group. In pro-active models, on the other hand, the participation of that group assumes great significance. It becomes a means by which to

> deepen the democratic legitimacy and reach of equality by incorporating civil society or relevant stakeholders into both the process of norm setting and its implementation.[154]

---

[148]   These are identified as the three aims which are characteristic of pro-active models of equality in Fredman, 'Changing the Norm' (n 103 above) 377–9.

[149]   Disability Discrimination (Public Authorities) (Statutory Duties) Regulations 2005 (SI 2966/2005) reg 2(2) and (3). See n 117 above and accompanying text.

[150]   DRC, *DDA 1995 Code of Practice: Rights of Access—Services to the Public, Public Authority Functions, Private Clubs and Premises* (London, Stationery Office, 2006) para 4.14.

[151]   Fredman, 'Changing the Norm' (n 103 above) 379. See also C McCrudden, 'Mainstreaming Equality in the Governance of Northern Ireland' (1999) *Fordham International Law Journal* 22; and O'Cinneide, 'A New Generation of Equality Legislation?' (n 104 above).

[152]   A term used by Fredman, 'Changing the Norm' (n 103 above).

[153]   *Ibid.*

[154]   *Ibid.*

The fact that anticipatory reasonable adjustment duties lack a strong participatory dimension is thus more characteristic of the individual rights, 'complaint led' model of equality, identified by Fredman, than of the pro-active model. The observation also applies to the enforcement method applicable to reasonable adjustment—a method which contrasts with the enforcement method applicable to the disability equality duty.

A second difference between the two duties thus relates to their enforcement methods. Anticipatory reasonable adjustment duties may be enforced only by way of actions for unlawful discrimination brought by individuals who have been disadvantaged as a result of non-compliance. In this sense the duties, although highly pro-active in nature, are 'complaints-led'. Their pro-active power would be enhanced were a mechanism to be introduced whereby they could be enforced by representative bodies or by the EHRC as well as by aggrieved individuals.

The enforcement of the disability equality duty, unlike the reasonable adjustment duty, lies either in the hands of individuals or organisations willing to bring actions for judicial review, or in the hands of the Equality and Human Rights Commission.

The different enforcement mechanisms of the two duties are closely linked to a third and fundamental difference between them. The reasonable adjustment duty is a duty not to discriminate. Failure to take the positive measures required by it therefore constitutes unlawful discrimination. This is not the case for the disability equality duty. Although that duty requires positive measures designed to facilitate disability equality, breach of it will not itself constitute unlawful discrimination.

A fourth distinction between the two duties concerns the extent to which they are outcome-orientated. The disability equality duty currently requires public bodies to have 'due regard' to principles of disability equality in all aspects of their functioning and decision-making. This language has been criticised for being insufficiently outcome-orientated—for placing weight on procedure rather than substance.[155] The anticipatory reasonable adjustment duty, on the other hand, is very clearly outcome-orientated in that it requires service providers to take reasonable steps to ensure that their provisions, criteria, practices and physical features do not make it impossible or unreasonably difficult for disabled people to access their services. It also requires service providers to take reasonable steps to provide auxiliary aids and services if that would facilitate the use of the services by disabled people.

A fifth important respect in which the two duties differ is that the anticipatory reasonable adjustment duty, in addition to its pro-active and group-orientated obligations, will often require a highly individualised assessment of the circumstances and needs of a particular disabled person. The disability equality duty, however, does not require such specificity. It operates entirely at the general level

---

[155] See nn 123–5 above and accompanying text.

and is concerned with the development of effective policies and practices designed to create an inclusive environment and to break down structural barriers in the way of disabled people. This departure of approach between the disability equality duty and the anticipatory version of the reasonable adjustment duty is still more marked in the case of the reactive version of that duty. Reactive reasonable adjustment is entirely concerned with the identification of an appropriate and reasonable response to the specific circumstances of a particular individual—although it should be remembered that such a response may well have the effect of removing a barrier (eg a set of steps or an inaccessibly designed website) which would otherwise have operated to disadvantage other disabled people.

It is clear, then, that there are differences between the disability equality duty and the reasonable adjustment duty. There are also similarities between them—particularly in the case of anticipatory reasonable adjustment. In addition, it is important to recognise that a successful implementation of the disability equality duty would necessarily overlap with the anticipatory element of reasonable adjustment duties. Indeed, this overlap is likely to encourage bodies subject to both duties to discharge them together—a process which is likely to benefit from the different strengths of each duty. It is likely to result in a process whereby duty-bearers involve disabled people in the development of their plans for removing disabling barriers and in which they are conscious of the obligation, not simply to have 'due regard' to the need to promote disability equality, but also to take definite steps to facilitate access and inclusion.

In addition, the effective discharge of the disability equality duty is likely to facilitate the making of reactive reasonable adjustments in individual cases. Accordingly, although its range and purpose differs from the reasonable adjustment duty, the disability equality duty has the potential greatly to enhance the extent to which timely adjustments are made in order to accommodate the requirements of disabled people. This is particularly important in the context of employment where, at present, there is no anticipatory reasonable adjustment duty.

5.2   Relationship with Positive Action

Reasonable adjustment duties are sometimes described as a form of positive action.[156] This classification is presumably based on the fact that such duties concern the taking of positive measures in order to place disabled people on an

---

[156] See eg K Monaghan, *Blackstone's Guide to the Disability Discrimination Legislation* (Oxford, Oxford University Press) 96. See also B Doyle, 'Enabling Legislation or Dissembling Law? The Disability Discrimination Act 1995' (1997) 60 *Modern Law Review* 64 at 74 where reasonable adjustments are described as a form of 'legally mandated positive action'. Elsewhere, however, Doyle insists that: 'reasonable accommodation must be seen as an integral part of the non-discrimination

equal footing with their non-disabled peers. Although this approach to reaso
able adjustments is by no means incorrect, its helpfulness is certainly questic
able.

The term 'positive action' is generally used, at least in Britain, to refer
measures which an organisation may choose to adopt, but which it is r
required to adopt, in an effort to reduce the obstacles confronting disadvantag
groups. Describing reasonable adjustment duties as a form of positive acti
therefore risks diluting the obligatory nature of the reasonable adjustment duti

Further, as indicated in the discussion of positive action above, the term
generally confined to measures adopted at a policy or organisational level rath
than extending to measures required to accommodate a particular individu
The description of reasonable adjustments as a form of positive action thus fa
adequately to capture the highly individualised assessment which reasona
adjustment duties will frequently entail.

There is another respect in which the measures required by reasonal
adjustment duties (particularly of the reactive kind) differ from those typica
adopted by way of positive action. The measures required under a reasona
adjustment duty will often be of an on-going nature (eg the services of a si
language interpreter or support worker). The measures which characterise po
tive action, by contrast, are generally of a one-off or time-limited nature.[157]

Finally, the nature of the disadvantage targeted by conventional positive acti
measures is very different from that which is tackled by reasonable adjustmo
duties. The former tends to be caused by general societal factors not clos
connected to the particular employer or other organisation taking the posit
action. Reasonable adjustment duties however, as was seen in chapter three, v
not arise unless the disadvantage is caused by an aspect of the relevant organi
tion's criteria, provisions, practices or physical features. Reasonable adjustmo
thus requires a causal link between disadvantage and organisational operatio
which is not generally to be found in relation to positive action.

The categorisation of reasonable adjustment duties as a form of positive acti
is therefore misleading. It carries with it the very real danger that it will dilute t
practical power and potency of the reasonable adjustment duties. It also ri
conceptual confusion. Reasonable adjustment duties are duties not to discrir
nate, breach of which constitutes unlawful discrimination. Although they requ
positive measures to be taken, so too does indirect discrimination. Categorisi
reasonable adjustments as a form of positive action is as unhelpful as categorisi
the actions required by indirect discrimination in that way. Conceptual clarity

---

standard' and that it 'should not be regarded as a species of affirmative action, thereby attract
heightened scrutiny, judicial suspicion and narrow application'—Doyle, *Disability, Discrimina,
and Equal Opportunities* (n 21 above) 245–6.

[157] See L Waddington and A Hendriks, 'The Expanding Concept of Employment and Discrimi
tion in Europe: From Direct and Indirect Discrimination to Reasonable Accommodation Discrim
tion' (2002) 8 *International Journal of Comparative Labour Law and Industrial Relations* 403 at 41

is suggested, will be enhanced by categorising reasonable adjustment simply as a form of non-discrimination requirement, akin to direct discrimination and indirect discrimination, rather than as a form of positive action.[158]

5.3 Relationship with Positive Discrimination

5.3.1 The British Experience

The relationship between reasonable adjustment and positive discrimination is a complex one. There are two ways in which they are often linked. First, the measure required by a reasonable adjustment duty in a particular case is sometimes regarded as a measure which amounts to positive discrimination. Second, the duties themselves are sometimes classified, on a generic basis, as a form of positive discrimination. On this view, such duties will necessarily require positive discrimination and their mere existence constitutes positive discrimination in favour of the targeted group. Before considering these two understandings of reasonable adjustment further, some attention will be given to the relevant statutory language and guidance.

According to section 18D(1) of the DDA,

> [s]ubject to any duty to make reasonable adjustments, nothing in this Part is to be taken to require a person to treat a disabled person more favourably than he treats or would treat others.

Recital 17 of the Employment Equality Directive similarly provides that, without prejudice to the reasonable accommodation duty set out in Article 5, nothing in that Directive requires employers to provide work or training to

> an individual who is not competent, capable and available to perform the essential functions of the post concerned or to undergo the relevant training.[159]

The predecessor of section 18D(1) (section 6(7)) did not contain an explicit mention of reasonable adjustment. It referred instead to 'the provisions of this section', which included the employment reasonable adjustment duties. It was interpreted by the Employment Tribunal in *Archibald v Fife*, however, as imposing a restriction on the range of measures which might be required under the reasonable adjustment duty. Such measures, in its view, had to be limited to those which did not involve treating a disabled person more favourably than others. Waiving a competitive interview requirement in order to redeploy an employee who had become disabled therefore lay beyond the demands of the duty.

---

[158] See, for a similar viewpoint, L Waddington, 'Reasonable Accommodation' in D Schiek, L Waddington and M Bell (eds), *Cases, Materials and Text on National, Supranational and International Non-Discrimination Law* (Oxford, Hart Publishing, 2007) 745–8; and Waddington and Hendriks, 'The Expanding Concept of Employment and Discrimination in Europe' (n 157 above).

[159] See ch 3, fnn 47–8 above and accompanying text.

The House of Lords in *Archibald* took a different view. Section 6(7)'s specifi cation that nothing in Part II of the Act should require disabled people to b treated more favourably than others was, it ruled, subject to the reasonabl adjustment duty. Nothing in the elaboration of the reasonable adjustment dut indicated that the measures it required were to be confined to ones which woul not confer more favourable treatment on the disabled person. Their Lordship also held that the statutory requirement[160] that all local authority appointment must be made on the basis of merit was subject to the reasonable adjustmen duty.[161] The question of whether it was reasonable in all the circumstances for th Council to transfer Ms Archibald without a competitive interview to a differen post, albeit one of a higher grade, was accordingly remitted to the Employmen Tribunal.

The *Archibald* ruling thus appears to provide some support for the first of th understandings of the relationship between positive discrimination and reason able adjustment set out at the beginning of this Section. It makes it clear that th reasonable adjustment duty may well require measures to be taken, in a particu lar case, which amount to the more favourable treatment of a disabled person The duty is therefore not limited, as Fife Council had argued,[162] to removin disadvantage through measures which would simply level the playing field an permit the merits of disabled people to be assessed on the same terms as those o non-disabled people. It may, in cases such as *Archibald*, require the removal o disadvantage through measures which deny entry to the playing field to anybod other than the disabled person in question. The aim of the duty is the removal o disadvantage but, in order to achieve this, it may occasionally be reasonable t take steps which require preference to be given to them in a selection process.

Archibald has generally been understood to rule that the reasonable adjust ment duty may sometimes require a departure from the merit principle amount ing to positive discrimination.[163] On closer inspection, however, it is not at a clear that this is a helpful or convincing interpretation. It tends to obscur significant limitations on the potential scope of the ruling. Indeed, so significan are these limitations that they seriously call into question the description of th treatment in *Archibald* as 'more favourable' and the existence, in that case, of an actual departure from the merit principle.

First, the disadvantage to which Ms Archibald was exposed was liability t dismissal because her newly acquired impairment made it impossible for her t continue in her previous role. This situates the *Archibald* ruling clearly within th context of the redeployment and retention of existing employees who becom disabled while in post. No analogous advantage or requirement to abandor

---

[160] Local Government and Housing Act 1989 s 7(2)(f).
[161] *Archibald v Fife Council* [2004] UKHL 32, [2004] IRLR 197, [69] (Baroness Hale).
[162] *Ibid*, [57] (Baroness Hale).
[163] For the view that it required 'positive discrimination' see eg R Harding-Hill and J Thomas 'Ruling Amounts to Positive Discrimination' (2007) 77 *Employment Law Journal* 5.

competitive selection has been, or is likely to be, identified in cases involving initial applications for work by people already disabled. In this sense it is possible to regard the obligation recognised in *Archibald* as one that operates to the advantage of all currently non-disabled employees in that it provides them with a safeguard against the possibility of the onset of a significant impairment. Such a perspective makes it difficult to view the treatment granted to Ms Archibald as more favourable than that of any other employee or as constituting a clear-cut violation of the merit principle.

Second, any departure from the merit principle, associated with the waiver of a competitive interview, would have amounted to a reasonable adjustment only if it could be regarded as a reasonable step to require of the Council. While Baroness Hale stressed that the issue of reasonableness must depend on all the circumstances of a particular case, she drew attention to several considerations that appeared to be relevant on the facts before her.[164] The Council's redeployment policies required competitive interviews only when the transfer in question was to a higher grade than that previously held by the employee in question. Thus, Ms Archibald would not have required such an interview had she been able to make a sideways or downwards move. However, given the physical nature of her impairment and the fact that her previous post had been a low-ranking manual one, the only move open to her was upwards to a clerical position. Manual workers who became physically disabled were, according to her Ladyship, thus placed in a particularly difficult position by the Council's redeployment policies. Further, regard should be had to the impact on the Council of appointing a qualified person to the relevant post without a competitive selection process. For posts of the grade in question, her Ladyship suggested, the impact was likely to be minimal—a factor which would therefore increase the likelihood of a non-competitive transfer being regarded as reasonable. This suggests that, where the post in question is a high-ranking one, requiring its holder to influence the policy and direction of an organisation, the waiver of a competitive selection process is less likely to be regarded as a reasonable step for the organisation to have to take.

Third, and again in relation to the reasonableness requirement, a crucial factor in *Archibald* was that Ms Archibald was qualified for the post in question. It is inconceivable that it could ever be regarded as reasonable to require the transfer of a disabled person to a post for which they were not qualified.

In summary then, the DDA reasonable adjustment duty does, at least in certain circumstances, require preference to be given to a disabled person in a selection process, despite the fact that they may not be the best-qualified person for the position in question. It is therefore tempting to regard the duty as requiring positive discrimination in such circumstances. It should not be forgotten, however, that these cases concern the treatment of existing employees who become disabled. If their treatment is compared with that of other employees, rather than

---

[164]   *Archibald v Fife Council* [2004] UKHL 32, [2004] IRLR 197, [70].

with that of potential applicants for the post in question, its classification as more favourable or as positive discrimination becomes problematic.

In the vast majority of cases, then, the measures required by reasonable adjustment duties do not violate the merit principle. While *Archibald* rules that this need not always be the case, it is certainly arguable that the measures required in that case did operate within the confines of that principle. Indeed, *Archibald* stands as an interesting case study in what meaning should actually be attached to the merit principle. It demonstrates that it is a principle which, although superficially simple, becomes profoundly challenging and elusive on closer analysis. Unsurprisingly, therefore, despite the fact that it has received very little judicial scrutiny,[165] the notion of merit has provoked lively academic debate.[166]

Turning now to the second way in which positive discrimination and reasonable adjustment are sometimes linked, it is not uncommon for reasonable adjustments generally to be categorised as positive discrimination.[167] Indeed, such a categorisation is to be found in both of the House of Lords decisions on the DDA.

In *Lewisham London Borough Council v Malcolm*,[168] where reasonable adjustments were not directly in issue, Lord Brown observed:

> The needs of the disabled are rather different and require sometimes to be met by positive action. As I noted at the outset, where Parliament is clearly intent not merely on levelling the playing field for the disabled but in securing positive discrimination in their favour it does so by requiring reasonable adjustments to be made to cater for their special difficulties.[169]

Similarly, in *Archibald* itself, Baroness Hale stated:

> It is common ground that the Act entails a measure of positive discrimination, in the sense that employers are required to take steps to help disabled people which they are not required to take for others.[170]

---

[165] A theme developed further in AR Kamp, 'The missing jurisprudence of merit' (2002) 11 *Boston University Public Interest Law Journal* 141.

[166] See eg the works referred to in n 6 above. See also N Daniels, 'Merit and Meritocracy' (1978) 7 *Philosophy and Public Affairs* 206; and R Fallon, 'To Each According to His Ability, From None According to His Race: The Concept of Merit in the Law of Antidiscrimination' (1980) 60 *Boston University Law Review* 815; J Morrison, 'Colorblindness, Individuality, and Merit: An Analysis of the Rhetoric against Affirmative Action' (1994) 79 *Iowa Law Review* 313; and M Selmi, 'Testing for Equality: Merit Efficiency and the Affirmative Action Debate' (1995) 42 *University of California Los Angeles Law Review* 1251.

[167] See eg H Collins, 'Discrimination, Equality and Social Inclusion (2003) 66 *Modern Law Review* 16 at 37; and A Burns, 'Reasonable Adjustments: The Calm after the Storm' (2004) 154 *New Law Journal* 1820.

[168] *Lewisham LBC v Malcolm* [2008] UKHL 43.

[169] *Ibid*, [114].

[170] *Archibald v Fife Council* [2004] UKHL 32, [2004] IRLR 197, [57]. See also *O'Hanlon Commissioners of Revenue and Customs* [2007] EWCA Civ 283 [22], where Hooper LJ observed that 'There is no doubt that the Act envisages a measure of positive discrimination in favour of thos suffering from a disability'.

This reflects an extremely broad understanding of the term 'positive discrimination'. Unlike more conventional uses of the term, it is not based on the conferring of preferences but on the taking of steps to help reduce or remove a job-related disadvantage that would otherwise limit the prospects of a particular individual. It stands in marked contrast to the very narrow interpretation of positive discrimination evident in the report of the Discrimination Law Review. According to that,

> [p]ositive discrimination in the workplace generally refers to making recruitment/ promotion decisions solely to redress the balance of representation of the under-represented group and irrespective of merit, for example, quotas.[171]

Worryingly, the authors of the Discrimination Law Review appear to endorse Baroness Hale's view that reasonable adjustments necessarily entail positive discrimination without acknowledging that she appears to have been using the term 'positive discrimination' in a different and much broader sense than the one in which they were using it.[172]

Although there currently appears to be little ill-will towards the reasonable adjustment duties in Britain, a perception that they require employers and others to discriminate positively in favour of disabled people is potentially dangerous. Attention has already been drawn to the keen awareness, displayed in the Equalities Review, the Discrimination Law Review and also the Government's response to the consultation on the latter, of the political sensitivity of the term 'positive discrimination'.[173] The authors of all these documents were at pains to emphasise that their recommendations did not amount to positive discrimination. This reflects an obvious perception that, in the minds of employers, service providers and the public at large, positive discrimination is associated with unmerited, unfair and undesirable preference-giving. Accordingly, the description of reasonable adjustment duties as forms of positive discrimination risks sacrificing public goodwill and inciting resentment. It is, in this regard, worth bearing in mind recent American experience.

5.3.2 The US Experience

In the United States, numerous commentators have drawn attention to the underlying similarities between reasonable adjustment (or accommodation) duties in favour of disabled people and affirmative action programmes conferring preferences on disadvantaged groups.[174] Both require disadvantage to be

---

[171] Department for Communities and Local Government, *Discrimination Law Review* (n 3 above) para 4.17.

[172] *Ibid*, para 4.41.

[173] See nn 82 and 87 above and accompanying text.

[174] See eg PS Karlan and G Rutherglen, 'Disabilities, Discrimination, and Reasonable Accommodation' (1996) 46 *Duke Law Journal* 1 at 12; S Schwab and S Willborne, 'Reasonable Accommodation of Workplace Disabilities' (2003) 44 *William and Mary Law Review* 1197; B Poitras Tucker, 'The ADA's Revolving Door: Inherent Flaws in the Civil Rights Paradigm' (2001) 62 *Ohio State Law Journal* 335;

recognised and different treatment to be given to the relevant individual or grou in response. These similarities have led some to classify reasonable accommoda tion duties as a form of affirmative action.[175] Indeed, they were classified in th way by the US Supreme Court in *Southeastern Community College v Davis*.[176]

Over the past few decades there has been a growing hostility towards th differential treatment required by affirmative action programmes.[177] Reasonabl accommodation duties, which, like affirmative action, were born out of claim for equality and civil rights also require differential treatment. Unsurprisingl therefore, they too have been the subject of controversy. In the words of Matthe Diller,

> the strategy of linking the goals of people with disabilities to a civil rights model doe not ... place questions concerning the treatment of people with disabilities in an area c broad social consensus around civil rights. Instead, it situates the issue of access t employment for people with disabilities in the midst of a hotly contested and long running battle. In short, with the passage of the ADA and the adoption of the civ rights model, people with disabilities find themselves on the front lines of a legal an cultural war.[178]

The reasonable accommodation duties have certainly not escaped unblemishe from the antipathy directed towards affirmative action. Sherwin Rosen, fo example, has argued that by 'forcing employers to pay for ... job accommoda tions that might allow workers with impairing conditions ... to compete on equ terms' it requires them 'to treat unequal people equally, thus discriminating i favor of the disabled'.[179] For some members of the law and economics movemen both affirmative action and reasonable accommodation obligations represen unwarranted and counterproductive interferences in the labour market, an emanate from a standpoint which is 'antilibertarian, antiutilitarian, and antima rket in [its] orientation'.[180] Such a viewpoint will be examined more closely in th next chapter.

---

and R Colker, 'Affirmative Action, Reasonable Accommodation and Capitalism: Irreconcilable Diffe ences?' in M Hauritz, C Sampford, S Blencowe (eds), *Justice for People with Disabilities: Legal an Institutional Issues* (Sydney, The Federation Press, 1998).

[175] See Karlan and Rutherglen, 'Disabilities, Discrimination, and Reasonable Accommodation' an Colker, 'Affirmative Action, Reasonable Accommodation and Capitalism: Irreconcilable Differences (both n 174 above).

[176] *Southeastern Community College v Davis* 442 US 397 at 411 (1979). See also, however, th qualification of this approach by Justice Marshall in *Alexander v Choate* 469 US 287 at 300 (1985).

[177] See eg R Colker, 'Whores, Fags, Dumb-Ass Women, Surly Blacks and Competent Heterosexu White Men: The Sexual and Racial Morality Underlying Anti-Discrimination Doctrine' (1995) 7 Ya *Journal of Law and Feminism* 195; S Sturm and L Guinier, 'The Future of Affirmative Actio Reclaiming the Innovative Ideal' (1996) 84 *California Law Review* 953; M Adams, 'The Last Wave c Affirmative Action' (1998) *Wisconsin Law Review* 1395.

[178] Diller, 'Judicial Backlash, the ADA and the Civil Rights Model' (n 78 above) 44.

[179] 'Disability Accommodation and the Labor Market' in C Weaver (ed), *Disability and Wor Incentives, Rights and Opportunities* (Washington, AEI Press, 1991) 18 at 29.

[180] R Epstein, *Forbidden Grounds: The Case Against Employment Discrimination Laws* (Bosto Harvard University Press, 1992) 8.

Reasonable accommodation duties would undoubtedly have attracted some hostility from critics even without their association with affirmative action. The 'backlash' against the ADA may, however, have been less marked had it been free from this association. It is therefore unsurprising that many commentators have been at pains to stress the distinctiveness of reasonable accommodation and the differences between it and affirmative action.[181]

In some respects, reasonable accommodation duties are more far-reaching than the type of commitments generally included in affirmative action plans. Whilst, in the employment context, the latter are often confined to initial appointments and promotions, the former extend to every aspect of the performance of a job affected by the impairment of a disabled person.[182] Further, reasonable accommodation duties require highly individualised, negotiated solutions designed to fit the needs of a particular person in particular circumstances. Affirmative action, on the other hand, generally operates on the basis of broad categories and groupings. Consequently, in the words of Professors Karlan and Rutherglen,

> [r]easonable accommodation does not perpetuate the stereotypes that it is designed to counteract. In traditional affirmative action plans, the same stereotypes that reinforce patterns of discrimination have supported the charge that affirmative action plans stigmatize the very groups that they are supposed to help.[183]

It has also been argued that the two concepts differ in their temporal focus. The focus of affirmative action tends to be on redressing imbalances arising from past discrimination.[184] The focus of reasonable accommodation, on the other hand, is on the removal of existing barriers—barriers which may take a multitude of forms (relating to issues such as physical structures, information technology, timetabling, transport, and general attitudes).[185] This distinction, however, is less convincing than it might at first appear. The under-representation addressed by affirmative action schemes is often caused by very real disadvantages which

---

[181] See eg ME Martin, 'Accommodating the Handicapped: The Meaning of Discrimination Under Section 504 of the Rehabilitation Act' (1980) 55 *New York University Law Review* 881 at 885; J Cooper, 'Overcoming Barriers to Employment: The Meaning of Reasonable Accommodation and Undue Hardship in the Americans with Disabilities Act' (1991) 139 *University of Pennsylvania Law Review* 1423; Anonymous, 'Toward Reasonable Equality: Accommodating Learning Disabilities Under the Americans with Disabilities Act' (1998) 111 *Harvard Law Review* 1560 at 1574; and MA Stein, 'Same Struggle, Different Difference: ADA Accommodations as Antidiscrimination' (2004) 153 *University of Pennsylvania Law Review* 579.

[182] Karlan and Rutherglen, 'Disabilities, Discrimination, and Reasonable Accommodation' (n 174 above) 38–9.

[183] *Ibid*, 40.

[184] See eg ME Martin, 'Accommodating the Handicapped: The Meaning of Discrimination Under Section 504 of the Rehabilitation Act' (1980) 55 *New York Law Review* 881 at 885–6.

[185] Anonymous, 'Toward Reasonable Equality: Accommodating Learning Disabilities Under the Americans with Disabilities Act' (n 181 above) 1574–5; MA Rebell, 'Structural Discrimination and the Rights of the Disabled' (1986) 74 *Georgia Law Journal* 1435 at 1453.

operate in the present, even though they may be accompanied by a history of exclusion and discriminatory treatment.[186]

Importantly, reasonable adjustment or accommodation is limited by two substantial constraints which are not generally applicable to affirmative action programmes. First, as its name indicates, reasonable accommodation is limited by the factor of reasonableness. Once an adjustment becomes sufficiently onerous, any obligation on an employer or service provider to carry it out will evaporate. Second, reasonable adjustment generally operates well within the confines of the merit principle. Unlike many US-style affirmative action programmes, its aim is not to give any form of advantage to members of the relevant group in selection processes.[187] Its primary purpose is rather to remove disadvantage and its concern is to ensure that disabled people have the chance to be considered fairly on their merits. It leaves those merits to be assessed, however, without allowance being made for any previous disadvantage which that person may have endured as a result of their impairment (eg in relation to their educational opportunities).[188]

These limitations have prompted powerful arguments for the need to supplement reasonable adjustment or accommodation duties with mandatory affirmative or positive action measures.[189] Without them, it has been suggested, progress towards meaningful disability equality would be unacceptably slow. Any such measures, however, might prove counter-productive unless care were taken to ensure that tokenism was avoided and that a clear focus on inclusion and the mainstream was maintained. Lessons may undoubtedly be learned from the British quota and reserved occupation schemes in this regard.

6. Conclusion

In conclusion, like the disability equality duty, reasonable adjustment duties require the taking of positive measures in favour of disabled people. There is a considerable overlap between anticipatory reasonable adjustment duties and the disability equality duty, both of which are pro-active in nature. They have different strengths, which, in combination, produce an obligation which is powerfully outcome-orientated and participatory in nature.

---

[186] Young, *Justice and the Politics of Difference* (n 5 above) 198.

[187] See further eg J Cooper, 'Overcoming Barriers to Employment: The Meaning of Reasonable Accommodation and Undue Hardship in the Americans with Disabilities Act' (1991) 139 *University of Pennsylvania Law Review* 1423 at 1429–33.

[188] L Waddington and M Diller, 'Tensions and Coherence in Disability Policy: The Uneasy Relationship Between Social Welfare and Civil Rights Models of Disability in American, European and International Employment Law' in M Breslin and S Yee (eds), *Disability Rights Law and Policy: International and National Perspectives* (Ardsley NY, Transnational Publishers inc, 2002) 275–6.

[189] See eg MC Weber, 'Beyond the Americans with Disabilities Act: A National Employment Policy for People with Disabilities' (1998) 46 *Buffalo Law Review* 123; and Waddington and Diller, 'Tensions and Coherence in Disability Policy' (n 188 above).

Conclusion

Positive action and positive discrimination measures, like reasonable adjustments, represent positive steps to counter disadvantage. As regards positive discrimination, British non-discrimination law relating to disability departs from the template laid down by the sex and race legislation. The asymmetrical structure of the DDA makes it possible to confer preferences on disabled people without fear of litigation. Organisations are thus permitted to treat disabled people more favourably than others and should be encouraged to consider ways in which they might usefully and appropriately take advantage of this entitlement. Such measures must be clearly differentiated from reasonable adjustments.

The DDA's reasonable adjustment duties represent another departure from the sex and race template. They require disability to be acknowledged and to play a role in the reasoning processes of employers and others. They therefore require a departure from the neutrality paradigm enshrined in the well-established symmetrical non-discrimination legislation. Under the SDA and the RRA, a failure to be neutral as to the relevant ground (in the sense of banishing it from the decision-making process) is likely to constitute unlawful discrimination. This perhaps helps to explain the worrying tendency to characterise reasonable adjustment duties as forms of positive discrimination.

Reasonable adjustment duties, unlike positive action (or positive discrimination) schemes, are mandatory and they generally operate well within the ambiguous confines of the merit principle. They are, in essence, not preference-giving but disadvantage-removing. Unless this is acknowledged and articulated, there is a risk not only of conceptual muddle but also of a potential backlash against British reasonable adjustment obligations.

Archibald ruled that such duties may, in very limited circumstances, require preference to be given to a disabled person in a selection process. The context, however, was that of redeployment after the onset of a disabling condition and not that of initial recruitment or of promotion. If properly understood, it is not therefore likely to attract the hostility often directed towards positive discrimination. If, however, the recent trend to refer to reasonable adjustments as a form of positive discrimination continues, there is a risk that that hostility will be roused. Attention will now be turned to a closer analysis of such potential hostility triggers and to ways in which a negative reaction against reasonable adjustment might be avoided or contained.

6

Reasonable Adjustments in Practice: Resistance and Response

1. Introduction

P REVIOUS CHAPTERS HAVE explored the qualities and boundaries of the concept of reasonable adjustment as it has emerged in the contexts of British human rights and non-discrimination jurisprudence. They have indicated that it is a legal tool which has a distinctive role to play in the process of shifting our society from one in which disabled people are largely excluded and marginalised to one in which disabled people are included and valued as equals. The concept of reasonable adjustment acknowledges and accepts the fact that responsibility for removing disabling barriers does not lie with the State alone—it lies with all social actors (whether they be employers, providers of goods or services, public authorities, landlords or private clubs). Reasonable adjustment obligations require all these to confront, and to take some responsibility for, the exclusionary effects of policies, practices and structures predicated on the assumption that people participating in them will have no significant physical, sensory, intellectual, psycho-social or other impairment. They require all to acknowledge the full range of functional variation amongst human beings and to take whatever steps are reasonable to facilitate the participation of individuals who depart from the accepted non-disabled norm.

Consequently, reasonable adjustment duties have the potential to effect significant change, not only for the disabled people in whose favour adjustments are made, but for the whole of society. Fulfilling this potential, however, is by no means straightforward or free from contention. It entails the elaboration of clear and strong legal rules and also their effective implementation. Effective implementation will happen only if the nature and purpose of the rules are understood and, to some degree, accepted, by those who are entitled to reasonable adjustments, by those who are required to make them, and by the judiciary who are charged with the task of interpreting and developing their conceptual boundaries. It will also require the existence of appropriate and affordable enforcement machinery.

This chapter will focus on potential resistance to the implementation of reasonable adjustment duties. It will draw heavily on the sizeable body of US literature on this issue—a body which has been enlarged by concerns emerging from a number of well-publicised studies which suggest that, since the Americans with Disabilities Act 1990 (ADA), the employment rates of disabled people have declined and their wages remained the same.[1] It has also been fuelled by a restrictive judicial approach to ADA claims.[2]

British reasonable adjustment duties have not as yet generated the wealth of literature which surrounds their older American counterparts. Neither have they attracted the same degree of concern and resistance. Statistics in Britain, unlike those in the United States, reveal a steady increase in the employment rate of disabled people in the years following the enactment of anti-disability-discrimination legislation (though this, of course, is not necessarily attributable to that legislation). In 1998 some 38 per cent of disabled people were employed—a figure which increased to 47 per cent by the end of 2007.[3] Further, evidence suggests that, while many British employers and service providers remain somewhat unclear as to the exact nature of reasonable adjustment duties,[4] the overwhelming majority of them regard the making of adjustments and alterations for disabled employees and customers not as an expensive burden but as a manifestation of best practice which is generally achievable with relative ease.[5] Despite evidence of an increasing tendency of employers to carry out adjustments for their disabled employees,[6] the employment situation of disabled

---

[1] See in particular T de Leire, 'The Wage and Employment Effects of the Americans with Disabilities Act' (2000) 35 *Journal of Human Resources* 691; and D Acemoglu and JD Angrist 'Consequences of Employment Protection? The Case of the Americans with Disabilities Act' (2001) 109 *Journal of Political Economy* 915. For analysis of such findings see eg DC Stapleton and RV Burkhauser (eds), *The Decline in Employment of People with Disabilities: A Policy Puzzle (Symposium Disability and Employment)* (2003) 42 *Industrial Relations* 1.

[2] The following studies found that claimants in ADA cases lost in 92% and 93% of cases respectively: American Bar Association, 'Study Finds Most Employers Win ADA Title I Judicial and Administrative Complaints' (1998) 22 *Mental and Physical Disability Law Reporter* 403; and R Colker 'The Americans with Disabilities Act: A Windfall for Defendants' (1999) 34 *Harvard Civil Rights and Civil Liberties Review* 99. For discussion of the factors underlying such figures, one of which may be judicial resistance to the ADA, see eg the essays in 'Backlash Against the ADA: Interdisciplinary Perspectives and Implications for Social Justice Strategies' (2000) 21 *Berkeley Journal of Employment and Labor Law* 1; W Wilkinson, 'Judicially Crafted Barriers to Bringing Suit Under the Americans with Disabilities Act' (1997) 38 *South Texas Law Review* 907; and MA Stein, 'The Law and Economics of Disability Accommodations' (2003) 53 *Duke Law Journal* 79.

[3] Department for Work and Pensions, *Public Consultation—Helping People Achieve their Full Potential: Improving Specialist Disability Employment Services* (London, Department for Work and Pensions, 2007) para 1.11. See also DRC, *The Disability Agenda: Creating an Alternative Future* (London, DRC, 2007); and Equal Opportunities Review, 'More Disabled People in Work Since DDA' (2003) 123 *Equal Opportunities Review* 4.

[4] S Roberts et al, *Responses to the Disability Discrimination Act in 2003 and Preparation for 2004 Changes*, Research Report No 202 (London, Department for Work and Pensions, 2004) para 3.2.4.

[5] *Ibid*, paras 2.6.2, 2.6.4 and 3.4.3.

[6] See eg N Stuart, A Watson and J Williams, '*How Employers and Service Providers are Responding to the DDA 1995*', Department for Work and Pensions In-House Report 96 (London, DWP, 2002); C Woodhams, *Employing Disabled Workers: An Investigation into Organisational Disability Policies and*

people in Britain remains very far from ideal—particularly for people with specific types of impairment.[7] A 2004 study reported that a third of employers regarded the appointment of a disabled employee as a 'major risk'.[8] This figure masks significant variation in the responses to people with different types of impairment—for instance, over 90 per cent of employers indicated that they would find it difficult or impossible to employ a person with a significant visual impairment.[9]

The British experience of reasonable adjustment to date therefore differs significantly from that of the United States. Despite this, the US debate clearly contains much of relevance to the effective implementation of reasonable accommodation or adjustment duties in other jurisdictions, including Britain. A careful analysis of that debate is likely to help inform relevant British policy and legislative development.

It should be stressed that while the subject cries out for a detailed and comprehensive comparative analysis, such an examination is beyond the scope of this chapter. The heavy reliance on American literature evident here is made necessary by the dearth of British material on the issue. That literature contains much of relevance to Britain but its grounding in a different social and economic context clearly requires extreme caution to be exercised when considering its implications for British law and policy.

Many of the concerns about reasonable adjustment or accommodation to be discussed here overlap. To assist discussion, however, they will be divided into four broad categories. First, concerns relating to the economic inefficiency of reasonable adjustment duties will be considered. Second, attention will be focused on concerns based on the view that the costs of reasonable adjustment are, in effect, inappropriately placed welfare benefits. They are, on this view, little more than the manifestation of an attempt by the State to shift costs that should be borne by the public purse onto private employers and other individuals. The third category concerns the closely related argument that reasonable adjustment duties require a form of special treatment going beyond what is required by equality principles. The fourth and final category embraces a range of concerns relating to the concept of 'reasonableness' and its role within these duties.

An attempt will be made, in relation to each category, to outline the relevant concerns about, and resistance to, the notion of reasonable adjustment or accommodation. This will, in each case, be followed by a discussion of possible

---

Practices (Manchester, Manchester Metropolitan University, 2003) available at www.ribm.mmu.ac.uk/ hrmob/managingdiversity/2003disabilitysurvey.pdf (last accessed 28 April 2008).

[7] See generally DRC, *The Disability Agenda* (n 3 above); and K Stanley, 'The Missing Million: The Challenges of Employing More Disabled People' in A Roulstone and C Barnes (eds), *Working Futures? Disabled People, Policy and Social Inclusion* (Bristol, The Policy Press, 2005).

[8] Roberts et al, *Responses to the Disability Discrimination Act in 2003 and Preparations for 2004 Changes* (n 4 above) para 2.7.

[9] *Ibid*, tbl 2.8.

responses to the relevant concerns. These may take the form of counter-arguments or of possible measures which might be adopted to minimise the risk of the concerns in question becoming breeding grounds of resistance and resentment towards the British reasonable adjustment duties.

2. Economic Inefficiency

2.1 Resistance

Official figures released shortly after the enactment of the ADA predicted that significant economic benefits would result from the increased participation of disabled people in society which the Act would facilitate.[10] These included considerable financial benefits to employers (resulting from the widened pool of talent available to them), to the State (because of the reduction in welfare payments which would result from the increased employment of disabled people) and to disabled people themselves who would be much more likely to achieve their full potential in the job market and thereby to gain financial independence. Other benefits, such as the increased level of disability awareness amongst the general public, were also mentioned.

Nevertheless, from that moment on, the economic efficiency of the ADA and its reasonable accommodation duties has been the subject of lively debate amongst commentators. The debate has focused on the employment provision set out in Title I and, as mentioned above, has been intensified by the publication of reports suggesting that the position of disabled people in the labour market has, if anything, deteriorated since the passage of the Act.[11]

On the basis of what is sometimes termed the 'neoclassical economic model of the labour market',[12] a number of scholars have condemned reasonable accommodation duties as inefficient. Proponents of this approach look to the efficient choices that would be made in an unregulated competitive market as a means of determining socially desirable outcomes. On this view, distorting the market by requiring inefficiency is likely to create social difficulties and to impose unacceptable burdens on particular sectors of society.

In the context of recruitment, efficiency will be maximised if the most productive candidate is selected. Discriminatory hostility towards, or irrational

---

[10] See eg Equal Employment Opportunity Commission, *Costbenefit Analysis of the US Adminis-tration in Adopting Regulations Under Title I of the Americans with Disabilities Act 1990* (EEOC 56 Federal Register 8578, 1991).

[11] See n 1 above.

[12] See eg Stein, 'The Law and Economics of Disability Accommodations' (n 2 above); and Donohue, 'Discrimination in Employment' in P Newman (ed), *The New Palgrave Dictionary of Economics and the Law* (London, Macmillan, 1998) 615–23. See more generally RA Posner, *Economic Analysis of Law* (Boston MA, Little, Brown and Company, 1998).

prejudice against, certain categories of worker (such as women, members of racial minorities or disabled people) may cause employers to make inefficient choices. If the most productive worker is a member of a disliked group, an employer may decide to appoint a less productive person instead. According to most proponents of the neoclassical model, such employers are likely to be penalised for this inefficiency by reduced profits—a penalty which may eventually drive them from the market place. In this sense, the pursuit of efficiency requires adherence to a basic principle of equality and, by focusing solely on the need to maximise productivity, employers will steer clear of liability for the forms of discrimination prohibited by sex and race legislation.[13]

Disability, however, is frequently regarded as raising different considerations. According to Richard Epstein, the 'unmistakable' costs of 'doing business with the disabled' should not be dismissed as irrational or arbitrary.[14] In his view,

> [e]ven if no one is at fault for X's disability, having to deal with X, given that disability, is costlier than having to deal with Y, who lacks that disability. Business is harder to conduct as the pace of transaction slows. Customers may find it inconvenient, unpleasant, or awkward to deal with persons who are deaf, blind, or palsied, or who have disfiguring marks or speech.[15]

He argues that the costs arising from the relative slowness of disabled employees and from the negative reactions of non-disabled people towards them should be taken into account in calculations of efficiency. Accordingly, a decision to refuse a post to a disabled person would not generally be inefficient and the relevant employer would not therefore be penalised for failing to make the most efficient choice.

In the context of disability, the situation is further complicated by the additional costs associated with reasonable accommodation. In an unregulated competitive market, it is argued, the needs of a disabled worker would be accommodated only where doing so would be efficient. An accommodation would be efficient if its net gain exceeded its net cost.

Thus, from the perspective of employers, providing an accommodation such as a sign language interpreter in order to facilitate the employment of a person with a hearing impairment would be efficient if the disabled person's productivity

---

[13] See eg CL Weaver, 'Incentives versus Controls in Federal Disability Policy' in CL Weaver (ed), *Disability and Work: Incentives, Rights and Opportunities* (Lanham and London, University Press of America, 1991); and SJ Schwab and SL Willborn, 'Reasonable Accommodation of Workplace Disabilities' (2003) 44 *William and Mary Law Review* 1197. For powerful arguments that antidiscrimination sex and race laws, as well as disability laws, impose real costs on employers, however, see C Jolls, 'Antidiscrimination and Accommodation' (2001) 115 *Harvard Law Review* 642; and MA Stein, 'Same Struggle, Different Difference: ADA Accommodations as Antidiscrimination' (2004) 153 *University of Pennsylvania Law Review* 579.

[14] R Epstein, *Forbidden Grounds: The Case Against Employment Discrimination Laws* (Cambridge MA, Harvard University Press, 1992) 486–8. For cogent criticism see Stein, 'The Law and Economics of Disability Accommodations' (n 2 above) 122–3.

[15] Epstein, *ibid*, 486. See also MA Schuman, 'The Wheelchair Ramp to Serfdom: The Americans with Disabilities Act, Liberty, and Markets' (1995) 10 *St John's Journal of Legal Commentary* 495.

sufficiently exceeded that of other potential non-disabled employees to cover the cost of the interpreter. It would also be efficient to provide the interpreter if the disabled person, though no more productive than other potential employees, were prepared to work for a sufficiently reduced wage to cover the interpreter's costs. Consequently, in such situations, disabled people themselves would bear the cost of accommodations. Other forms of accommodation, such as the installation of a ramp, may benefit others and thereby facilitate access by customers or future employees. Such considerations would enter into the efficiency calculation and may well encourage employers to bear a share of the expense.[16]

The cost of accommodations would thus be one of the factors to be weighed in the work-choice balance of a disabled person. That cost would need to be added to the costs resulting from loss of income from benefits, the set up costs associated with preparing for and travelling to work and the cost of inability to participate in non-work activities due to the time or energy absorbed by work. These factors, which militate against decisions to work, need to be weighed against the benefits of work—foremost amongst which is likely to be salary. A similar equation underlies the work-choices of the entire population. In the case of disabled people, however, decisions to work are less likely to be efficient. This is because, for them, the costs are likely to be higher than for non-disabled people and, the benefits, in terms of salary, are likely to be lower. Such considerations, it is argued, make it less likely to be efficient for a disabled person to work in an unregulated market than it would be for a non-disabled person and consequently help to explain why they are more likely to be unemployed than their non-disabled counterparts.[17]

Duties to make accommodations, according to members of this school of thought, become particularly problematic when accompanied by non-discrimination principles which prevent the payment of a lower wage to a disabled person for whom the employer has provided accommodations. In the words of Sherwin Rosen, '[t]hen the burden of accommodation expense is shifted to others, and distortions in efficient resource allocation decisions result'.[18]

Commentators have drawn attention to a variety of undesirable and, as they would argue, unacceptable consequences which would flow from the distortion of the market introduced by mandatory reasonable accommodation duties coupled with prohibitions against wage reduction. Some have argued that, regardless of any benefit that disabled people themselves may gain from such an approach, an unacceptable cost would fall on others. In particular, as will now be discussed, there is concern that the cost would unduly burden employers and that it would unduly burden fellow non-disabled workers.

---

[16] See further Weaver, 'Incentives versus Controls in Federal Disability Policy' (n 13 above) 8–9.
[17] See further S Rosen, 'Disability Accommodation and the Labor Market' in Weaver (ed) *Disability and Work: Incentives, Rights and Opportunities* (n 13 above) 23–6.
[18] *Ibid*, 26.

Richard Epstein, in one of the early and seminal works on this issue, drew attention to the unfair burden which reasonable accommodation duties would place on employers. According to him, the imposition of such duties 'necessarily impedes the operation and efficiency of firms'[19] by forcing them to bear the costs of an inefficient social policy. Despite the fact that the ADA contains an exemption for employers with fewer than 15 employees, there remains some concern that the burdens imposed on smaller businesses will be particularly severe.[20]

Concern about the impact of reasonable accommodation duties on employers is evident, not only in academic literature, but also in some judicial pronouncements. In the European context, this is well illustrated by the ruling of the Irish Supreme Court in the case of *Re Article 26 and the Employment Equality Bill*.[21] The Supreme Court was there required to assess the constitutionality of the Employment Equality Bill 1996, which sought to introduce anti-discrimination protection on the basis of nine specified grounds, one of which was disability. It would have required employers to 'do all that was reasonable to accommodate' the needs of a disabled employee or applicant, subject to the limit of 'undue hardship'.[22] The court accepted that the Bill's reasonable accommodation provisions were designed to further the 'totally laudable aim'[23] of promoting 'equality in the workplace between the disabled and their more fortunate fellow citizens'.[24] In its view the cost of furthering that aim—unlike costs arising from the production process (such as those relating to health and safety or environmental pollution)—should not fall on employers but be borne instead by society as a whole. The Bill, however, imposed the entire cost on employers and this, according to the court, was 'so contrary to reason and fairness' as to amount to an 'unjust attack' on the constitutional rights of employers to enjoy their property and their freedom to make a living.[25]

---

[19] Epstein, *Forbidden Grounds* (n 14 above) 484.
[20] See generally TH Barnard, 'The Americans with Disabilities Act: Nightmare for Employers and Dream for Lawyers?' (1990) 64 *St John's Law Review* 229; and L Lavelle, 'The Duty to Accommodate: Will Title I of the Americans with Disabilities Act Emancipate Individuals With Disabilities Only to Disable Small Businesses?' (1991) 66 *Notre Dame Law Review* 1135.
[21] *Re Article 26 and the Employment Equality Bill* [1997] 2 Irish Reports 321. See generally G Quinn and S Quinlivan, 'Disability Discrimination: The Need to Amend the Employment Equality Act 1998 in Light of the EU Framework Directive on Employment' in C Costello and E Barry (eds), *Equality in Diversity: The New Equality Directives* (Oxford and Dublin, Irish Centre for European Law, 2003).
[22] Employment Equality Bill ss 16(3) and 35(4).
[23] *Re Article 26 and the Employment Equality Bill* [1997] 2 Irish Reports 321 at 367 (Hamilton CJ).
[24] *Ibid*, 366 (Hamilton CJ).
[25] Under Arts 40(3) and 43 of the Irish Constitution. The language quoted in the text was accepted as representing the correct approach in this case—see [1997] 2 Irish Reports 321 at 334 (Hamilton CJ, quoting *Tuohy v Courtney* [1994] 3 Irish Reports 1 at 47).

The Employment Equality Bill was consequently ruled to be repugnant to th Constitution. It was allowed to become law only after the reasonable accomm dation provisions had been modified so as to restrict their scope to accommod tions which imposed no more than a 'nominal' cost on employers.[26] Europe Community law has since resulted in the lifting of the nominal cost restriction relation to employment[27] but it remains in operation in the context of goods ar services.[28]

Commentators such as Sherwin Rosen, while accepting that disabled peop themselves may well benefit from reasonable accommodation duties, argue th the cost of accommodations will fall most heavily on workers with similar ski to those of the disabled people who are accommodated. Employers, it is su gested, will shift the cost of accommodations onto the general pool of su workers by reducing their average wage or by depriving them of collater benefits which would otherwise have been provided (such as 'on-the-job-trainir programs, special housing or transportation programs for unskilled workers, job counselling and medical treatment'[29]). As disabled people in work tend to l situated in jobs which are less skilled and already generally poorly paid, it argued that the cost of accommodations will fall disproportionately on relative poor non-disabled workers.[30]

The concerns arising from the inefficiency of reasonable accommodatic duties considered thus far have related to the impact of such duties on employe and on fellow workers. Concerns have also been expressed that reasonab accommodation duties will have a negative impact on disabled people then selves. On this view, in order to avoid incurring the expense of accommodatio or the need to pass that expense on to non-disabled workers, employers w become increasingly reluctant to employ disabled people. Consequently, th employment prospects of disabled people—particularly those perceived to be i need of on-going or expensive accommodations—will decline, with the resu that it will become still more difficult for disabled people to find work.[31] I Epstein's words,

> once coercion replaces informal accommodation, we should expect employers to ta steps to minimize their losses, and public agencies to take steps to counteract th tendency, and for the cycle of evasion, resentment, and regulation to continue witho closure.[32]

---

[26] Employment Equality Act 1998 s 16(3)(c). For discussion of the meaning of this phrase s Quinn and Quinlivan, 'Disability Discrimination' (n 21 above) 230–32.
[27] The Equality Act 2004 (Ireland) amends s 16(3) of the Employment Equality Act 1998 l replacing the reference to 'nominal' with a reference to 'disproportionate burden'.
[28] Equal Status Act 2000 (Ireland).
[29] Weaver, 'Incentives versus Controls in Federal Disability Policy' (n 13 above) 12.
[30] See eg Rosen, 'Disability Accommodation and the Labor Market' (n 17 above).
[31] See in particular C Jolls, 'Accommodation Mandates' (2000) 53 *Stanford Law Review* 223 274–5; and Weaver, 'Incentives versus Controls in Federal Disability Policy' (n 13 above) 11–12.
[32] Epstein, *Forbidden Grounds* (n 14 above) 487.

The same desire on the part of employers to reduce the risk of having to make costly accommodations, it is argued, is likely to affect the recruitment potential of various groups of currently non-disabled candidates. Employers are likely to be more reluctant to employ people who are considered likely to become disabled in the future. According to Carolyn Weaver,

> [t]his would suggest a bias toward younger, higher-income, better-educated workers in preference to older, lower-income, more poorly educated ones.[33]

Such a view reinforces the concerns, described above, about the impact of reasonable accommodation duties on relatively poor non-disabled workers.

The concerns emanating from the neoclassical school may be summed up as follows:

> While promoting the employment of [disabled people] may be a highly desirable social goal, the antidiscrimination-reasonable accommodation approach is a costly and inefficient way of doing so and is likely to have highly undesirable distributional consequences.[34]

The coupling of mandatory accommodation duties with restrictions on wage reductions is regarded as particularly problematic. Some commentators call simply for the abandonment of this aspect of the ADA.[35] Others go further and argue for the repeal of all the ADA's employment provisions.[36] Epstein goes still further and calls for the abandonment of all regulatory intervention designed to counter discrimination.[37] The part of this budget that would have been devoted to disability should instead, he suggests, be devoted to 'programs that deal with rehabilitation, training, and counselling and direct assistance' or to 'grants to certain firms to allow them to offer employment to particular classes of disabled workers'.[38]

2.2 Response

2.2.1 Overview

Reasonable accommodation duties, such as those contained in the ADA and the DDA, may be defended against these neoclassical efficiency-based attacks in a number of ways. Evidence has been produced which appears to contradict some of the economic predictions of the critics, and evidence which appears to support their views has been challenged. Many of the assumptions which underlie their

---

[33] Weaver, 'Incentives versus Controls in Federal Disability Policy' (n 13 above) 12.
[34] *Ibid*, 7.
[35] See eg *ibid*, 5–7.
[36] See eg CJ Willis, 'Title I of the Americans with Disabilities Act: Disabling the Disabled' (1995) 25 *Cumberland Law Review* 715.
[37] Epstein, *Forbidden Grounds* (n 14 above).
[38] *Ibid*, 484.

attack have been questioned. In addition, attention has been drawn to the importance of considering other social goods, alongside that of economic efficiency. There is also an argument—which has particular resonance in the British context—as to the role and relevance of State-funded assistance with the costs of adjustments. Such issues will now be considered in a little more depth.

2.2.2 Weaknesses in the Supporting Evidence

Turning first to the statistical evidence that appears to support the predictions the neoclassicists, defenders of the ADA have urged caution in the interpretation of reports indicating a drop in the employment of disabled people since the passage of the Act.[39] The determination of who is disabled, for the purposes such reports, is generally based on what is often referred to as the 'work disability measure.[40] According to this, a person is disabled if they declare that they have health condition which prevents them working or which limits the amount type of work they can do. This measure, it has been argued, may produce misleading information if used to track the employment effects of the ADA.[41]

The key problem with the use of the work disability measure in this context that it requires not simply the presence of some form of health condition impairment but also a perception that that condition places constraints on one ability to work. Consequently, disabled people who have found employment may not report themselves as having a work disability in this sense. They would therefore place themselves outside the class of disabled people being examined the relevant reports. Further, the numbers of unemployed people in that class are likely to have swelled since 1990 if the stigma of attributing limitations to an impairment or health condition has decreased. Thus, although the proportion people with a work disability who are unemployed may have increased according to the reports, this may reveal more about the establishment and composition that class than it does about a decline in the employment prospects of disabled people.

2.2.3 Unfounded Assumptions Leading to Inaccurate Calculations

Challenges have also been mounted against several of the assumptions on which neoclassical calculations of efficiency are based. One such assumption is that disabled workers will necessarily be less productive than non-disabled workers

---

[39] See n 1 above.

[40] See further D Kruse and L Schur, 'Employment of People with Disabilities Following the ADA' (2003) 42 *Industrial Relations* 31.

[41] See eg C Kirchner, 'Looking Under the Street Lamp: Inappropriate Uses of Measures Just Because They are There' (1996) 7(1) *Journal of Disability Policy Studies* 77; S Schwochau and P Blanck, 'The Economics of the Americans with Disabilities Act, Part III: Does the ADA Disable the Disabled?' (2000) 21 *Berkeley Journal of Labor and Employment Law* 271; and Kruse and Schur 'Employment of People with Disabilities Following the ADA' (n 40 above).

Michael Stein[42] has drawn attention to the fact that, while this might be true of some disabled workers, it is an inaccurate and unhelpful generalisation. He points to a number of empirical studies, carried out before the ADA, which indicate that the productivity rates of disabled and non-disabled workers were broadly equivalent.[43] It should be noted, however, that it is often difficult to obtain precise assessments of individual productivity—a fact which may allow unfounded generalisations about disabled people to flourish and to become entrenched.[44]

Stein also criticises traditional neoclassical scholarship for its failure to recognise productivity-related distinctions that are crucial to the operation of the ADA and its reasonable accommodation duties. Such scholarship, he argues, focuses on the net-productivity of a worker and includes in this calculation the cost of any accommodations they might require. For its purposes, therefore, there is no relevant distinction between the following three examples of disabled people, all of whom have the same net-productivity which is lower than that of the average non-disabled worker:

1. A worker with a disability who does not require an accommodation but who is less productive than a non-disabled peer;

2. The equally productive disabled worker, provided with a reasonable accommodation; or

3. The comparatively hyper-productive worker with a disability provided with a proportionately hyper-reasonable accommodation expense.[45]

The distinctions between these three scenarios would, however, be crucial for the application of the ADA. Person (1) would, Stein argues, fall outside the statute's protection, as she would not be able to perform the essential functions of the job even with the benefit of an accommodation. Person (2) would be entitled to ADA protection and to the reasonable accommodation in question. Person (3), while extremely productive once an accommodation was provided, would be entitled to that accommodation and hence to ADA protection only if providing the accommodation were regarded as reasonable (a question which would depend in part on the extent of the resources available to the employer). An efficiency analysis

---

[42] MA Stein, 'Rational Market Decisions and Unemployed Workers with Disabilities' in L Pickering Francis and A Silvers (eds), *Americans with Disabilities: Exploring Implications of the Law for Individuals and Institutions* (New York, Routledge, 2000) 198.

[43] See eg RA Lester and DW Caudill, 'The Handicapped Worker: Seven Myths' (1987) 41 *Training and Development Journal* 50; GE Stevens, 'Exploding the Myths about Hiring the Handicapped' (1986) 63 *Personnel* 57; and, more generally, R Greenwood and VA Johnson, 'Employer Perspectives on Workers with Disabilities' (1987) 53 *Journal of Rehabilitation* 37.

[44] See further Schwab and Willborn, 'Reasonable Accommodation of Workplace Disabilities' (n 13 above) 1220–27.

[45] Stein, 'The Law and Economics of Disability Accommodations' (n 2 above) 133. See also Schwab and Willborn, *ibid*, 1229–33.

that fails to recognise these distinctions, so fundamental to the concept reasonable accommodation, thus appears to be a somewhat blunt instrume with which to gauge its success.

Another, not unrelated, assumption which underlies arguments of the neocla sical critics is the view that accommodations will necessarily be expensive ar burdensome for employers. However, a number of US (and also British[46]) studi have demonstrated that, in the vast majority of cases, this is not so. According one such study, of the accommodations it covered, 72 per cent were cost free, I per cent cost less than US$100, 10 per cent cost less than US$500, and only or per cent cost more than US$500.[47] According to another,[48] in only 18.7 per ce of cases in which an accommodation was made in connection with the retentic of a newly-disabled employee or the promotion of a disabled employee, d employers feel that the costs were not exceeded by the benefits. This study al revealed that the net benefits of accommodations tended to be perceived to l greater when made for a person with a 'substantial' limitation, as required und the ADA's definition of disability, than when made for a person with a less degree of impairment who may well not be covered by the statute. In addition, found that accommodations made for people on higher salaries were perceived be more beneficial than those made for less senior employees.

While there is undoubtedly a need for further empirical work in this area, such studies as there have been clearly demonstrate that accommodating disabl workers may yield a range of potential economic benefits for employers i addition to the increased productivity of the disabled worker in question. The is evidence of a lower turnover rate amongst disabled employees who ha received accommodations and meeting the impairment-related needs of a newl disabled existing employee clearly facilitates their retention. Thus, providir reasonable accommodations or adjustments is likely to reduce significantly th costs associated with recruiting and training new members of staff.[50] There a

[46] Roberts et al, *Responses to the Disability Discrimination Act in 2003 and Preparation for 20 Changes* (n 4 above) tbl 2.11.

[47] PD Blanck, 'Communicating the Americans with Disabilities Act, Transcending Complian 1996 Follow-Up Report on Sears, Roebuck and Co' (Annenberg WA, Program Report, 199 discussed in PD Blanck, 'The Economics of the Employment Provisions of the Americans wi Disabilities Act: Workplace Accommodations' (1997) 46 *Depaul Law Review* 877 at 902. See also t President's Committee on the Employment of People with Disabilities *Report to Congress on the J Accommodation Network* (26 July 1995), reporting that the typical cost of an accommodation w US$200.

[48] H Schartz, K Schartz, DJ Hendricks and PD Blanck, 'Workplace Accommodations: Empiric Study of Current Employees' (2006) 75 *Mississippi Law Journal* 917.

[49] A point emphasised by Schartz et al, *ibid*, 942–3; and also by Stein, 'The Law and Economics Disability Accommodations' (n 2 above) 108–9.

[50] See further ES Fabian, 'Reasonable Accommodations for Workers with Serious Mental Illne Type, Frequency, and Associated Outcomes' (1993) *Psychosocial Rehabilitation Journal* 163; PD Blan and MW Marti, 'Attitudes, Behaviour and the Employment Provisions of the Americans wi Disabilities Act' (1997) 42 *Villanova Law Review* 345; Blanck, 'The Economics of the Employme Provisions of the Americans with Disabilities Act' (n 47 above); Schartz et al, 'Workplace Accomm dations' (n 48 above).

also likely to be additional positive 'ripple' effects in terms of increased dedication and diversity and improved corporate culture.[51]

These potential benefits of accommodations or adjustments, additional to the increased productivity of the individual recipient, are rarely acknowledged in the writings of the efficiency critics. It is admittedly far from easy to quantify such benefits in financial terms. This, however, does not mean that they should be ignored in economic assessments of reasonable accommodation or adjustment duties. Including them in such assessments, however, would undoubtedly weaken the efficiency-based attack which has been launched against those duties.

In addition, as Cass Sunstein[52] has recently argued, there is a tendency to concentrate on the costs which making the accommodation would impose on the employer and to ignore the costs that failure to make it would impose on the relevant disabled person. According to Sunstein, costs of the latter type often take the form of daily humiliations associated with exclusion and stigmatisation. Such costs should be incorporated into any systematic cost-benefit analysis of the situation. The fact that this form of cost is not easily quantified does not of itself justify excluding it from the equation.

Another, more easily calculable, factor relevant to the efficiency of making accommodations is publicly-funded financial assistance. There are surprisingly few references to this in the academic efficiency literature. Indeed, given that public funds are available to cover at least a substantial proportion of the cost of the majority of accommodations, the assertion that the expense of making accommodations falls entirely on employers appears to be somewhat misleading. This assertion, however, is made with puzzling persistence by commentators on both sides of the debate. The issue of State funding for accommodations is an extremely important one, which will be returned to in Section 2.2.6 below.

2.2.4 Incomplete Information within the Market

Another criticism frequently levelled at the application of neoclassical economic theory to the ADA relates to its fundamental underlying premise of a perfect market. It assumes that the market functions rationally to determine prices

---

[51] See, eg, Blanck, 'The Economics of the Employment Provisions of the Americans with Disabilities Act' (n 47 above) 405.

[52] CR Sunstein, 'Cost-Benefit Analysis Without Analyzing Costs or Benefits: Reasonable Accommodation, Balancing and Stigmatic Harms', John M Olin Center for Law and Economics Working Paper No 325 (2nd Series), Public Law and Legal Theory Working Paper No 149 (2007). I am grateful to Lisa Waddington for bringing this article to my attention. See also S Fredman, 'Disability Equality: A Challenge to the Existing Anti-Discrimination Paradigm?' in A Lawson and C Gooding (eds), *Disability Rights in Europe: From Theory to Practice* (Oxford, Hart Publishing, 2005) 208–11; and, for similar criticisms of the tendency to focus on the costs of a specific organisation without factoring in costs and benefits falling on others, J Humphries and J Rubery, 'Some Lessons for Policy' in J Humphries and J Rubery (eds), *The Economics of Equal Opportunities* (Manchester, Equal Opportunities Commission, 1995) 399.

efficiently on the basis of free bargaining and full and accurate information. Those employers who operate on the basis of inadequate information, or on the basis of irrational prejudice or distaste, are regarded as inefficient and, it assumed, will therefore be penalised by the operation of market forces.

In the context of disability and the labour market, however, the assumption that complete and accurate information is disseminated to all relevant actors misplaced. Indeed, the shortfall in the dissemination of disability-related information is so great that it has been described by commentators such as Stein amounting to a 'market failure'. Aside from the many disability-specific concern (which will be outlined in the following paragraphs) there is a more general concern that the application of the neoclassical model, though well suited to the financial market, does not transfer with ease to the labour market.[54]

Significant examples of disability-related informational shortfall among employers have already been touched upon in the previous Section. Unsurprisingly perhaps, employers tend to share the misplaced assumptions of the neoclassical theorists considered there. Thus, evidence suggests that employers generally underestimate the potential productivity of disabled people and that they overestimate the cost of accommodations.[55] The significant under-use of the subsidi available to employers of disabled people also suggests a lack of relevant knowledge and a consequent startling information shortfall.[56] This is likely to be echoed by a high level of ignorance of the potential benefits of providing accommodations which have been identified in the work of Peter Blanck and others.[57]

Neoclassicist approaches have reflected misconceptions about disability which are similar to those which operate within the labour market. Consequently neoclassicist writing has been slow to acknowledge the possibility that the market failure associated with inadequate dissemination of information and understanding will result in inefficiency. Instead, current market attitudes and practices ten to be endorsed, with the result that reasonable accommodation duties a condemned as inefficient.

---

[53]   See further WJ Baumol and AS Blinder, *Economics: Principles and Policy* (Cincinnati O Thomson Learning, 1998) 226–8 and 313–14.

[54]   See eg Stein, 'Rational Market Decisions and Unemployed Workers with Disabilities' (n above) 196, who points out that the labour market lacks the financial market's extensive, a rigorously enforced, reporting requirements. He also observes that the ready liquidity of financ market commodities, unlike that of individual workers, facilitates the application of the neoclassi model.

[55]   See eg M Baldwin and WG Johnson, 'Labor Market Discrimination Against Men w Disabilities' (1994) 29 *Journal of Human Resources* 1; M Baldwin, LA Zeager and PR Flacco, 'Gend Differences in Wage Losses from Impairments: Estimates from the Survey of Income and Progr Participation' (1994) 29 *Journal of Human Resources* 865. See also JN Shklar, *American Citizenship: 7 Quest for Inclusion* (Cambridge MA, Harvard University Press, 1991) 63–101; and G Kavka, 'Disabil and the Right to Work' in Pickering Francis and Silvers (eds), *Americans with Disabilities* (n 42 abov

[56]   See n 90 below and accompanying text.

[57]   See nn 41–8 above and accompanying text.

Ironically, however, the reasonable accommodation duties themselves fulfil an important role in facilitating the dissemination of relevant information within the labour market. The ADA duties, like those of the DDA, require employers to engage in an interactive dialogue with disabled employees in order to identify the accommodations which should be provided.[58] This process is designed to facilitate the exchange of information relevant to the impairment-related needs of the disabled individual and to the means by which their potential, within the particular work setting in question, might best be fulfilled. In both the United States and in Britain, assistance in this process is available cost-free from agencies able to provide information as to the range of available publicly funded subsidies and to provide more formalised mediation in the event of disagreements.[59]

In theory at least, the final recourse to litigation and judicial pronouncement provides another means of disseminating information to a large audience about the real costs and benefits of accommodations. However, the effectiveness of litigation as a tool for addressing the market failure brought about by disability-related information deficits has been questioned, at least in the United States.[60] Nevertheless, once questions of reasonableness and undue hardship reach a court, employers are forced to produce information about their financial and other circumstances and to set against them the real costs of the contested accommodation. In this sense such litigation, or the threat of it, has a powerful 'information forcing' function not dissimilar to that of a well-developed objective justification defence in indirect discrimination rules.[61] This information-forcing aspect of reasonable accommodation duties is by no means always welcome. Indeed, the discomfort engendered by the idea that, in order to take advantage of an undue hardship defence, businesses would need to reveal financial details to strangers was an important factor in the decision of the Irish Supreme Court to strike down the Employment Equality Bill.[62]

---

[58] Regulations Relating to Labor (Ch XIV—Equal Employment Opportunity Commission) 29 CFR 1630.2 (o)(3), 1630.9 (2002). See generally S Silverman, 'The ADA Interactive Process: The Employer and Employee's Duty to Work Together to Identify a Reasonable Accommodation is More Than a Game of Five Card Stud' (1998) 77 *Nebraska Law Review* 281; AM Barancik, 'Determining Reasonable Accommodations Under the ADA: Why Courts Should Require Employers to Participate in an "Interactive Process"' (1999) 30 *Loyola University of Chicago Law Journal* 513; and AR Brown, 'Mental Disabilities Under the ADA: The Role of Employees and Employers in the Interactive Process' (2002) 8 *Washington University Journal of Law and Policy* 341.

[59] See eg, in the US, the Job Accommodation Network and the Equal Employment Opportunity Commission; and, in England and Wales, the Disability Employment Advisory Service and the Equality and Human Rights Commission.

[60] For doubts as to the effectiveness of US litigation in this regard see eg Stein, 'Same Struggle, Different Difference' (n 13 above) fn 659–60 and accompanying text.

[61] See further PS Karlen and G Rutherglen, 'Disabilities, Discrimination and Reasonable Accommodation' (1996) 46 *Duke Law Journal* 1 at 32–3; and H Collins, 'Discrimination, Equality and Social Inclusion' (2003) 66 *Modern Law Review* 16 at 38.

[62] *Re Article 26 and the Employment Equality Bill* [1997] 2 Irish Reports 321 at 368. For criticism see Quinn and Quinlivan, 'Disability Discrimination' (n 21 above), who argue that Irish employers are subject to heavy regulation and therefore already required to reveal such details to outsiders.

2.2.5 Fairness and Market Unresponsiveness

Neoclassical economic theory, as has been seen, is built on the underlyin premise of market perfection. According to it, employers whose decisions a tainted by inadequate information, irrational prejudice or distaste will be pena ised for their inefficiency by the operation of market forces. These forces w ensure that competitors whose decisions are untainted by such inefficiency w prosper and eventually drive their inefficient rivals from the marketplace togeth with their tainted decision-making practices.

It is, however, far from clear that market forces do in fact operate to discipli discriminatory or unfair practices in this way. Indeed, were it not for t prevalence and persistence of discriminatory prejudice in the unregulated ma ketplace, it is doubtful that any employment-related non-discrimination legisl tion would ever have been enacted. It seems likely that, as long as t discriminatory prejudices and preferences are shared by the general publi market forces may even operate to reward discriminatory employers and penali those who make decisions according to principles of equality and fairness.

Stein argues that the neoclassicist attack on the ADA is normatively flaw because, in its endorsement of the status quo produced by market forces, reinforces the stereotypes and prejudices the statute was intended to counteract. It endorses a medical or individual model perspective on disability, according which social policy should focus exclusively on the cure, correction or suppo (through welfare or charity) of disabled individuals. It does not adopt the soci model perspective, cherished by campaigners for disability equality, which dra attention to the disabling impact of socially-created barriers. Adherence to medical or individual model perspective, which locates the problem of disabili entirely within the individual, is likely to generate far less discomfort abo placing the cost of an inaccessible workplace on a disabled person than adherence to a social model perspective, which locates the problem of disabili within social structures and practices.[64]

Neoclassical law and economics scholars have long been criticised for the exclusive focus on wealth maximisation and their consequent marginalisation issues of fairness and morality.[65] It has been argued that, in disregarding su issues, neoclassicists take insufficient account of the distinction between t functions of economics and of law. Whereas the primary function of the form is predictive, law (at least the equality and human rights type of law at issue her

---

[63] Stein, 'Rational Market Decisions and Unemployed Workers with Disabilities' (n 42 abo 196–7.

[64] *Ibid*, 201–02. See also ch 1, section 5 above.

[65] See eg JL Coleman, *Markets, Morals and the Law* (Cambridge, Cambridge University Pre 1988) particularly 111–22; MC Nussbaum, 'The Costs of Tragedy: Some Moral Limits of Cost-Bene Analysis' (2000) 29 *Journal of Legal Studies* 1005; and HS Richardson, 'The Stupidity of t Cost-Benefit Standard' (2000) 29 *Journal of Legal Studies* 971. See also HF Chang, 'A Liberal Theory Social Welfare: Fairness, Utility and the Pareto Principle' (2000) 110 *Yale Law Journal* 173.

has an important persuasive or expressive role to play in bringing about behavioural, normative and social change.[66] The task of the ADA, the DDA and other such statutes is thus to effect a moral and attitudinal shift. Such laws express the clear view that employers, service providers, educators and other social actors have the responsibility to identify and attempt to remove barriers which obstruct the path of disabled people wishing to participate in life's mainstream. In this sense it is an educative role which, if successful, will promote a shift in thinking away from the medical model approach—for which the neoclassicists have been criticised—towards a more social model perspective. In the process, it is often argued, it will open up the market to allow entry to a hitherto largely excluded group and, in so doing, inject a greater degree of fairness and rationality into its operation.[67]

In sum, neoclassicist law and economics scholars have been criticised for paying insufficient regard to the expressive, normative function of law. Their focus on wealth maximisation lies at the root of their condemnation of the ADA's imposition of reasonable accommodation duties together with its insistence on equal pay. Regardless of whether allowing disabled people to sell their labour for a lower price than other workers would in fact be economically efficient, it would risk undermining the expressive function of the ADA. Bribing employers to appoint or retain disabled workers in this way would, in Stein's words, 'reinforce the devaluation of those individuals begot by unfounded stereotypes, and so continue market failure', thereby reducing 'whatever social good and external benefits can arise from equal pay and occupational dignity'.[68]

2.2.6 General Societal Economic Benefit and State Funding

In addition to the charge that they fail to give adequate recognition to the potential benefits of accommodations to employers, neoclassical efficiency theorists such as Epstein have been criticised for not sufficiently taking into account the wider economic benefits of accommodations. There is a high welfare cost attached to the non-employment of disabled people. Studies have suggested that the increased employment of disabled people is beneficial to the general economy and demonstrated a very strong link between their employment and general tax

---

[66] See eg KG Dau-Schmidt, 'Legal Prohibitions as More than Prices: The Economic Analysis of Preference Shaping Policies in the Law' in RP Malloy and CK Braun (eds), *Law and Economics: New and Critical Perspectives* (New York, Peter Lang Publishers, 1995) 153; RP Malloy, *Law and Market Economy: Reinterpreting the Values of Law and Economics* (Cambridge, Cambridge University Press, 2000) 8–11; A Geisinger, 'A Belief Change Theory of Expressive Law' 88 *Iowa Law Review* 35 (2002); MA Stein, 'Under the Empirical Radar: An Initial Expressive Law Analysis of the ADA' (2004) 90 *Virginia Law Review* 1151; and A Geisinger and MA Stein, 'A Theory of Expressive International Law' (2007) 60 *Vanderbilt Law Review* 77.

[67] See eg G Quinn, 'The Human Rights of People with Disabilities Under EU Law' in P Alston (ed), *The EU and Human Rights* (Oxford, Oxford University Press, 1999) 291–3.

[68] Stein, 'Rational Market Decisions and Unemployed Workers with Disabilities' (n 42 above) 197.

reductions.[69] Efficiency critics, as has been seen, are unlikely to accept that su
benefits will be achieved through a strategy of mandatory accommodation duti
because, in their view, such duties are not likely to promote the employment
disabled people.

Amy Wax—while accepting that the question of whether the ADA has pr
moted the employment of disabled people to date is contentious—suggests th
any failure of the ADA to increase employment amongst disabled people is like
to be the result of inadequate enforcement.[70] She draws attention to cases
which it would be efficient for society as a whole (taking into account facto
such as reduced taxes) for a disabled person to be appointed to a particul
position (if able to perform its core elements), but in which it would not
efficient for the employer in question to appoint them because their net produ
tivity (taking into account the costs of accommodations) would fall short of th
of a non-disabled candidate. Wax criticises the tendency of neoclassical theoris
to concentrate solely on the labour market when calculating the efficiency of t
ADA. She writes:

> In predicting that mandates that disturb the 'rational' operation of labor markets w
> always produce welfare-reducing inefficiencies, these analysts conveniently overlook t
> fact that, without the ADA, many disabled persons might be wastefully unemploy
> and would require support from the rest of us.[71]

A greater priority, she argues, should be given to what is efficient for society as
whole and not simply to what is efficient for employers.[72] While this may ha
been the aim of the ADA, Wax observes that the statute places the costs
employment-related disability accommodations on employers and not on socie
as a whole. This raises the question of whether it is appropriate or fair f
employers to pay for what may, in those cases in which a disabled employee is le
productive, be in the interests of society at large but not in the interests of t
employers themselves. According to Wax, fairness (rather than efficiency) m
thus require shifting the financial burden of an accommodation, which does n
benefit an employer, to society more generally—through, for instance, the t
system.[73]

---

[69] See the studies cited by Stein, 'The Law and Economics of Disability Accommodations' (
above) fn 181 (suggesting that Californian tax payers paid US$629 a month less in tax for eve
disabled person who was employed).

[70] AL Wax, 'Disability, Reciprocity, and "Real Efficiency": A Unified Approach' (2003) 44 *Willi*
and Mary Law Review 1421 at 1427.

[71] *Ibid*, 1437.

[72] *Ibid*, 1433–7. See also SR Bagenstos, 'The Americans with Disabilities Act as Welfare Refor
(2003) 44 *William and Mary Law Review* 921.

[73] *Ibid*, 1450–51.

Moss and Malin[74] have used such arguments as a platform from which to argue that the costs of all employment accommodations should be funded by the State. They take the view that requiring employers to pay for reasonable accommodations gives them an incentive to avoid employing disabled people—the cost of accommodations making disability discrimination rational. In order to achieve the ADA's goals of equality and workplace integration, they argue, it is therefore essential that the costs of accommodations be paid entirely from federal funds by way of grants made to relevant employers.

A different approach to the role of State funding of employment accommodations is taken by Michael Stein. While agreeing that the State should fund some such accommodations, he insists that the obligation to pay for reasonable (and therefore mandatory[75]) accommodations should fall on employers alone. State funding should be restricted to paying for accommodations which fall outside the parameters of reasonableness and which employers would therefore be under no obligation to make. The question of whether or not an accommodation is reasonable should, he suggests, be decided according to efficiency-based considerations. Accommodations should therefore be regarded as reasonable only if they allow the employer to profit from the employment of the disabled person in question—even if they would profit less than they would have done had they employed an equivalent non-disabled person instead. In cases where the employer derives no benefit from the accommodation, but it would nevertheless represent a net social gain to have the disabled person in employment, the accommodation would be unreasonable and therefore not required under the ADA.[76] However, in such cases State funding should be provided to support the employment of the disabled person in question.[77]

---

[74] SA Moss and DA Malin, 'Public Funding for Disability Accommodations: A Rational Solution to Rational Discrimination and the Disabilities of the ADA' (1998) 33 *Harvard Civil Rights and Civil Liberties Law Review* 197.

[75] Americans with Disabilities Act 1990, 42 USC s 12112(b)(5)(A).

[76] Stein suggests ('The Law and Economics of Disability Accommodations' (n 2 above) 175) that there may still be reason to 'compel an employer to make an accommodation' when 'an employer cannot profit from retaining a worker with a disability due to her accommodation cost' if that produces a net social benefit gain. However, this point is not expanded upon. The issue of whether the suggested compulsion should be achieved through the ADA or through other means is not discussed. Neither is the question of whether this form of mandatory unreasonable accommodation should be limited to cases of employment retention or whether it should apply more broadly to include recruitment.

[77] These two types of case ('semi-efficient accommodations' and 'social benefit gain accommodations' respectively) fall into the middle category of Stein's spectrum of accommodations—a category he terms 'socially efficient accommodations' because it achieves a form of Kaldor-Hicks efficiency in which the total gain is greater than the total loss even though employers will not have benefited to the extent they would have done by employing a non-disabled person. The top category of accommodations in this spectrum is termed 'wholly efficient accommodations' because the relevant accommodations achieve Pareto optimality in that employers, the disabled person and society at large all gain from them. Such accommodations make employment possible for disabled people whose net-productivity is at least equivalent to that of their non-disabled counterparts. The bottom category is termed 'wholly inefficient mandates' because it is cheaper to support the disabled person on benefits than to pay for the accommodations necessary to allow them to work. In such

Stein's approach is grounded in his commitment to the view that the reasonable accommodation obligation is a non-discrimination measure and that compliance with it is required by fundamental principles of equality. It therefore belongs alongside the other more familiar and well-established non-discrimination concepts of direct and indirect discrimination (or disparate treatment and disparate impact). Employers are required to bear the costs arising from the demands of these other non-discrimination measures and should therefore also be required to pay for the costs arising from reasonable accommodation. A system which did not require them to pay for reasonable accommodations would risk signalling that those accommodations were not, in fact, essential requirements of equality and non-discrimination. In his words,

> [w]here a policymaker believes that the equality line falls ... will inform where she draws the lines between cost bearers. If accommodations effectuate equality, then it will seem appropriate to lay the costs for those accommodations at the feet of employers. On the other hand, if reasonable accommodations are really redistributive devices however laudable, then it would be more apposite to have the general tax base bear those costs.[78]

Similar views on the issue of State funding are expressed by Matthew Diller. According to him,

> the civil rights approach places the responsibility for the necessary changes on individual employers. The premise of civil rights law is that the provision of equal opportunity and equal access is a basic responsibility of every employer, government program and public accommodation. The idea of socializing the cost through public funding of compliance by private entities cuts against the grain–it suggests that the responsibility for effectuating equality is collective rather than individual. This ... highlights the fact that advocates for and among people with disabilities have made strategic decision to cast the claim for government protection as an issue of civil right rather than simply as an appeal for a social welfare program, or an investment in the labor force.[79] (footnotes omitted)

The commitment of Stein and Diller to the categorisation of reasonable accommodation as a non-discrimination measure is to be welcomed. It does not appear to be shared by Moss and Malin, who, by contrast, refer to reasonable accommodation as a form of disparate treatment (or direct discrimination) in favour of disabled people.[80] This may, in part, explain their greater willingness to contemplate the possibility of State-funded reasonable accommodation. It is suggested, however, that the provision of State funding for reasonable accommodations

---

cases, according to Stein, the accommodation would be unreasonable and one for which the State should provide no funding. For further explanation of Pareto and Kaldor-Hicks efficiencies, Posner, *Economic Analysis of Law* (n 12 above) s 1.2.

   [78]   Stein, 'The Law and Economics of Disability Accommodations' (n 2 above) 136.
   [79]   M Diller, 'Judicial Backlash, the ADA and the Civil Rights Model' (2000) 21 *Berkeley Journal Employment and Labor* 19 at 33–4.
   [80]   Moss and Malin, 'Public Funding for Disability Accommodations' (n 74 above) 197.

not inconsistent with the view that they are non-discrimination measures. Further, the British experience of such a funding system provides no evidence to support the concern that it might undermine the view that making reasonable accommodations represents an integral element of the provision of equality.

Indeed, it might well be argued that the provision of a generous State subsidy towards the costs of accommodations, such as that established by the British Access to Work scheme, actually operates to facilitate and hasten the achievement of equality. Such subsidies have the potential to enhance the power and the practical impact of reasonable adjustment duties very considerably. The availability of additional resources to employers pushes the limits of what steps will be considered reasonable for them to take and thereby reduces the barrier against the employment of a disabled person created by the expense of an adjustment.

The active involvement of the State in facilitating adjustments is, it is suggested, entirely consistent with the social model's emphasis on the removal of socially-created barriers—barriers which make the physical structure of the workplace, its equipment or its information systems inaccessible to disabled people. It is also consistent with calls for a greater synthesis between the strategies of civil rights and social welfare.[81] Further, it may be regarded as a demonstration of positive steps which States might take to support and strengthen the social and economic rights of their citizens[82]—the employment-related rights of their disabled people. It should also be noted that it is an approach which, in Britain, is not confined to the context of disability. The funding of statutory maternity leave provided by the State may be regarded as a manifestation of the same broad strategy—a strategy which aims to promote equality in the workplace.[83] Such a strategy acknowledges that the implementation of principles of non-discrimination is a responsibility which is collective as well as individual, and that it raises questions of distributive as well as of corrective justice.

In addition, and perhaps more significantly for present purposes, the provision of State-funded subsidies is likely to reduce the economic concerns which may be aroused by reasonable accommodation or adjustment duties and so help to reduce the risk of resistance and resentment. The different approaches taken to subsidies in Britain and in the United States may well have had a significant influence on the generation of the different degrees of economically-based criticism which the duties have attracted in the two countries. For this reason, it is worth revisiting the differences between the two funding systems and considering their possible implications.

---

[81] L Waddington and M Diller, 'Tensions and Coherence in Disability Policy: The Uneasy Relationship Between Social Welfare and Civil Rights Models of Disability in American, European and International Employment Law' in ML Breslin and S Yee (eds), *Disability Rights Law and Policy: International and National Perspectives* (Ardsley NY, Transnational Publishers Inc, 2002).

[82] Fredman, 'Disability Equality' (n 52 above) 215–18.

[83] See generally S Fredman, 'A Difference with Distinction: Pregnancy and Parenthood Reassessed' (1994) 110 *Law Quarterly Review* 106; and C Palmer et al, *Maternity and Parental Rights: A Guide to Parents' Legal Rights at Work* (London, Legal Action Group, 2006) ch 6.

The British Access to Work scheme, details of which were provided in chapter three above,[84] was recently described by the Department for Work and Pensions as 'one of our most popular and successful labour market programmes'.[85] It makes government funding available to assist employers with the cost of adjustments for disabled workers. It also assists disabled people who are self-employed and, in some circumstances, provides funding for the costs of transport to work. For the year 2006–07, some £60,000,000 was spent on the Access to Work scheme in the provision of support to approximately 40,000 disabled people.[86] In a 2001 survey, 9 out of 10 users of the scheme stated that it met all or most of their needs and nearly half indicated that they would not be able to work without it.[87]

The British subsidy scheme differs from that adopted in the United States, which was also explained in chapter three, in a number of important respects.

The first important respect in which the British Access to Work scheme contrasts with the US tax credit system relates to the point of delivery. The Access to Work subsidy is available to employers at the time when the support or adjustment is purchased. Under the US system, however, the subsidy is available only retrospectively. This difference has a number of repercussions on the making of reasonable adjustments or accommodations.

The fact that US employers are able to recover reasonable accommodation subsidies only retrospectively gives them more freedom and flexibility to proceed with purchasing the reasonable accommodations. In Britain, the process of applying for Access to Work funding can slow down this process. Indeed, such delays have resulted in the withdrawal of job offers made to disabled people and in them being unable to perform the job to which they were appointed.[88]

Other implications of this difference in approach work in favour of the British system. The fact that Access to Work makes funding available from the outset creates a simpler financial structure for employers than does the US system, under which money has to be recovered at a later point through the tax system. Unlike the US system, it also makes it absolutely clear from the start that the employer is not paying the entire bill. In addition, the British approach perhaps makes it easier to factor the availability of State funding into assessments of the

---

[84] Ch 3, fnn 110–12 above and accompanying text.

[85] Department for Work and Pensions, *Helping People Achieve their Full Potential* (n 3 above) para 5.0.

[86] *Ibid*, para 5.1.

[87] P Thornton, M Hirst, H Arksey and N Tremlett, *Users' Views of Access to Work: Final Report of a Study for the Employment Service*, Research and Development Report ESR72 (Sheffield, Employment Service, 2001).

[88] See eg *Kenny v Hampshire Constabulary* [1999] IRLR 76 (EAT), discussed in ch 3, fnn 57–62 above and accompanying text; and *Williams v J Walter Thomson Group* [2005] EWCA Civ 133, discussed in ch 4, fnn 68–9 above and accompanying text. See also Department for Work and Pensions, *Helping People Achieve their Full Potential* (n 3 above) para 5.7 where delay in securing relevant support is identified as a concern raised by many Access to Work recipients, and paras 11–14 where action taken to date to address the problem is described.

reasonableness of adjustments than it would be under the US system, where such assistance is available only at some point after the purchase of the accommodation.

The second significant difference between Access to Work and the US tax credit scheme relates to the funding structure used in the two systems. In the United States, the tax credit system allows businesses to recover some of the cost of disability-related adjustments which do not exceed a specified upper limit—currently US$5,000 or US$15,000 depending on which of the schemes is applicable.[89] Under Access to Work on the other hand, although employers are expected to foot the entire bill for relatively cheap adjustments and to share the costs of more expensive ones, they will never be required to pay more than a specified upper limit—currently £10,000. Once the costs exceed this amount, the State will pay them in full. There is no upper limit on the amount of Access to Work funding available in any particular case.

This difference in approach is likely to have a significant impact on the attitudes of employers in the two countries—at least on the attitudes of those employers who are aware of the subsidy schemes.[90] British employers are offered a safety net which is not offered to US employers. This, it would appear, should make them more willing to contemplate recruiting or retaining an employee who will need on-going and expensive adjustments.

A third difference between the two schemes relates to their coverage. Outside ministerial government departments, the Access to Work scheme is available to all employers and covers all types of adjustment. In the United States, however, although subsidies for the costs of physical alterations are available to all employers, this is not the case for other types of accommodation. For them, the subsidies are restricted to small businesses. Larger businesses are therefore likely to have to pay the entire bill for expensive and on-going accommodations (such as the provision of a sign-language interpreter or a reader). The implications of this departure of approach between the two systems are very similar to those discussed in the previous paragraph and will not therefore be repeated here.

These differences between the US and British State subsidy schemes may help to explain the different degrees of economically-based hostility that reasonable adjustment or accommodation duties have attracted in the two countries. The Access to Work scheme appears to have played a vital role in the process of introducing the British duties and securing their acceptance. The Government,

---

[89] See generally ch 3, fnn 114–17 above and accompanying text.

[90] In Britain, research suggests that 74% of employers had never heard of the Access to Work scheme—C Goldstone and N Meager, *Barriers to Employment for Disabled People* (London, Department for Work and Pensions, 2002). In the US, according to General Accounting Office, *Business Tax Incentives: Incentives to Employ Workers with Disabilities Receive Limited Use and Have an Uncertain Impact* (GAO-03–39, December 2002) 2 (discussed in Stein, 'The Law and Economics of Disability Accommodations' (n 2 above) 124–5), these schemes were severely under-used, with only 'a very small proportion' of businesses actually taking advantage of them.

however, is currently consulting on proposals to alter the scheme.[91] Worryingly one of these proposals is the withdrawal of Access to Work funding from the public sector.[92] Such a change would seem likely to trigger inevitable resentmen Either disabled people wishing to obtain or retain public sector work would nee to accept a much reduced level of support or the bounds of reasonableness woul be pushed way beyond the limits of comfort for public sector bodies—bodie which will all too often already be financially hard-pressed.

3. Displaced Welfare Benefits for A Protected Group

3.1 Resistance

Another reason which is often given for resistance to reasonable accommodatio duties is the tendency to regard them not as instruments designed to ensur equality and fairness but as mechanisms for transferring the costs of providin disability subsidies or welfare benefits from the State to employers, servic providers and others. Perceiving reasonable accommodations or adjustments a equivalent to privately-funded welfare benefits is clearly likely to raise question as to their economic efficiency. This approach is therefore closely linked to th arguments considered in the previous Section and the tendency at issue here ca often be found in the writings of adherents to the neoclassical model of law an economics. Thus, according to Carolyn Weaver, reasonable accommodatio provisions represent a 'wrong-headed' attempt to promote disability employmer by what amounts to 'a mandated benefit program'.[93] Similarly, Sherwin Rose condemns their inclusion in the ADA as an 'ill-advised' but 'politically easy' wa to

> shift a public burden off the budget at a time when the government budget [was] i deficit and there [was] widespread public distaste for greater taxation.[94]

This tendency to regard reasonable accommodation as a form of 'special' benefi rooted in principles of welfare and philanthropy rather than equality, is n confined to theorists. Various commentators have developed a powerful accoun

---

[91] Department for Work and Pensions, *Helping People Achieve their Full Potential* (n 3 above).
[92] *Ibid*, paras 5.23–5.25. See also para 20 where it is suggested that the Government 'might wa to encourage the largest employers to pay the entire cost of some or all of the workplace adjustmen of their staff'. These proposals emerge from Cabinet Office Strategy Unit, *Improving the Life Chanc of Disabled People* (London, Stationery Office, 2005) recommendation 7.10.
[93] Weaver, 'Incentives versus Controls in Federal Disability Policy' (n 13 above) 15.
[94] Rosen, 'Disability Accommodation and the Labor Market' (n 17 above) 29. See also W C 'Disability and a Workfare-Welfare Dilemma' in Weaver (ed), *Disability and Work: Incentives, Righ and Opportunities* (n 13 above) 43–5; and JM Van de Walle, 'In the Eye of the Beholder: Issues Distributive and Corrective Justice in the ADA's Employment Protection for Persons Regarded Disabled' (1998) 73 *Chicago-Kent Law Review* 897.

of its influence over the US judiciary. Michael Stein, for instance, has argued that, for many judges, reasonable accommodation is regarded not as an issue of equality but as the dispensation of humanitarian support, which must therefore compete with other claims to social largess.[95] It calls upon 'the better angels of our nature',[96] which prompt sympathy for those with physical and mental impairments and is thus redolent of pity and altruism rather than social justice.

Similarly, Matthew Diller has argued that the pattern of 'narrow and begrudging'[97] judicial interpretations of the ADA is inconsistent with adherence to a civil rights approach to the Act. It appears instead to reflect an understanding according to which reasonable accommodations are equated with privileges akin to welfare benefits, to be conferred on members of a tightly circumscribed protected class. In his words,

> [t]he failure of many judges to fully embrace the concept of equality reflected in the ADA has led courts to construe the statute in ways that make no sense as a matter of civil rights policy ... [I]n the absence of a grounding in principles of equality, the ADA can only be read as a means of dispensing subsidies to a targeted group of people. Seen from this vantage point, the case law has a certain coherence, although not the coherence intended by the framers of the law.[98]

One of those framers, Robert Burgdorf, has himself lamented the 'unnecessary complexity, harsh technicalities and niggardly standards' which have been generated by the dominance in judicial thinking of what he terms a 'special treatment or preferred group' approach.[99]

The reverberations caused by a judicial perception of reasonable accommodations as a form of special treatment or welfare subsidy are likely to be felt throughout the framework of disability equality law, extending well beyond the construction of reasonable accommodation duties themselves. Threshold issues, concerning the establishment of entitlement or membership of the protected class, are particularly susceptible. Burgdorf[100] documents four ways in which US courts have restricted the limits of the entitled class, which he regards as inconsistent with the original civil rights mission of the ADA. Although a detailed analysis of these developments is beyond the scope of this book, a brief reference to them is instructive.

---

[95] Stein, 'Same Struggle, Different Difference' (n 13 above) fn 629–30 and accompanying text.
[96] *Board of Trustees of University of Alabama v Garrett*, 531 US 356 at 375–7 (2001) (Kennedy J). See further A Soifer, 'Disabling the ADA: Essences, Better Angels, and the Unprincipled Neutrality Claim' (2003) 44 *William and Mary Law Review* 1285.
[97] Diller, 'Judicial Backlash, the ADA and the Civil Rights Model' (n 79 above) 23.
[98] *Ibid*, 47–8.
[99] RL Burgdorf, '"Substantially Limited" Protection from Disability Discrimination: The Special Treatment Model and Misconstructions of the Definition of Disability' (1997) 42 *Villanova Law Review* 409 at 413.
[100] *Ibid*. See also A Soifer, 'The Disability Term: Dignity, Default and Negative Capability' (2000) 47 *University of California Los Angeles Law Review* 1279.

Title I of the ADA defines a person with a disability as somebody who has physical or mental impairment that substantially limits one or more of the majc life activities'; as somebody who has had a history of such an impairment; or a somebody who is regarded as having such an impairment.[101] In addition, for th purposes of employment, they must be 'qualified' in the sense that they are ab to perform the essential functions of the job whether with or without a reasor able accommodation.[102] This definition was drawn from the Rehabilitation A 1973 in order to ensure consistency between the two Acts and to redu complexity.[103]

The first restrictive interpretation to which Burgdorf refers concerns the nee to show the substantial limitation of a major life activity.[104] In a number of case courts have identified the relevant life activity as being that of work and hav refused to confer the status of 'disabled' on claimants who have not proved the inability to carry out, not just the one job in question, but also a broad range other jobs. This requirement has been applied so strictly that, according Burgdorf, it has contributed to rulings that people with a range of seriou impairments (including cancer, haemophilia, HIV infection, diabetes, the loss an eye, a removed larynx and avascular necrosis leading to hip and should replacements) are not disabled for the purposes of the ADA or the Rehabilitatic Act 1973.[105] Because such claimants are denied entry into the protected class disabled people, their cases fail without the alleged discriminatory conduct of th defendants ever being examined.

An example of a case in which the central issue should arguably have bee reasonable accommodation, but which failed because of this 'one-job-is-no enough' requirement, is *Wooten v Farmland Foods*.[106] In this case, Mr Wooter who worked as a ham-boner, developed bilateral carpal tunnel syndrome, inflan mation and tendonitis in his left arm and shoulder. When his supervisors learne of medical advice that Wooten should not work in a cold environment an should be given only limited lifting tasks, he was fired expressly on grounds of h disability. Nevertheless, the Eighth Circuit dismissed his ADA case because he w not disabled within the meaning of the ADA. This was because his impairmer was regarded as one which would prevent him from carrying out too 'narrow' range of jobs.[107]

As Burgdorf observes, it is 'difficult to see' how such decisions

---

[101] Americans with Disabilities Act 1990, 42 USC s 12102(2).
[102] *Ibid.*
[103] See generally RL Burgdorf, 'The Americans with Disabilities Act: Analysis and Implications o' Second-Generation Civil Rights Statute' (1991) 26 *Harvard Civil Rights and Civil Liberties Law Revi* 413 at 441–52.
[104] See Burgdorf, '"Substantially Limited"' (n 99 above) 439–69.
[105] *Ibid*, 540–41. See also RA Bales, 'Once is Enough: Evaluating when a Person is Substantia Limited in her Ability to Work' (1993) 11 *Hofstra Labor Law Journal* 203 at 235–42.
[106] *Wooten v Farmland Foods*, 58 F 3d 382 (8th Cir 1995).
[107] *Ibid*, 386.

further any conceivable policy of the ADA ... which seeks to eliminate discrimination against employees and to get employers to make accommodations.[108]

If, however, accommodations are equated with welfare benefits, the approach becomes more understandable.[109] On that view the approach helps to ensure that entitlement will be conferred on only those people who are perceived to be in genuine need. A person whose impairments do not prevent them obtaining other work is not perceived to be in such need, even if that work is not of a type they would otherwise have chosen and which does not therefore allow them to fulfill their own personal potential. Entitlement to reasonable accommodation is thus preserved for those who would not otherwise be able to work and is not considered appropriate for those who could avoid the need for it by changing jobs. Indeed, refusals to grant ADA protection to people falling into the latter category have sometimes been accompanied by judicial assertions that the Act must not be allowed to become 'a handout to those who are in fact capable of working in substantially similar jobs'.[110] Diller suggests that it is the perception that such people are needlessly imposing demands on their existing employer, rather than looking for alternative work, which seems to provoke judicial anger and impatience.[111]

The second restrictive interpretation given to the definition of disability, addressed by Burgdorf, concerns impairments which are temporary in nature.[112] Although the ADA itself does not specify that a relevant disability must be long-term, such a requirement was included in the Regulations produced by the Equal Employment Opportunity Commission in 1992.[113] Burgdorf argues that, like the previous requirement, this one has been developed by the courts in an overly harsh manner so as to exclude people with serious impairments (such as epilepsy, depression and arthritis).[114] Ironically, such 'harsh and inequitable rulings'[115] have sometimes been defended by courts on the ground that, in enacting the ADA, Congress intended to protect only 'the truly disabled'.[116] Their effect, however, is again to evict people with severe impairments, who feel that they have been badly treated, from the protected class, thereby removing the question of their entitlement to reasonable accommodations from judicial scrutiny.

---

[108] Burgdorf, '"Substantially Limited"' (n 99 above) 544.
[109] See further Diller, 'Judicial Backlash, the ADA and the Civil Rights Model' (n 79 above) 48–9.
[110] *Sutton v United Airlines*, 130 F 3d 893 (10th Cir 1997), affirmed, 527 US, 119 S Ct 2139 (1999); and *Hileman v City of Dallas*, 115 F3d 352 at 354 (5th Cir 1997).
[111] Diller, 'Judicial Backlash, the ADA and the Civil Rights Model' (n 79 above) 48–9.
[112] Burgdorf, '"Substantially Limited"' (n 99 above) 469–89.
[113] Equal Employment Opportunity Commission, 'Technical Assistance Manual for the Americans with Disabilities Act' II.5. See also (1997) 29 CFR s 1630.2(j)(l).
[114] Burgdorf, '"Substantially Limited"' (n 99 above) 546–7.
[115] *Ibid*, 548.
[116] See eg *Sutton v New Mexico Department for Children, Youth and Families*, 922 F Supp 516 at 519 (DNM 1996); and, in the context of the one-job-is-not-enough requirement, *Forrisi v Bowen*, 794 F 2d 931 at 934 (4th Cir 1986).

The third restriction on entitlement to ADA protection, considered by Burg dorf, concerns what he terms 'judicial estoppel'.[117] A number of cases have hel that an unemployed disabled person claiming to be unable to work for tk purposes of obtaining social security benefits is thereby estopped from claimin to be a 'qualified' person for the purposes of the employment provisions of tk ADA.[118] While this approach has now been rejected by the Supreme Court,[1] Diller explains its appeal by reference to his theory that reasonable accommoda tions tend to be perceived as welfare benefits. On this basis, without tk intervention of judicial estoppel, claimants would be allowed to argue that the were entitled to reasonable accommodation and thereby to maintain a form « 'double dipping'.[120]

The judicial estoppel approach places disabled people unable to obtain wor due to discriminatory obstacles 'between a rock and a hard place'[121] or in a impossible 'catch 22' situation. It overlooks the point—so fundamental to disabi ity equality law—that the provision of reasonable accommodation (and tk removal of other discriminatory barriers) may make a crucial difference to tk ability of a disabled person to work. In other decisions, which have not estoppe the ADA claim, the burden of proving that reasonable accommodation will mal this crucial difference has been placed on the claimant[122]—an approach which, a Stein has argued, demonstrates the existence of an assumption that disable people are 'inauthentic workers'.[123]

The last of Burgdorf's examples of restrictive interpretations of entitlemer criteria again relates to the question of whether or not a person is a 'qualifie« individual with a disability.[124] He criticises a number of rulings according t which former employees, who have left employment due to the onset of impai ments, have been held not to be 'qualified' as they can no longer perform tk essential functions of the job. Consequently, such former employees have bee held to be outside the protective scope of the ADA and therefore unable to rely c that statute to challenge the denial to them of employment-related benefits suc as health insurance or pension plans.[125] As Judge Anderson has pointed out (in dissenting judgment), however, the 'counter-intuitive' and quite 'surprising' resu

---

[117] Burgdorf, '"Substantially Limited"' (n 99 above) 489–506.
[118] See eg the decision of the Third Circuit in *McNemar v Disney Stores Inc*, 91 F 3d 610 (3d C 1996), cert denied, 117 S Ct 958 (1997).
[119] *Cleveland v Policy Management Systems Corp*, 526 US 795, 119 S Ct 1597 (1999).
[120] Diller, 'Judicial Backlash, the ADA and the Civil Rights Model' (n 79 above) 48.
[121] M-K Zachary, 'Between A Rock and Hard Place—Disability Benefits and/or ADA Relie (1997) *Labor Law Journal* 115.
[122] See eg *Cleveland v Policy Management Systems Corp*, 526 US 795 (1999).
[123] Stein, 'Same Struggle, Different Difference' (n 13 above) 604 and accompanying text. See al V Schultz, 'Life's Work' (2000) 100 *Columbia Law Review* 1881.
[124] Burgdorf, '"Substantially Limited"' (n 99 above) 506–11 and 554–9.
[125] See eg the decision of the Eleventh Circuit in *Gonzales v Garner Food Services Inc*, 89 F 3d 15 (11th Cir 1996); 104 F 3d 373 (11th Cir 1996); 117 S Ct 1822 (1997). See also, for similar reasoning the context of s 504 of the Rehabilitation Act 1973, *Beauford v Father Flanagan's Boys' Home*, 831 F. 768 (8th Cir 1987).

of such rulings is to confer ADA protection on the fringe benefits of current employees but to terminate that protection abruptly when an employee leaves— because of retirement or disability—'at precisely the time that those benefits are designed to materialize'.[126]

Through these 'illogical and counter-intuitive doctrines', Burgdorf reports, cases in which people believe they have experienced serious discrimination are derailed.[127] Not only is the result 'antithetical to the purposes of the federal non-discrimination statutes' but it positively

> suggests to employers that there are huge loopholes that will enable them to escape with impunity when they have violated the requirements of non-discrimination laws.[128]

The focus of scrutiny is not the alleged discriminatory conduct of employers and others but the medical conditions and abilities of claimants. This approach is far more consistent with assessments of entitlement to welfare benefits[129] than it is with a meaningful attempt to gauge whether there has been a violation of principles of equality and non-discrimination.

Elaborating on this point, Diller has argued that ADA claimants appear to many judges not as 'potential victims' but as 'supplicants' whose 'moral worth and need' must be probed before benefits may be dispensed to them.[130] If found to be unworthy, they risk being regarded merely as 'whiners making excuses for poor performance' and attempting to 'capitalize' on their medical conditions.[131] So intense and intrusive is the level of scrutiny directed at claimants that the process has been likened to rape cases in which the victims often feel that they are themselves on trial.[132] Diller concludes:

> In sum, rather than viewing ADA cases as disputes about fundamental civil rights, many judges treat them as requests for special benefits made by employees who are performing poorly. They are both unsympathetic to these requests and, at some level, annoyed that Congress has compelled the federal judiciary to hear them. The result has been a body of case law that is disastrous for ADA plaintiffs.[133]

In Britain, the DDA also requires claimants to establish that they are (or have been) disabled as a precondition of protection. The DDA definition is narrower than that of the ADA in that it does not cover cases in which a person, though not

---

[126] *Gonzales v Garner Food Services Inc*, 89 F 3d 1523 at 1532 (11th Cir, 1996).
[127] Burgdorf, '"Substantially Limited"' (n 99 above) 567.
[128] *Ibid.*
[129] See further eg D Stone, *The Disabled State* (London, Macmillan, 1985); and J Handler and Y Hasenfeld, *The Moral Construction of Poverty* (Newbury Park, Sage Publications, 1991).
[130] Diller, 'Judicial Backlash, the ADA and the Civil Rights Model' (n 79 above) 48.
[131] *Ibid*, 50. See generally WK Olson, *The Excuse Factory: How Employment Law is Paralyzing the American Workplace* (New York, The Free Press, 1997) 114.
[132] Burgdorf, '"Substantially Limited"' (n 99 above) 561.
[133] *Ibid*, 50–51. See also, for the view that the US judiciary has resorted to an impressive degree of inventiveness in order to develop the law in a manner which stifles its fundamental aims, B Poitras Tucker, 'The ADA's Revolving Door: Inherent Flaws in the Civil Rights Paradigm' (2001) 62 *Ohio State Law Journal* 335.

actually disabled, is discriminated against because they are wrongly perceived to be disabled. Further, the DDA, unlike the ADA, contains an explicit requirement that impairments must be long-term.[134] Various other significant limitations on the scope of disability imposed by the DDA were removed by the DDA 2005.[135] On the other hand, some elements of the ADA's approach to definition and qualification which have proved to be particularly problematic are absent from the DDA. There is, for instance, no need for a claimant to demonstrate that, in addition to being disabled, they are 'qualified' in the ADA sense.[136] Ability to work is not included in the list of normal day-to-day activities that must be substantially affected by an impairment.[137] Although its absence has avoided some of the difficulties which have arisen under the ADA, problems have been created by the question of whether an impairment which affects one's ability to carry out a particular job should be regarded as affecting one's ability to carry out a normal day-to-day activity.[138]

The DDA definition of disability, like that of the ADA, has generated a considerable body of case law and it has caused more DDA cases to perish than has any other reason. Failure to comply with it has been estimated to defeat almost a fifth of all DDA tribunal cases.[139] Evidence also suggests that, at least in employment disputes, defendants often deliberately choose to challenge the disabled status of a claimant as a strategy designed to intimidate and pressurise them into settling or withdrawing the case.[140]

---

[134] For discussion of some of the difficulties which have arisen in the application of this requirement, see F Reynold and A Palmer, 'What Place for Hindsight in Deciding Whether a Claimant was Disabled?' (2007) 36 *Industrial Law Journal* 486.

[135] See eg the need for a mental impairment to be 'clinically well-recognised' which was removed by the DDA 2005 s 18.

[136] For criticism of the 'qualified' individual requirement under US law see eg Burgdorf, '"Substantially Limited"' (n 99 above) 421–3; A Silvers and MA Stein, 'Disability, Equal Protection, and the Supreme Court: Standing at the Crossroads of Progressive and Retrogressive Logic in Constitutional Classification' (2002) 35 *University of Michigan Journal of Law Reform* 81 at 121–3.

[137] DDA sch 1 para 4(1).

[138] In *Quinlan v B&Q*, EAT/1386/97, for instance, a man who could not lift heavy weights at work following heart surgery was held not to be disabled because he was capable of lifting everyday objects. This sharp division between work activities and normal day-to-day activities has, however, been diluted by subsequent cases—see eg *Law Hospital NHS Trust v Rush* [2001] IRLR 611; and *Cruickshank v VAW Motorcast Ltd* [2002] IRLR 24.

[139] N Meagre et al, *Monitoring the Disability Discrimination Act 1995* (London, Department for Education and Employment, 1999) 126. See also, for criticism of the DDA definition, C Woodhams and S Corby, 'Defining Disability in Theory and Practice: A Critique of the British Disability Discrimination Act 1995' (2003) 32 *Journal of Social Policy* 1.

[140] J Hurstfield et al, *Monitoring the Disability Discrimination Act 1995: Phase 3* (London, DRC 2004) 121. See also the discussion in N Meager and J Hurstfield, 'Legislating for Equality: Evaluating the Disability Discrimination Act 1995' in A Roulstone and C Barnes (eds), *Working Futures? Disabled People, Policy and Social Inclusion* (Bristol, The Policy Press, 2005) 83–4.

The DDA definition cases are not free of unnecessarily restrictive and technical judicial reasoning.[141] Nonetheless such reasoning, particularly in the judgments of higher-level courts, appears to be a great deal less prevalent than it has been in ADA definition cases. Judicial calls for the DDA's definition of disability to be interpreted purposively,[142] however, have been hampered by highly technical and restrictive statutory language.

The tendency to equate reasonable adjustments with welfare benefits does not therefore emerge as clearly from British cases as it does from US jurisprudence. Such an assumption, however, appears to underlie the essential framework of the DDA with its strict definitional requirements. Neither does it appear to be very far removed from observations, such as those of Baroness Hale in *Archibald*, that the DDA requires reasonable adjustments 'to cater for the special needs of disabled people'.[143] Her Ladyship added, quite correctly (if regrettably), that the fact that DDA protection is expressly limited to those whose impairments have a substantial and long-term adverse effect on their ability to carry out day-to-day activities means that 'the Act is concerned with addressing the special needs of those with serious handicaps'[144] and not with the prohibition of discrimination against people with a lesser degree of impairment. While the actual decision in *Archibald* reflected an expansive and purposive approach, such language may reveal underlying assumptions encouraged by the structure of the statute, which—as the American experience demonstrates—may prove to be stifling and counter-productive in the long-term. It is disappointing that such language appears in the judgments of Baroness Hale because her understanding of disability equality issues, as reflected in her discussion of the relevant law in *Lewisham*[145] and in *Archibald*,[146] seems to be stronger than that of most, if not all, of the other law lords.

The absence of a statutory definition of disability does not guarantee an expansive interpretation of the phrase. This is illustrated by the decision of the European Court of Justice in *Chacón Navas v Eurest Colectividades SA*.[147] It was

---

[141]   See eg EAT ruling in *McNicol v Balfour Rail Maintenance* [2002] IRLR 711 (CA); and the first instance rulings in *Vicary v Commissioner of Police of the Metropolis* [2001] ICR 105 (ET); *Abadeh v BT* [2001] ICR 156 (ET); and *Kirton v Tetrosyl* [2003] IRLR 353 (ET).

[142]   See eg *Goodwin v Patent Office* [1999] IRLR 44; *Vicary v British Telecommunications* [1999] IRLR 680; and *Paterson v Commissioner of Police of the Metropolis* [2007] IRLR 763 (EAT) [70].

[143]   *Archibald v Fife Council* [2004] UKHL 32, [2004] IRLR 197, [47]. See also her judgment in *Lewisham LBC v Malcolm* [2008] UKHL 43 where, at [75], the phrase 'special needs' is repeated and where she describes the *Novacold* interpretation of disability-related discrimination (which she endorses) as requiring landlords, employers and others to be 'kinder' to disabled people than to others.

[144]   *Ibid*, [48].

[145]   *Lewisham v Malcolm* [2008] UKHL 43.

[146]   *Archibald v Fife Council* [2004] UKHL 42.

[147]   Case C-13/05 *Chacón Navas v Eurest Colectividades SA*, [2006] ECR I-6467. For criticism, see L Waddington, 'Case C-13/05 *Chacón Navas* v *Eurest Colectividades SA*, judgment of the Grand Chamber of 11 July 2006' (2007) 44 *Common Market Law Review* 487; and DL Hosking, 'A High Bar for EU Disability Rights' (2007) 36 *Industrial Law Journal* 228.

there required to provide guidance on the extent to which sickness should b
regarded as a 'disability' for the purposes of the Framework Directive. Althoug
that Directive contains no definition of 'disability', the Court ruled that the terr
should be understood to require satisfaction of three conditions which are no
dissimilar from those of the DDA. First, there must be a physical or menta
impairment which causes a limitation of functioning; second, that limitatio
must restrict their ability to participate in professional life; and, third, th
impairment must be likely to continue for a long time.[148] The decision of th
European Court of Justice in *Coleman v Attridge Law*,[149] however, reveals a
expansive approach to the issue of extending protection from disability discrimi
nation to non-disabled people who are directly discriminated against or harasse
on grounds of the disability of another.

3.2 Response

3.2.1 Equality

The obvious response to suggestions that reasonable accommodations are, i
effect, special disability benefits akin to welfare entitlements is the counter
assertion that they are in fact an integral element of non-discrimination. Descrip
tions of disabled people, and their rights to be free from discrimination, a
'special' are unhelpful and potentially dangerous.[150] They threaten to undermin
the idea that the claims of disabled people to non-discriminatory treatmer
(including reasonable accommodation) are simply claims for equal consideratio
and respect. They are claims grounded not in principles of benevolence or charit
but in notions of equality and social justice.

The relationship between equality and reasonable accommodation will b
explored in more detail in the next Section and will therefore not be furthe
developed here. The remainder of this Section will be devoted instead to
consideration of factors which might foster the view that reasonable accommo
dations are akin to welfare benefits and to methods by which such factors, c
their problematic tendencies, might be tackled.

3.2.2 Protected Class Approach

As has been explained above, equating reasonable accommodation with welfar
benefits has an impact on decisions as to who falls within the limits of th
statutorily-defined protected class and thereby gains entitlement. In this way, th

---

[148] *Ibid*, [43] and [45].
[149] Case C-303/06 *Coleman v Attridge Law*, 17 July 2008.
[150] See further PJ Rubin, 'Equal Rights, Special Rights, and the Nature of Antidiscrimination Law
(1998) 97 *Michigan Law Review* 564 at 567; Burgdorf, '"Substantially Limited"' (n 99 above) 534
and 568; and JA Nelson (ed), *The Disabled, the Media, and the Information Age* (Westport C
Greenwood Press, 1994).

statute is interpreted and developed in ways which may not always have been intended by the original drafters. Further, as was suggested above in the context of Britain, the structure and language of a statute may themselves nurture the view that reasonable accommodation represents a form of special disability benefit.

Commentators have argued that the very existence of a narrowly-defined protected class injects a welfare-ist dimension into anti-disability-discrimination legislation.[151] In the United States, the decision to include the protected class approach in section 504 of the Rehabilitation Act 1973 appears to have been heavily influenced by its location within a statute dealing principally with rehabilitation.[152] For reasons of consistency and simplicity, calls for an alternative approach prohibiting discrimination 'on the basis' of having a disability[153] were rejected, and the protected class approach was carried over into the ADA. Its presence in the ADA then undoubtedly contributed to its inclusion in the British DDA. The decision of Congress to import the Rehabilitation Act approach into the ADA, however, has been condemned as 'negligent' in view of the fact that

> although the definition itself was meant to be neutral, that is, not read within the context of the Rehabilitation Act, the legal-cultural accretion of established welfarist classification continues to influence post-ADA Supreme Court decisions. Accordingly, the prevailing characterization of people with disabilities as a group is one of incompetence.[154]

A well-defined protected class is clearly essential for purposes of defining entitlement to rehabilitation and welfare. In that context, particular benefits and programmes will be targeted at specific categories of people and it is therefore essential that there should be a mechanism for determining whether or not a particular applicant falls within a relevant category. In this context, then, a degree of scrutiny of the nature and severity of the impairments of an applicant, together with the ways in which it has affected their ability to perform various functions, will be inevitable.

In civil rights legislation, however, the existence of such a class is likely to prove problematic. As considered above, it prevents people from challenging discriminatory behaviour if their impairments are not deemed to be sufficiently serious to bring them within the designated class, even though they are regarded as sufficiently serious to attract less favourable treatment at the hands of alleged

---

[151] Burgdorf, '"Substantially Limited"' (n 99 above) 426–7. See also Silvers and Stein, 'Disability, Equal Protection, and the Supreme Court' (n 136 above).

[152] See further Burgdorf, '"Substantially Limited"' (n 99 above) 420–21.

[153] See eg Burgdorf, '"Substantially Limited"' (n 99 above); and C Bell, 'Eliminating Discrimination Against Physically and Mentally Handicapped Persons: A Statutory Blueprint' (1984) 8 *Mental and Physical Disability Law Reporter* 64; and *On the Threshold of Independence* (National Council on the Handicapped, Washington DC, 1988).

[154] Silvers and Stein, 'Disability, Equal Protection, and the Supreme Court' (n 136 above) 85.

discriminators. This gives free rein to employers and others to discriminate against people with impairments provided that their impairments are not judged to be too serious.

Further, the need to establish membership of a protected class inevitably focuses attention on the characteristics and circumstances of plaintiffs, thereby endorsing medicalised investigations into atypical biology. The demoralising and often embarrassing experience of being the subject of such courtroom investigations is an experience which victims of other forms of discrimination are spared. As Burgdorf observes, in cases of race, religious or sex discrimination, the focus would not be on

> the relative darkness or lightness of the plaintiff's skin, how religious the plaintiff was, how feminine or masculine the plaintiff was or on the plaintiff's job performance (unless the pleadings raised poor performance as a justification for the defendants' conduct),[155]

but would instead be on the allegedly discriminatory conduct of the defendant. The result of the designated class requirement is a shift of focus away from the allegedly discriminatory conduct and towards the medical condition of an individual. It thus runs entirely counter to the thrust of the social model of disability, which draws attention to the ways in which people with impairments are disabled by socially-created barriers.[156] Under the protected class approach the existence and nature of such barriers, together with the practicality of their removal, are issues that take second place to those relating to the existence, nature and impact of particular medical conditions.[157]

The current approach reflects a 'minority group' conception of disability. This is enshrined in the preamble of the ADA, according to which disabled people constitute a

> discrete and insular minority, who have been faced with restrictions and limitations, subjected to a history of purposeful unequal treatment, and relegated to a position of political powerlessness in our society.[158]

While this conception of disability was highly influential in the campaign for civil rights legislation in the United States,[159] it is problematic—not least because of

---

[155] Burgdorf, '"Substantially Limited"' (n 99 above) 560–61. See, for discussion of the stereotypes arising from atypical biology which have plagued other groups seeking protection from anti-discrimination legislation, Silvers and Stein, 'Disability, Equal Protection, and the Supreme Court' (n 136 above); and Stein, 'Same Struggle, Different Difference' (n 13 above).

[156] See generally JE Bickenbach, 'The ADA v the Canadian Charter of Rights: Disability Rights and the Social Model of Disability' and A Silvers, 'The Unprotected: Constructing Disability in the Context of Antidiscrimination Law' both in Pickering Francis and Silvers (eds), *Americans with Disabilities* (n 42 above).

[157] See further A Asch, 'Critical Race Theory, Feminism, and Disability: Reflections on Social Justice and Personal Identity' in PD Blanck (ed), *Disability Rights* (Aldershot, Ashgate, 2005) 449–50.

[158] See Americans with Disabilities Act 1990, 42 USC s 12101(a)(1) and (7).

[159] See generally IK Zola, 'Towards the Necessary Universalizing of a Disability Policy' (1989) 67 *Millbank Quarterly* 401; RK Scotch, 'Politics and Policy in the History of the Disability Rights

its dependence on some rigid differentiation between those who are disabled and those who are not. There is therefore an increasing move towards a 'human variation' or 'universalist' conception of disability.[160] Such a conception stresses the fact that impairment is not confined to a discrete and separate class and the fact that the entire population benefits from societal structures constructed so as to facilitate access and inclusion because

> we are all abnormal, disabled, impaired, deformed and functionally limited, because, truth be told, that is what it means to be a human being.[161]

A universalist approach, however, is inconsistent with strict definitional requirements such as those which currently operate in the ADA and in the DDA.[162]

In summary, the need to show that one falls within a tightly circumscribed definition of disability before one can claim the protection of non-discrimination law appears to foster (as well as to emerge from) the idea that the entitlement in question is equivalent to some form of welfare benefit reserved only for members of a special protected class. Any solution to this problem needs to refocus attention on the discriminatory conduct or exclusionary barriers, instead of on the impairments of an individual. This might be achieved by removing such restrictions on the statutory notion of 'disabled person' as the need for an impairment to be long-term or to have a substantial effect on ability to carry out day-to-day activities.[163] Protection should also be extended to those who are discriminated against because, although not themselves disabled, they are regarded as having an impairment or because of their association with a person who has an impairment[164]—a measure which may, in any event, be required in order to ensure compliance with the Employment Equality Directive as interpreted in *Coleman*.[165] Only if the DDA is amended in these ways will it reflect the notion that '[n]on-discrimination is a guarantee of equality. It is not a special service reserved for a select few'.[166]

Movement' (1989) 67 *Milbank Quarterly* 380; and H Hahn, 'Antidiscrimination Laws and Social Research on Disability: The Minority Group Perspective' (1996) 14 *Behavioral Sciences and the Law* 41.

[160] See eg R Scotch and K Shriner, 'Disability as Human Variation: Implications for Policy' (1997) 549 *Annals of the American Academy of Political and Social Science* 148; M Stein, 'Disability Human Rights' (2007) 95 *California Law Review* 75; and A Asch, 'Critical Race Theory, Feminism, and Disability: Reflections on Social Justice and Personal Identity' (2001) 62 *Ohio State Law Journal* 391.

[161] JE Bickenbach, 'Minority Rights or Universal Participation: The Politics of Disablement' in M Jones and LA Basser-Marks (eds), *Disability, Divers-ability and Legal Change* (London, Martinus Nijhoff, 1999) 114.

[162] See generally Fredman, 'Disability Equality' (n 52 above) 206.

[163] As was recommended by the DRC in *Consultation on Definition of Disability in Anti-Discrimination Law* (London, DRC, 2006).

[164] As was also recommended by the DRC, *ibid*; and also by B Hepple, M Coussey and T Choudhury, *Equality: A New Framework* (Oxford, Hart Publishing, 2000) para 2.68.

[165] Case C-303/06 *Coleman v Attridge Law*, OJ C 237 of 30 September 2006, p 6 (17 July 2008).

[166] Burgdorf, '"Substantially Limited"' (n 99 above) 568.

3.2.3 Individualised Nature of Reasonable Accommodations

Another factor which may foster the tendency to regard reasonable accommodations as a form of subsidy or welfare benefit is the fact that they are frequently highly individualised in nature. This is particularly the case in the contexts of employment and education—the two areas which tend to be the most heavily litigated and therefore to occupy a predominant place in public consciousness. The process of identifying a reasonable accommodation in such cases will often involve a detailed consideration of the needs and circumstances of a particular disabled individual.

This process differs significantly, in nature and purpose, from that of determining whether an individual is disabled in the sense required in order to benefit from statutory coverage. Unlike the latter, its purpose is not the exclusionary one of filtering out potential claimants. Its purpose is, rather, to ensure that any accommodations made for a disabled individual will be appropriate to their needs and thus facilitate their efficiency and participation to the fullest extent possible.

Nevertheless, like the process of applying the definition of disability, it focuses attention on the particular disabled person and the effects of their impairment. It acknowledges their difference, albeit as an essential preliminary to the removal of relevant disabling barriers. Consequently, this process risks fostering the impression that disabled people are different from their non-disabled peers and in need of special treatment. There is a risk that provision made by way of reasonable accommodation will be perceived not as a practical manifestation of equality but as the provision of a specialised impairment-related aid (not far removed from a wheelchair or a white cane).

Individualised inquiries are clearly essential in any meaningful system of effective reasonable accommodation. The risk of misperception to which they might give rise, however, may be reduced. Two strategies by which this risk reduction might be achieved will now be outlined.

First, while retaining the current individualised inquiry process, more emphasis might be given to the group dimension of disability discrimination or to what is sometimes termed 'pan-disability theory'.[167] Such a strategy would help to dispel the assumption that disability is an entirely individualised problem emerging from the specific medical condition of a particular person. It would draw attention instead to the disabling impact of procedures and designs developed without regard to the needs of people who deviate from the physical or mental norm. In so doing, it would focus attention on the negative impact of externally-created barriers and encourage the view that those barriers, rather than the individual's own impairments, should be identified as the primary source of the relevant problem.

---

[167] See, eg MA Stein and ME Waterstone, 'Disability, Disparate Impact, and Class Actions' (2006) 56 *Duke Law Journal* 861.

In the United States, it has been argued that this sharpened focus on pan-disability issues should be achieved through greater reliance on principles of disparate impact (or indirect discrimination) and class action in the employment field.[168] In Britain, the DDA's concept of anticipatory reasonable adjustment is already at work in non-employment fields. Its clear focus on the group dimension of disabling barriers is now supplemented by the public sector disability equality duty. As has already been argued, however, effort must continue to be devoted to maximising the reach and the effectiveness of these tools. Anticipatory reasonable adjustment duties should therefore be extended to the arena of employment. The introduction of a system permitting representative or class actions would also have considerable potential to emphasise and tackle the group dimension of disabling and exclusionary barriers.[169]

Lewisham London Borough Council v Malcolm[170] contains a heart-breaking example of the low profile which is sometimes given to group-based mechanisms for tackling disability discrimination. The following passage appears in the judgment of Lord Brown:

> Disabilities are too diverse in their nature for the concept to lend itself easily to the notion of indirect discrimination—the imposition of requirements ostensibly neutral but in fact having a disproportionate and unjustifiable impact on those sought to be protected. What indirect discrimination against the disabled would equate to, say, a requirement for employees to be at least six feet tall—presumably indirectly discriminatory against both women (sex) and those of Asian origins (race)? The needs of the disabled are rather different.[171]

In addition to extending and strengthening the anticipatory reasonable adjustment duty, it is therefore important that efforts are made to raise awareness of it amongst the judiciary.

Secondly, awareness-raising efforts might usefully be devoted to the promotion of a social model understanding of disability and its implications for reasonable adjustment law. According to this, adjustments to the external environment, to equipment or to policies or practices are required, not principally because of the impairments of a person whom they would otherwise disadvantage, but because they were initially designed for use only by non-disabled people. The reasonable accommodation duty is thus a mechanism through which the legitimacy of providing only for an unstated non-disabled norm may be challenged.[172] Rather

---

[168] *Ibid.*
[169] See ch 4, fnn 184–6 above and accompanying text.
[170] *Lewisham LBC v Malcolm* [2008] UKHL 43.
[171] *Ibid*, [114].
[172] See generally RK Murphy, 'Reasonable Accommodation and Employment Discrimination under Title I of the Americans with Disabilities Act' (1991) 64 *Southern California Law Review* 1607; M Minow, *Making All the Difference: Inclusion, Exclusion and American Law* (Ithaca NY, Cornell University Press, 1990); and M Minow, 'Learning to Live with the Dilemma of Difference: Bilingual and Special Education' (1985) 48 *Law and Contemporary Problems* 160.

than an instrument of charity or welfare, it is thus a potentially powerfu instrument of social change. This point is expressed succinctly by Burgdorf in th following words:

> Properly understood ... reasonable accommodation is not a special service for ind viduals with disabilities. It is a method for eliminating discrimination that inheres i the planning and organization of societal opportunities based on expectations c certain physical and mental characteristics. It is a necessary device for achieving rea equal opportunity, not deviating from it.[173]

This, again, is an issue which will be explored further in the following Section.

4. More Than Equal Treatment

4.1   Resistance

Some reference has already been made, in the preceding chapter, to the tendenc to refer to reasonable adjustment or accommodation as a form of positive actior positive discrimination or, in US terminology, 'affirmative action'. As will b evident from that discussion, the lack of precision as to the conceptual bounda ries of these various notions hampers any attempt to achieve clarity and resolu tion. Nevertheless, an attempt was made in that chapter to impose some structur on the debate and to situate reasonable adjustment within the broader concep tual landscape of positive measures designed to counter disadvantage. It wa argued that it should be regarded as a clear non-discrimination requirement an that it should not therefore be classified as a form of positive action or positiv discrimination. The focus of the current discussion is not the complex interpla between these concepts as such, but the view which underlies many of th attributions of labels such as 'positive discrimination' or 'affirmative action' t obligations to make reasonable adjustments or accommodations—the view tha what is required is more favourable treatment than that which is received b others and treatment which goes beyond what would be required by principles c equality.

There is clearly a significant overlap between the tendency to regard reasonab accommodation as a form of more than equal treatment and the view, examine in the previous Section, that reasonable adjustment or accommodation const tutes some form of special disability specific benefit. The division inserte between this Section and the last may thus appear somewhat artificial. It hoped, however, that considering these two closely related and often overlappin perspectives separately will facilitate clarity of analysis.

---

[173] Burgdorf, "'Substantially Limited'" (n 99 above) 533.

It should be stressed at the outset that the categorisation of reasonable accommodation as a form of more-than-equal treatment does not necessarily result in resistance to the imposition of relevant duties. A number of commentators have insisted that reasonable accommodation duties are a form of more favourable treatment whilst advocating powerfully for their retention and development.[174] The view that reasonable accommodation goes beyond the dictates of equality, however, often triggers resentment and resistance, and it is for this reason that it will be considered here.

Reasonable accommodation obligations require duty-bearers to identify barriers which physical structures or standard processes and procedures may create for disabled people, and to take reasonable steps to remove them. The structures and processes in question, although obstructive to a disabled person, will generally be unproblematic for people without impairments, as it is for such people that they will have been designed. Different aspects of the environment will present different obstacles for different people with different impairments. Further, different people with the same impairment may require different measures in order to remove the same barrier. One visually impaired person, for instance, may need to access printed material in Braille whereas another may need to access it electronically or via an audio recording. Thus, while many barriers may be anticipated, the reactive element of reasonable accommodation duties requires duty-bearers to take into account all the circumstances of a particular individual (including the barriers which disadvantage them) and to respond appropriately.[175]

Duty-bearers are therefore unquestionably required to notice and to respond to physical and mental impairment. They cannot simply insist on providing all customers, employees, pupils or members with identical facilities and identical treatment. In this sense, reasonable accommodation duties require duty-bearers to treat disabled people differently from how they treat others.

The differential treatment required by reasonable accommodation duties constitutes the soil in which the more-than-equal treatment view of reasonable accommodation is rooted. It is nurtured by the popular belief that non-discrimination rules are essentially concerned with the prohibition of treatment which differentiates between people on the basis of a prohibited ground. This belief, together with its consequences, are described by Jolls in the following words:

---

[174] See eg Schwab and Willborn, 'Reasonable Accommodation of Workplace Disabilities' (n 13 above).

[175] See, for further discussion of the highly individualised nature of many reasonable accommodation claims, PS Miller, 'Disability Civil Rights and a New Paradigm for the Twenty-First Century: The Expansion of Civil Rights Beyond Race, Gender and Age' (1998) 1 *University of Pennsylvania Journal of Labor and Employment Law* 511; and Karlen and Rutherglen, 'Disabilities, Discrimination and Reasonable Accommodation' (n 61 above) 10–11.

> The canonical idea of 'antidiscrimination' ... condemns the differential treatment of otherwise similarly situated individuals on the basis of race, sex, national origin, or other protected characteristics. Starting from this perspective, legal requirements that actors take affirmative steps to 'accommodate' the special, distinctive needs of particular groups, such as individuals with disabilities, by providing additional benefits or allowances to them strike many observers as fundamentally distinct from, broader than, and often less legitimate than legal requirements within the canonical 'antidiscrimination' category.[176]

Consequently, reasonable accommodation obligations are often set firmly apart from what are regarded as 'real anti-discrimination'[177] laws, which feature only the more familiar notions of direct and indirect discrimination (or, in US terminology, disparate treatment and disparate impact).[178] This division is summed up succinctly by Schwab and Willborn.[179] They suggest that the dominant thrust of sex and race legislation is a 'sameness' model of discrimination, according to which it is required that people are to be treated in the same way regardless of their sex or race. The distinctive approach of disability legislation, however, is a 'difference' model, which requires employers and others 'to treat individuals with disabilities differently and more favourably than others'.[180]

Thus, while traditional anti-discrimination laws are felt to require equal treatment, reasonable accommodation laws are regarded as requiring something more. Classic anti-discrimination laws are regarded as cost-free in that they will operate only where a claimant is similarly situated to, and thus equally as productive as, relevant comparators. A reasonable accommodation law, on the other hand, 'necessarily entails an element of more favourable treatment'.[181] It requires duty-bearers to incur costs and is accordingly regarded as redistributive in nature.[182] Statutes such as the ADA and the DDA are thus felt to go 'well beyond' what is required by traditional civil rights laws and to mandate the

---

[176] Jolls, 'Antidiscrimination and Accommodation' (n 13 above) 643 (footnotes omitted).

[177] *Erickson v Board of Governors of State Colleges and Universities for Northeastern Illinois University*, 207 F 3d 945 at 951 (7th Cir 2000) (Easterbrook J).

[178] See eg Rosen, 'Disability Accommodation and the Labor Market' (n 17 above) 21; S Issacharoff and J Nelson, 'Discrimination with a Difference: Can Employment Discrimination Law Accommodate the Americans with Disabilities Act?' (2001) 79 *North Carolina Law Review* 307; Karlen and Rutherglen, 'Disabilities, Discrimination and Reasonable Accommodation' (n 61 above); and Schwab and Willborn, 'Reasonable Accommodation of Workplace Disabilities' (n 13 above).

[179] Schwab and Willborn, 'Reasonable Accommodation of Workplace Disabilities' (n 13 above). See also Karlen and Rutherglen, 'Disabilities, Discrimination and Reasonable Accommodation' (n 61 above).

[180] Schwab and Willborn, 'Reasonable Accommodation of Workplace Disabilities' (n 13 above) 1200.

[181] *Archibald v Fife Council* [2004] UKHL 32, [2004] IRLR 197, [45] (Baroness Hale).

[182] See eg M Kelman, *Strategy or Principle? The Choice between Regulation and Taxation* (Michigan, The University of Michigan Press, 1999); M Kelman, 'Market Discrimination and Groups' (2001) 53 *Stanford Law Review* 833; Issacharoff and Nelson, 'Discrimination with a Difference' (n 178 above) 311–14; and, for general discussion of this approach, Stein, 'Same Struggle, Different Difference' (n 13 above).

'unequal treatment of equals'.[183] Diller sums up the impact of what he considers to be a widespread judicial adherence to this view as follows:

> Simply put, many judges are not strongly imbued with the notion that basic civil rights are at stake in ADA cases. Many do not harbour a sense that the employer who refuses to provide an accommodation has in fact violated someone's basic civil rights ... —judges are reluctant to label employers who fail to provide accommodations as wrongdoers for carrying on their business as usual.[184]

Those who adopt this view are often uncomfortable with the mandatory nature of reasonable accommodation. They argue that the nature of the entitlement it confers should be weaker than the entitlement conferred by real anti-discrimination legislation. The latter, which is concerned with ensuring equality and is cost-free, should confer unqualified rights to equal treatment. The former, however, is concerned with more favourable treatment and the redistribution of precious resources. The entitlements conferred by it should therefore be available on a basis which is not mandatory but rather highly discretionary and contingent on other competing claims and priorities.[185] This perception of reasonable accommodation as requiring more than equal treatment links it to concepts such as affirmative action and positive discrimination. Judicial, political and popular resistance to these concepts was explored in the previous chapter.

4.2 Response

The sharp divide between non-discrimination principles and reasonable adjustment or accommodation principles—which underlies many of the arguments that the latter go beyond equality—has been challenged. Jolls,[186] for instance, has drawn attention to the fact that indirect discrimination (or disparate impact) laws frequently operate as accommodation measures. She also demonstrates that, like the reasonable accommodation obligation, the direct discrimination (or disparate treatment) obligation to appoint the best-qualified person for a post despite their race, gender or religion, often entails costs. These may be incurred where the recruitment of members of a hitherto excluded group requires the provision of additional facilities (such as women's toilets or uniforms of different sizes) or where the presence of an employee from an under-represented group is likely to deter customers who have preferences for more conventional types of worker. She concludes that

---

[183] Weaver, 'Incentives versus Controls in Federal Disability Policy' (n 13 above) 6. See also Rosen, 'Disability Accommodation and the Labor Market' (n 17 above) 21.
[184] Diller, 'Judicial Backlash, the ADA and the Civil Rights Model' (n 79 above) 46.
[185] See eg Kelman, 'Market Discrimination and Groups' (n 182 above) 852.
[186] Jolls, 'Antidiscrimination and Accommodation' (n 13 above).

it is hard to resist the conclusion that antidiscrimination and accommodation are overlapping rather than fundamentally distinct categories, despite the frequent claims of commentators to the contrary.[187]

Stein has taken Joll's arguments a stage further.[188] He argues (as have European commentators such as Waddington and Hendriks[189]) that rather than regarding reasonable accommodation as a legal category which overlaps with that of non-discrimination, it should itself be categorised as a non-discrimination measure. Like Jolls, he rejects the validity of the distinction so often made between non-discrimination and accommodation on grounds that the latter, but not the former, imposes costs on employers and service providers. He asserts that all civil rights laws necessarily engender cost because their purpose is to 'change an instantiated and prejudicial status quo'[190] and this can be achieved only through the spending of money. Cost, therefore, cannot be used to differentiate accommodation in kind from non-discrimination. Like concepts used in sex and race legislation, reasonable accommodation is a legal tool developed in order to address the artificial exclusion of protected groups from employment, education and other areas of social life and, as such, it is a necessary and fundamental mechanism for achieving equality for disabled people.[191]

Nevertheless, for many there is a stumbling block in the way of accepting the notion that reasonable adjustment obligations are genuine non-discrimination devices, essential to securing meaningful equality for disabled people. This is the idea—so central to the view that reasonable adjustment goes beyond equality and requires more favourable treatment—that its aim is to remedy or compensate for deficiencies within the disabled individual him or herself. The usefulness and appropriateness of this individual deficiency view of reasonable adjustment however, are open to challenge. Such an understanding focuses attention on the way in which people with impairments deviate from the physical and mental norm around which societies have generally been constructed, and fosters the view that, in requesting adjustments, disabled people are demanding special concessions and facilities for which non-disabled people are not entitled to apply.

A number of commentators have urged that, in place of this individual deficiency-based approach to reasonable adjustment, an alternative approach should be adopted, according to which reasonable adjustment is regarded as

---

[187] *Ibid,* 645. See also H Hahn, 'Disputing the Doctrine of Benign Neglect: A Challenge to the Disparate Treatment of Americans with Disabilities' in Pickering Francis and Silvers (eds), *American with Disabilities* (n 42 above).

[188] Stein, 'Same Struggle, Different Difference' (n 13 above) 622.

[189] L Waddington and A Hendriks, 'The Expanding Concept of Employment Discrimination in Europe: From Direct and Indirect Discrimination to Reasonable Accommodation Discrimination' (2002) 18 *International Journal of Comparative Labour Law and Industrial Relations* 403.

[190] Stein, 'Same Struggle, Different Difference' (n 13 above) 599–604. See also Diller, 'Judicial Backlash, the ADA and the Civil Rights Model' (n 79 above) 47.

[191] See also A Silvers, 'Formal Justice' in A Silvers, D Wasserman and MB Mahowald (eds) *Disability, Difference, Discrimination. Perspectives on Justice in Bioethics and Public Policy* (Lanham, Rowman & Littlefield Publishers, 1998) 132.

means of addressing shortcomings in the external environment.[192] This alternative approach would be grounded on the acknowledgement that many of society's structures and procedures have been designed without regard to the needs of people with impairments. They are not therefore neutral in nature but operate, however unintentionally, to disadvantage and exclude disabled people. Thus, in line with a social model approach to disability, reasonable accommodation rules should be viewed as mechanisms for addressing extrinsic shortcomings in the external environment rather than as mechanisms for addressing intrinsic deficiencies within disabled individuals themselves. Arguably, the language of 'reasonable adjustment' or 'reasonable modification' directs attention to these extrinsic shortcomings more clearly than does the language of 'reasonable accommodation'. The latter phrase appears to direct attention to the need to accommodate particular individuals whereas the former phrases place more emphasis on the need to change the environment around them.

Adoption of this alternative social model approach to reasonable adjustment allows, and indeed requires, that concept to sit comfortably alongside other concepts of non-discrimination and equality law. Care should be taken, however, to ensure that such a conception of reasonable adjustment does not become fault dependent. Reasonable adjustment should clearly be available in cases where the relevant barrier would not exist had thought been given to the needs of disabled people during the design or development of the structure or procedure. However, reasonable adjustment should also be available in some cases in which every care was taken to comply with principles of universal design and hence to have regard to the needs of the majority of disabled people. Such a case might involve an employee whose visual impairment requires a degree of lighting which deviates significantly from that generally regarded as optimal, or a pupil whose physical impairment requires a desk or other piece of equipment to be designed on a more individual basis. Although the avoidance and removal of anticipated barriers will greatly reduce the need to make reasonable adjustments on an individualised responsive basis, it will never entirely remove that need.

Once reasonable adjustment is perceived to be a means of removing such externally-created obstacles as it is reasonable to remove, the importance of its role in creating equality of opportunity for disabled people becomes apparent.[193] A reasonable adjustment to a building (such as the installation of a lift or a

---

[192] See eg Murphy, 'Reasonable Accommodation and Employment Discrimination under Title I of the Americans with Disabilities Act' (n 172 above); C Feldblum, 'Antidiscrimination Requirements of the ADA' in LO Gostin and HA Beyer (eds), *Implementing the Americans with Disabilities Act: Rights and Responsibilities of All Americans* (Baltimore, Brookes, 1993) 36–7; Burgdorf, '"Substantially Limited"' (n 99 above) 533; Silvers, 'Formal Justice' (n 191 above) 132; Diller, 'Judicial Backlash, the ADA and the Civil Rights Model' (n 79 above) 41; and Stein, 'Same Struggle, Different Difference' (n 13 above) fnn 18–30.

[193] It is often suggested that the underlying rationale of reasonable accommodation duties is the promotion of equality of opportunity. See eg Quinn, 'The Human Rights of People with Disabilities Under EU Law' (n 67 above) 291–2; P Blanck, E Hill, CD Siegal and M Waterstone, *Disability Civil Rights Law and Policy* (St Paul Mn, West Group, a Thomson Business, 2004) paras 23.6–23.7.

ramp), or to a timetable (such as the rescheduling of a class to a ground-floor room) will grant a person with physical impairments the opportunity to attend a course alongside her non-disabled peers. Without such adjustments, however, a flight of stairs would deny her that opportunity while having no effect on the opportunity available to others. In the absence of a reasonable adjustment requirement, the scheduling of a course at the top of a flight of steps constitutes as effective a ban on wheelchair users as does the presence of an eligibility criterion that students must have no mobility impairments.[194] A philosophy according to which the latter, but not the former, is regarded as a violation of equality principles would thus appear to be superficial and unjust. What is at issue here is essentially the difference between a strictly formal notion of equality, in which identical treatment is required, and one which is more substantive in nature.

The tendency to regard equality as demanding the same, and not different, treatment is thus overly restrictive. Indeed, insistence on identical treatment, against the backdrop of a society largely constructed without regard to people with impairments, would inevitably perpetuate inequality and exclusion. It would mean requiring people with physical impairments to access their bank or shop via steps they were unable to negotiate; it would mean requiring people with visual impairments to take examinations via the medium of print which they were able neither to read nor write; and it would mean requiring people with hearing impairments to answer a standard telephone which they were unable to hear. The description of such identical treatment as 'equal' treatment thus appears somewhat ironic.

Burgdorf[195] has drawn attention to the fact that employers and service providers routinely devote considerable energy and resources to accommodating the needs of non-disabled employees and customers. Employees, for instance, may be provided with a comfortable office including a desk, a chair, good lighting, a plush carpet, a telephone and a computer. Customers may be provided with shopping trolleys, signs, audible announcements, parking facilities and shopping bags. Such accommodations are, he argues, generally based on the assumption that employees and customers will have standard physical and mental characteristics. Reasonable accommodation may thus be viewed as

> simply the same type of accommodation that is provided generally, but ... tailored to the actual needs of the particular [person] for whose benefit it is made.[196]

He concludes that

[194] See Silvers, 'Formal Justice' (n 191 above) 127.
[195] Burgdorf, '"Substantially Limited"' (n 99 above) 530–33.
[196] *Ibid*, 532.

requiring reasonable modifications of facilities, policies, practices and procedures is certainly not asking anything extraordinary or beyond the bounds of that which is already being supplied to other[s].[197]

It is, on this view, simply demanding that equal consideration be given to their needs and requirements—a demand which may be regarded as a demand for a more meaningful form of 'equal treatment' than that which would emerge from identical treatment.[198]

As has already been mentioned, the meaning of the concept of equality has generated a lively debate which has spanned many centuries. The emergence of non-discrimination law in the last half century has given rise to thought-provoking explorations of the concepts of equality that lie at its foundations. The purpose of this discussion, however, is not to outline or to probe these debates. Neither is it to defend the use of the principle of 'equality', as opposed to a principle such as 'dignity',[199] 'diversity'[200] or 'social inclusion'[201] as a guiding light in the development of reasonable adjustment duties. It is, rather, simply to demonstrate the illogicality and injustice which flow from regarding reasonable accommodation as distinct from, and less important than, more familiar non-discrimination concepts such as direct and indirect discrimination.

5. Reasonableness

5.1 Insufficiently Radical

5.1.1 Resistance

A number of proponents of disability equality have drawn attention to the relatively limited nature of the concept of reasonable adjustment or accommodation.[202] This concept, it is argued, is premised on the acceptance of a non-disabled norm from which some departures will be required in order to

---

[197] *Ibid*, 533.

[198] See further Waddington and Diller, 'Tensions and Coherence in Disability Policy' (n 81 above) 275. See also ch 2, section 2.2 above.

[199] G Moon and R Allen, 'Dignity Discourse in Discrimination Law: A Better Route to Equality?' [2006] *European Human Rights Law Review* 610.

[200] See further L Barmes and S Ashtiany, 'The Diversity Approach to Achieving Equality: Potential and Pitfalls' (2003) 4 *Industrial Law Journal* 32.

[201] Collins, 'Discrimination, Equality and Social Inclusion' (n 61 above).

[202] See in particular MT McCluskey, 'Rethinking Equality and Difference: Disability Discrimination in Public Transportation' (1988) 97 *Yale Law Journal* 863 at 871–2; MC Weber, 'Beyond the Americans with Disabilities Act: A National Employment Policy for Persons with Disabilities' (1998) 46 *Buffalo Law Review* 123 at fnn 120–23 and accompanying text; Waddington and Diller 'Tensions and Coherence in Disability Policy' (n 81 above) 275–8; and C O'Cinneide, 'A New Generation of Equality Legislation? Positive Duties and Disability Rights' in Lawson and Gooding (eds), *Disability Rights in Europe* (n 52 above) 223–4.

accommodate the needs of people with impairments. Because such departures will be required only if they are deemed to be 'reasonable', they will necessarily be modest and limited. A departure from normal practice will not be deemed reasonable, and therefore not required, if it would inflict an undue level of hardship on the duty-bearer.

The notion of 'reasonableness' thus represents a compromise. It anticipates and legitimises failures to achieve the ideal. The prominence of its role in disability equality legislation has therefore, on occasion, attracted the suspicion of campaigners for the complete removal of all disabling barriers.[203] Accordingly, unlike the forms of resistance to the concept of reasonable adjustment already considered, this one is to be found within elements of the Disability Movement itself.

5.1.2 Response

A number of points may be raised in order to address this concern. Before these are considered further, however, it is important to acknowledge that the term 'reasonable' is one which is inherently ambiguous and used in different jurisdictions to convey different meanings. In Britain the fact that an adjustment must be 'reasonable' requires it to be both one which is effective and also one which does not impose any form of undue burden on the duty-bearer. Interestingly, the Netherlands has chosen to implement reasonable accommodation duties, as is required by the Employment Equality Directive, in such a way as to make no reference to the term 'reasonable'. It simply requires that effective accommodations should be made provided that they do not impose a disproportionate burden on the duty-bearer.[204] The net substantive effect of this type of formulation may not differ from that achieved by formulations based on the notion of 'reasonableness'. The former type of formulation, however, may well help to allay some of the concerns which the term 'reasonable' incites in disability activists. The case for abandoning the reference to 'reasonable' in the British formulation nevertheless appears unconvincing given the familiarity of the term 'reasonable adjustment' and the minimal practical effect of such a change. Further, it seems likely that the focus of such concerns would simply shift from the concept of 'reasonableness' to that of 'disproportionate burden'.

In response to concerns about the insufficiently radical nature of reasonable adjustment duties it may be argued, first, that such duties should not be expected to operate alone. As is stressed by many of the commentators who have drawn

---

[203] See eg S Prideaux, *Good Practice for Providing Reasonable Access to the Physical Built Environment for Disabled People* (Leeds, Disability Press, 2006) 38–9.

[204] Act on Equal Treatment on the Grounds of Disability or Chronic Illness, Art 2. For discussion, see L Waddington, 'Reasonable Accommodation' in D Schiek, L Waddington and M Bell (eds), *Cases, Materials and Texts on National, Supranational and International Non-Discrimination Law* (Oxford, Hart Publishing, 2007) 658–62; and L Waddington, 'Implementing the Disability Provisions of the Framework Employment Directive: Room for Exercising National Discretion' in Lawson and Gooding (eds), *Disability Rights in Europe* (n 52 above) 126–8.

attention to the 'able-bodied orientation'[205] of concepts such as reasonable adjustment, it is important to supplement reasonable adjustment duties with measures such as affirmative or positive action programmes and appropriate income support. On this view, the fact that the concept of reasonable adjustment is inherently limited does not necessarily provide grounds for the argument that it is intrinsically deficient or dangerous. It does provide grounds, however, for the argument that, in order to break down disabling barriers effectively, it must be supplemented by the adoption of other methods for promoting disability equality, such as programmes of positive or affirmative action.

Second, reference should be made to the mandatory nature of reasonable adjustment in countries such as Britain and the United States. Without this obligatory quality, it is highly likely that the question of the reasonableness of the vast majority of potential adjustments would never even be considered. Without the qualification injected by the term 'reasonableness', it would clearly have been politically and economically impossible to place the concept of reasonable adjustment on a mandatory footing. The need to excuse duty-bearers from the responsibility of making unreasonable adjustments seems an entirely fair and sensible price to pay for placing them under an obligation to make reasonable ones.

Third, it may well be possible to incorporate specific standards, based on principles of universal design, within the concept of reasonable adjustment. Indeed, this occurs within the DDA. For example, duty-bearers, in certain situations, will not be deemed to have fulfilled their obligations to take reasonable steps to remove physical barriers unless they have complied with the accessibility standards laid down in the Building Codes.[206] This allows a degree of certainty, in the form of specific standards, to be injected into the apparently nebulous concept of reasonableness.

Fourth, it should be noted that whilst the concept of 'reasonableness' carries with it the flavour of compromise, it has the merit of obliging duty-bearers to apply their minds to the problem of disabling barriers and to think constructively about possible solutions. This, not unimportant, aspect of the duty must be discharged even in cases where the favoured adjustment is regarded as unreasonable.

5.2 Uncertainty

5.2.1 Resistance

It will by now be clear that British employers, service providers and others who are subjected to reasonable adjustment duties will be legally obliged to make any adjustment which is reasonable. They will, however, be under no obligation to

---

[205] Weber, 'Beyond the Americans with Disabilities Act' (n 202 above) 148.
[206] See ch 3, fnn 131–5 above and accompanying text.

make an adjustment which is unreasonable. The divide between reasonable a⟩ unreasonable thus separates cases in which failure to make an adjustment w result in potentially expensive liability for discrimination from those in which will be regarded as entirely legitimate. The point at which this divide is locate however, may be extremely difficult to predict and is likely to vary from case case in accordance with the particular factual scenarios in question. A simi⟩ predictive difficulty attends the US reasonable accommodation duties despite t fact that, unlike the British duties, they also employ a notion of 'undue har ship'.[207] In the words of Chai Feldblum,

> [u]nderstandably, businesses want certainty; it is hard for an employer to imagⁱ providing reasonable accommodation if the employer can never be sure whethe⟩ particular accommodation would ultimately be required under the law or not.[208]

So potent is the problem of determining the reasonableness of accommodatio⟩ that it has been described as the 'great unsettled question' of the ADA. Predictably, therefore, concern has been expressed about the uncertainty inhere⟩ in the notion of reasonable adjustment or accommodation.[210] This uncertainty is argued, is likely to result in conflicting expectations and understandings an⟩ consequently, in an unwelcome increase in the number of disputes and cases.

Although some guidance on the identification of relevant factors is available Britain, as well as in the United States, this does not rule out the possi⟩ relevance of other additional factors. Neither does it provide a ranking of t relative importance of the various factors or of their inter-relationship mᴏ generally. Richard Epstein, having noted the consequent uncertainty of su provisions, goes on to observe:

> Obviously the relevant considerations on cost and accommodation cannot be reduc to a formula of the sort that says 'stop at red lights' or 'pay your taxes in accordance w the rate structure found in Schedule X'. But the utter want of precision is not treated, it should be, as a reason for jettisoning the system altogether.[211]

5.2.2 Response

The first response to commentators such as Epstein, who argue that the uncᴇ tainty of 'reasonableness' renders concepts such as reasonable adjustme⟩

---

[207] See ch 3, fn 128 above and accompanying text.
[208] C Feldblum, 'Employment Protections' (1991) 69 *The Milbank Quarterly (Supplement)* 81 95. See also RA Vassel, 'The Americans with Disabilities Act: The Cost, Uncertainty and Inefficien⟩ (1994) 13 *Journal of Law and Commerce* 397 at 406–10.
[209] Karlen and Rutherglen, 'Disabilities, Discrimination and Reasonable Accommodation' (n above) 8.
[210] See eg Weaver, 'Incentives versus Controls in Federal Disability Policy' (n 13 above) 9–11; SB Epstein, 'In Search of a Bright Line: Determining when an Employer's Hardship Becomes "Undᵘ under the Americans with Disabilities Act' (1995) 48 *Vanderbilt Law Review* 391; and Epstᴇ *Forbidden Grounds* (n 14 above) 489–91.
[211] Epstein, *ibid*, 489–90.

unworkable and dangerous, is that it is this very uncertainty that generates the flexibility which is essential to any system of meaningful disability equality.[212] Without such flexibility, the needs and specific circumstances of individual disabled people would become legally invisible. Impairments, and their effects on the lives of particular people, are infinitely varied. If the law is to have any role in tackling the removal of disabling barriers, it is essential that it should provide some mechanism for the identification of the specific barriers which operate to disadvantage a particular disabled person. The reactive form of the reasonable adjustment duty is ideally suited to this task.[213]

A second response to accusations of unworkable uncertainty relates to forms of reasonable adjustment obligation other than the reactive duty. The degree of uncertainty associated with these other forms of duty is, on any view, unlikely to prove problematic. The anticipatory reasonable adjustment duty, for instance, requires attempts to be made to remove the barriers which are likely to be encountered by broad groups of disabled people whose needs may be anticipated. Because the particular circumstances of a specific disabled person will not be relevant in such cases, much clearer guidance (from Codes of Practice or bodies such as the Equality and Human Rights Commission) could and should be made available.

Further, as discussed in chapter four, it is possible to regard statutory schemes relating to issues such as maternity or parental leave as very particularised forms of the duty to make adjustments. In such schemes, there is virtually no uncertainty as to what is required of duty-bearers. The adjustments to which claimants are entitled are precisely defined and are the same for all members of the relevant group. The role played by the concept of reasonableness here is not an explicit one. The desire to require duty-bearers to take reasonable steps to accommodate the needs of particular sectors of society, however, would appear to provide the underlying rationale for such schemes.

Third, it is important to recognise that assessments of reasonableness are not confined to the operation of reasonable adjustment duties. In Britain, as in many other countries, the concept of reasonableness plays a powerful role in many other areas of law.[214] Its role is particularly prominent in rules governing liability for torts such as negligence. Judges and other arbitrators are accordingly no strangers to the general concept and its application. In the United States, scholars such as Schwab and Willborn[215] have criticised the tendency to regard the determination of the reasonableness of accommodations as a process which is entirely distinct from the determination of reasonableness for the purposes of

---

[212] See also on this point L Waddington, *Disability, Employment and the European Community* (Appledoorn Netherlands, MAKLU, 1995) 172–3.
[213] For criticism of this flexibility argument, see Epstein, 'In Search of a Bright Line' (n 210 above) 444–5.
[214] See further GP Fletcher, 'The Right and the Reasonable' (1985) 98 *Harvard Law Review* 949.
[215] Schwab and Willborn, 'Reasonable Accommodation of Workplace Disabilities' (n 13 above) 1264–8.

tort law. Greater reference to approaches used in the latter context would, in th
view, assist in the development of clearer guidance and standards in the form

5.3   The Inegalitarian Tendency of Reasonableness

5.3.1 Resistance

Reasonableness, then, is a concept with which judges and others required
arbitrate on the reasonableness of adjustments will be familiar. Schwab a
Willborn, as has just been mentioned, draw attention to the assistance which su
arbitrators may derive from the elaboration of reasonableness in other le
contexts. In particular, they refer to the attractiveness of reliance on the notio
'reasonable person', so familiar to tort lawyers, and attribute the appeal of t
construct to the fact that it is objective; that it directs attention away from t
passions of the particular disputants; that it balances interests from the perspe
tive of an average member of the community; and that it provides a means
laying down community standards with relevance extending far beyond t
particular facts of an individual case.[216] The appeal of such a construct, howev
is by no means universally acknowledged.

There is a powerful body of literature devoted to the exposure of the inega
tarian impact which the reasonable person (who grew out of the 'reasonal
man') has had on the various areas of law in which s/he has operated.[217] T
reasonable person is often endowed with qualities of averageness
ordinariness—attributes which are inherently conservative and therefore unlik
to yield results which alter or challenge the status quo. Thus, the reasona
person of half a century ago would not have anticipated that a blind pers
might walk unaccompanied along a pavement and would consequently ha
taken no additional steps to protect such a person from the risk of falling int
hole.[218] As a result, blind people injured by falling into such unprotected ho
would have no redress in negligence, and society at large would be given
responsibility to accept their presence (and their independent mobility) as
simple part of day-to-day existence.

The averageness of the reasonable person would thus appear to render him
inappropriate arbiter of delicate equality-related issues. Too often it will end
him with the very prejudices and stereotypical notions which equality law v
intended to challenge. As Mayo Moran explains,

---

[216]   *Ibid*, 1267–8.
[217]   See in particular M Moran, *Rethinking the Reasonable Person* (Oxford, Oxford University Pr
2003).
[218]   See *Haley v London Electricity Board* [1965] AC 778 (discussed in A Lawson, 'Mind the G
Normality, Difference and the Danger of Disablement through Law' in Lawson and Gooding (e
Disability Rights in Europe (n 52 above). See also, for an excellent discussion of this issue in the
context, J tenBroek, 'The Right to Live in the World: The Disabled in the Law of Torts' (1966)
California Law Review 841.

if the reasonable person characteristically holds common or ordinary beliefs and attitudes, then precisely because discrimination is constituted by widely shared beliefs about the lesser humanity of certain others, the reasonable person standard will actually tend to build discrimination into the legal standard itself.[219]

To date, the reasonable person has not made an appearance in the British law on reasonable adjustments. His introduction would, it is suggested, add little apart from additional complexity and potential confusion. His absence, however, does not free the subject of concerns such as those just outlined.

The broad, contextual nature of the notion of reasonableness grants, to the official arbitrators of relevant disputes, a powerful role in the application and development of the concept of reasonable adjustment. In Britain, this role falls to the Employment Tribunals and the courts. To date, judicial rulings on reasonable adjustments have been refreshingly expansive. However, unless careful and on-going efforts are made to counter the unconscious biases and misplaced assumptions which such people are likely to share with the general population, there will clearly be a danger that decisions on the reasonableness of adjustments will be unnecessarily restrictive and that they may even run counter to the very purpose of disability equality legislation.

5.3.2 Response

Acceptance of the validity of the concerns outlined here does not necessarily entail a rejection of the reasonableness standard. It does require a degree of caution and care, however. Such a standard should be adopted only where it is appropriate and where less flexible concepts would provide an inadequate solution. It is suggested, for reasons developed elsewhere in this chapter, that the flexibility and responsiveness of the notion of reasonableness does indeed constitute an essential element of adequate disability equality legislation.

Concerns about the non-egalitarian tendencies of reasonableness also demand the taking of appropriate steps to guard against the possibility that relevant decision-makers will inject their own subconscious prejudices and unfounded assumptions into their assessments of reasonableness. The British response of issuing Codes of Practice, setting out guidance on the practical application of the concept of reasonable adjustment, illustrated by clear examples, is one extremely important such step. Alone, however, it would be inadequate. Other essential measures include the raising of awareness, amongst arbitrators of reasonableness, of fundamental principles of disability equality (such as the social model) and the general aims of equality legislation. Purpose clauses have not traditionally

---

[219] 'The Reasonable Person and the Discrimination Inquiry' in S Tierney (ed), *Accommodating Cultural Diversity* (Aldershot, Ashgate, 2007) 149. See also R Allen and G Moon, 'Substantive Rights and Equal Treatment in Respect of Religion and Belief: Towards a Better Understanding of the Rights, and their Implications' [2000] *European Human Rights Law Review* 580 at 600–01.

accompanied British legislation. Nevertheless, the addition of a clearly and carefully drafted purpose clause to any future single Equality Act may well assist greatly in this regard.[220]

The Judicial Studies Board, responsible for the training of judges, has produced a reference guide on equality issues. The production of such guides, accompanied by relevant training events, is undoubtedly of great value. So too is experience and familiarity. So great is the value of the latter, indeed, that there is a very strong argument for allowing non-employment cases under the DDA to be heard by Employment (or 'Equality') Tribunals instead of the County or Sheriff Courts. The former have much greater experience of dealing with equality issues than do the latter and are therefore more likely to be familiar with the underlying principles and purposes of the legislation.[221] Nevertheless, the need for greater disability awareness, even in these tribunals, is stressed by empirical studies which indicate that tribunals and officials are often insufficiently aware of the access needs of disabled litigants and of the ways in which they may be disproportionately disadvantaged by the operation of standard legal processes and proceedings.[222]

6. Conclusion

In this chapter a range of issues has been addressed. What links them is their potential to impede the effective development and application of reasonable adjustment duties by generating bodies of resentment or resistance. The fact that there is little evidence to suggest that such bodies currently exist in Britain must not be permitted to induce complacency. Carelessness in relation to the issues discussed here might, at any time, cause them to lumber into being and to wreak havoc in the relatively young and tender pastures of disability equality law.

A number of specific legal reforms have been suggested. For the reasons set out above, these would help to minimise the risk of a backlash against reasonable adjustment obligations. They include: the reformulation of the current DDA definition of disability and its role as a threshold entry requirement for protection; the extension of anticipatory reasonable adjustment duties to employment; the use of a legislative purpose clause; the introduction of a mechanism for class or representative actions; and the transfer of DDA non-employment cases to Equality Tribunals. In addition, care must be taken to ensure that the mainstreaming function of the public sector disability equality duty is preserved and strengthened.

---

[220] This idea was rejected in Government Equalities Office, *The Equality Bill: Government Response to the Consultation* (London, Stationery Office, 21 July 2008) ch 14.

[221] Hepple, Coussey and Choudhury, *Equality: A New Framework* (n 164 above) paras 4.2–4.17. See generally ch 3, fnn 280–82 above and accompanying text.

[222] Meager and Hurstfield, 'Legislating for Equality' (n 140 above) 87.

Conclusion

Efforts should not be confined to the enactment of specific legal reforms. It is likely that one highly significant factor underlying the current British tolerance of reasonable adjustment duties is the system of State funding set up to support them. Under the Access to Work scheme, as has already been explained, no funds will be made available to help employers with the costs of relatively low-cost adjustments. Once the cost reaches a certain figure, however, the expectation is that it will be met from State funds regardless of the size or wealth of the employer. This provides a reassuring safety net to British employers. The fact that such a safety net is not provided to US employers may have fuelled and intensified some of the economics-based attacks on reasonable accommodation duties considered in Sections 2 and 3 above. Care should therefore be taken to preserve and strengthen British funding schemes such as Access to Work. In particular, efforts need to be made to ensure that applications, particularly for extensive support, are processed as quickly as possible, as delay may result in the applicant losing a job.[223]

Finally, effort must continue to be devoted to the task of awareness raising. Public attention should be drawn, on an on-going basis, to the disabling effect of apparently neutral societal structures, practices and assumptions. Reasonable adjustment duties have a vital role to play in dismantling these barriers and, where reasonable, ensuring that disabled people are provided with the support and equipment which will allow them to study, to work and to play. Such duties represent an essential element of a meaningful concept of equality and should not be regarded as providing treatment which is special or more than equal.

---

[223] This was the reason Mr Kenny was refused employment in *Kenny v Hampshire Constabulary* [1999] IRLR 76 (EAT) and it was also a significant factor in the difficulties which led to Ms Williams claim in *Williams v J Walter Thomson Group* [2005] EWCA Civ 133.

7

Conclusion

T HE BRITISH CONCEPT of reasonable adjustment represents what the Disability Rights Commission has described as 'one of the success stories of employment and social legislation'.[1] In Britain, unlike in the United States,

[i]t has received a favourable response from employers and service providers on the one hand, and from the tribunals and courts on the other. The culmination of this from a jurisprudential standpoint was *Archibald v Fife Council* [and *Roads v Central Trains*], but there have been no appellate decisions in which the concept has been interpreted restrictively or met with hostility.[2]

It is to be hoped that this continues and that reasonable adjustment is thereby spared the fate which befell disability-related discrimination in *Lewisham London Borough Council v Malcolm*.[3]

The 'success' of British reasonable adjustment law has been achieved despite the fact that the Disability Discrimination Act 1995 was, in its first incarnation, marred by considerable weaknesses[4] and that it was born into what was a distinctly unpromising political climate.[5]

The DDA has undoubtedly been considerably strengthened by subsequent amendments. These have widened its coverage to include important areas originally excluded from its scope, such as education, transport and public functions. Further, reasonable adjustment duties have been introduced into parts of the Act in which they did not originally operate.[6] In addition, changes required

---

[1] Disability Rights Commission, *Initial Submission to the Discrimination Law Review* (London, DRC, 2006) para 1.1.3.

[2] *Ibid* (footnotes omitted).

[3] *Lewisham LBC v Malcolm* [2008] UKHL 43.

[4] See generally B Doyle, 'Enabling Legislation or Dissembling Law? The Disability Discrimination Act 1995' (1997) 60 *Modern Law Review* 64; and C Gooding, *Blackstone's Guide to the Disability Discrimination Act 1995* (London, Blackstone Press, 1996).

[5] See generally R Colker, 'Affirmative Action, Reasonable Accommodation and Capitalism: Irreconcilable Differences?' in M Hauritz, C Sampford and S Blencowe (eds), *Justice for People with Disabilities: Legal and Institutional Issues* (Sydney, The Federation Press, 1998).

[6] Such duties were introduced into the sections dealing with the selling, letting and management of premises by s 13 of the Disability Discrimination Act 2005.

by the Employment Equality Directive[7] have resulted in the streamlining of such duties in the areas of employment and post-16 education. Weaknesses and bewildering complexities nevertheless remain. Before considering some of these weaknesses and complexities, it is worth reflecting on some of the factors which might help to explain why the concept of reasonable adjustment has, at least until now, thrived in Britain. Only if these factors are identified will the importance of their continued operation be appreciated.

It is possible that one of the apparent weaknesses in the DDA might itself have contributed to the development of the notion of anticipatory reasonable adjustment—a notion which does not appear to have yet emerged outside Britain and one which has tremendous potential as a tool in the struggle for disability equality. This apparent weakness is the absence of the concept of indirect discrimination. In its absence, duties to make anticipatory reasonable adjustments have been developed as the primary mechanism for tackling group-based disadvantage. Ironically, as was explained in chapter four, the concept of anticipatory reasonable adjustment is likely to prove a more powerful device for tackling such disadvantage than is the British concept of indirect discrimination. For this reason, the failure of the Act to prohibit indirect discrimination may in fact prove to be a strength rather than a weakness. Some of the work which might have been done by a concept of indirect discrimination, however, has until now been done by the concept of disability-related discrimination. The shrinkage of this latter concept effected in *Lewisham*[8] therefore leaves an unfortunate gap.

Factors outside the DDA itself also seem likely to have played a significant part in the success of the reasonable adjustment duties. One such factor may be found in the enactment of another statute—the Human Rights Act 1998—shortly after the DDA. The appearance of this Act significantly raised the profile of human rights issues amongst the judiciary, and may well have increased its willingness to depart from rigid adherence to notions of identical treatment. As was explained in chapter two, the idea that different treatment must sometimes be given to differently situated individuals—an idea which has recently manifested itself in the form of the explicit reasonable accommodation obligation imposed by the UN Convention on the Rights of Persons with Disabilities—is an idea which is fundamental to human rights principles. It is this same idea which underlies and defines the concept of reasonable adjustment under the DDA.

Another factor which has undoubtedly played an important part in shaping the approach of the judiciary to reasonable adjustment is the existence of the DDA codes of practice.[9] Indeed, this factor is also likely to have operated to

---

[7] Directive 2000/78/EC establishing a general framework for equal treatment in employment and occupation, [2000] OJ L 303/16.

[8] *Lewisham LBC v Malcolm* [2008] UKHL 43.

[9] See generally N O'Brien, 'The UK Disability Rights Commission and Strategic Law Enforcement: Transcending the Common Law Mind' in A Lawson and C Gooding (eds), *Disability Rights in Europe: From Theory to Practice* (Oxford, Hart Publishing, 2005) 259–60.

develop the understanding and influence the attitudes of employers, providers of goods and services and other duty-bearers. As Connolly has pointed out, these codes are more detailed than those relating to sex and race and contain more practical examples.[10] This may well have increased their usefulness. Further, as was seen in chapter three, they have been used to flesh out and to clarify many reasonable adjustment issues that were left unclear in the DDA itself. The importance of this explanatory function is particularly pronounced given the fact that the concept of reasonable adjustment did not exist in British non-discrimination law prior to the DDA.

Another important factor, closely linked to the previous one, is the work of the Disability Rights Commission (DRC). Not only was the DRC responsible for drawing up the DDA codes of practice from its establishment in 2000, but it also played a significant part in reasonable adjustment litigation. It presented persuasive and ultimately successful arguments in the two leading reasonable adjustment cases of *Archibald v Fife Council*[11] and *Roads v Central Trains*.[12] In both of these cases, which were considered in chapter three, an expansive and purposive approach was taken to the interpretation and development of reasonable adjustment duties. These decisions therefore stand in stark contrast with the more recent disability-related discrimination case of *Lewisham London Borough Council v Malcolm*.[13]

The DRC was replaced by the broader Equality and Human Rights Commission in October 2007. It is to be hoped that this new Commission will continue to exercise the same clear guiding influence over the legal development of reasonable adjustment law as did its predecessor—a prospect which cannot be taken for granted given the significant structural and personnel changes involved.[14]

The success of British reasonable adjustment to date also owes much to the availability of substantial financial assistance from the State with the costs of adjustments. Such assistance is provided in the contexts of post-16 education (through the disabled student's allowance)[15] and of employment, in both of which the ability of disabled people to participate may well depend on the making of expensive individualised adjustments. The financial assistance for

---

[10] M Connolly, *Townshend-Smith on Discrimination Law: Text, Cases and Materials* (London, Cavendish, 2004) 464.

[11] *Archibald v Fife Council* [2004] UKHL 32, [2004] IRLR 197.

[12] *Roads v Central Trains* [2004] EWCA Civ 1540.

[13] *Lewisham LBC v Malcolm* [2008] UKHL 43.

[14] See generally L Sayce and N O'Brien, 'The Future of Equality and Human Rights in Britain: Opportunities and Risks for Disabled People' (2004) 19 *Disability and Society* 663; and, on the role of such bodies more generally, G Moon, 'Enforcement Bodies' in D Schiek, L Waddington and M Bell (eds), *Cases, Materials and Text on National, Supranational and International Non-Discrimination Law* (Oxford, Hart Publishing, 2007).

[15] Adjustments in the form of the provision of auxiliary aids or services and the making of physical alterations are not covered by the DDA's pre-16 education provisions. They are dealt with instead by the special educational needs system and are funded by local education authorities.

employment-related adjustments is provided through the Access to Work scheme, the importance of which bears repetition here.

The funding provided to an employer through Access to Work increases as the cost of the adjustment rises and it is subject to no upper limit. Its existence is factored into assessments of the reasonableness of potential adjustments. It therefore operates to transform what would otherwise have been an unreasonable adjustment into a reasonable one, and thereby makes it mandatory. The chances of crucial modifications being made, or support being provided, are accordingly significantly increased. Such modifications and support will be a vital prerequisite of many disabled people finding work of a type they wish to perform and for which they are qualified.

Access to Work thus ensures that the employment prospects of disabled people are enhanced whilst, at the same time, protecting employers from heavy financial burdens. Without it, the level of support or modification deemed to be reasonable would almost certainly drop significantly. The fear of being required to pay for expensive adjustments un-cushioned by Access to Work funding is also likely to plant the seeds of resistance to reasonable adjustment in the minds of employers—a resistance which may well spread to others including the judiciary. In short, Access to Work has provided the DDA with a powerful bulwark against the type of backlash experienced by the Americans with Disabilities Act 1990, and has been a significant factor in the success of British reasonable adjustment. The Government's proposal to withdraw Access to Work funding from the public sector and possibly from large private employers is therefore extremely worrying.[16]

Having considered some of the factors which help to explain the strength of the reasonable adjustment concept in Britain, attention will now be turned to some of the legal weaknesses and complexities which continue to hamper it. These have been explored in depth elsewhere in this book. The present discussion will therefore be brief.

First, a number of problems relating to the design of reasonable adjustment duties themselves may be identified. For instance, the DDA provides that reasonable adjustment duties in different parts of the Act will arise in different circumstances. The Discrimination Law Review's proposal to subject all such duties to the single trigger of 'substantial disadvantage' would remove the current inconsistency and complexity and is therefore to be welcomed.[17]

---

[16] Department for Work and Pensions, *Public Consultation—Helping People Achieve their Full Potential: Improving Specialist Disability Employment Services* (London, DWP, 2007) paras 5.23–5.25.

[17] Department for Communities and Local Government, *Discrimination Law Review—A Framework for Fairness: Proposals for a Single Equality Bill for Great Britain* (London, Stationery Office, 2007) paras 1.58–1.59.

Another problem is located in the continuing existence of a number of justification defences for failures to make reasonable adjustments. The justification defence for such failures, which originally operated in relation to employment, was removed by the 2003 Regulations implementing the Employment Equality Directive 2000. Reasonable adjustment law would be greatly improved were such defences to be removed from all parts of the Act.

Another problem connected with the current formulation of reasonable adjustment duties relates to the scope of both the anticipatory and the reactive duties. As has been argued in many parts of this book, anticipatory reasonable adjustment duties should be extended to the employment sphere. These should not replace the existing entirely reactive duty but should supplement it. In addition, as was argued in chapter three, a duty which is entirely reactive in nature should be introduced into the education context to run alongside the existing anticipatory duty.

These reforms are particularly important but were not addressed by the Discrimination Law Review. Indeed, that Review makes no mention whatsoever of the important concept of anticipatory reasonable adjustment—an omission which is more than disappointing. In its response to the Discrimination Law Review, the Government did acknowledge the existence of anticipatory duties but refused to extend them into the employment context.[18]

Second, various other features of the DDA have the potential to operate so as to weaken the interpretation and enforcement of reasonable adjustment duties. As discussed in the previous chapter, the definition of disability is one such feature. The expansion of this definition may well help to safeguard the positive approach to reasonable adjustment which the judiciary has adopted to date.

In addition, there is currently no mechanism for enforcing reasonable adjustment duties other than through an action brought by a person who has been disadvantaged as a result of non-compliance. The introduction of a mechanism for class or representative actions would therefore be helpful and would seem particularly appropriate in the context of the anticipatory reasonable adjustment duty. The transfer of DDA non-employment cases to Equality Tribunals would also seem likely to reduce the disincentives which currently appear to deter disadvantaged individuals from bringing cases.

Accordingly, although the British concept of reasonable adjustment has in many ways proved to be a success story, there is scope for it to be further strengthened, streamlined and safeguarded. The legislative amendments suggested here would simplify and harmonise reasonable adjustment law; increase its strength and effectiveness; and facilitate its enforcement and practical realisation. The issue of its practical realisation raises the question of its role. What precisely is the function of reasonable adjustment duties?

---

[18]   See ch 3, fnn 313–14 above and accompanying text.

Conclusion

It has been argued throughout this book that the function of reasonable adjustment is to tackle discrimination. Descriptions of it as a form of positive action or positive discrimination are therefore unhelpful, confusing and potentially damaging. Its purpose is to counter the disadvantage resulting from the application of conditions and expectations designed for the non-disabled norm to a person with an impairment. In this sense it is tempting to regard it as a legal instrument which is perfectly designed to implement the social model of disability. It appears to have been finely crafted so as to identify and chip away at socially-created barriers which prevent individuals with impairments from participating in society as full and equal citizens. Radical social model theorists, however, may baulk at the suggestion that any instrument designed only to chip away at social barriers in this somewhat piecemeal fashion, limited by the confines of reasonableness, should be regarded as a perfect tool of the social model.[19] Nevertheless, if appropriately nurtured and developed, reasonable adjustment has the potential to effect wide-reaching and profound social change.

While there are certainly grounds for some optimism as to the power of reasonable adjustment duties to dismantle social barriers, it is important to remain mindful of their limitations. Failure to do so will encumber the concept with the weight of unrealistically high expectations. It is also likely to distract attention from the importance of implementing other legal and policy measures designed to tackle and break down such barriers. Insufficient regard to the limitations of reasonable adjustment as a mechanism for achieving social change is also liable to result in the attribution of blame for inadequate progress to the operation of that concept, when the causes will in fact be more complex and multifaceted.

It is important, indeed, to recognise the limited role not only of the reasonable adjustment concept but also of non-discrimination law more generally.[20] The pace of change associated with individualised concepts such as direct discrimination and reactive reasonable adjustment is likely to be slow. Group-based concepts such as indirect discrimination and anticipatory reasonable adjustment clearly have the potential to bring about change more quickly. Indeed, the

---

[19] See eg M Oliver, *Understanding Disability: From Theory to Practice* (Basingstoke, MacMillan, 1996).

[20] See generally B Hepple, 'Have Twenty-Five Years of the Race Relations Acts in Britain been a Failure?' in B Hepple and E Szysczak (eds), *Discrimination: The Limits of the Law* (London, Mansell, 1990); DA Young and R Quibell (eds), 'Why Rights are Never Enough: Rights, Intellectual Disability and Understanding' (2000) 15 *Disability and Society* 747; M Russell, 'What Disability Civil Rights Cannot Do: Employment and Political Economy' (2002) 17 *Disability and Society* 117; AI Batavia, 'Ten Years Later: The ADA and the Future of Disability Policy' in L Pickering Francis and A Silvers (eds), *Americans with Disabilities: Exploring Implications of the Law for Individuals and Institutions* (New York, Routledge, 2000); and M Jones and LA Basser Marks, 'The Limitations on the Use of Law to Promote Rights: An Assessment of the Disability Discrimination Act 1992' in M Hauritz, C Sampford and S Blencowe (eds), *Justice for People with Disabilities: Legal and Institutional Issues* (Sydney, The Federation Press, 1998).

concept of anticipatory reasonable adjustment holds particular promise in this regard. So too does the positive equality duty.

Equality and non-discrimination laws, however well crafted and carefully implemented, can never achieve meaningful social change in isolation. Their effectiveness will depend on the wider policy context in which they operate. Accordingly, in relation to disability, policies concerning independent living, housing, benefit entitlements, transport, employment services and health and safety are likely to have a significant impact.[21] Disabling social barriers will be removed only if concerted efforts are made across all these areas. One of the key strengths of anticipatory reasonable adjustment, and also of the disability equality duty, is that principles of disability equality are placed at the heart of policy-making processes in all these different contexts.

Nevertheless, statistics indicate that there is no room for complacency and that progress towards the full inclusion of disabled people in the life of mainstream society in Britain is still painfully slow. This point emerges clearly from the following passage:

> In 2007 there are more working age disabled adults in poverty than children or pensioners. A quarter of children living in poverty have a disabled parent ... Official figures suggest only 6% of formal volunteers and 4.3% of public appointees are disabled people ... Whilst the overall employment rate for disabled people increased from 43% in 1998 to 50% in 2005, some groups lag behind: for instance, the rate for people with mental health problems increased from 15% in 1998 to 20% in 2005. Disabled people are overwhelmingly in low paid, low status jobs, and across all levels the average pay gap is 10% ... The numbers of people being placed by their local authorities into increasingly costly residential or nursing care has risen steeply over the past ten years ... Nine out of ten people with a learning disability report physical and verbal abuse as a feature of daily life ... Three times as many disabled as non-disabled 19 year olds are currently not in any employment, education or training and disabled people age 16–24 are twice as likely to have no formal qualifications.[22]

In addition, it is worth noting that the income of a disabled person in Britain is, on average, less than half that of a non-disabled person[23] and that over half of families with a disabled child are thought to live in or on the margins of poverty.[24] Over 90 per cent of employers believe that it would be difficult or

---

[21] See further A Paz-Fuchs, *Welfare to Work* (Oxford, Oxford University Press, 2008); RF Drake, 'Disabled People, New Labour, Benefits and Work' (2000) 20 *Critical Social Policy* 421; and J Davies and W Davies, 'Reconciling Risk and the Employment of Disabled Persons in a Reformed Welfare State' (2000) 29 *Industrial Law Journal* 347.

[22] DRC, *The Disability Agenda: Creating an Alternative Future* (London, DRC, 2007) Introduction (footnotes omitted). See also *ibid*, Section 3.6.

[23] E Bardasi, SP Jenkins and J Rigg, *Disability, Work and Income: A British Perspective*, Working Paper No 2000–36 (London, Institute for Social and Economic Research, 2000).

[24] N Smith et al, *Disabled People's Costs of Living: More Than You Might Think* (York, Joseph Rowntree Foundation, 2004).

impossible to employ a visually impaired person[25] and 50 per cent of the population would feel 'uncomfortable' were a person with depression to live next door to them.[26]

Much work therefore remains to be done. Reasonable adjustment is only one of the tools which should be used to perform that work. It is nevertheless a vital one. Degener and Quinn thus concluded their comparative review of disability equality law with the following words about the concept of reasonable adjustment or accommodation:

> This, the crowning achievement of the ADA, is the critical element that permeates all effective legislation. Clearly, significant work needs to be done in educating people across different legal cultures about the nature and operation of this concept, without which legislation will either fail or not achieve as much as it could.[27]

As has been seen, reasonable adjustment in essence requires that relevant difference in circumstance be identified and that it be responded to in the form of appropriately different treatment. Although compliance with principles of universal design[28] will reduce the need for particular adjustments to be made, it will never remove the need for such adjustments. There will always be instances where environments constructed around principles of universal design create obstacles for a person with particular impairments. Further, universal design does not generally address the need for assistance to be offered to disabled people in order to allow them to access a particular facility or service. For instance, a visually impaired person is likely to need assistance with locating items in a supermarket or with changing trains in an unfamiliar station however well designed that shop or station might be.

In the words of David Lepofsky, the crux of the duty to accommodate is a 'spirit of change and flexibility'.[29] It is the driving force behind the construction of a model of disability equality which is not built on the need to comply with a dominant norm but which 'requires adaptation and change'.[30] The dialogue and flexibility which characterise reasonable adjustment allow the immense variation

---

[25] S Roberts et al, *Responses to the Disability Discrimination Act in 2003 and Preparation for 2004 Changes* (London, DWP, 2004) table 2.8. See also P Simkiss, 'Work Matters: Visual Impairment, Disabling Barriers and Employment Options' in A Roulstone and C Barnes (eds), *Working Futures? Disabled People, Policy and Social Inclusion* (Bristol, The Policy Press, 2005).

[26] National Centre for Social Research, *British Social Attitudes: Perspectives on a Changing Society*, 23rd Report (London, Sage, 2007).

[27] T Degener and G Quinn, 'A Survey of International, Comparative and Regional Disability Law Reform' in ML Breslin and S Yee (eds), *Disability Rights Law and Policy: International and National Perspectives* (Ardsley NY, Transnational Publishers Inc, 2002) 120.

[28] See generally R Imrie, 'From Universal to Inclusive Design in the Built Environment' in J Swain, S French, C Barnes and C Thomas (eds), *Disabling Barriers—Enabling Environments* (London, Sage, 2004).

[29] D Lepofsky, 'The Duty to Accommodate: A Purposive Approach' (1992) 1 *Canadian Labor Law Journal* 1 at 21.

[30] S Fredman, 'Disability Equality: A Challenge to the Existing Anti-Discrimination Paradigm?' in Lawson and Gooding (eds), *Disability Rights in Europe* (n 9 above) 203.

of individual impairment and social circumstance to be factored into the demands of non-discrimination law. This flexibility carries with it certain difficulties, foremost amongst which are problems associated with uncertainty and with litigation and judicial interpretation.

Outside the area of disability, there appears to be less need for such a high degree of flexibility. The range of disadvantage resulting from interaction between social and physical environments and the characteristics associated with the particular ground of discrimination (such as religion, sex or race) is likely to be much more limited than the range of disadvantage resulting from the interaction between such environments and physical, sensory, intellectual or psychosocial impairment. The solutions are therefore likely to be more predictable and less individualised in nature. For these reasons, it was argued in chapter four that the highly flexible concept of reasonable adjustment need not be extended beyond disability. Where a need exists for adjustments to be made in non-disability contexts, it might be met instead by the introduction of specific measures permitting or requiring the making of relevant types of adjustment on a more tightly circumscribed basis.

The flexibility inherent in the notion of reasonable adjustment renders it particularly vulnerable in the event of a backlash. Every care must therefore be taken to guard against the occurrence of such a backlash in Britain. The fact that British reasonable adjustment has to date been a 'success story' is no guarantee that it will continue to be one. Effort must be made to preserve those factors which have contributed to its success and steps must also be taken to further strengthen and safeguard its operation and development.

Reasonable adjustment has a crucial role to play in the dismantling of the social barriers which disable people with impairments. In Britain, its power has been significantly enhanced by the emergence of the notion of anticipatory reasonable adjustment. Indeed, if the 'crowning glory' of the Americans with Disabilities Act 1990 was the concept of reasonable accommodation, the 'crowning glory' of British reasonable adjustment law is undoubtedly this concept of anticipatory reasonable adjustment—a concept which seems likely to find its way into the promised EC Directive on goods and services and from there into the domestic law of all EU countries. The fact that such an innovative and potentially powerful equality concept has received so little academic attention is perhaps partially explained by the fact that it has not yet appeared in the employment arena—the traditional stamping ground of the majority of equality lawyers.[31] This, however, cannot explain the unforgiveable silence of the Discrimination Law Review on the point.

In conclusion, the road travelled by British reasonable adjustment law from the Disability Discrimination Act 1995 to the present has been a relatively smooth

---

[31] See generally N Bamforth, 'Conceptions of Anti-Discrimination Law' (2004) 24 *Oxford Journal of Legal Studies* 693 at 693–4.

one. This has allowed it to gather strength and momentum. It now faces a crossroads. It may be shepherded down an even better road—a road smoothed by continued Access to Work funding and by appropriate legislative amendments, including the extension of anticipatory reasonable adjustment to employment. It may, on the other hand, be about to face a bumpier ride. What must not be forgotten is that every bump will profoundly shake the lives of disabled people in Britain.

Index